AF852771

Ultimate BigQuery for Data Engineering

Master BigQuery, Data Modeling, dbt, Dataflow, Apache Beam, Streaming Analytics, BigQuery ML, and Production Data Engineering

Dinak Lal

www.orangeava.com

Copyright © 2026, Orange Education Pvt Ltd, AVA®

All rights reserved. No part of this book may be reproduced, stored in a retrieval system, or transmitted in any form or by any means, without the prior written permission of the publisher, except in the case of brief quotations embedded in critical articles or reviews.

Every effort has been made in the preparation of this book to ensure the accuracy of the information presented. However, the information contained in this book is sold without warranty, either express or implied. Neither the author nor **Orange Education Pvt Ltd** or its dealers and distributors, will be held liable for any damages caused or alleged to have been caused directly or indirectly by this book.

Orange Education Pvt Ltd has endeavored to provide trademark information about all of the companies and products mentioned in this book by the appropriate use of capital. However, **Orange Education Pvt Ltd** cannot guarantee the accuracy of this information. The use of general descriptive names, registered names, trademarks, service marks, etc. in this publication does not imply, even in the absence of a specific statement, that such names are exempt from the relevant protective laws and regulations and therefore free for general use.

First Published: July 2026

Published By: Orange Education Pvt Ltd, AVA®

Address: 9, Daryaganj, Delhi, 110002, India

275 New North Road Islington Suite 1314 London,

N1 7AA, United Kingdom

ISBN (PBK): 978-81-69646-29-1

ISBN (E-BOOK): 978-81-69646-30-7

Scan the QR code to explore our entire catalogue

www.orangeava.com

Get a Free eBook

We hope you're enjoying your recent book purchase! Your feedback is incredibly valuable to us and helps other readers discover books that truly make a difference.

If you found this book useful or enjoyable, we'd greatly appreciate it if you could leave a short review with a 5-star rating on Amazon. Your review supports our work and allows us to reach more learners worldwide.

As a thank-you, we're happy to offer you a **free digital copy of this book** plus a **30% discount code** for your next purchase on our official websites:

www.orangeava.com

www.orangeava.in (For the Indian Subcontinent).

☑ **How it works:**

Leave your review on Amazon, take a screenshot of the confirmation or use the following link to submit the claim and email it to **info@orangeava.com.** Once received the required detail, we will send your rewards within 24 hours, **along with one month free subcription to the book on AVA SkillShelf!**

Claim Form
https://rebrand.ly/4d2477

Thank you for your support–it truly means a lot to us.

Enjoy 1 Month of Free Access to AVA SkillShelf!

The future belongs to lifelong learners. With AVA SkillShelf, you go beyond reading books and start building real, job-ready skills curated by industry experts.

Your membership unlocks **200+ learning products** covering AI, Cloud, Python, Cybersecurity, Data Science, DevOps, and more—all in one platform. Our bestselling technical books are transformed into structured courses designed for practical, real-world application.

Learn directly from experienced professionals and published authors, with no filler—just actionable insights. Earn **verified digital certifications** to strengthen your CV, LinkedIn profile, and professional credibility.

Learn anytime, anywhere, on any device, at your own pace. Ideal for students, professionals, career switchers, and tech leaders.

For full access to all current and future courses, choose our **Annual Membership**. Simply scan the QR to get started!

For 1 month Free access, simply refer to the steps on the previous page titled: Get a Free ebook!

https://www.avaskillshelf.com/

Downloading the code bundles and colored images

Please follow the links or scan the QR codes to download the **_Code Bundles and Images_** of the book:

https://github.com/ava-orange-education/Ultimate-BigQuery-for-Data-Engineering

The code bundles and images of the book are also hosted on **_https://rebrand.ly/6fp9pln_**

In case there's an update to the code, it will be updated on the existing GitHub repository.

Errata

We take immense pride in our work at **Orange Education Pvt Ltd**, and follow the best practices to ensure the accuracy of our content to provide an indulging reading experience to our subscribers. Our readers are our mirrors, and we use their inputs to reflect and improve upon human errors, if any, that may have occurred during the publishing processes involved. To let us maintain the quality and help us reach out to any readers who might be having difficulties due to any unforeseen errors, please write to us at:

errata@orangeava.com

Your support, suggestions, and feedback are highly appreciated.

Dedicated To

My Beloved Family for Their Love and for Accepting That "One More Page" Means I Will See Them in Three Hours.

My Mentors and Friends, Who Guided My Journey from "SELECT" to

Actual Data Engineering.

And to Myself, for All Those Sleepless Nights, Countless Cups of Coffee,

And the Stubborn Belief That Every Error Message is Just a Learning

Opportunity in Disguise.

About the Author

Dinak Lal is a data engineer with over 9 years of experience working with cloud data platforms. He started his career in data analytics – writing SQL, building dashboards, and working closely with business teams. Over time, he moved into data engineering, building pipelines and warehouse architectures across AWS, GCP, and Azure.

Dinak holds a Master of Technology in Computer Science from IIIT Guwahati, Assam and a Bachelor of Technology from Government Engineering College, Wayanad, Kerala. He is a Databricks Certified Data Engineer Professional.

His own transition from analyst to engineer is what motivated this book. He found plenty of tutorials on individual tools but very little guidance on how they work together in production. This book is his attempt to fill that gap – a practical, hands-on guide that covers the full journey from SQL queries to production data platforms on Google Cloud.

Outside work, Dinak is a competitive chess player – a national-level prize winner at the ISTE Chess Competition – who plays soccer as a hobby and is a voracious reader.

About the Technical Reviewers

Akash Jatangi is a fintech product leader with deep experience building scalable credit, onboarding, and financial infrastructure products. He currently serves as a Senior Staff Product Manager at Intuit, where he works on the Intuit Business Credit Card, and helps expand access to credit for small businesses through modern origination and onboarding systems.

Previously, Akash was the Director of Product at Deserve, where he led product strategy for credit card origination platforms powering multiple innovative consumer credit programs. Earlier in his career, Akash co-founded AutoVRse, an enterprise VR/AR company in India, where he led product vision, commercialization, and early enterprise growth. He holds an M.S. in Product Management from Carnegie Mellon University and dual degrees in Computer Science and Economics from BITS Pilani. Akash is passionate about fintech, product strategy, data-driven systems, and practical technology adoption.

Madhu Agrahara Gopalakrishna is a Senior Principal Engineer based in Cupertino, California, with more than 20 years of experience in secure storage architecture, filesystem security, distributed systems, and embedded multimedia. He currently leads enterprise security initiatives at Dell Technologies. His areas of focus include Data-at-Rest and Over-the-Wire encryption, TLS 1.3 modernization, FIPS compliance, post-quantum cryptography, key management integration, anomaly detection, and cybersecurity.

Madhu is the inventor of 10 U.S. patents in filesystem security that have been incorporated into globally deployed enterprise storage platforms. His expertise spans cryptography, clustered systems, Kubernetes, and low-level software development using C, C++, Python, and Go. He holds a Bachelor of Engineering degree in Electronics and Communication from Dr. A.I.T., Bengaluru, India.

Acknowledgments

There are a few people I want to thank for the continued and ongoing support they have given me during the writing of this book. First and foremost, I would like to thank my family for continuously encouraging me throughout this journey – I could have never completed this book without their support, especially when I disappeared into my laptop for entire weekends.

I am grateful to the companies and teams I have worked with throughout my career, which gave me the practical knowledge that shaped this book. The challenges I faced building production data platforms became the foundation for the hands-on labs and patterns you will find in these chapters.

Thank you to the data engineering community – the countless blog posts, YouTube videos, and open-source contributors who unknowingly became my teachers. I gratefully acknowledge the technical reviewers whose expertise and attention to detail significantly improved the quality and accuracy of this book. Their real-world insights from building production systems helped ensure the content reflects the current industry practices.

My gratitude also goes to the editorial team at Orange Education Pvt Ltd for being supportive enough to provide me the time needed to complete this comprehensive guide. Data engineering is a vast and rapidly evolving field, and they understood that covering everything from basic concepts to production streaming architectures required both depth and real-world examples.

Finally, I thank every reader who picks up this book. Your commitment to learning and growing as a data engineer is what makes this field so rewarding.

Preface

Modern data engineering is not just writing SQL anymore – it is building systems that ingest, transform, and serve data reliably at scale. This book covers BigQuery and the tools around it on Google Cloud. BigQuery handles the analytics, but using it effectively in production means understanding the full ecosystem – dbt for transformations, Apache Beam and Dataflow for batch and stream processing, Cloud Composer for orchestration, and Pub/Sub for real-time messaging. Most professionals know pieces of this stack. Few understand how they work together. That is the gap this book fills.

Every chapter includes runnable code, real performance numbers, and production patterns – not simplified demos. You will work with e-commerce datasets, see actual query costs and bytes scanned, and build complete pipelines you can adapt to your own projects.

The book assumes basic SQL knowledge and access to a Google Cloud account. Some Python helps for the Beam and Spark chapters but is not required for most of the book.

This book is divided into 15 chapters.

Chapters 1 and 2 cover the foundations – what data engineering looks like today, where BigQuery fits, and how it works internally. Understanding slots, columnar storage, and the execution engine will change how you approach everything that follows.

Chapter 3 walks through getting data into BigQuery – console uploads, Cloud Storage loads, file formats, Data Transfer Service, and streaming ingestion with Pub/Sub.

Chapters 4 and 5 focus on modeling and optimization. You will compare nested, star schema, and denormalized approaches with actual performance data, and then see how partitioning and clustering can reduce scan costs dramatically.

Chapter 6 digs into cost engineering – using INFORMATION_SCHEMA to find expensive queries, choosing between pricing models, and leveraging materialized views and BI Engine.

Chapter 7 introduces dbt. This is where the book shifts from individual queries to building modular, tested, documented transformation pipelines. The lab builds a complete ELT system with staging, intermediate, and smart layers.

Chapters 8 and 9 cover Apache Beam with Dataflow and Spark with BigQuery. You can build batch and streaming pipelines, and learn when each tool is the right choice.

Chapter 10 brings orchestration with Cloud Composer – coordinating BigQuery, Dataflow, and dbt into automated workflows with retry logic and failure handling.

Chapter 11 tackles security, governance, and data quality – from IAM and row-level security to data quality assertions in SQL.

Chapter 12 shows how to train ML models using SQL in BigQuery, and deploy them to Vertex AI for real-time serving.

Chapter 13 builds a production streaming pipeline end to end – Pub/Sub, Beam windowing, late data handling, and live BigQuery dashboards.

Chapter 14 is the capstone project. You will be able to build a complete enterprise warehouse with incremental models, automated testing, and CI/CD deployment using GitHub Actions.

Chapter 15 looks at where data engineering is heading – streaming-first architectures, Data Mesh, and AI-native platforms.

Thus, by the end of the book, you will have all the skills to build production data platforms on Google Cloud – not just understand them.

DID YOU KNOW

Did you know that Orange Education Pvt Ltd offers eBook versions of every book published, with PDF and ePub files available? You can upgrade to the eBook version at **www.orangeava.com** and as a print book customer, you are entitled to a discount on the eBook copy. Get in touch with us at: **info@orangeava.com** for more details.

At **www.orangeava.com**, you can also read a collection of free technical articles, sign up for a range of free newsletters, and receive exclusive discounts and offers on Print Books and eBooks.

PIRACY

If you come across any illegal copies of our works in any form on the internet, we would be grateful if you would provide us with the location address or website name. Please contact us at **info@orangeava.com** with a link to the material.

ARE YOU INTERESTED IN AUTHORING WITH US?

If there is a topic that you have expertise in, and you are interested in either writing or contributing to a book, please write to us at **business@orangeava.com**. We are on a journey to help developers and tech professionals to gain insights on the present technological advancements and innovations happening across the globe and build a community that believes Knowledge is best acquired by sharing and learning with others. Please reach out to us to learn what our audience demands and how you can be part of this educational reform. We also welcome ideas from tech experts and help them build learning and development content for their domains.

REVIEWS

Please leave a review. Once you have read and used this book, why not leave a review on the site that you purchased it from? Potential readers can then see and use your unbiased opinion to make purchase decisions. We at Orange Education would love to know what you think about our products, and our authors can learn from your feedback. Thank you!

For more information about Orange Education, please visit **www.orangeava.com**.

Table of Contents

CHAPTER 1
Data Engineering Basics and BigQuery's Role

Introduction

Data engineering is the part of data work that makes everything else possible. Dashboards, reports, and Machine Learning (ML) models all depend on data being collected, processed, and stored reliably. When those underlying systems are poorly designed, problems show up everywhere—with slow queries, missing data, rising costs, and fragile pipelines.

This chapter will introduce the basics of data engineering and explain how modern data systems are typically put together. Rather than focusing on tools right away, it starts with the core ideas: how data moves through pipelines, how different processing approaches are used, and how analytical storage fits into the picture. From there, the chapter will explain where BigQuery fits in a Google Cloud-based data platform and why many teams use it as their primary analytical warehouse.

The goal here is not depth, but rather orientation. By the end of the chapter, you should have a clear mental model that will make the more detailed chapters easier to follow.

Structure

In this chapter, we will cover the following topics:

- Core Responsibilities of Data Engineering
- Understanding Data Pipelines
- Batch Processing versus Streaming Processing
- From Processing to Storage

- Analytical Storage Layers
- Data Warehouses
- Lake and Lakehouse Approaches
- The Cloud Data Platform Landscape
- Core Data Services on Google Cloud
- BigQuery in the Modern Data Stack
- Ideal Use Cases for BigQuery

Core Responsibilities of Data Engineering

At a high level, data engineering is about getting data from point A to point B in a useful form. In practice, that usually means moving data from operational systems into analytical systems where it can be queried, aggregated, and analyzed.

A data engineer typically works on problems such as:

- Collecting data from applications, databases, and external sources.
- Designing pipelines that transform raw data into clean datasets.
- Choosing where and how data should be stored.
- Ensuring that pipelines run reliably with recoverability from failures.
- Balancing performance, scalability, and cost.

Unlike application development, data engineering often runs in the background. When things are working well, it is barely noticed. However, when things go wrong, the impact is felt across teams.

Understanding Data Pipelines

A data pipeline describes the path data takes from its source to its destination. Most pipelines follow a similar pattern, even if the tools differ.

A simple pipeline might appear in this manner:

Imagine you are building an e-commerce analytics platform. Orders come in from your application database, clickstream events arrive from your website, and product catalog updates flow from an inventory system. Each of these sources needs to be collected, cleaned, and combined into a single dataset where analysts can answer questions such as "which products are trending this week?" or "what is our conversion rate by region?" That is what a data pipeline does—it turns scattered and messy inputs into something useful.

1. Data is generated by a source system, such as an application or database.
2. Data is ingested into a central platform.
3. Transformations clean, filter, or enrich the data.
4. The processed data is stored for analysis.

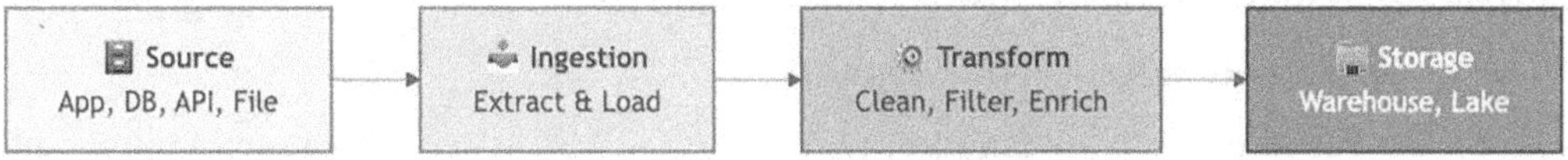

Figure 1.1: *Stages of a Data Pipeline*

In real systems, pipelines are rarely simple or static. New data sources are added, schemas change, and business requirements evolve. Owing to this, pipelines need to be designed with change and failure in mind.

This is why data engineering focuses heavily on automation, monitoring, and repeatability.

Batch Processing versus Streaming Processing

One of the first questions data engineers face is whether data should be processed in batches or streams. The answer depends on how quickly the data is needed and how it will be used.

Batch Processing

Batch processing collects data over a period of time and processes it together. Common examples include daily reports, hourly summaries, or historical backfills.

Batch pipelines tend to share the following traits:

- Data is processed on a schedule.
- Results are not required immediately.
- Systems are easier to reason about and debug.
- Failures can often be retried safely.

Batch processing is still the most common approach for analytics and reporting.

Tip: *When starting a new analytics project, default to batch processing unless there is a clear requirement for real-time insights. This simplifies design and reduces operational complexity.*

Streaming Processing

Streaming processing handles data continuously as it arrives. This approach is used when data needs to be available quickly or when events are generated at high volume.

Streaming systems typically involve:

- Continuous ingestion of events,
- Lower latency requirements,
- Handling late or out-of-order data, and
- More operational complexity.

Many modern platforms support both batch and streaming pipelines, depending on the use case.

As a practical rule of thumb, choose batch processing when data freshness of minutes-to-hours is acceptable and operational simplicity matters, as this covers the majority of analytics, reporting, and ML training workloads. Choose streaming when the business requires sub-second reaction times (for example, fraud detection, live personalization, or real-time monitoring) and when the team is prepared to handle the added complexity of windowing, late data, and always-on infrastructure. When in doubt, start with a batch and migrate specific use cases to streaming as the need becomes clear.

From Processing to Storage

Whether data arrives through batch jobs or streaming pipelines, it eventually needs a place to land. The processing layer handles extracting, cleaning, and transforming data. But once that work is done, the question becomes where the data should live so that analysts, dashboards, and downstream systems can actually use it.

This is where the choice of storage layer becomes critical. The system that stores your processed data determines how fast queries run, how much you pay for storage and compute, and how easily teams can access what they need. Operational databases that power applications are not designed for this kind of work—they excel at handling individual transactions, not scanning millions of rows to answer a business question.

Analytical Storage Layers

Once data has been processed, it needs somewhere to live. The databases that power everyday applications are not built for the kind of questions analysts ask. Those systems are tuned for quick and targeted operations, such as "Look up this customer,"

"Update that order," or "Check an account balance." They are fast when you need one record at a time.

Analytical work is different. Instead of fetching a single row, you are scanning millions of them. You are grouping, filtering, joining tables, and asking questions such as "What were our top-selling products last quarter across all regions?" Try running that on a transactional database, and you will either wait a long time or bring the system to its knees.

That is why analytical storage layers exist. They are designed from the ground up for a different access pattern–reading large chunks of data quickly, compressing it efficiently, and spreading the work across many machines at once. The way you store your data shapes everything downstream: how fast your queries run, how much you spend, and how painful (or painless) it is for teams to get the answers they need.

Historically, analytical systems were built on tightly managed, on-premises data warehouses that required careful capacity planning and long setup cycles. As data volumes grew and workloads became more unpredictable, these systems struggled to scale efficiently. Cloud-native warehouses emerged to address these limitations by separating storage from compute and automating infrastructure management–a shift that changed how teams approach analytical platforms.

Over time, two main approaches have emerged: data warehouses and data lakes. Each has its strengths and trade-offs, and the right choice depends primarily on what you are trying to build.

Data Warehouses

Data warehouses are designed for analytical queries rather than transactional workloads. They store structured data, optimized for scans, aggregations, and joins.

Modern cloud data warehouses typically offer:

- **Columnar Storage**: Data is stored by column rather than by row, which dramatically improves performance for queries that only need a subset of columns.
- **Separation of Storage and Compute**: Storage and processing resources scale independently, allowing teams to store large amounts of data without paying for idle compute.
- **Automatic Scaling**: The system adjusts resources based on query complexity and concurrency.
- **SQL-Based Access:** Analysts and engineers interact with data using familiar SQL syntax.

BigQuery is a cloud-native example of this type of system. It handles infrastructure management automatically, allowing teams to focus on data modeling and query design rather than server provisioning.

Lake and Lakehouse Approaches

Some architectures store data in object storage using open formats and process it with different engines. These approaches are often referred to as "data lakes" or "lakehouses."

A data lake is a storage layer that holds raw data in open file formats (such as Parquet or JSON) without enforcing schema or structure upfront–it prioritizes flexibility and low-cost storage. Meanwhile, a lakehouse builds on top of a data lake by adding warehouse-like capabilities, such as ACID transactions (guarantees that data writes are atomic, consistent, isolated, and durable), schema enforcement, and optimized query performance through open table formats, including Apache Iceberg or Delta Lake. In short, a data lake stores everything; a lakehouse organizes it.

While they provide flexibility, they also introduce additional complexity around governance, performance tuning, and maintenance. Choosing the right approach depends on the organization's needs and capabilities.

In practice, lakehouse architectures often rely on open table formats such as Delta Lake, Apache Iceberg, or Apache Hudi. These formats add features that raw object storage lacks, including ACID transactions, schema evolution, and time travel. Teams typically choose a lakehouse approach when they need to support multiple processing engines (for example, Spark, Presto, Flink, and so on) on the same data, or when they want to avoid vendor lock-in. Yet that flexibility comes at a cost–more moving parts, more tuning, and more decisions that a managed warehouse such as BigQuery handles for you.

The Cloud Data Platform Landscape

Every major cloud provider offers a similar set of building blocks for data platforms. The names may differ, but the categories are consistent, as demonstrated in *Table 1.1*:

Category	**AWS**	**Azure**	**Google Cloud**
Object Storage	S3	Blob Storage	Cloud Storage
Streaming Ingestion	Kinesis	Event Hubs	Pub/Sub
Batch/Stream Processing	Glue, EMR	Data Factory, Synapse	Dataflow, Dataproc
Data Warehouse	Redshift	Synapse Analytics	BigQuery

Orchestration	Step Functions, MWAA	Data Factory	Cloud Composer

Table 1.1: *Data Platform Building Blocks across Major Clouds*

The architectural patterns are largely the same across clouds. Data lands in object storage, gets processed through batch or streaming pipelines, and ends up in a warehouse for analysis. Orchestration tools tie everything together.

This book primarily focuses on Google Cloud, so the examples and deep dives use Google Cloud Platform (GCP) services. However, the concepts transfer. If you understand how to build a data platform on GCP, you will recognize the same patterns on AWS or Azure as well.

Core Data Services on Google Cloud

Google Cloud provides a set of services that are commonly combined to build data platforms, which are as follows:

Service	**Purpose**
Cloud Storage	Storing raw and intermediate data files
Pub/Sub	Event ingestion and message delivery
Dataproc	Apache Spark-based processing workloads
Dataflow	Batch and streaming data processing
BigQuery	Analytical storage and querying
Cloud Composer	Workflow orchestration

Table 1.2: *Core Google Cloud Data Services*

These services are designed to work together, but each plays a specific role in the overall architecture.

BigQuery in the Modern Data Stack

In most Google Cloud architectures, BigQuery sits at the analytical layer. It is where cleaned and processed data is stored and queried by analysts, dashboards, and downstream systems.

A common pattern appears in this manner:

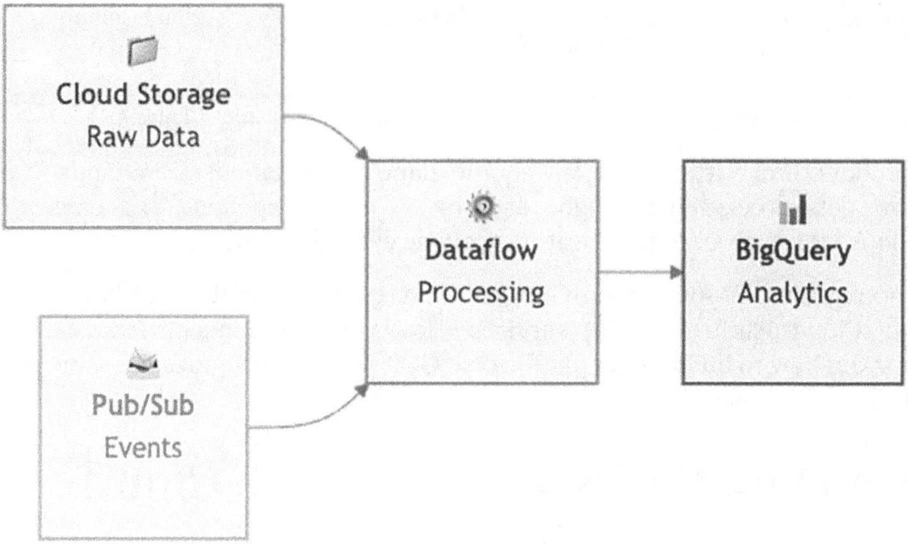

Figure 1.2: *Common Data Flow Pattern on Google Cloud*

- Raw data lands in Cloud Storage.
- Events flow through Pub/Sub and Dataflow.
- Transformations prepare the data for analysis.
- Final datasets are stored in BigQuery.

As BigQuery is fully managed, teams do not need to provision servers or manage storage manually. This shifts the focus from infrastructure to data modeling and query design.

Ideal Use Cases for BigQuery

BigQuery works particularly well for the following scenarios:

- Large-scale analytical queries
- Business intelligence and reporting
- SQL-based transformation workflows
- Analytics over historical and semi-structured data
- Multi-team or multi-tenant environments

It is not designed for transactional workloads or frequent row-level updates. Knowing what BigQuery is not built for saves headaches later.

Conclusion

This chapter introduced the basic concepts behind data engineering and showed how BigQuery fits into modern cloud-based data platforms. We covered data pipelines, processing models, storage layers, and the role BigQuery plays within Google Cloud architectures.

With this foundation in place, the next chapter will take a closer look at BigQuery, focusing on how it stores data, executes queries, and scales analytical workloads.

Points to Remember

- Data engineering focuses on building reliable data systems.
- Batch and streaming processing serve different needs.
- Analytical storage is optimized for querying, and not for transactions.
- BigQuery is designed for large-scale analytics.
- Architecture decisions affect performance and cost.

Multiple Choice Questions

1. Which processing approach runs on a schedule and handles data in groups?
    a. Streaming processing
    b. Batch processing
    c. Real-time processing
    d. Manual processing
2. What type of storage is BigQuery?
    a. Transactional database
    b. Object storage
    c. Analytical data warehouse
    d. File system
3. Which is NOT a characteristic of cloud data warehouses?
    a. Columnar storage
    b. Frequent row-level updates

   c. Separation of storage and compute
   d. SQL-based access
4. Which GCP service handles workflow orchestration?
   a. BigQuery
   b. Dataflow
   c. Cloud Composer
   d. Pub/Sub
5. What does a data pipeline do?
   a. Only stores data
   b. Moves and transforms data from source to destination
   c. Only visualizes data
   d. Deletes old data

Answers

1. b
2. c
3. b
4. c
5. b

Questions

1. What is the main difference between batch and streaming processing?
2. Why are transactional databases not suitable for analytical workloads?
3. What are the trade-offs between data warehouses and lakehouse architectures?
4. How does separation of storage and compute benefit cloud data warehouses?
5. What types of workloads is BigQuery best suited for?
6. Why did cloud-native warehouses emerge to replace on-premises systems?

7. What factors should be considered when choosing between batch and streaming processing?

Key Terms

- **Data Pipeline**: The path data takes from source to destination, including ingestion and transformation steps.
- **Batch Processing**: Processing data in scheduled intervals rather than continuously.
- **Streaming Processing**: Processing data continuously as it arrives.
- **Data Warehouse**: Storage system optimized for analytical queries, not transactions.
- **Lakehouse**: Architecture combining data lake flexibility with warehouse features.
- **BigQuery**: Google Cloud's fully managed, serverless analytical data warehouse.
- **Columnar Storage**: Storing data by column rather than row for faster analytical queries.
- **Orchestration**: Coordinating and scheduling the execution of data pipeline tasks.

CHAPTER 2

Inside BigQuery Storage, Compute, and Execution

Introduction

The previous chapter established where BigQuery fits in a modern data platform–it is the analytical warehouse where processed data lands and gets queried. You saw how it sits downstream of ingestion and transformation pipelines, serving as the foundation for reporting, dashboards, and analytics. Now, it is time to look at what makes BigQuery work the way it does.

Most BigQuery users never think about what happens after they hit "Run query." The interface is simple–type SQL and get results. For a while, that simplicity is enough. However, as data volumes grow, more teams start querying the same datasets, and monthly bills climb, that black box becomes a problem. Queries that used to finish in seconds now take minutes. Costs which seemed predictable suddenly spike. Pipelines that ran smoothly start hitting resource limits.

You cannot fix what you do not understand. This chapter will look beneath that simple interface, explaining how BigQuery stores data, allocates compute, and executes queries at scale. The goal is not to memorize implementation details, but rather to build an understanding of why certain designs and query patterns behave in a certain way. When you understand how BigQuery thinks, you can write better queries, design better schemas, and avoid the performance as well as cost traps that catch most teams by surprise.

By the end of this chapter, you will understand the architectural decisions that shape BigQuery's performance characteristics–knowledge that will inform every schema, query, and pipeline decision you make going forward.

Structure

In this chapter, we will cover the following topics:

- BigQuery as a Serverless Analytical Warehouse
- Separation of Storage and Compute
- Columnar Storage and Metadata Pruning
- Dremel Execution Model and Distributed Query Processing
- Query Lifecycle and Execution Stages
- Slots, Reservations, and Workload Management
- Caching and Acceleration Features
- Impact of Internals on Performance and Cost

BigQuery as a Serverless Analytical Warehouse

BigQuery is a fully managed and serverless analytics platform. In practical terms, this means that you do not provision machines, manage disks, or tune clusters. You focus on data design and query logic, while the service scales resources behind the scenes to execute workloads.

This is a fundamental shift from traditional data warehouses. In systems such as Teradata or on-premises SQL Server, performance tuning often meant adjusting server configurations, adding nodes to a cluster, or rebalancing data across disks. Teams spent significant time on capacity planning–estimating how much hardware they would need six months out.

BigQuery eliminates most of the operational overhead. There are no servers to size, no disks to monitor, and no clusters to rebalance. However, this does not mean that performance is automatic or that costs take care of themselves. The serverless model changes where performance problems show up. In traditional systems, slow queries often point to overloaded servers or missing indexes. In BigQuery, performance is influenced more by the following aspects:

- How much data your query scans,
- How efficiently the query can be parallelized across workers,
- How compute capacity (slots) is allocated to your workload, and
- Whether your schema design allows BigQuery to skip irrelevant data.

Understanding these factors is what separates teams that use BigQuery effectively from those who struggle with unpredictable costs and slow queries.

Separation of Storage and Compute

A key design principle in BigQuery is the separation of storage and compute. Storage persists your tables and metadata in Google's Colossus distributed file system, while compute is allocated on demand to run queries. This separation allows BigQuery to scale query execution without requiring teams to scale storage infrastructure.

To understand why this matters, consider a traditional data warehouse. Storage and compute are tightly coupled—your data lives on the same machines that process queries. If you need more storage, you often have to add more compute nodes, even if your query workload has not changed. If you need more query performance, you might have to reorganize how data is stored across nodes. BigQuery decouples these concerns entirely.

Your data sits in Colossus, which is compressed and organized in a columnar format. When you run a query, BigQuery spins up the compute resources needed to execute it, reads only the relevant data from storage, processes it, and returns results. When the query finishes, those compute resources are released.

From a data engineering perspective, this design has two practical benefits:

First, storage can grow independently without forcing capacity planning for compute. You can store petabytes of historical data without paying for idle compute resources. You only pay for compute when queries actually run.

Second, multiple workloads can run concurrently because compute is not tied to a single fixed cluster. Your data team can run exploratory queries while your ELT pipelines load new data and your dashboards refresh—all without competing for the same physical resources.

This separation is why BigQuery can handle unpredictable workloads efficiently. However, it also means that you need to think differently about optimization. Instead of tuning servers, you can optimize for how much data gets scanned and how efficiently queries can be parallelized.

Columnar Storage and Metadata Pruning

BigQuery stores data in a columnar format. Instead of storing full rows, values for each column are stored in contiguous blocks. This is ideal for analytical queries where only a subset of columns is needed.

Here is why this matters in practice:

Imagine that you have a table with 100 columns and 1 billion rows. An analyst writes:

```
SELECT user_id, purchase_amount, purchase_date
FROM orders
WHERE purchase_date = '2024-01-15'
```

In a row-based storage system, the database would need to read all 100 columns for every row, even though the query only needs 3 of them. That is a massive amount of unnecessary I/O.

In BigQuery's columnar storage, only the three columns that are referenced in the query are read from disk. The other 97 columns are never touched. This can reduce the amount of data scanned by 95% or more, which directly translates to faster queries and lower costs.

Columnar storage also supports strong compression. Since values in a column tend to share similar patterns—dates follow date formats, status codes repeat, numeric ranges cluster—BigQuery can compress them far more efficiently than row-based storage. It is common to see compression ratios of 10:1 or better on real datasets.

However, columnar layout is only part of the story. BigQuery also relies on metadata to reduce unnecessary reads.

When you partition a table by date or cluster it by frequently filtered columns, BigQuery maintains metadata about the min/max values in each storage block. When a query includes a filter such as `WHERE purchase_date = '2024-01-15,'` BigQuery checks this metadata and skips any blocks that do not contain data from that date.

This is called pruning, and it is one of the most powerful cost-saving features in BigQuery.

Consider a table with three years of daily data, which is partitioned by date. A query that filters on a single day will scan only 1/1095th of the table—assuming that data is evenly distributed. Without partitioning, BigQuery would scan the entire table.

Tip: *Most cost and performance issues in BigQuery are tied to how much data a query scans. Columnar layout helps, but schema design and query patterns determine whether pruning and partition elimination are effective. We will cover partitioning and clustering strategies in more detail in Chapter 5, Partitioning, Clustering, and Optimization.*

Dremel Execution Model and Distributed Query Processing

BigQuery's SQL engine is based on Google's Dremel architecture, designed for interactive analysis over large datasets. Dremel executes queries by breaking them into stages and distributing those stages across many workers.

At a high level, the engine parses and optimizes the query, builds an execution plan, and runs the plan as a directed graph of operators. Operators include scans, filters, joins, aggregations, and shuffles. Each stage can be parallelized, allowing BigQuery to process large amounts of data efficiently.

Let us make this concrete with the following simple query:

```
SELECT region, SUM(sales) AS total_sales
FROM orders
WHERE order_date >= '2024-01-01'
GROUP BY region
```

Here is what happens under the hood:

Stage 1: Scan and Filter

Hundreds or thousands of workers read the orders table in parallel from Colossus storage. Each worker scans its assigned portion of the data, applies the `WHERE` filter, and keeps only the rows that match.

Stage 2: Shuffle

The filtered data is redistributed (shuffled) across workers so that all rows for each region end up on the same worker. This is necessary because `GROUP BY` requires all sales for a given region to be aggregated together.

Stage 3: Aggregate

Each worker computes the `SUM(sales)` for its assigned regions.

Stage 4: Return Results

The final aggregated results are sent back to the client.

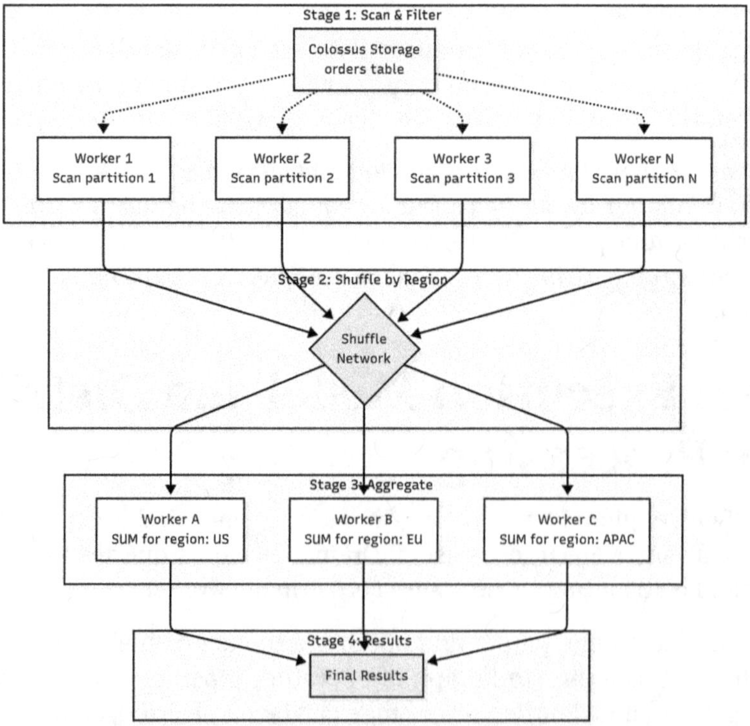

Figure 2.1: *Distributed Execution of a GROUP BY Query across Multiple Stages*

Each stage can be parallelized, allowing BigQuery to process large amounts of data efficiently. However, not all stages parallelize equally well.

Scans parallelize beautifully–BigQuery can throw thousands of workers at reading data. Shuffles are more expensive as they involve moving data across the network. Large joins and aggregations can create bottlenecks if data is heavily skewed toward certain keys.

This is why query design matters. Queries that minimize shuffles, avoid cross joins, and work with well-distributed data run faster and cost less. Queries that force BigQuery to move massive amounts of data between stages will be slow and expensive, no matter how many slots you throw at them.

Query Lifecycle in BigQuery

When you run a query in BigQuery, it goes through a predictable lifecycle. Understanding these steps helps in diagnosing slow queries or unexpected costs.

The journey from SQL text to results involves the following distinct phases:

- **Parsing and Validation**: BigQuery checks syntax and verifies that referenced datasets, tables, and columns exist. If you reference a table that does not exist or misspell a column name, the query fails here before any resources are consumed.
- **Optimization**: The engine rewrites parts of the query to make it more efficient. This might involve reordering joins, pushing filters down closer to the data source, or eliminating redundant operations. BigQuery's optimizer is sophisticated, but it is not magic–poorly written queries can still perform badly.
- **Scheduling**: The execution plan is broken into stages and scheduled across available compute resources (slots). If slots are not immediately available, the query waits in a queue. This is where you will see delays if your project is hitting slot limits.
- **Execution**: Workers scan data from Colossus storage, shuffle intermediate results between stages, and compute final outputs. This is where most of the time and cost is spent. The execution details panel in the BigQuery UI shows you exactly what happened during this phase.
- **Results and Storage**: Results are returned to the client and may be cached for repeated execution. If the same query runs again within 24 hours and the underlying data has not changed, BigQuery can return cached results instantly at no cost.

The following is a practical example of why understanding this lifecycle matters:

You run a query that takes 45 seconds. Is that slow? It depends on where the time is spent. To illustrate:

- If 40 seconds are in execution and you are scanning terabytes of data, that is actually fast.
- If 40 seconds are in scheduling because you are waiting for slots, you have a capacity problem.
- If the query completes in 2 seconds but you are scanning unnecessary data, you have a cost problem even though it feels fast.

The execution details in the BigQuery console break down time spent in each stage. Learn to read this information–it is the fastest way to diagnose performance issues.

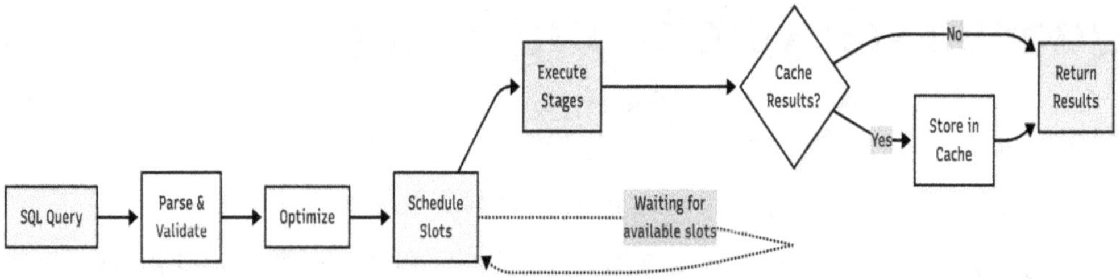

***Figure 2.2**: Query Lifecycle from Submission to Results*

Tip: *When diagnosing slow queries, check the execution details first. If most time is in scheduling, you have a slot availability problem–either optimize concurrent queries or consider reservations. If most time is in execution with high bytes scanned, you need better partitioning or query optimization. If the query is fast but expensive, you are scanning unnecessary data. The execution details tell you which problem you are solving.*

Slots, Reservations, and Workload Management

Slots are the basic unit of compute capacity used to execute queries in BigQuery. You can think of a slot as a portion of processing resources available to run query stages in parallel.

However, what does that actually mean?

When BigQuery executes a query, it breaks the work into stages (as seen in the earlier section). Each stage needs compute resources–CPU, memory, and network bandwidth–to process data. A slot represents a bundle of these resources. The more slots are available to your query, the more work can happen in parallel, and generally the faster your query completes.

- **On-Demand Pricing:** BigQuery allocates slots automatically for your queries. You get access to a shared pool of up to 2,000 slots per project, even though the actual number available at any moment depends on overall demand. You pay only for the scanned data, and not for slot usage directly.
- **Capacity-Based Pricing (Reservations):** Organizations purchase a fixed number of slots (a minimum of 100) and manage them through reservations. This gives you guaranteed capacity and predictable costs. You pay for the slots whether you use them or not, but you get consistent performance and can isolate workloads.

Here is when reservations start to make sense:

Imagine your data team runs three types of workloads, including:

- Daily ELT pipelines that must complete by 8 AM,
- Ad-hoc analyst queries throughout the day, and
- Dashboard refreshes every 15 minutes.

In the case of on-demand pricing, these workloads compete for slots from the shared pool. During busy periods, your critical ELT job might get queued behind someone's exploratory query, causing it to miss its deadline.

With reservations, you can create separate slot pools, such as:

- 300 slots for ELT pipelines (high priority)
- 150 slots for dashboards (medium priority)
- 50 slots for ad-hoc queries (low priority)

Now, your ELT jobs always have capacity, dashboards stay responsive, and analyst queries do not interfere with production workloads. This is called workload isolation, and it becomes essential as teams and data volumes grow.

Practical Considerations: Slots do not make bad queries fast. If your query scans 10 TB unnecessarily, throwing more slots at it will not fix the underlying problem. Slots help with parallelism, not with inefficiencies.

Slot usage is reported in the BigQuery console. If you consistently see queries waiting for slots, you either need to optimize your queries to use fewer slots or consider moving to reservations for guaranteed capacity.

For data engineering teams, slot management becomes important when multiple pipelines run concurrently–daily ELT jobs, ad-hoc analyst queries, and scheduled reporting all competing for resources. Workload isolation ensures critical jobs complete on time without being affected by interactive queries.

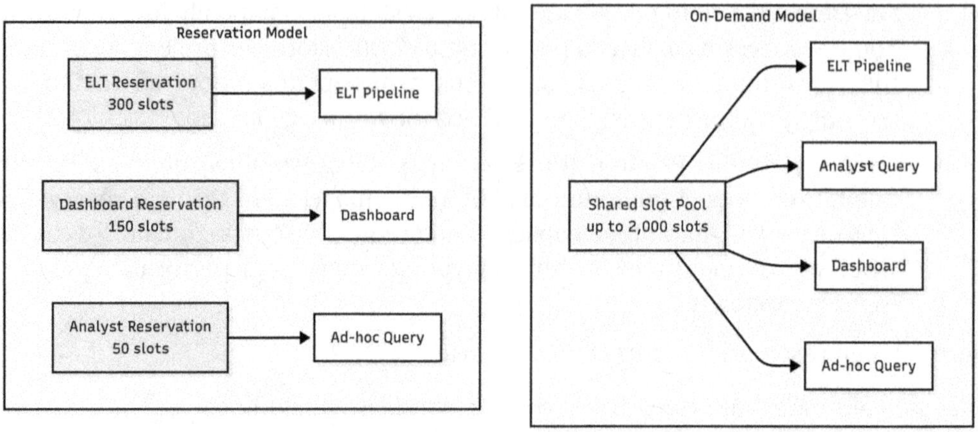

Figure 2.3: *On-Demand versus Reservation-Based Slot Allocation*

Tip: *Start with on-demand pricing. Only move to reservations when you have predictable workloads and can demonstrate that slot contention is causing real problems. Reservations add complexity and fixed costs–ensure that you need them before committing.*

Caching and Acceleration Features

BigQuery includes caching and acceleration features that can significantly reduce query time and cost in the right scenarios. Understanding when these features help and when they do not is key to using them effectively.

Query Results Cache

The query results cache can return results instantly when the same query is executed again, and the underlying data has not changed. This is useful for repeated dashboard queries and iterative exploration.

Here is how it works:

When you run a query, BigQuery stores the results for 24 hours in your personal cache. If you run the same query again, BigQuery conducts the following checks:

- Is the query text identical?
- Has the underlying data changed?
- Have any of the referenced tables been modified?

If all checks pass, BigQuery returns the cached results immediately. You pay nothing, and the query completes in milliseconds instead of seconds or minutes. Note that the cache is per-user, not per project. If your colleague runs the identical query, they will get a cache miss and pay normally, and their first run becomes their own cache. We will see this confirmed in *Chapter 6, Performance and Cost Engineering*, where we will measure cache behavior directly.

When the Cache Helps:

- Dashboards that refresh frequently with the same queries.
- Analysts iterating on visualizations without changing the underlying query.
- Scheduled reports that run multiple times before data updates.

When the Cache Does Not Help:

- Queries with timestamps or random values (they are never identical).
- Tables that are constantly being updated.
- Queries that use non-deterministic functions such as **`CURRENT_TIMESTAMP()`**.

Example:

```
-- This query will cache well
SELECT region, SUM(sales)
FROM orders
WHERE order_date = '2024-01-15'
GROUP BY region

-- This query will NEVER cache (CURRENT_DATE() changes daily)
SELECT region, SUM(sales)
FROM orders
WHERE order_date = CURRENT_DATE()
GROUP BY region
```

Tip: *Design your dashboard queries to be cache-friendly. Use explicit date filters instead of relative dates whenever possible, and avoid functions that return different values on each execution.*

Materialized Views

Materialized views can precompute and maintain aggregated results, reducing repeated computation for common patterns.

Think of a materialized view as a query result that BigQuery keeps up to date automatically. You define the aggregation once, and BigQuery maintains it as the underlying data changes.

Example Scenario. Your analysts frequently run queries, such as:

```
SELECT
  product_id,
  DATE_TRUNC(order_date, MONTH) as month,
```

```
  SUM(quantity) as total_quantity,
  SUM(revenue) as total_revenue
FROM orders
GROUP BY product_id, month
```

This scans the entire orders table every time. If orders have billions of rows, that is expensive. Instead, create a materialized view:

```
CREATE MATERIALIZED VIEW monthly_product_sales AS
SELECT
  product_id,
  DATE_TRUNC(order_date, MONTH) as month,
  SUM(quantity) as total_quantity,
  SUM(revenue) as total_revenue
FROM orders
GROUP BY product_id, month
```

Now, when analysts query this aggregation, BigQuery reads from the much smaller materialized view instead of scanning the full orders table. BigQuery automatically refreshes the view as new data arrives.

Trade-offs:

- Materialized views cost money to maintain (storage and refresh compute).
- They add complexity to your data model.
- They are best for aggregations that are queried frequently and change slowly.

Note: *Do not create materialized views for every aggregation. Use them sparingly for high-value, frequently - accessed patterns. Each materialized view adds maintenance overhead.*

BI Engine

BI Engine can accelerate certain dashboard workloads by keeping optimized data structures in memory. BI Engine is an in-memory analysis service that works alongside BigQuery. You allocate a certain amount of memory (starting at 1 GB), and BI Engine caches frequently accessed data in a format optimized for fast aggregation and filtering.

When BI Engine Helps:

- Interactive dashboards with sub-second latency requirements.
- Queries that scan the same tables repeatedly.
- Workloads with high concurrency (many users querying simultaneously).

When It Does Not Help:

- Queries that scan large amounts of data that do not fit in the allocated memory.

- Infrequent queries that do not benefit from caching.
- Workloads where query results cache already provides good performance.

BI Engine is most useful for business intelligence tools such as Looker, Tableau, or Data Studio, where users expect instant response times.

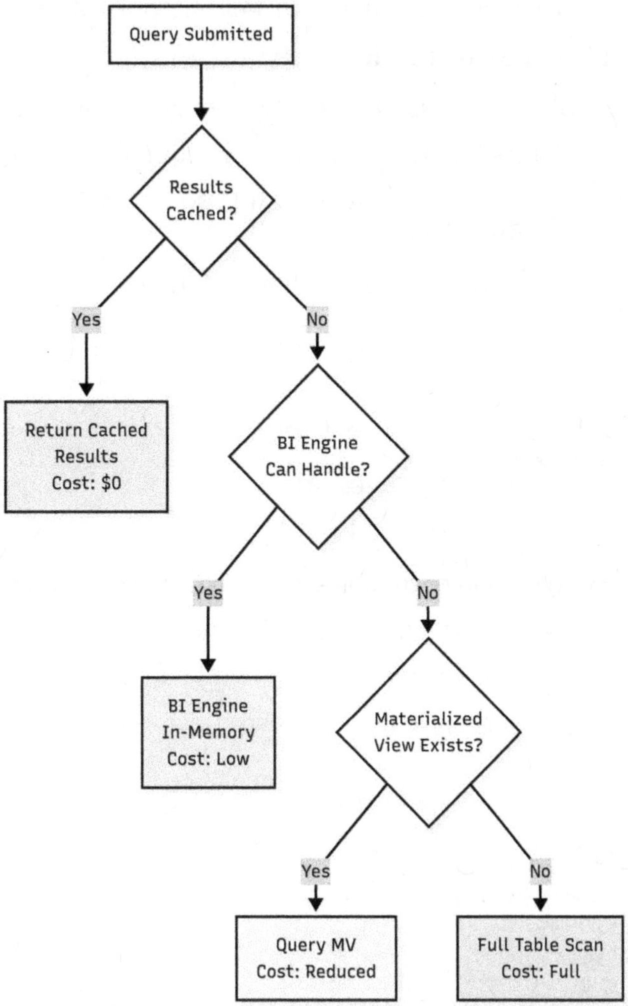

Figure 2.4: *BigQuery's Caching and Acceleration Hierarchy*

Impact of Internals on Performance and Cost

The internal architecture of BigQuery leads to a few consistent principles that repeatedly show up in real-world usage.

Queries are Fast When They:

- Scan less data through partitioning, clustering, and selective column reads,
- Avoid expensive shuffles by using appropriate join strategies and pre-aggregation, and
- Parallelize efficiently by working with well-distributed data.

Queries Become Slow and Costly When They:

- Scan wide tables unnecessarily (**`SELECT *`** when you only need a few columns),
- Perform large cross joins (joining tables without proper filters), and
- Require heavy repartitioning during execution (**`GROUP BY`** on high-cardinality columns with skewed data).

The following concrete example ties everything together:

Bad query:

```
SELECT *
FROM orders o
CROSS JOIN products p
WHERE o.order_date >= '2020-01-01'
```

This query:

- Scans every column in both tables (columnar storage does not help),
- Creates a massive cross join (every order × every product),
- Forces a huge shuffle operation, and
- Will be slow and expensive no matter how many slots you have.

Better query:

```
SELECT
  o.order_id,
  o.product_id,
  p.product_name,
  o.quantity
FROM orders o
JOIN products p ON o.product_id = p.product_id
WHERE o.order_date = '2024-01-15'  -- Partition filter
```

This query:

- Reads only the columns needed,
- Uses a proper join condition,
- Filters on a partitioned column (scans only one day's data), and
- Allows BigQuery to prune irrelevant data and parallelize efficiently.

The difference in cost and performance can be 100x or more.

In later chapters, we will apply these principles through schema design (*Chapter 4, Modeling for Scale*), partitioning and clustering strategies (*Chapter 5, Partitioning, Clustering, and Optimization*), and cost-focused query patterns (*Chapter 6, Performance and Cost Engineering*). For now, the key takeaway is that BigQuery rewards designs that reduce scanned bytes, allowing the engine to work in parallel.

Understanding these internals is not about memorizing implementation details–it is about building intuition for why certain patterns work, and others do not. When you understand how BigQuery stores data, allocates compute, and executes queries, you can make better decisions about schema design, query optimization, and capacity planning.

Conclusion

This chapter explained how BigQuery works under the hood, focusing on the architectural decisions that shape its performance characteristics.

We started with BigQuery's serverless model and what it means in practice–with no servers to manage, but a different set of performance considerations centered on data scanned and parallelization rather than hardware tuning. The separation of storage and compute emerged as a key design principle, enabling independent scaling and concurrent workloads without the capacity planning constraints of traditional warehouses.

We explored how columnar storage and metadata pruning work together to reduce scan costs, showing why schema design and query patterns matter more than raw compute power, especially when it comes to performance.

The Dremel execution model revealed how BigQuery distributes query work across stages–through scans, shuffles, and aggregations–and why understanding these stages allows you to write queries that parallelize efficiently. We walked through the query lifecycle from submission to results, highlighting where delays typically occur and how to diagnose them using execution details.

Slots and reservations showed up as the mechanism for compute allocation, with practical guidance on when workload isolation becomes necessary and when on-demand pricing is sufficient.

Finally, we covered BigQuery's caching and acceleration features–such as query results cache, materialized views, and BI Engine–explaining when each provides value and when unnecessary complexity is added. The consistent theme throughout has been that BigQuery rewards designs that minimize data scanned and maximize parallelization.

Understanding these internals is not about memorizing implementation details; rather, it is about building the intuition needed to make good decisions about schemas, queries, and capacity as your data platform grows.

With this foundation in place, the next chapter will focus on getting data into BigQuery, covering the ingestion patterns and tools that feed the warehouse we have just explored.

Points to Remember

- BigQuery's serverless model eliminates infrastructure management but shifts performance focus to data scanned and query parallelization.
- Separation of storage and compute enables independent scaling and concurrent workloads without capacity planning constraints.
- Columnar storage and metadata pruning reduce scan costs when schema design supports selective queries through partitioning and clustering.
- BigQuery executes SQL using a distributed, stage-based execution model where shuffles are often the most expensive operation.
- Slots represent compute capacity and influence concurrency—reservations provide workload isolation when needed.
- Query results cache, materialized views, and BI Engine can dramatically improve performance for the right workloads but add complexity.
- Performance and cost optimization in BigQuery centers on reducing bytes scanned and enabling efficient parallelization.

Multiple Choice Questions

1. What is the main benefit of separating storage and compute in BigQuery?
   a. Faster transactional updates
   b. Independent scaling of storage and query execution
   c. Automatic row-level indexing
   d. Fixed cluster sizing
2. Why does columnar storage benefit analytical workloads?
   a. It optimizes single-row updates.
   b. It stores all fields together for fast inserts.
   c. It reads only the columns needed for a query.
   d. It requires no compression.

3. Which component represents compute capacity for query execution in BigQuery?
   a. Buckets
   b. Slots
   c. Partitions
   d. Tables
4. Which feature can return results instantly when the same query is executed again, and data has not changed?
   a. Query results cache
   b. Partitioning
   c. Clustering
   d. Sharding
5. What generally drives cost in BigQuery's on-demand pricing model?
   a. Number of tables
   b. Bytes scanned by queries
   c. Number of datasets
   d. Number of columns
6. Which of the following queries will NOT benefit from the query results cache?
   a. `SELECT region, SUM(sales) FROM orders WHERE date = '2024-01-15' GROUP BY region`
   b. `SELECT * FROM products WHERE category = 'Electronics'`
   c. `SELECT COUNT(*) FROM users WHERE signup_date = CURRENT_DATE()`
   d. `SELECT product_name FROM products WHERE product_id = 12345`
7. Which operation in the Dremel execution model is typically the most expensive?
   a. Parsing
   b. Scanning
   c. Shuffling
   d. Caching

8. When does it make sense to move from on-demand pricing to reservations?
   a. As soon as you start using BigQuery
   b. When you have predictable workloads and slot contention issues
   c. Only for small projects
   d. Never, on-demand is always better
9. What happens during the shuffle stage of query execution?
   a. Data is deleted from storage.
   b. Data is redistributed across workers for aggregation.
   c. Query syntax is validated.
   d. Results are cached.
10. What is the minimum number of slots you can purchase with reservations?
    a. 10
    b. 50
    c. 100
    d. 500

Answers

1. b
2. c
3. b
4. a
5. b
6. c
7. c
8. b
9. b
10. c

Questions

1. How does separating storage and compute change how teams think about scaling analytics systems?
2. What role does metadata pruning play in BigQuery query performance?
3. What are slots, and when would a team consider using reservations?
4. Why do shuffles and repartitioning often increase query time and cost?
5. When are query caching and materialized views most useful?

Key Terms

- **Columnar Storage**: A storage layout that stores values by column, enabling efficient scans for analytical queries.
- **Metadata Pruning:** Skipping blocks of data that cannot match query filters, reducing bytes scanned.
- **Dremel**: Google's distributed query architecture that powers interactive analytics in BigQuery.
- **Query Stages**: Execution steps that break a query into parallelizable units of work.
- **Slot**: A unit of compute capacity used to execute query workloads in BigQuery.
- **Reservation**: A capacity management construct used to allocate slots to specific teams or workloads.
- **BI Engine**: An in-memory analysis service that caches frequently accessed data in optimized structures for sub-second dashboard query performance.
- **Materialized View**: A precomputed query result that BigQuery maintains automatically as underlying data changes, reducing repeated computation for common aggregation patterns.
- **Colossus**: Google's distributed file system where BigQuery stores table data in compressed, columnar format.
- **Execution Plan**: The optimized sequence of operations BigQuery will perform to execute a query, represented as a directed graph of operators.
- **Bytes Scanned:** The primary cost driver in BigQuery's on-demand pricing model, representing the amount of data read from storage to execute a query.
- **Serverless**: A cloud computing model where infrastructure is fully managed by the provider, eliminating the need for capacity planning or server provisioning.

- **Shuffle**: The operation of redistributing data across workers during query execution, typically required for GROUP BY and JOIN operations. Often the most expensive stage due to network transfer.
- **Query Results Cache:** A feature that stores query results for 24 hours per user and returns them instantly if the same user runs the same query again and the underlying data has not changed.
- **Separation of Storage and Compute:** An architectural pattern where data storage and query processing use independent, scalable resources rather than being coupled on the same hardware.

CHAPTER 3
Getting Data into BigQuery

Introduction

The previous chapter explained how BigQuery stores and processes data internally. Now, it is time to get data into the system so that you can actually use it.

Ingestion is where most data platforms either gain trust or lose it. When data arrives reliably, on time, and in the expected format, teams build confidence in the platform. When loads fail silently, schemas drift unexpectedly, or data goes missing, that confidence erodes quickly.

This chapter will focus on the practical side of ingestion–how to actually load data into BigQuery, what works well, and what typically goes wrong. We will start with the simplest approach–uploading a CSV file through the console–and work toward more production-ready patterns involving cloud storage, managed transfers, and streaming pipelines.

The goal is not to cover every ingestion option exhaustively. It is to give you enough hands-on experience and context to choose the right approach for your workload and avoid the common mistakes that may cause problems later.

By the end of this chapter, you will know how to load data into BigQuery by using multiple methods, understand when each approach makes sense, and recognize the design patterns that make ingestion reliable in production.

Structure

In this chapter, we will cover the following topics:

- Loading Your First CSV File through the BigQuery Console
- Loading Data from Cloud Storage (GCS) for Production Workflows
- Understanding File Formats

- Handling Schema Mismatches and Data Quality Issues
- Loading Data with SQL and Command Line
- BigQuery Data Transfer Service (DTS) for Managed Recurring Loads
- Streaming Ingestion Patterns with Pub/Sub and Dataflow
- Storage Write API for High-Throughput Streaming
- Batch versus Streaming: Choosing the Right Approach

Prerequisites and Environment Setup

Before you load data, you need access to BigQuery. This takes about five minutes if you are new to Google Cloud.

Quick Setup

Complete these steps to prepare your Google Cloud environment before loading your first dataset.

1. **Create a Google Cloud Project:** Go to "console.cloud.google.com" and sign in with your Google account. Click the project dropdown at the top, then "`NEW PROJECT`". Name it "bigquery-learning" and click "`CREATE`." Note the auto-generated Project ID–you will use this in queries throughout the book.

2. **Enable BigQuery:** Open the navigation menu (≡) and go to **`BigQuery`** → **`SQL workspace`**. If prompted, click "`ENABLE API`." The BigQuery console opens automatically.

3. **Enable Billing (Optional):** Go to "`Billing`" in the navigation menu and link a billing account. New Google Cloud accounts typically receive free credits to get started. BigQuery also offers a free tier that includes monthly storage and query processing allowances, which are more than enough for all examples in this chapter.

   Alternatively, you can use the BigQuery sandbox, which requires no billing account and provides limited free access sufficient for all examples in this chapter.

4. **Verify That It Works:** In the BigQuery console, run the following query:

```
SELECT 'Ready!' as status, @@project_id as project
```

If you see results, your environment is ready.

What You Will Use

This chapter uses the BigQuery console (the web interface) for all examples. It is the easiest way to learn, as you get immediate visual feedback. Later in this chapter, we will also introduce the **bq** command-line tool for production workflows.

Now, you are ready to load your first file.

Loading Your First CSV File through the BigQuery Console

The fastest way to understand BigQuery ingestion is to load a file and see what happens. We will start with a CSV file containing sample order data.

Step 1: Preparing the Data

Here is a simple CSV file with a few sample orders:

```
order_id,customer_name,order_date,amount,status,
product_category,quantity,shipping_country
1001,Alice Johnson,2024-01-15,150.50,completed,Electronics,2,USA
1002,Bob Smith,2024-01-16,200.00,pending,Books,5,Canada
1003,Charlie Brown,2024-01-17,75.25,completed,Clothing,1,UK
...
```

The file includes different data types: integers (**order_id**, **quantity**), decimals (**amount**), dates (**order_date**), and strings (**customer_name**, **status**, **product_category**, **shipping_country**). This variety is useful for seeing how BigQuery handles schema detection.

Step 2: Create a Dataset

Before loading data, you need a dataset, which is BigQuery's equivalent of a database or schema in traditional systems.

In the BigQuery console:

1. Click on your project name in the left panel.
2. Click "**CREATE DATASET.**"
3. Dataset ID: **ingestion_test**
4. Location: Choose the region that is closest to you.
5. Click "**Create dataset.**"

Datasets are organizational containers. Tables live inside datasets, and access control is typically managed at the dataset level.

Step 3: Upload the CSV File

Now, load the CSV file in the following manner:

1. Click on your **`ingestion_test`** dataset.
2. Click "**`CREATE TABLE.`**"
3. Source: "**`Upload`**"
4. Select your CSV file.
5. Table name: **`orders_local`**
6. Check "**`Auto detect`**" under Schema.
7. Click **"`Create table.`"**

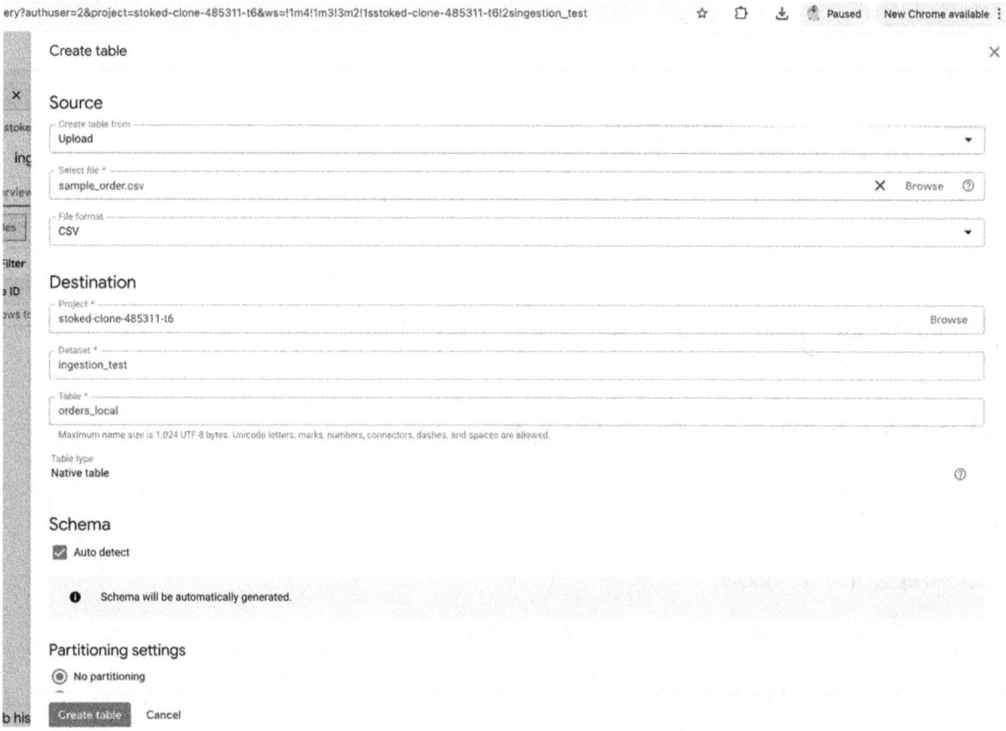

Figure 3.1: *The BigQuery Upload Interface for CSV Files—with the "Auto Detect" Option to Infer Column Names and Types*

The upload typically completes in a few seconds for small files. For this 30-row CSV, the job finishes almost immediately. BigQuery handles larger files in the same way—the job is queued, executed by workers, and you get a notification when it completes.

Step 4: Review the Detected Schema

After the load finishes, click on the **`orders_local`** table and go to the "**`Schema`**" tab.

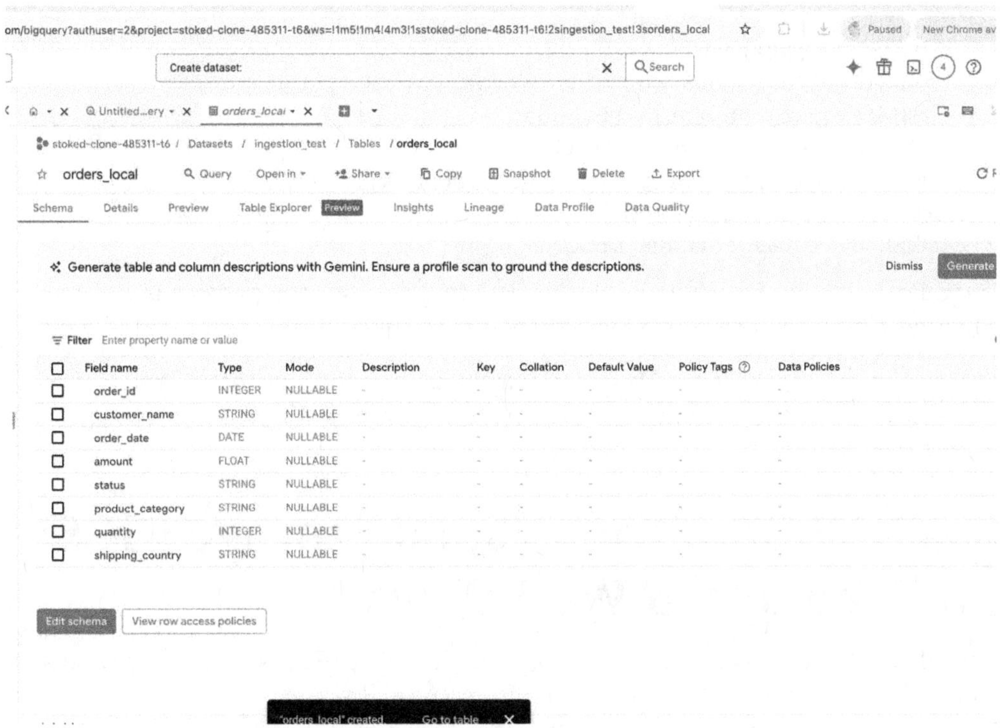

***Figure 3.2**: BigQuery's Auto-Detected Schema for the "Orders" Table*

BigQuery's schema detection worked well in the following ways:

- **`order_id`** and quantity were detected as **`INTEGER`**.
- **`amount`** was detected as **`FLOAT`**.
- **`order_date`** was detected as **`DATE`**.
- Text fields were detected as **`STRING`**.
- All fields were set to **`NULLABLE`** (the default).

This level of accuracy is typical when CSV files follow standard conventions–ISO date formats, consistent delimiters, and clean data. Schema detection becomes less reliable with messy real-world files that mix formats or include inconsistent values.

Step 5: Query Your Data

Now that the data is loaded, you can query it in the following manner:

```
SELECT
  product_category,
  COUNT(*) as order_count,
  SUM(amount) as total_revenue,
  AVG(amount) as avg_order_value
FROM `your-project.ingestion_test.orders_local`
GROUP BY product_category
ORDER BY total_revenue DESC
```

The query runs immediately. While this is a tiny dataset, the pattern is the same for tables with billions of rows—write SQL and get results.

Tip: *The fully qualified table name format is "`project.dataset.table`." You can omit the project if you are querying tables in the current project, but including it makes queries more portable.*

Loading Data from Cloud Storage (GCS) for Production Workflows

Uploading files through the console works for quick tests and small datasets, but production ingestion typically loads data from Cloud Storage. This approach separates data staging from the load process, making it easier to automate, retry, and audit.

Cloud Storage (GCS)

GCS acts as a staging area between source systems and BigQuery. Files land in GCS buckets, and BigQuery loads them from there. This design has the following advantages:

- Files can be validated or transformed before loading.
- Multiple systems can read the same staged files.
- Failed loads can be retried without re-extracting from the source.
- GCS provides durability and versioning for loaded files.
- Automation tools can trigger loads when new files arrive.

The integration between GCS and BigQuery is tight. BigQuery reads directly from GCS without copying files, and the load process is optimized for this path.

Step 1: Upload a File to GCS

First, create a GCS bucket and upload your CSV file in the following steps:

1. In Google Cloud Console, open **`Cloud Storage`** → **`Buckets`**.
2. Click **`CREATE BUCKET`**.
3. Name in this manner: your-name-bigquery-data (must be globally unique).
4. Location: Choose the same region as your BigQuery dataset.
5. Click **`Create.`**
6. Upload your **`sample_order.csv`** file to the bucket.

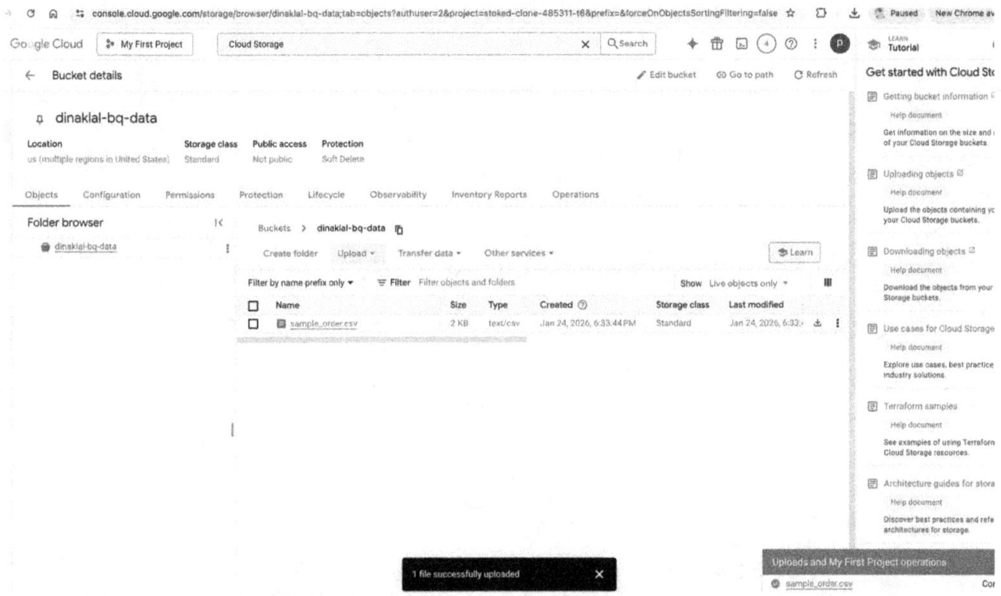

Figure 3.3: A CSV File Uploaded to a Cloud Storage Bucket, Ready to be Loaded into BigQuery

Tip: *Keep your GCS buckets and BigQuery datasets in the same region. Cross-region data movement adds latency and can incur egress charges.*

Step 2: Load from GCS into BigQuery

Now, load the file from GCS:

1. In BigQuery, click **`CREATE TABLE`**.
2. Source: "**`Google Cloud Storage`**"
3. Select file by browsing to "**`gs://your-bucket/sample_order.csv`**"

4. File format: **CSV**
5. Table name: **orders_from_gcs**
6. Schema: **Auto detect**
7. Click **Create table**.

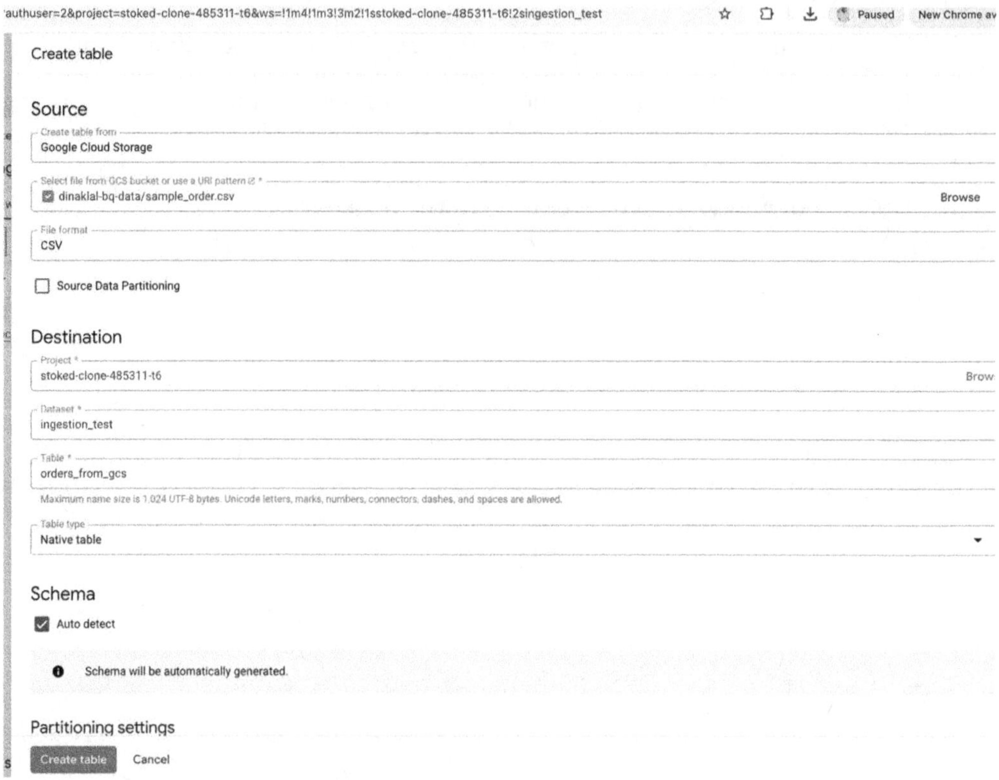

***Figure 3.4:** The Process of Loading a Table from GCS is Nearly Identical to Local Upload–with the GCS Path as Source*

The load completes quickly–often faster than uploading through the console, as BigQuery reads directly from GCS without an intermediate transfer step.

Step 3: Verify the Load

Check that both tables contain the same data:

```
-- Compare row counts
SELECT 'orders_local' as source, COUNT(*) as rows
FROM `your-project.ingestion_test.orders_local`
UNION ALL
SELECT 'orders_from_gcs' as source, COUNT(*) as rows
FROM `your-project.ingestion_test.orders_from_gcs`
```

Both should show 30 rows. The data is identical—only the load path differs.

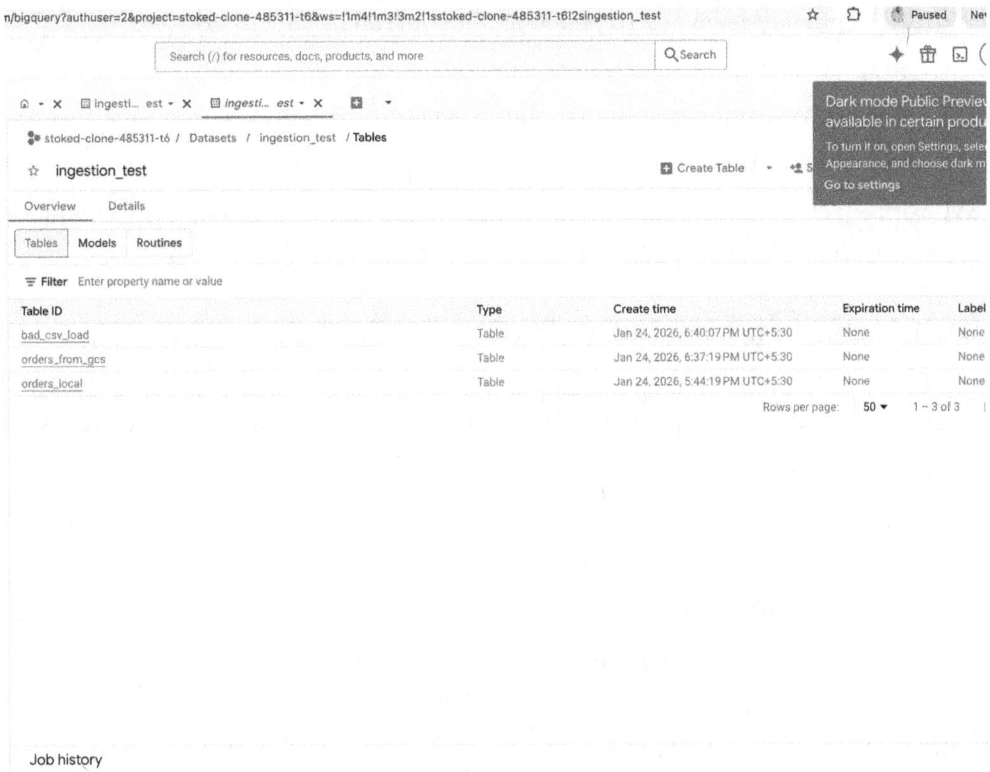

Figure 3.5: *Tables Loaded into BigQuery from Both Local Upload and GCS—Visible in the Dataset Explorer*

Understanding File Formats

BigQuery supports several file formats, and the choice matters for performance, cost, and operational simplicity.

CSV: Simple but Limited

CSV is the most common format for data exchange. It is human-readable, widely supported, and easy to generate from spreadsheets and databases.

Strengths:

- Universal compatibility
- Easy to inspect and debug
- Simple to generate from any system

Weaknesses:

- No embedded schema (types must be inferred or specified)
- Inefficient storage (no compression by default)
- Ambiguity around delimiters, quotes, and null values
- Slow to parse for large files

CSV works well for small datasets, ad-hoc transfers, and initial prototyping. For production systems with large volumes, columnar formats are usually better.

Parquet: Optimized for Analytics

Parquet is a columnar file format designed for analytical workloads. It stores data by column rather than by row, which aligns perfectly with how BigQuery stores data internally.

Strengths:

- Columnar layout reduces scan costs
- Built-in compression (typically 5-10x smaller than CSV)
- Embedded schema (no type ambiguity)
- Efficient for queries that read a subset of columns

Weaknesses:

- Not human-readable
- Requires tools to generate and inspect
- Slightly more complex to produce from source systems

Parquet is the preferred format for production batch ingestion. The storage savings and query performance improvements typically outweigh the added complexity of generating Parquet files.

Avro: Schema Evolution Friendly

Avro is a row-based format with an embedded schema. It is commonly used in streaming systems and data pipelines where schema evolution is frequent.

Strengths:

- Embedded schema travels with the data
- Good support for schema evolution
- Compact binary format
- Wide ecosystem support (for example, Kafka, Hadoop, and Spark)

Weaknesses:

- Row-based layout is less efficient for analytics than columnar formats
- Not as widely adopted as Parquet for batch analytics

Avro is a solid choice when interoperability matters or when schemas change frequently, and you want the schema definition to stay with the data.

JSON: Flexible but Expensive

BigQuery supports newline-delimited JSON (NDJSON), where each line is a separate JSON object.

Strengths:

- Flexible schema
- Easy to generate from APIs and applications
- Supports nested structures naturally

Weaknesses:

- Verbose and inefficient storage
- Slower to parse than binary formats
- Type inference can be unreliable

JSON is useful for semi-structured data or when the schema is highly variable. For structured analytical data, Parquet or Avro are better choices.

Recommendations

For most production ingestion:

- Use Parquet for batch loads of structured data.
- Use Avro when schema evolution is frequent, or interoperability is important.
- Use CSV for small datasets, quick tests, or when source systems cannot produce better formats.
- Use JSON for semi-structured or highly nested data.

Handling Schema Mismatches and Data Quality Issues

Real-world data is messy. Source systems change, files arrive with unexpected values, and schemas drift over time. A robust ingestion process needs to handle these issues without breaking.

Handling Bad Data

Let us see how BigQuery handles a CSV file with type mismatches. Here is a file where some numeric columns contain text:

```
order_id,customer_name,order_date,amount
1001,Alice,2024-01-15,150.50
1002,Bob,not-a-date,200.00
1003,Charlie,2024-01-17,not-a-number
```

When schema auto-detection notices inconsistent values, it may infer a wider type (often STRING) or fail the job depending on the file and settings.

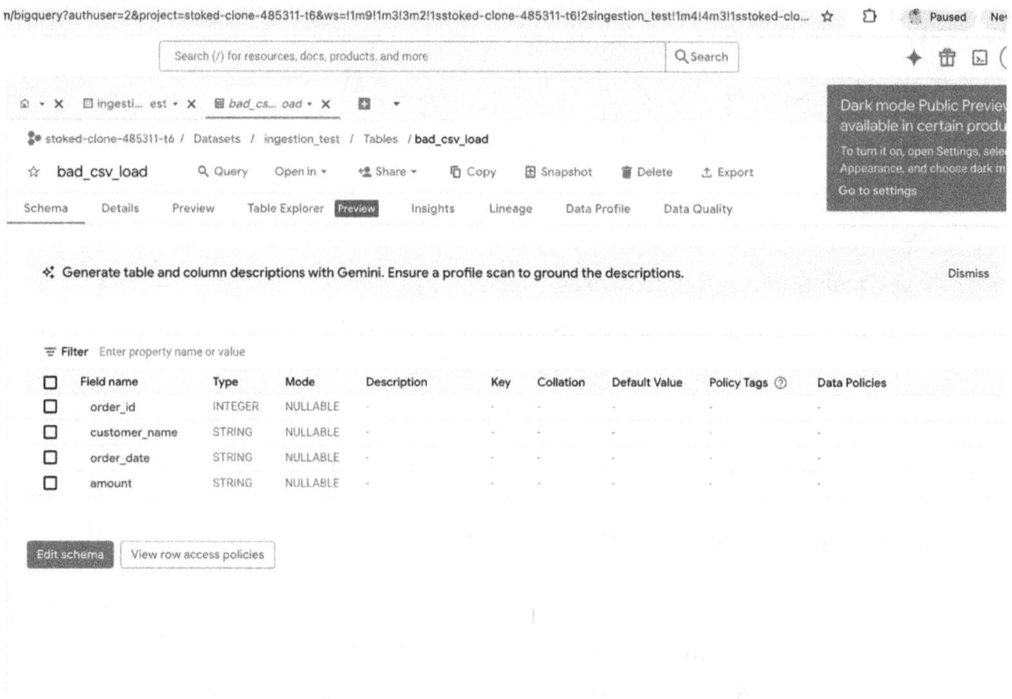

Figure 3.6: *Schema Detection for a CSV with Mixed Types*

This behavior is both helpful and dangerous in the following ways:

- **Helpful:** The load does not fail, and you can inspect the data to understand what went wrong.
- **Dangerous:** You might not notice that numeric columns became strings, leading to incorrect query results later.

Controlling Error Handling

BigQuery provides the following settings to control how errors are handled during loads:

- **Max Bad Records:** Allow up to N rows to fail without failing the entire load. Useful when a small percentage of rows have issues but most of the data is clean.
- **Schema Mismatch Behavior:** Choose whether to fail the load or coerce types when values do not match the expected schema.

The following example uses the **`bq`** command-line tool:

```
bq load \
  --source_format=CSV \
  --skip_leading_rows=1 \
  --max_bad_records=10 \
  --autodetect \
  project:dataset.table \
  gs://bucket/file.csv
```

With **`--max_bad_records=10`**, up to 10 rows can fail without failing the entire load. The bad rows are logged, and the rest of the data is loaded successfully.

Note: *Be careful with permissive error handling in production. Silently dropping bad rows can lead to data loss that is hard to detect. A better pattern is to load raw data permissively into a staging table, then validate and clean it before promoting to production tables.*

Loading Data with SQL and the Command Line

So far, we have used the BigQuery console to load data. For production workflows, engineers typically use SQL statements or the **`bq`** command-line tool instead, as both allow automation, version control, and integration with orchestration systems such as Cloud Composer.

Loading with SQL

BigQuery supports a "**`LOAD DATA`**" statement for loading files from GCS in the following manner:

```
LOAD DATA INTO `project.dataset.orders_raw`
FROM FILES (
  format = 'CSV',
```

```
  skip_leading_rows = 1,
  uris = ['gs://my-bucket/orders/*.csv']
);
```

This approach works well when:

- You are already writing SQL for transformations.
- You want to load multiple files matching a pattern.
- You are using scheduled queries to automate ingestion.

Loading with the bq Command-Line Tool

The **bq** tool is BigQuery's command-line interface, included with the Google Cloud SDK. If you installed the SDK during the "Prerequisites" section, you already have it. Engineers prefer **bq** over the console for production workflows because commands can be scripted, automated, version-controlled, and integrated into orchestration tools such as Cloud Composer.

The console remains ideal for exploration and debugging, while **bq** is the tool of choice when reliability and repeatability matter.

```
bq load \
  --source_format=PARQUET \
  --time_partitioning_field=order_date \
  --clustering_fields=product_category,shipping_country \
  project:dataset.orders_partitioned \
  gs://my-bucket/orders/*.parquet
```

This command:

- Loads all Parquet files matching the pattern.
- Creates a table partitioned by **order_date**.
- Clusters the data by **product_category** and **shipping_country**.
- Can be run from scripts, CI/CD pipelines, or orchestration tools.

The **bq** tool is useful for automation, especially when you need features that are not available in the console, such as partitioning and clustering during the initial load.

BigQuery Data Transfer Service (DTS) for Managed Recurring Loads

The BigQuery Data Transfer Service (DTS) provides managed and recurring ingestion from supported sources. Instead of writing custom scripts to schedule and monitor loads, you configure a transfer and let Google handle the operational details.

When to Use DTS?

DTS works well when:

- The source system is already supported (such as Google Ads, YouTube, Salesforce, AWS S3, and so on).
- You need recurring loads on a schedule.
- You want Google to handle retries, monitoring, and alerting.
- The data can be loaded as-is without complex transformations.

DTS becomes limiting when:

- You need custom transformations before loading.
- The source requires custom authentication or API calls.
- You need fine-grained control over error handling.
- The integration does not exist or does not support the fields you need.

Common Use Cases

- **Scheduled Loads from GCS:** DTS can load files from GCS on a schedule. This is useful when files arrive regularly (for instance, daily exports or hourly logs), and you want automated ingestion without writing the orchestration code.
- **SaaS Integrations:** DTS supports direct transfers from advertising platforms (such as Google Ads or Campaign Manager), analytics tools (such as Google Analytics), and other SaaS products. These integrations handle API authentication, pagination, and incremental loading automatically.
- **Cross-Cloud Transfers**: DTS can load data from AWS S3 or Azure Blob Storage, making it easier to build multi-cloud analytics platforms.

Setting up a Transfer

The following steps show how to set up a recurring load from GCS:

1. In BigQuery, go to "`Data transfers`"
2. Click "`CREATE TRANSFER`"
3. Source: "`Google Cloud Storage`"
4. Schedule: Daily, hourly, or custom `cron` expression
5. Destination Dataset: Choose where data should land
6. File Pattern: `gs://bucket/path/*.csv`
7. File Format: `CSV, JSON, Avro, or Parquet`
8. Click "`Save`"

DTS runs the transfer on schedule, logs the results, and sends notifications if transfers fail. You can view transfer history and re-run failed transfers from the console.

Tip: *Start with DTS when it supports your use case. Only build custom ingestion pipelines when DTS does not provide the flexibility you need.*

Recommended Pattern: Layered Ingestion

A production-ready ingestion design typically uses multiple layers:

Layer 1: Raw Ingestion

- Load data with minimal validation.
- Accept schema mismatches by using STRING for ambiguous columns.
- Goal: Capture what the source system produced.

Layer 2: Staging and Validation

- Apply type conversions and cleaning logic.
- Flag or reject rows that do not meet quality rules.
- Goal: Normalize schema and catch data quality issues.

Layer 3: Curated Tables

- Analytics-ready tables with stable schemas.
- Business logic and transformations applied.
- Goal: Provide reliable data for downstream consumers.

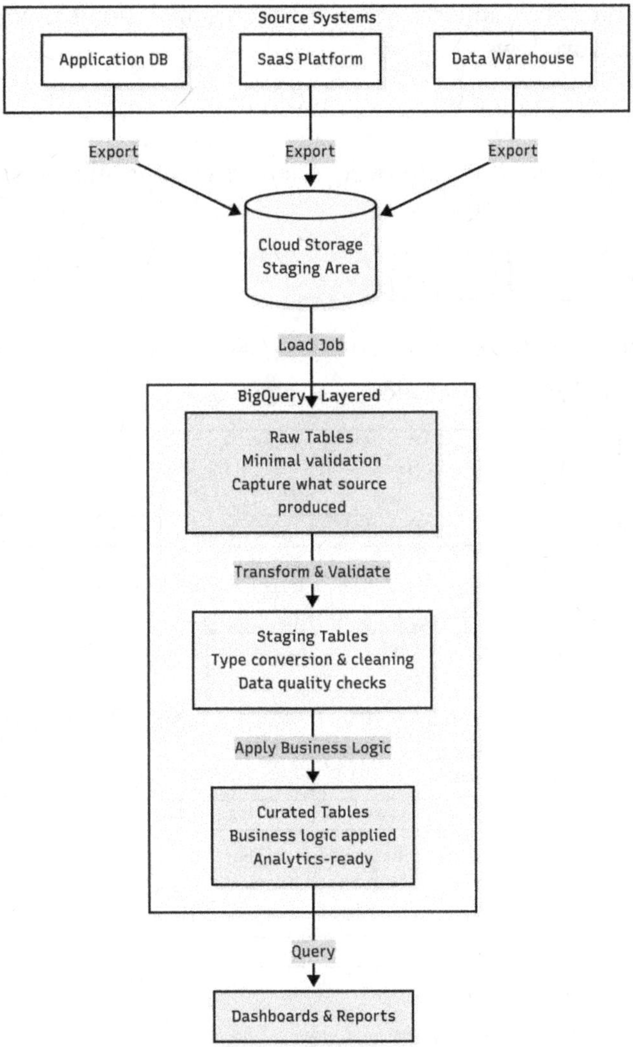

Figure 3.7: *Layered Batch Ingestion Workflow–Showing Data Flowing from Source Systems through GCS into BigQuery's Three-Layer Structure*

This layered approach makes backfills easier and reduces the risk of breaking dashboards when upstream systems change unexpectedly.

Streaming Ingestion Patterns with Pub/Sub and Dataflow

So far, we have focused on batch ingestion–loading data on a schedule using files. This covers most analytical workloads. However, some use cases require data to appear in BigQuery with low latency, within seconds or minutes rather than hours. Streaming ingestion is used for real-time dashboards, operational monitoring, fraud detection, and event-driven workflows.

Streaming ingestion is fundamentally different from batch. Instead of collecting data into files and loading them periodically, events flow continuously from sources into BigQuery. This section will cover when streaming makes sense and how to implement it on Google Cloud.

Pub/Sub and Dataflow

The most common streaming pattern on Google Cloud is:

`Event Source → Pub/Sub → Dataflow → BigQuery`

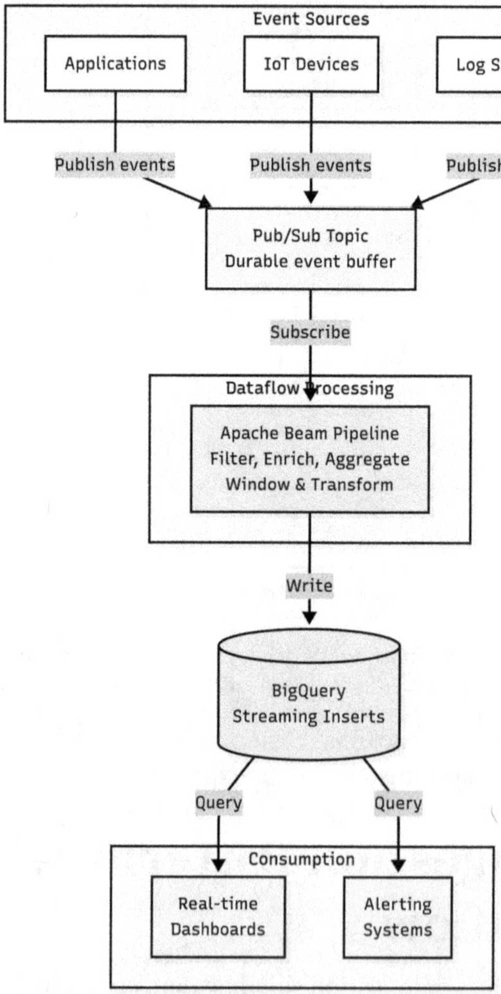

Figure 3.8: *Streaming Ingestion Architecture–Showing How Events Flow from Sources through Pub/Sub and Dataflow into BigQuery for Real-Time Analytics*

Pub/Sub acts as a durable buffer for events. Producers publish messages to Pub/Sub topics, and consumers read from subscriptions. This decouples producers from consumers and gracefully handles bursty traffic.

Dataflow processes the events using Apache Beam pipelines. It can filter, enrich, aggregate, and validate data before writing to BigQuery. Dataflow handles windowing, late data, and exactly-once semantics.

BigQuery receives the processed events as streaming inserts or batch writes, depending on the pipeline configuration.

This architecture is reliable, scalable, and well-supported by Google Cloud's managed services.

A Simple Streaming Pipeline

A minimal Dataflow pipeline that reads from Pub/Sub and writes to BigQuery is as follows:

```
import apache_beam as beam
from apache_beam.options.pipeline_options import PipelineOptions
def run():
    options = PipelineOptions()
    with beam.Pipeline(options=options) as p:
        (p
         | 'Read from Pub/Sub' >> beam.io.ReadFromPubSub(
             subscription='projects/my-project/subscriptions/my-sub')
         | 'Parse JSON' >> beam.Map(lambda msg: json.loads(msg))
         | 'Write to BigQuery' >> beam.io.WriteToBigQuery(
             'my-project:dataset.table',
            schema='order_id:INTEGER,amount:FLOAT,timestamp:TIMESTAMP',
             write_disposition=beam.io.BigQueryDisposition.
WRITE_APPEND))
```

This pipeline:

- Reads messages from a Pub/Sub subscription,
- Parses JSON payloads, and
- Writes rows to a BigQuery table.

Dataflow handles scaling, checkpointing, and retries automatically. We will cover Dataflow pipelines in detail in *Chapter 8: Apache Beam and Dataflow*.

Storage Write API for High-Throughput Streaming

For workloads that need higher throughput than legacy streaming inserts, BigQuery provides the Storage Write API. It is designed for applications that continuously write large volumes of data.

Key Features

- **Exactly-Once Semantics**: The API supports deduplication, reducing the risk of duplicate rows when retries occur.
- **Schema-Aware Writes:** Data is validated against the destination table schema before being written.
- **Parallel Streams:** Multiple write streams can write to the same table concurrently, increasing throughput.
- **Lower Cost:** The Storage Write API is more cost-effective than legacy streaming inserts for high-volume workloads.

Use Cases for Storage Write API

Use the Storage Write API when:

- You are writing more than a few thousand rows per second.
- You need exactly-once guarantees.
- You are building a custom producer that writes directly to BigQuery.
- Cost efficiency matters for high-volume streaming.

For most teams, Pub/Sub + Dataflow is simpler to operate and provides enough throughput. The Storage Write API is best used when you have outgrown simpler approaches or when you are building specialized ingestion systems.

Batch versus Streaming: Choosing the Right Approach

The choice between batch and streaming ingestion depends on latency requirements, operational complexity, and cost.

Batch Ingestion is Enough

Batch ingestion is the right choice when:

- Data can arrive on a schedule (for instance, hourly, daily, or weekly).

- Queries do not need to reflect the last few minutes of data.
- Simplicity and cost-effectiveness are priorities.
- Backfills and reprocessing are common.

Most analytical workloads fall into this category. Dashboards that refresh hourly do not need streaming. Historical analysis does not need real-time data. Batch ingestion is simpler, cheaper, and easier to troubleshoot.

Streaming is Necessary

Streaming ingestion makes sense when:

- Data must appear in BigQuery within seconds or minutes.
- Operational dashboards need live metrics.
- Alerting or automation depends on recent events.
- The business requirement for low latency is clear and justified.

Streaming systems are more complex to build and operate. They require handling late data, managing state, and monitoring pipeline health. Only adopt streaming when the business value justifies the added complexity.

Tip: *Start with batch ingestion. Add streaming only when you have a clear requirement and can justify the operational overhead. Many teams overestimate their need for real-time data.*

Conclusion

This chapter covered the practical aspects of getting data into BigQuery–from uploading your first CSV file to designing production-ready ingestion pipelines.

We started with the simplest approach–loading a CSV through the console–and saw how BigQuery's schema auto-detection works in practice. The detection handled dates, decimals, integers, and strings correctly, making it easy to get started without manually defining schemas.

Loading from GCS proved to be faster and more flexible than local uploads, and the tight integration between GCS and BigQuery made the process straightforward. We explored different file formats and saw why Parquet is typically preferred for production batch loads.

Handling bad data revealed an important behavior: BigQuery will coerce types to STRING rather than fail the load when it encounters mismatches. This flexibility is useful but requires careful monitoring to avoid silent data quality issues. A layered ingestion pattern–raw, staging, curated–manages schema changes and data quality in production systems.

We covered the BigQuery DTS for managed recurring loads and introduced streaming ingestion patterns using Pub/Sub and Dataflow. The Storage Write API provides a high-throughput option for custom streaming producers.

Finally, we discussed when to choose batch versus streaming ingestion. Batch is simpler, cheaper, and sufficient for most analytical workloads. Streaming adds complexity and should only be adopted when low latency is a clear business requirement.

With these ingestion foundations in place, the next chapter will focus on how to model data inside BigQuery for efficient analytics and long-term maintainability.

Points to Remember

- Schema auto-detection works reliably for clean CSV files with standard formats, correctly identifying dates, decimals, integers, and strings.
- Loading from GCS is faster and more production-ready than local uploads, with tight integration between GCS and BigQuery.
- Parquet is the preferred format for production batch loads due to columnar layout, compression, and embedded schema.
- BigQuery coerces mismatched types to STRING rather than failing loads, which helps with flexibility but requires monitoring for data quality.
- Layered ingestion (raw → staging → curated) manages schema changes and protects downstream consumers.
- BigQuery Data Transfer Service (DTS) provides managed recurring loads for supported sources, reducing operational overhead.
- Pub/Sub and Dataflow form a reliable streaming pattern for low-latency ingestion with transformations.
- Batch ingestion is simpler and sufficient for most analytical workloads–adopt streaming only when low latency is a clear business requirement.

Multiple Choice Questions

1. What happened when BigQuery's schema auto-detection encountered a CSV with mixed types in a column?

    a. The load failed with an error

    b. BigQuery converted the column to STRING

    c. BigQuery skipped the problematic rows

    d. BigQuery created separate tables for each type

2. Which file format is generally preferred for large analytical batch loads into BigQuery?
   a. CSV
   b. Parquet
   c. TXT
   d. XML
3. Which service is commonly used to stage batch ingestion files before loading into BigQuery?
   a. Pub/Sub
   b. Cloud Storage (GCS)
   c. Cloud Composer
   d. Cloud Functions
4. What is a key advantage of BigQuery Data Transfer Service (DTS)?
   a. It provides custom transformations by default.
   b. It supports managed recurring ingestion from supported sources.
   c. It replaces the need for SQL.
   d. It disables schema validation.
5. In a typical streaming pattern, which component acts as the event buffer?
   a. BigQuery
   b. Pub/Sub
   c. Cloud Storage (GCS)
   d. Looker Studio
6. Which BigQuery feature is designed for high-throughput streaming writes with lower overhead than legacy streaming inserts?
   a. Data Transfer Service
   b. Storage Write API
   c. BigQuery ML
   d. BI Engine

7. What is the recommended approach when starting a new analytics project?
    a. Always use streaming ingestion
    b. Start with batch ingestion and add streaming only when needed
    c. Use both batch and streaming from the beginning
    d. Avoid Cloud Storage (GCS) and load directly
8. What does the "max bad records" setting control?
    a. Maximum table size
    b. Number of rows that can fail without failing the entire load
    c. Maximum query execution time
    d. Number of concurrent load jobs
9. Why is Parquet preferred over CSV for production loads?
    a. It is human-readable.
    b. It has columnar layout, compression, and embedded schema.
    c. It is easier to generate.
    d. It works better with spreadsheets.
10. What is the purpose of a layered ingestion pattern (raw → staging → curated)?
    a. To increase storage costs
    b. To make queries slower
    c. To handle schema changes and protect downstream consumers
    d. To avoid using Cloud Storage (GCS)

Answers

1. b
2. b
3. b
4. b
5. b
6. b

7. b
8. b
9. b
10. c

Questions

1. Why is loading from Cloud Storage (GCS) preferred over local file uploads for production ingestion?
2. How did BigQuery handle the CSV file with mixed types, and why is this behavior both helpful and dangerous?
3. What are the advantages of Parquet over CSV for production batch loads?
4. What is a layered ingestion pattern, and how does it help manage schema changes?
5. When should you choose streaming ingestion over batch ingestion?
6. What role does Pub/Sub play in a streaming ingestion architecture?
7. How does the BigQuery Data Transfer Service differ from custom ingestion pipelines?

Key Terms

- **Batch Ingestion:** Loading data on a schedule in discrete loads rather than continuously.
- **Streaming Ingestion:** Loading data continuously as events arrive with low latency.
- **Schema Auto-Detection:** BigQuery's ability to infer column names and types from file contents.
- **Cloud Storage (GCS):** Google's object storage service, commonly used to stage files before loading into BigQuery.
- **Parquet:** A columnar file format optimized for analytical workloads and efficient storage.
- **Avro**: A row-based file format with embedded schema, commonly used for interoperability and schema evolution.
- **CSV**: Comma-separated values format, simple and widely supported but inefficient for large analytical datasets.

- **BigQuery Data Transfer Service:** A managed service for recurring ingestion from supported sources.
- **Pub/Sub:** A messaging service used to publish and buffer streaming events.
- **Dataflow**: A managed Apache Beam service for batch and streaming data processing.
- **Storage Write API:** A BigQuery API designed for high-throughput, schema-aware streaming writes.
- **Write Stream**: A stream used by the Storage Write API to write data into a destination table.
- **Schema Evolution:** The process of handling changes to fields, types, or structure over time.
- **Layered Ingestion:** A pattern that separates raw ingestion, staging/validation, and curated tables to manage schema changes and data quality.
- **Max Bad Records**: A load setting that allows up to N rows to fail without failing the entire load job.

CHAPTER 4
Modeling for Scale

Introduction

The previous chapter showed you how to get data into BigQuery–CSV uploads, Cloud Storage loads, and streaming inserts. You learned how schema auto-detection works, how bad data gets handled, and how different loading methods compare. However, once the data lands in BigQuery, the next question emerges: how should you structure it?

This is not an academic question. The way you model your data directly affects query performance, storage costs, and also how easy it is to write and maintain SQL. Get it wrong, and you will spend months refactoring production tables while your team complains about slow dashboards and expensive queries.

Traditional data warehouses pushed you toward star schemas–normalized dimension tables joined to fact tables. It is a pattern that has been around for decades, and it works. However, BigQuery is not a traditional warehouse. It has native support for nested and repeated fields through **STRUCT** and **ARRAY** types so that you can store hierarchical data without flattening it into multiple tables.

So, which approach should you use? Nested structures that keep related data together? Flat star schemas that separate dimensions from facts? Or fully denormalized wide tables that duplicate data but eliminate joins?

The answer is not that "it depends" followed by some vague advice. This chapter will walk through a hands-on comparison of all three approaches using the same dataset. You will see actual query performance numbers–bytes processed, bytes billed, and slot time–for identical queries run against nested, flat, and wide table structures. By the end, you will know when to use each approach and why.

Structure

This chapter will cover the following topics:

- The Three Modeling Approaches
- Building the Test Dataset
- Query Performance Comparison

- Use Case for Each Approach
- Organizing Your Data Warehouse
- Partitioning and Clustering
- Schema Evolution

The Three Modeling Approaches

Before diving into performance comparisons, let us look at what each modeling approach actually means in BigQuery.

Nested Structure (STRUCT + ARRAY)

BigQuery's native approach uses **STRUCT** for nested objects and **ARRAY** for repeated fields. This allows you to store hierarchical data in a single table without flattening it.

Here is an order table with nested customer and items:

```
CREATE TABLE orders_nested (
  order_id INT64,
  order_date DATE,
  customer STRUCT<
    customer_id INT64,
    name STRING,
    email STRING,
    country STRING
  >,
  items ARRAY<STRUCT<
    product_id INT64,
    product_name STRING,
    category STRING,
    quantity INT64,
    price FLOAT64
  >>,
  total_amount FLOAT64,
  status STRING
);
```

A single row contains everything about an order–the customer details nested as a **STRUCT**, and all order items stored as an **ARRAY** of **STRUCTs**. No joins are needed to get the complete picture.

When You Query It:

- Access nested fields with dot notation: **customer.name, customer.country**

- Flatten arrays with **UNNEST**: **FROM orders_nested, UNNEST(items) AS item**
- Use **ARRAY_LENGTH** to count items without unnesting

Storage Characteristics:

- One row per order, regardless of how many items
- Related data stays together (better compression)
- No duplicate customer information across rows

Star Schema (Flat Tables)

The traditional data warehouse approach separates dimensions from facts. For the same order data, you would create four tables in the following way:

```
-- Fact table: orders
CREATE TABLE orders_flat (
  order_id INT64,
  order_date DATE,
  customer_id INT64,  -- Foreign key
  total_amount FLOAT64,
  status STRING
);

-- Fact table: order items
CREATE TABLE order_items_flat (
  order_id INT64,       -- Foreign key
  product_id INT64,     -- Foreign key
  quantity INT64,
  price FLOAT64
);
-- Dimension: customers
CREATE TABLE customers (
  customer_id INT64,
  name STRING,
  email STRING,
  country STRING
);

-- Dimension: products
CREATE TABLE products (
  product_id INT64,
  product_name STRING,
  category STRING
);
```

This is the normalized approach. Customer data lives in one place, product data in another, and fact tables reference them through foreign keys.

When You Query It:

- JOIN tables to reconstruct relationships
- Filter on dimensions before joining (more efficient)
- Update dimension data once, affects all related facts

Storage Characteristics:

- Multiple rows per order (one per item in **`order_items_flat`**)
- No duplicate customer or product data
- More tables to manage, but cleaner separation

Wide Denormalized Table

The fully flattened approach duplicates everything into a single table in the following manner:

```
CREATE TABLE orders_wide AS
SELECT
  o.order_id,
  o.order_date,
  o.status,
  o.total_amount,
  -- Customer fields (duplicated for every item)
  c.customer_id,
  c.name AS customer_name,
  c.email AS customer_email,
  c.country AS customer_country,
  -- Item fields (one row per item)
  oi.product_id,
  p.product_name,
  p.category AS product_category,
  oi.quantity,
  oi.price,
  oi.quantity * oi.price AS line_total
FROM orders_flat o
JOIN customers c ON o.customer_id = c.customer_id
JOIN order_items_flat oi ON o.order_id = oi.order_id
JOIN products p ON oi.product_id = p.product_id;
```

Every row contains the complete denormalized data–order details, customer details, and item details–in one place. If an order has 5 items, the customer information gets duplicated 5 times.

When You Query It:

- No joins needed, as everything is already there

- Simple **SELECT** with **GROUP BY** for aggregations
- Fastest query execution (no join overhead)

Storage Characteristics:

- Most rows (one per order item)
- Significant data duplication (customer and order info repeated)
- Largest storage footprint
- Simplest queries

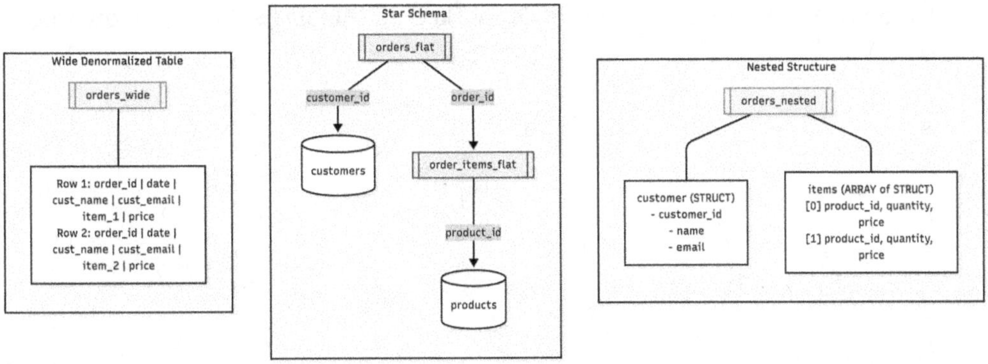

***Figure 4.1**: Comparing Modeling Approaches*

Building the Test Dataset

To compare these approaches fairly, you need the same data modeled in all three formats. Here is how to set it up as mentioned in this section.

Creating the Nested Table

Start with the nested structure. This requires understanding **STRUCT** and **ARRAY** syntax:

```
CREATE TABLE `your-project.dataset.orders_nested` (
  order_id INT64,
  order_date DATE,
  customer STRUCT<
    customer_id INT64,
    name STRING,
    email STRING,
    country STRING
  >,
  items ARRAY<STRUCT<
    product_id INT64,
```

```
        product_name STRING,
        category STRING,
        quantity INT64,
        price NUMERIC
      >>,
      total_amount NUMERIC,
      status STRING
    );
```

The schema shows up in BigQuery with expandable sections for the **STRUCT** and **ARRAY** fields. Click the arrow next to **customer**, and you will see the nested fields. Click **items,** and you will see that it is marked as "**REPEATED**" with its own nested structure.

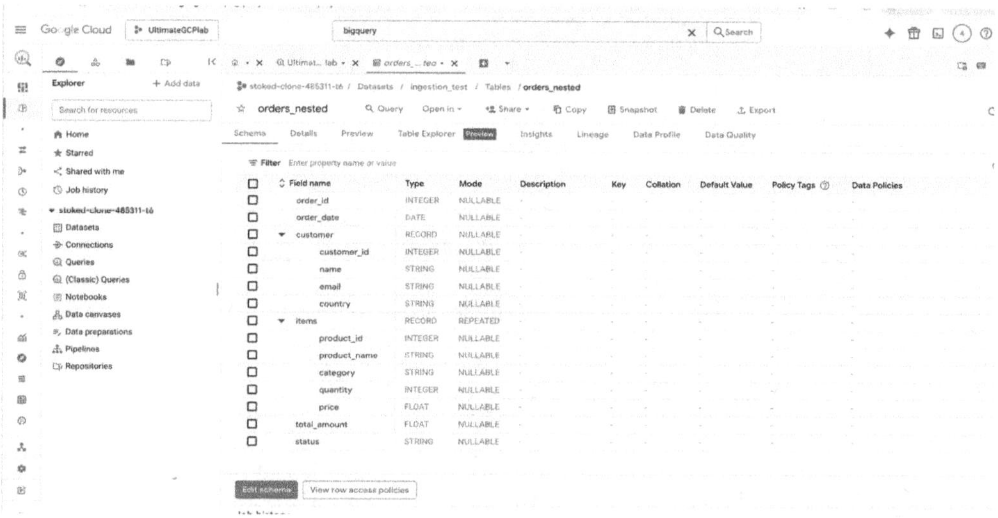

***Figure 4.2**: Schema of Nested Table Showing STRUCT and ARRAY Types in BigQuery UI*

Inserting the nested data requires array literals in the following manner:

```
INSERT INTO orders_nested VALUES
(1001, '2024-01-15',
 STRUCT(101, 'Alice Johnson', 'alice@email.com', 'USA'),
 [STRUCT(501, 'Laptop', 'Electronics', 1, 1200.00),
  STRUCT(502, 'Mouse', 'Electronics', 2, 25.00)],
 1250.00, 'completed');
```

The square brackets [] define the array, and each STRUCT inside represents one order item. This single INSERT creates a row with two items nested inside it.

Creating the Star Schema Tables

The flat approach requires four separate "**CREATE**" statements and four separate "**INSERT**" operations in the following way:

```
-- Create all four tables
CREATE TABLE orders_flat (
  order_id INT64,
  order_date DATE,
  customer_id INT64,
  total_amount NUMERIC,
  status STRING
);
CREATE TABLE order_items_flat (
  order_id INT64,
  product_id INT64,
  quantity INT64,
  price NUMERIC
);
CREATE TABLE customers (
  customer_id INT64,
  name STRING,
  email STRING,
  country STRING
);
CREATE TABLE products (
  product_id INT64,
  product_name STRING,
  category STRING
);
```

Then, insert the data separately in the following way:

```
-- Insert orders
INSERT INTO orders_flat VALUES
(1001, '2024-01-15', 101, 1250.00, 'completed');
-- Insert order items (two rows for order 1001)
INSERT INTO order_items_flat VALUES
(1001, 501, 1, 1200.00),
(1001, 502, 2, 25.00);
-- Insert customer (once)
INSERT INTO customers VALUES
(101, 'Alice Johnson', 'alice@email.com', 'USA');
-- Insert products (once each)
INSERT INTO products VALUES
(501, 'Laptop', 'Electronics'),
(502, 'Mouse', 'Electronics');
```

More tables to manage, but the data is normalized. Customer 101 appears once in the customers table, even if they have multiple orders.

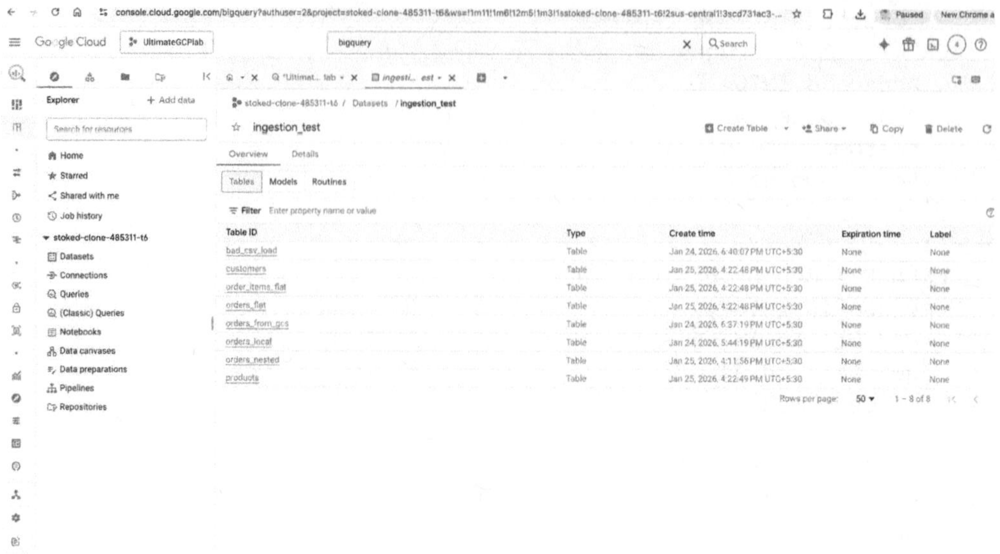

***Figure 4.3**: Star Schema Tables in BigQuery UI Showing All Four Tables*

Creating the Wide Table

The wide table is typically created from the star schema using a "**CREATE TABLE AS SELECT**" with all the joins in the following way:

```
CREATE TABLE orders_wide AS
SELECT
  o.order_id,
  o.order_date,
  o.status,
  o.total_amount,
  c.customer_id,
  c.name AS customer_name,
  c.email AS customer_email,
  c.country AS customer_country,
  oi.product_id,
  p.product_name,
  p.category AS product_category,
  oi.quantity,
  oi.price,
  oi.quantity * oi.price AS line_total
FROM orders_flat o
JOIN customers c ON o.customer_id = c.customer_id
JOIN order_items_flat oi ON o.order_id = oi.order_id
JOIN products p ON oi.product_id = p.product_id;
```

This single statement creates a wide table by joining all four-star schema tables.

The result is a fully denormalized structure, in which every row contains complete information about one order item, including duplicated customer and order data.

For the test dataset, insert 5 orders with varying numbers of items in the following way:

```
Order 1001: 2 items (Alice, Electronics)
Order 1002: 2 items (Bob, Books)
Order 1003: 1 item (Charlie, Clothing)
Order 1004: 3 items (Alice again, Electronics)
Order 1005: 2 items (Diana, Sports)
```

This provides 10 total order items across 5 orders from 4 customers—small enough to understand, and large enough to see patterns.

A Note on Scale: *This test uses a tiny dataset (for instance, 5 orders and 10 items) to illustrate the baseline mechanics and make the patterns visible. In production, you would be working with millions or billions of rows. The specific byte counts and millisecond timings will scale up, but the relative patterns hold and often amplify at larger scales. The principles you learn here apply regardless of data size.*

Query Performance Comparison

Now comes the interesting part—running the same queries against all three table structures and comparing the results. BigQuery's job information panel shows the following three key metrics:

- **Bytes Processed:** How much data BigQuery actually read from storage
- **Bytes Billed:** What you pay for (minimum 10 MB per table scanned in on-demand pricing)
- **Slot Milliseconds:** Compute time used (affects query speed and concurrency)

These numbers will tell you which approach is more efficient for different query patterns.

Query 1: Get All Orders with Customer Names

This is the simplest query: get order details with customer information.

Nested Version:

```
SELECT
  order_id,
  order_date,
  customer.name AS customer_name,
  customer.country,
  total_amount,
```

```
  status
FROM orders_nested
ORDER BY order_date;
```

Dircct access to nested fields. No joins or **UNNEST** are needed because we are not touching the items array.

Flat Version:

```
SELECT
  o.order_id,
  o.order_date,
  c.name AS customer_name,
  c.country,
  o.total_amount,
  o.status
FROM orders_flat o
JOIN customers c ON o.customer_id = c.customer_id
ORDER BY o.order_date;
```

Requires a join between "**orders_flat**" and "**customers**" to get the customer name.

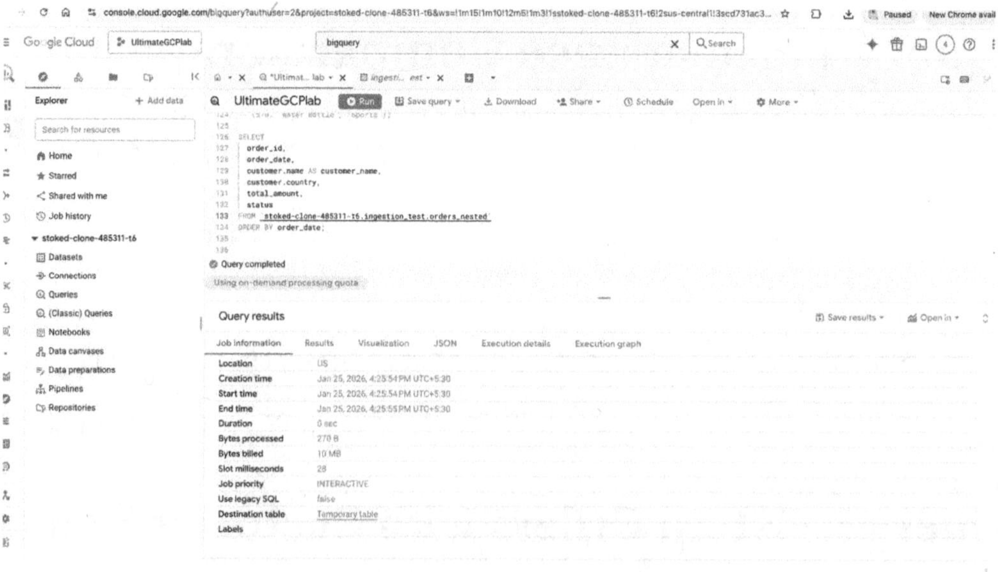

***Figure 4.4**: Job Information for Query 1–Nested Version*

Results from This Test:

- **Nested**: 270 B processed, 10 MB billed, 52 slot-ms

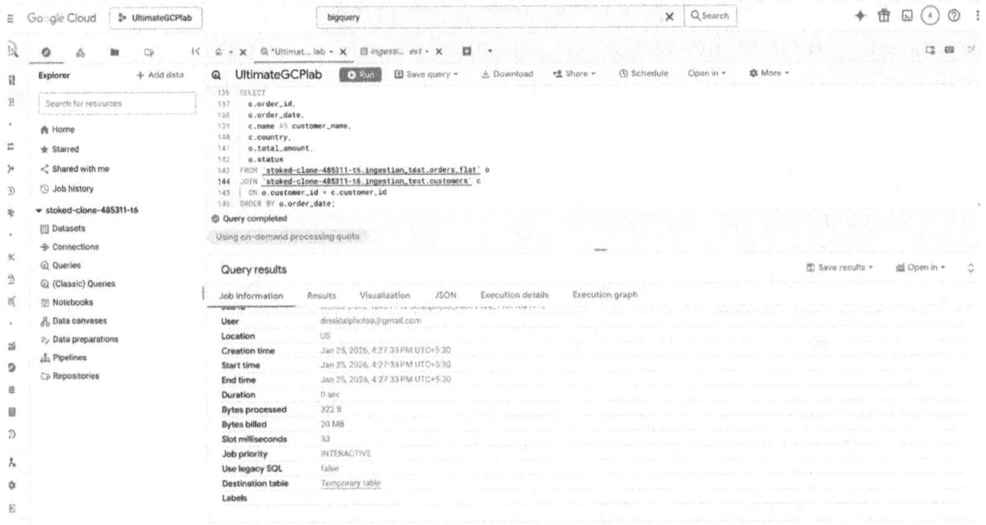

***Figure 4.5**: Job Information for Query 1–Flat Version (Star Schema)*

Results from This Test:

- **Flat**: 322 B processed, 20 MB billed, 33 slot-ms

The nested version processed less data (270 B versus 322 B in this test) and got billed for less (10 MB versus 20 MB), but it used more compute time (52 slot-ms versus 33 slot-ms). The pattern holds regardless of data size: single-table queries hit the 10 MB minimum once, while multi-table queries multiply that minimum. For simple queries on small datasets, the join in the flat version executed faster despite reading more data.

Query 2: Get Order Items with Product Details

Now, we need to flatten the data to see individual order items.

Nested Version:

```
SELECT
  order_id,
  order_date,
  customer.name AS customer_name,
  item.product_name,
  item.category,
  item.quantity,
  item.price,
  item.quantity * item.price AS line_total
FROM orders_nested,
UNNEST(items) AS item
ORDER BY order_id, item.product_name;
```

The **UNNEST** operation flattens the items array, creating one output row per item. The comma after "**orders_nested**" is shorthand for a "**CROSS JOIN**" with the unnested array.

Flat Version:

```
SELECT
  o.order_id,
  o.order_date,
  c.name AS customer_name,
  p.product_name,
  p.category,
  oi.quantity,
  oi.price,
  oi.quantity * oi.price AS line_total
FROM orders_flat o
JOIN customers c ON o.customer_id = c.customer_id
JOIN order_items_flat oi ON o.order_id = oi.order_id
JOIN products p ON oi.product_id = p.product_id
ORDER BY o.order_id, p.product_name;
```

Three joins are required: orders to customers, orders to **order_items**, and **order_items** to products.

Results from This Test:

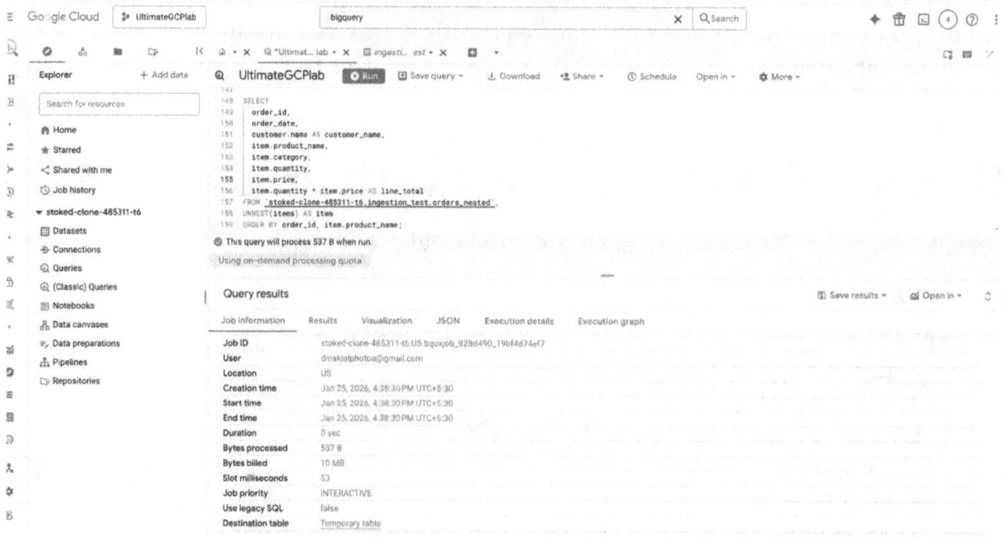

Figure 4.6: *Job Information for Query 2–Nested Version with UNNEST*

Results:

- **Nested**: 537 B processed, 10 MB billed, 53 slot-ms

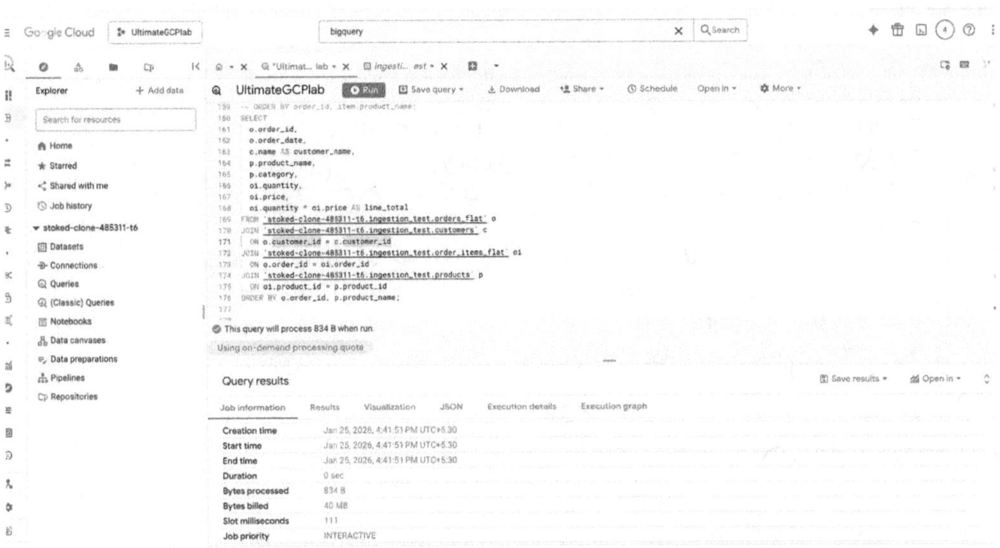

***Figure 4.7**: Job Information for Query 2–Flat Version with Multiple JOINs*

Results:

- **Flat**: 834 B processed, 40 MB billed, 111 slot-ms

The gap widens. The nested version processed 35% less data (537 B versus 834 B in this test), got billed for 75% less (10 MB versus 40 MB), and used half the compute time (53 slot-ms versus 111 slot-ms). This pattern demonstrates that when you need to work with nested data, keeping it nested is more efficient than splitting it across multiple tables and joining them back together.

Query 3: Revenue by Product Category

Aggregation queries show a different pattern.

Nested Version:

```
SELECT
  item.category,
  COUNT(DISTINCT order_id) AS order_count,
  SUM(item.quantity) AS total_quantity,
  SUM(item.quantity * item.price) AS total_revenue
FROM orders_nested,
UNNEST(items) AS item
GROUP BY item.category
ORDER BY total_revenue DESC;
```

UNNEST the items, then group by category. The aggregation happens after flattening.

Flat Version:

```
SELECT
  p.category,
  COUNT(DISTINCT o.order_id) AS order_count,
  SUM(oi.quantity) AS total_quantity,
  SUM(oi.quantity * oi.price) AS total_revenue
FROM orders_flat o
JOIN order_items_flat oi ON o.order_id = oi.order_id
JOIN products p ON oi.product_id = p.product_id
GROUP BY p.category
ORDER BY total_revenue DESC;
```

Join the tables, then group by category.

Results from This Test:

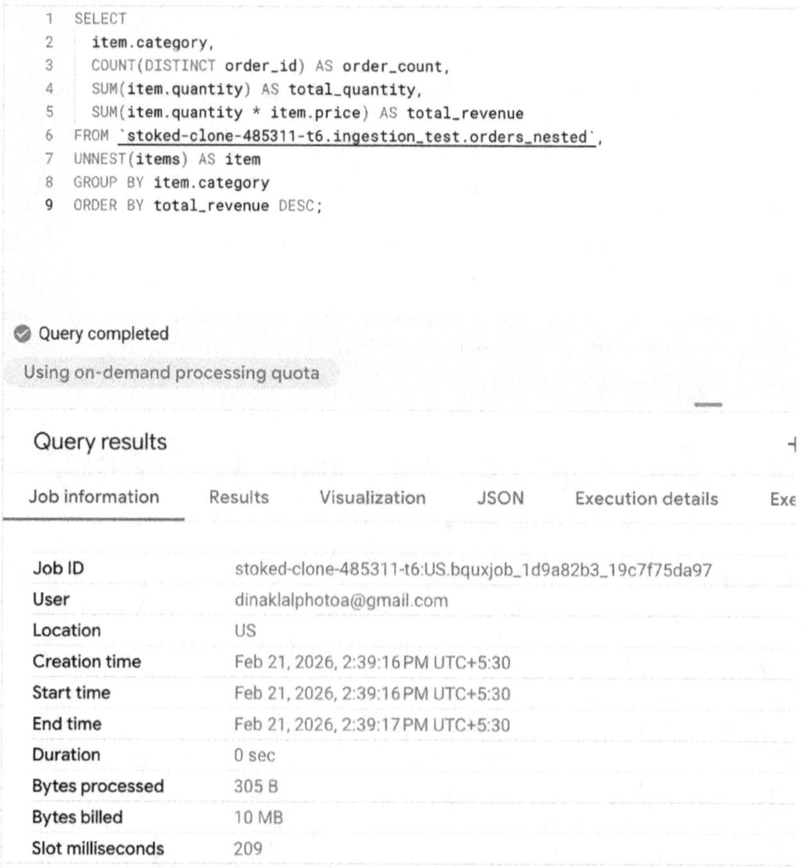

Figure 4.8: *Nested Version with UNNEST and GROUP BY*

Results:

- Nested: 305 B processed, 10 MB billed, 209 slot-ms

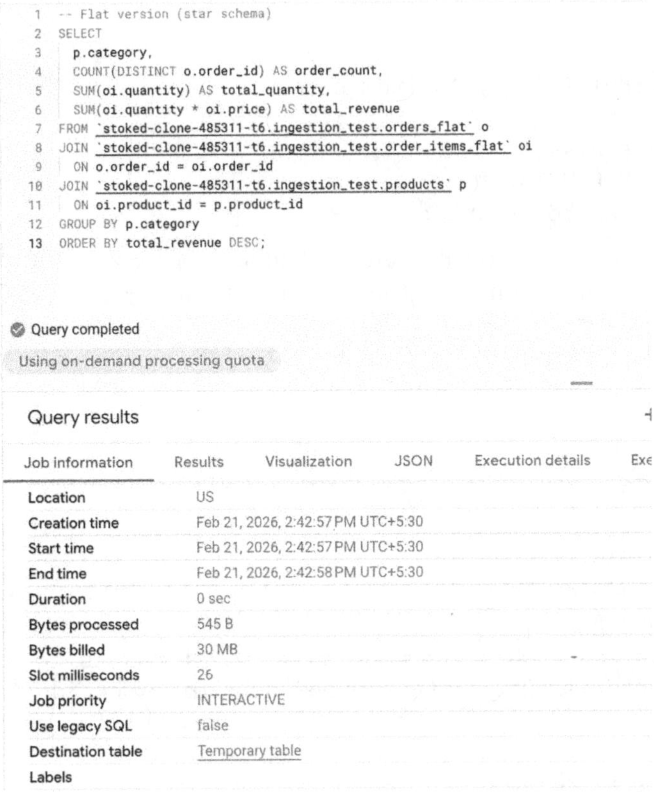

***Figure 4.9**: Flat Version with JOINs and GROUP BY*

Results:

- **Flat**: 545 B processed, 30 MB billed, 26 slot-ms

Here is where it gets interesting. The nested version still processed less data (305 B versus 545 B in this test) and got billed less (10 MB versus 30 MB), but used significantly more compute time (209 slot-ms versus 26 slot-ms). The **UNNEST** operation followed by **GROUP BY** required more processing than the flat version's joins and aggregation.

For aggregation queries, the flat version's higher data scan is offset by more efficient grouping operations. This pattern appears consistently when aggregating nested data.

Query 4: Orders with More than 2 Items

Filtering on array properties shows another use case.

Nested Version:

```
SELECT
  order_id,
  order_date,
  customer.name,
  ARRAY_LENGTH(items) AS item_count,
  total_amount
FROM orders_nested
WHERE ARRAY_LENGTH(items) > 2
ORDER BY item_count DESC;
```

ARRAY_LENGTH allows you to filter on the number of items without unnesting the array. This is a unique advantage of the nested structure—you can ask questions about the array itself.

Flat Version:

```
SELECT
  o.order_id,
  o.order_date,
  c.name,
  COUNT(*) AS item_count,
  o.total_amount
FROM orders_flat o
JOIN customers c ON o.customer_id = c.customer_id
JOIN order_items_flat oi ON o.order_id = oi.order_id
GROUP BY o.order_id, o.order_date, c.name, o.total_amount
HAVING COUNT(*) > 2
ORDER BY item_count DESC;
```

The flat version requires joining to **order_items**, grouping by order, counting rows, and filtering with **HAVING**—more complex SQL for the same result.

Results from This Test:

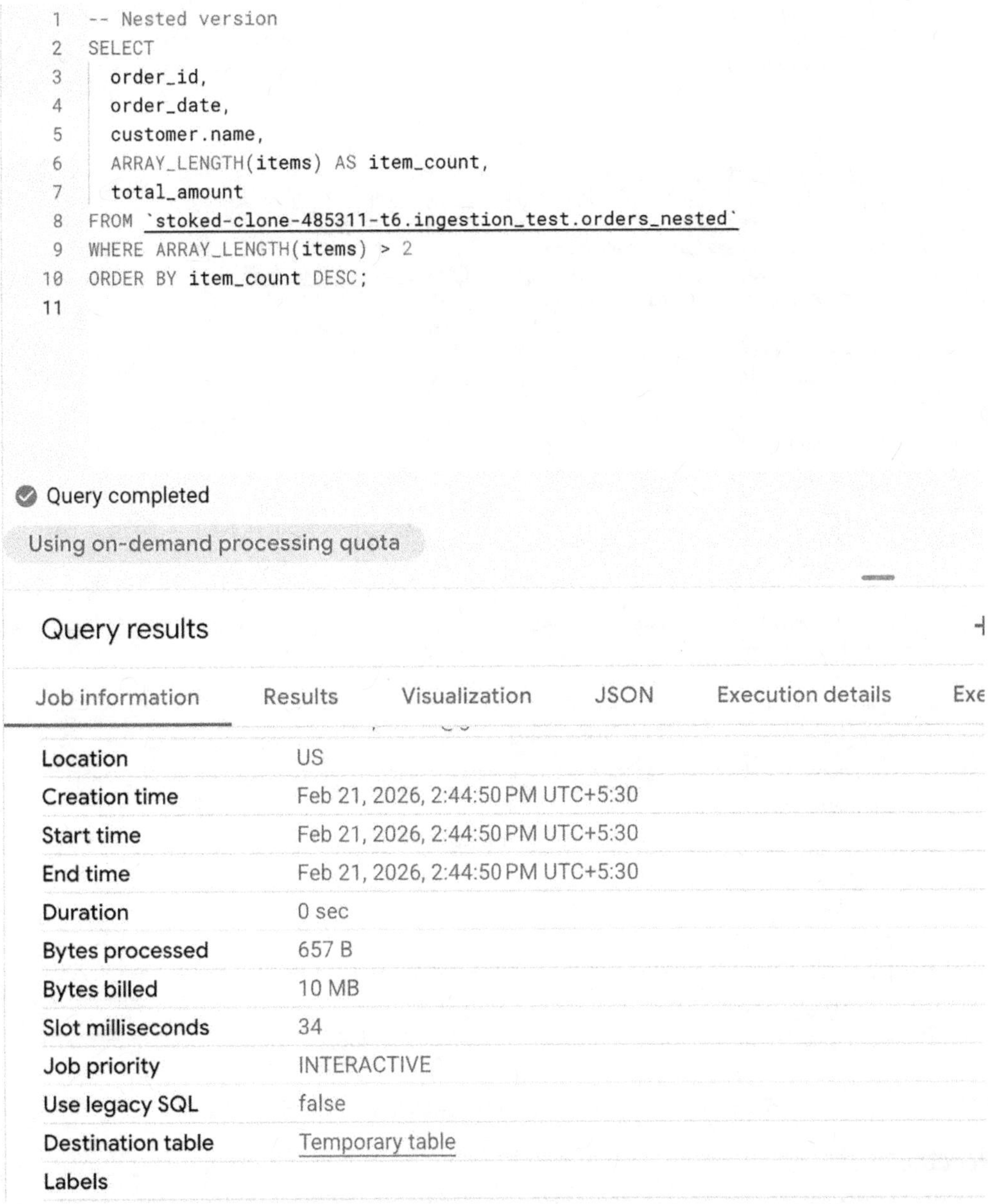

Figure 4.10: *Nested Version Using* ARRAY_LENGTH

Results:

- **Nested**: 657 B processed, 10 MB billed, 34 slot-ms

```sql
-- Flat version (star schema)
SELECT
  o.order_id,
  o.order_date,
  c.name,
  COUNT(*) AS item_count,
  o.total_amount
FROM `stoked-clone-485311-t6.ingestion_test.orders_flat` o
JOIN `stoked-clone-485311-t6.ingestion_test.customers` c
  ON o.customer_id = c.customer_id
JOIN `stoked-clone-485311-t6.ingestion_test.order_items_flat` oi
  ON o.order_id = oi.order_id
GROUP BY o.order_id, o.order_date, c.name, o.total_amount
HAVING COUNT(*) > 2
ORDER BY item_count DESC;
```

Query completed

Using on-demand processing quota

Query results

Job information | Results | Visualization | JSON | Execution details | Exe

Job ID	stoked-clone-485311-t6:US.bquxjob_2a6c3c68_19c7f7c42c4
User	dinaklalphotoa@gmail.com
Location	US
Creation time	Feb 21, 2026, 2:46:16 PM UTC+5:30
Start time	Feb 21, 2026, 2:46:16 PM UTC+5:30
End time	Feb 21, 2026, 2:46:16 PM UTC+5:30
Duration	0 sec
Bytes processed	327 B
Bytes billed	30 MB
Slot milliseconds	40
Job priority	INTERACTIVE

***Figure 4.11**: Flat Version with GROUP BY and HAVING*

Results:

- **Flat**: 327 B processed, 30 MB billed, 40 slot-ms

Surprisingly, the flat version processed less data (327 B versus 657 B in this test) but still got billed more (30 MB versus 10 MB) due to the 10 MB minimum per table scanned. The compute time was similar (34 slot-ms versus 40 slot-ms).

The nested version's advantage is simpler SQL and lower billing, not raw performance. The pattern shows that **`ARRAY_LENGTH`** operations are efficient, but the billing difference comes from scanning fewer tables.

Wide Table Performance

Now, test the same revenue-by-category query against the wide table in the following manner:

```
SELECT
  product_category,
  COUNT(DISTINCT order_id) AS order_count,
  SUM(quantity) AS total_quantity,
  SUM(line_total) AS total_revenue
FROM orders_wide
GROUP BY product_category
ORDER BY total_revenue DESC;
```

No joins. No **UNNEST**. Just a simple **SELECT** with **GROUP BY**.

Results from This Test:

***Figure 4.12**: Wide Table Query Results Showing Fastest Execution Time*

- **Wide**: 345 B processed, 10 MB billed, 17 slot-ms

Compare this to the same query on the other structures:

- **Nested**: 305 B processed, 10 MB billed, 209 slot-ms
- **Flat**: 545 B processed, 30 MB billed, 26 slot-ms
- **Wide**: 345 B processed, 10 MB billed, 17 slot-ms

The wide table wins on compute time by a significant margin—17 slot-ms compared to 209 slot-ms for nested and 26 slot-ms for flat. It processed a moderate amount of data (345 B between nested and flat) and got billed the minimum 10 MB.

For aggregation queries, the wide table's lack of joins and `UNNEST` operations makes it the fastest option. This pattern holds at scale: pre-joined data eliminates query-time overhead. The tradeoff is storage, as you are duplicating customer and order data for every order item.

Performance Patterns

Looking at all four queries together reveals clear patterns. Here is a summary of the test results:

Performance Comparison Matrix

Query	Approach	Bytes Processed	Bytes Billed	Slot-ms	Notes
Query 1: Orders with customer names	Nested	270 B	10 MB	52	Simple access, no UNNEST
	Flat	322 B	20 MB	33	One JOIN, faster execution
Query 2: Order items with details	Nested	537 B	10 MB	53	UNNEST required
	Flat	834 B	40 MB	111	Three JOINs
Query 3: Revenue by category	Nested	305 B	10 MB	209	UNNEST + GROUP BY (slow)
	Flat	545 B	30 MB	26	JOINs + GROUP BY (fast)
	Wide	345 B	10 MB	17	No JOINs (fastest)
Query 4: Orders with >2 items	Nested	657 B	10 MB	34	ARRAY_LENGTH (efficient)
	Flat	327 B	30 MB	40	GROUP BY + HAVING

Table 4.1: *Performance Comparison*

Key Patterns: The specific byte counts will vary with data size, but the relative pattern holds: nested scans read less data, as it stores related information together in fewer columns.

Bytes Processed:

- Nested consistently processes the least data (270-657 B in these tests)
- Flat processes more due to multiple table scans (322-834 B)
- Wide is in the middle (345 B for the aggregation query)

Bytes Billed:

- Nested: 10 MB (scans one table, hits 10 MB minimum once)
- Flat: 20-40 MB (scans 2-4 tables, each hits 10 MB minimum)
- Wide: 10 MB (scans one table, hits 10 MB minimum once)

Note on Pricing Models: *The 10 MB minimum per table applies to on-demand pricing, which is how most teams start with BigQuery. However, enterprise teams typically use capacity pricing (such as flat-rate slots or BigQuery Editions), through which you can pay for compute capacity over time rather than bytes scanned. Under capacity pricing, the slot-ms metric becomes more important than bytes billed—where lower slot-ms means better query concurrency and throughput on your fixed capacity.*

Slot Milliseconds (Compute Time):

- Nested is fast for simple queries (34-53 slot-ms) but slow for aggregations (209 slot-ms in this test).
- Flat is consistent (26-111 slot-ms) but slower for multi-join queries.
- Wide is fastest for aggregations (17 slot-ms) due to no joins or `UNNEST`.

The compute pattern shows that operation type matters more than data size. UNNEST + GROUP BY is expensive, while pre-joined data is fast.

The billing pattern is important. BigQuery charges a minimum of 10 MB per table scanned. If your query touches four tables and each processes only 100 bytes, you still get billed for 40 MB. This is why the flat version consistently shows higher billing—every join adds at least another 10 MB.

The compute pattern matters for concurrency. Slot milliseconds determine how many queries you can run simultaneously. If you have 100 slots available and a query uses 200 slot-ms, it occupies those slots for 200 milliseconds. Faster queries (lower slot-ms) mean better concurrency and more queries per second.

Use Case for Each Approach

The performance data points to clear use cases for each modeling approach.

Use Nested Structures When:

- **Your data is naturally hierarchical.** Events with properties, orders with line items, and users with sessions–these map cleanly to `STRUCT` and `ARRAY` types. Keeping them nested matches the domain model and simplifies queries.
- **BigQuery reads only the specific `STRUCT` fields** that you `SELECT`–for example, `SELECT customer.name` scans just that field, not the entire customer `STRUCT`–so always use explicit field paths instead of `SELECT *` to minimize bytes scanned.
- **You want to minimize billing.** Nested structures hit the 10 MB minimum once per query, while star schemas multiply that minimum across every table scanned. For small-to-medium datasets, this difference adds up.
- **You need to query array properties.** `ARRAY_LENGTH`, `ARRAY_AGG`, and array filtering work directly on nested data without requiring joins or subqueries. If you frequently ask "how many items per order" or "which orders have more than X items," nested structures make this trivial.
- **Your queries mostly retrieve complete records.** If you are building APIs that return full order details, user profiles with all their data, or event records with all properties, nested structures give you everything in one scan.
- **You are loading from JSON or Avro.** These formats already have nested structures. Loading them into nested BigQuery tables preserves the structure without flattening and re-joining.

Avoid Nested Structures When:

- You need to update individual nested records frequently (BigQuery does not support partial updates).
- Your arrays can grow unboundedly (BigQuery has a 100 MB row size limit).
- Most queries only need a few fields from deeply nested structures (you will scan the whole row anyway).

Use Star Schema When:

- **You need to update dimension data.** If customer addresses change, product names get updated, or category hierarchies shift, star schemas allows you to update the dimension table once and have it reflect across all related facts. Nested structures would require updating every row that contains that customer or product.
- **Different teams own different dimensions.** The customer team manages the customers table, the product team owns products, and the analytics team works with facts. Clear table boundaries make ownership and access control straightforward.

- **You are migrating from a traditional warehouse.** If you already have star schema ETL pipelines, dbt models, and BI tools configured for dimensional modeling, keeping that structure in BigQuery reduces migration risk.
- **Your queries frequently filter on dimensions before joining.** BigQuery can push down filters and reduce the data scanned before performing joins. If you often query "orders from US customers" or "sales of electronics products," filtering the dimension table first is efficient.
- **You want to reuse dimensions across multiple fact tables.** The same customers table can join to orders, support tickets, and subscription events. The same products table works for sales, inventory, and returns. Nested structures would duplicate this dimension data in every fact table.

Avoid Star Schemas When:

- Your queries always need data from multiple tables (you will pay the join cost every time).
- Dimension tables are small and rarely change (the normalization overhead is not worth it).
- You are building real-time dashboards where query speed matters more than storage costs.

Use Wide Denormalized Tables When:

- **Query speed is the top priority.** Wide tables eliminate joins and UNNEST operations, giving you the fastest query execution. If you are powering real-time dashboards, public-facing analytics, or high-concurrency applications, the performance gain is worth the storage cost.
- **Your queries are repetitive and predictable.** If 90% of your queries follow the same pattern–group by category, filter by date range, aggregate revenue–a wide table optimized for that pattern will outperform other approaches.
- **You are building materialized views or aggregation tables**. Wide tables work well as pre-computed aggregations. Run the expensive joins once during the materialization process, then query the wide table quickly. Note that BigQuery's materialized views have limitations–they support only specific aggregate functions (for example, SUM, COUNT, AVG, MIN, MAX, and so on) and have restrictions on JOINs and subqueries. For complex aggregations, you may need to build and refresh wide tables manually.
- **Storage cost is acceptable.** BigQuery storage is cheap. If your wide table is 10 GB and saves 100 milliseconds per query on a dashboard that runs 1000 times per day, the storage cost is negligible compared to the performance benefit.

- **You are using BI tools that struggle with joins.** Some BI tools generate inefficient SQL for multi-table queries. A wide table gives them a single table to work with, allowing them to focus on filters and aggregations.
- **Alternative for dashboards: BI Engine**. Before building massive wide tables for dashboard performance, consider BigQuery's BI Engine—an in-memory analysis service that accelerates queries from BI tools. BI Engine can provide sub-second response times on star schema queries without requiring denormalization. It is particularly effective for dashboards with repetitive query patterns. The trade-off is cost (BI Engine capacity is billed separately) versus the engineering effort of maintaining wide tables.

Avoid Wide Tables When:

- Data changes frequently (you will need to rebuild the wide table often).
- You need flexibility in how you slice the data (wide tables are optimized for specific query patterns).
- Storage costs matter more than query speed (wide tables use the most storage).
- You need to update individual records (updates affect many duplicated rows).

Organizing Your Data Warehouse

Once you understand the performance trade-offs between nested, star schema, and wide tables, the next challenge is organizing dozens or hundreds of tables, so that your team can actually find and use them. This section will cover practical patterns for common data types and how to structure your warehouse for clarity and maintainability.

Common Data Patterns and Use Case for Each Approach

Different types of data naturally fit different modeling approaches. Here is how to think about the most common patterns you will encounter.

Event Data

Event streams from applications, clickstreams, or IoT devices are naturally hierarchical. Each event has properties, and those properties can be complex.

Nested Approach (Recommended):

```
CREATE TABLE events (
  event_id STRING,
  event_time TIMESTAMP,
  user_id STRING,
  event_type STRING,
  properties STRUCT<
    page_url STRING,
    referrer STRING,
    device STRING,
    browser STRING,
    custom_fields ARRAY<STRUCT<
      key STRING,
      value STRING
    >>
  >
);
```

This matches how events are generated. Your application logs a JSON object, which lands in BigQuery with the same structure. The following queries such as "show me all **page_view** events with their URLs" are simple:

```
SELECT
  event_time,
  user_id,
  properties.page_url,
  properties.device
FROM events
WHERE event_type = 'page_view'
  AND DATE(event_time) = '2024-01-15';
```

The alternative–flattening events into multiple tables–creates complexity without benefit. You would need an events table, an **event_properties** table, and complex joins to reconstruct what was originally a single JSON object.

Product Catalogs

Product data often has attributes that vary by category. Electronics have specifications, clothing has sizes and colors, and books have authors and ISBNs.

Nested Approach for Flexible Attributes:

```
CREATE TABLE products (
  product_id INT64,
  name STRING,
  category STRING,
  base_price NUMERIC,
  attributes ARRAY<STRUCT<
```

```
      attribute_name STRING,
      attribute_value STRING
    >>
  );
```

This handles varying attributes without creating a sparse table with hundreds of mostly-null columns.

Star Schema for Stable Dimensions:

```
CREATE TABLE products (
  product_id INT64,
  name STRING,
  category_id INT64,
  brand_id INT64,
  base_price NUMERIC
);
CREATE TABLE categories (
  category_id INT64,
  category_name STRING,
  parent_category_id INT64
);
CREATE TABLE brands (
  brand_id INT64,
  brand_name STRING,
  country STRING
);
```

If categories and brands are managed separately and change independently, normalizing them makes sense.

Wide Table for Analytics:

```
CREATE TABLE product_analytics AS
SELECT
  p.product_id,
  p.name,
  c.category_name,
  b.brand_name,
  p.base_price,
  COALESCE(s.total_sales, 0) AS total_sales,
  COALESCE(s.units_sold, 0) AS units_sold
FROM products p
LEFT JOIN categories c ON p.category_id = c.category_id
LEFT JOIN brands b ON p.brand_id = b.brand_id
LEFT JOIN (
  SELECT product_id, SUM(revenue) AS total_sales, SUM(quantity) AS
units_sold
  FROM sales
```

```
  GROUP BY product_id
) s ON p.product_id = s.product_id;
```

Pre-join everything for fast dashboard queries.

User Profiles

User data accumulates over time—with profile information, preferences, activity history, and derived attributes.

Nested Approach for Complete Profiles:

```
CREATE TABLE user_profiles (
  user_id STRING,
  email STRING,
  created_at TIMESTAMP,
  profile STRUCT<
    first_name STRING,
    last_name STRING,
    country STRING,
    timezone STRING
  >,
  preferences STRUCT<
    email_notifications BOOL,
    theme STRING,
    language STRING
  >,
  activity_summary STRUCT<
    last_login TIMESTAMP,
    total_sessions INT64,
    total_purchases INT64,
    lifetime_value NUMERIC
  >
);
```

One row per user with all their data nested. Queries that need the complete profile get it in one scan.

Star Schema for Separate Concerns:

```
CREATE TABLE users (
  user_id STRING,
  email STRING,
  created_at TIMESTAMP,
  country STRING
);
CREATE TABLE user_preferences (
  user_id STRING,
  preference_key STRING,
```

```
  preference_value STRING,
  updated_at TIMESTAMP
);
CREATE TABLE user_sessions (
  session_id STRING,
  user_id STRING,
  session_start TIMESTAMP,
  session_end TIMESTAMP,
  page_views INT64
);
```

Separate tables allow you to update preferences without touching session data, and vice versa. Better for systems where different services own different parts of the user data.

Time-Series Data

Metrics, logs, and sensor data arrive continuously, which are queried by time ranges.

Nested Approach for Grouped Metrics:

```
CREATE TABLE metrics (
  timestamp TIMESTAMP,
  source STRING,
  metrics STRUCT<
    cpu_percent FLOAT64,
    memory_mb FLOAT64,
    disk_io_mb FLOAT64,
    network_mb FLOAT64
  >
) PARTITION BY DATE(timestamp)
CLUSTER BY source;
```

All metrics for a given timestamp and source are stored together. Partitioning by date and clustering by source makes time-range queries efficient.

Wide Table for Pre-Aggregated Metrics:

```
CREATE TABLE metrics_hourly AS
SELECT
  TIMESTAMP_TRUNC(timestamp, HOUR) AS hour,
  source,
  AVG(metrics.cpu_percent) AS avg_cpu,
  MAX(metrics.cpu_percent) AS max_cpu,
  AVG(metrics.memory_mb) AS avg_memory,
  MAX(metrics.memory_mb) AS max_memory
FROM metrics

GROUP BY hour, source;
```

Pre-aggregate to hourly buckets for dashboard queries that do not need second-by-second granularity.

Partitioning and clustering matter more than the modeling approach for time-series data. Whether you use nested structures or flat tables, partition by date and cluster by your most common filter columns. This reduces the data scanned far more than any modeling choice.

Layered Data Architecture and Naming Conventions

As your warehouse grows beyond a few tables, organization becomes critical. Without clear structure, analysts waste time searching for the right table, duplicate work by creating redundant datasets, and make mistakes by joining incompatible data.

Subject areas group tables around business domains. Instead of organizing by technical sources (such as **"kafka_raw"**, **"postgres_sync"**, and **"api_dumps"**), organize by business function (such as **"sales"**, **"marketing"**, **"finance"**, and **"product"**). This is sometimes called a layered or medallion architecture.

A Practical Dataset Layout:

```
raw_*            -- Raw ingestion (minimal transformation)
  raw_kafka
  raw_postgres
  raw_api
staging_*        -- Cleaned and typed (one dataset per source)
  staging_orders
  staging_customers
  staging_products
mart_sales       -- Curated sales analytics
  fact_orders
  fact_order_items
  dim_customers
  agg_daily_revenue
mart_marketing   -- Curated marketing analytics
  fact_campaigns
  fact_conversions
  dim_channels
mart_finance     -- Curated finance analytics
  fact_transactions
  fact_invoices
  dim_accounts
```

This structure makes the intent obvious. When someone sees **mart_sales.fact_orders**, they know that it is curated sales data, and not raw ingestion. When they see **staging_orders**, they know that it is cleaned but not yet modeled for analytics.

Naming Conventions Matter:

- Use prefixes that indicate purpose: `raw_, staging_, mart_`
- Use suffixes that indicate type: `_fact, _dim, _agg`
- Be consistent: if you use `fact_orders` in sales, use `fact_campaigns` in marketing, not `campaigns_fact`

Document table grain explicitly. Add a description to every major table that states what one row represents:

- "One row per order item" (not per order, per item)
- "One row per user per day" (not per user, per day)
- "One row per campaign impression" (not per campaign, per impression)

Unclear grain is the source of most analytical errors. When someone joins two tables with different grains without realizing it, they get duplicate rows and wrong metrics.

Hybrid Approaches in Practice

You do not have to pick one modeling approach for your entire warehouse. Mix them based on what each table needs.

Example: E-commerce Data Warehouse

```
orders (nested)
├── order_id
├── order_date
├── customer_id (reference to dimension)
├── items ARRAY<STRUCT<...>>
└── shipping STRUCT<...>
customers (dimension)
├── customer_id
├── name
├── email
└── country
products (dimension)
├── product_id
├── name
├── category_id
└── attributes ARRAY<STRUCT<...>>
categories (dimension)
├── category_id
├── name
└── parent_category_id
order_analytics (wide, materialized daily)
```

```
├── order_date
├── customer_country
├── product_category
├── order_count
├── revenue
└── units_sold
```

Orders use nested structures because each order naturally has multiple items and shipping details. Customers, products, and categories are dimensions that get reused and updated independently. The **`order_analytics`** table is a wide denormalized view, rebuilt daily for fast dashboard queries.

This hybrid approach uses each modeling pattern where it makes sense, such as:

- Nested for hierarchical transactional data
- Star schema for reusable dimensions
- Wide denormalized for high-performance analytics

Common Modeling Mistakes and Their Solutions

Even with good intentions, certain patterns create problems at scale. The following are some mistakes that cause the most pain and fixes to avoid them.

Mistake 1: `SELECT *` in Curated Tables

Wide curated tables are helpful, but selecting all columns encourages unnecessary scanning and creates hidden dependencies.

```
-- Bad: Creates a 50-column table when analysts only use 10
CREATE TABLE mart_sales.orders_wide AS
SELECT *
FROM raw_orders o
JOIN dim_customers c ON o.customer_id = c.customer_id
JOIN dim_products p ON o.product_id = p.product_id;
```

Fix: *Select only the columns your workload needs. If analysts primarily filter by date, customer country, and product category, include those plus the metrics they aggregate. Do not include every customer field and every product field just in case.*

Mistake 2: Too Many Micro-Tables

Splitting everything into tiny, normalized tables creates join-heavy queries and makes the model hard for analysts to navigate.

```
-- Overkill: Separate tables for attributes with little analytical value
dim_customer
dim_customer_address
```

```
dim_customer_phone
dim_customer_preferences
dim_customer_loyalty_tier
```

Fix: *Group related attributes together. Unless you have a specific reason to separate them (such as different update frequencies, different access controls, or reuse across multiple facts), keep them in one-dimension table.*

Mistake 3: Ignoring Table Grain

When the grain is unclear, metrics become inconsistent, and duplicates appear.

```
-- Ambiguous: Is this one row per order or one row per order item?
CREATE TABLE orders_summary AS
SELECT
  order_id,
  customer_id,
  order_date,
  product_id,
  revenue
FROM ...
```

Fix: *State the grain explicitly in the table description and make it obvious in the table name. If it is one row per order item, call it **`fact_order_items`**. If it is one row per order, call it **`fact_orders`**. Add a description: "Grain: one row per item per order."*

Mistake 4: Denormalizing Frequently Changing Attributes

Copying dimension attributes into fact tables works for stable data, but creates consistency problems for data that changes often.

```
-- Problem: Customer addresses change, but old orders still show old
addresses
CREATE TABLE fact_orders AS
SELECT
  order_id,
  order_date,
  customer_id,
  customer_address,  -- This will be wrong after customer moves
  revenue
FROM ...
```

Fix: *Only denormalize attributes that are stable or where you explicitly want to capture the value at transaction time. For customer addresses, either keep them in a dimension table or use a Slowly Changing Dimension (SCD) pattern if you need history.*

Why This Matters: BigQuery uses a copy-on-write architecture for DML operations (such as **`UPDATE`**, **`DELETE`**, **`MERGE`**, and so on). When you update a row, BigQuery does not modify it in place—it creates a new version of the affected storage blocks. This makes updates expensive, especially on wide denormalized tables. Additionally,

BigQuery has daily DML quota limits per table (typically 1,500 operations per day). Frequent updates to denormalized fact tables can hit these limits quickly.

Mistake 5: No Partitioning on Large Tables

Without partitioning, every query scans the entire table, even if it only needs one day of data.

```
-- Expensive: Scans all data even for single-day queries
CREATE TABLE events (
  event_time TIMESTAMP,
  user_id STRING,
  event_type STRING,
  properties STRUCT<...>
);
```

Fix: *Partition by date on any table that grows continuously and is queried by time ranges. This is especially critical for event data, logs, and time-series metrics.*

```
CREATE TABLE events (
  event_time TIMESTAMP,
  user_id STRING,
  event_type STRING,
  properties STRUCT<...>
) PARTITION BY DATE(event_time)
CLUSTER BY event_type, user_id;
```

Mistake 6: Over-Nesting

Nested structures are powerful, but deeply nested data becomes hard to query and understand.

```
-- Too complex: Three levels of nesting
CREATE TABLE orders (
  order_id INT64,
  customer STRUCT<
    customer_id INT64,
    addresses ARRAY<STRUCT<
      address_id INT64,
      address_lines ARRAY<STRING>,
      city STRING
    >>
  >,
  items ARRAY<STRUCT<...>>
);
```

Fix: *Keep nesting to a maximum of two levels. If you need more complexity, consider whether a star schema with separate tables would be clearer.*

Why This Matters: BigQuery's storage engine (based on Google's Dremel) uses a columnar format with a shredding and assembly algorithm to handle the nested data. Deeply nested structures require more complex shredding and reassembly operations, which increases query overhead. Additionally, BigQuery has a 100 MB row size limit–deeply nested arrays can hit this limit faster than you would expect.

Partitioning and Clustering

Regardless of which modeling approach you choose, partitioning and clustering have a bigger impact on query performance than the table structure itself.

Partitioning divides a table into segments based on a column value, typically a date. When you query with a date filter, BigQuery only scans the relevant partitions.

```
CREATE TABLE orders_nested (
  order_id INT64,
  order_date DATE,
  customer STRUCT<...>,
  items ARRAY<STRUCT<...>>,
  total_amount NUMERIC,
  status STRING
)
PARTITION BY order_date;
```

Now, queries with **`WHERE order_date = '2024-01-15'`** or **`WHERE order_date BETWEEN '2024-01-01' AND '2024-01-31'`** only scan the relevant partitions. If your table has a year of data and you query one day, that means you scan 1/365th of the table.

Clustering sorts data within partitions based on specified columns. This improves performance for queries that filter or aggregate on those columns.

```
CREATE TABLE orders_nested (
  order_id INT64,
  order_date DATE,
  customer STRUCT<...>,
  items ARRAY<STRUCT<...>>,
  total_amount NUMERIC,
  status STRING
)
PARTITION BY order_date
CLUSTER BY status, customer.country;
```

Queries that filter on **`status`** or **`customer.country`** will scan less data because BigQuery can skip blocks that do not contain matching values.

Partition and cluster your tables based on how you query them, not based on the modeling approach. A nested table with good partitioning and clustering will outperform a poorly partitioned star schema, and vice versa.

Schema Evolution

Tables change over time. You add columns, rename fields, or restructure nested data. How you handle schema evolution depends on your modeling approach.

Adding Columns

The following are a few methods to add columns to tables:

Adding Columns to Flat Tables:

```
ALTER TABLE orders_flat
ADD COLUMN discount_amount NUMERIC;
```

Simple and safe. Existing rows get NULL for the new column.

Adding Fields to Nested Structures:

```
ALTER TABLE orders_nested
ADD COLUMN customer.loyalty_tier STRING;
```

BigQuery supports adding fields to **STRUCT** types. Existing rows get **NULL** for the new field.

Adding Elements to Arrays:

You cannot alter the schema of an **ARRAY** directly. Instead, you would need to recreate the table or use a view to add computed fields:

```
CREATE OR REPLACE VIEW orders_with_item_count AS
SELECT
  *,
  ARRAY_LENGTH(items) AS item_count
FROM orders_nested;
```

Renaming Columns

BigQuery now supports direct column renaming:

```
ALTER TABLE orders_flat RENAME COLUMN customer_id TO client_id;
```

This is a metadata-only operation that completes immediately without copying data. However, renaming fields inside a **STRUCT** is not supported–those require recreating the table with the following new structure:

```
CREATE TABLE orders_nested_v2 AS
SELECT
  order_id,
  order_date,
  STRUCT(
```

```
      customer.customer_id,
      customer.name AS customer_name,   -- renamed
      customer.email,
      customer.country
    ) AS customer,
    items,
    total_amount,
    status
  FROM orders_nested;
```

Then, drop the old table and rename the new one.

Schema evolution is easier with star schemas because you are changing one table at a time. With nested structures, you are modifying the entire row structure, which can be more complex. However, for most additive changes (such as adding columns or fields), both approaches work fine.

Conclusion

Data modeling in BigQuery is not about following a single best practice; rather, it is about matching the structure to your query patterns and operational needs.

Nested structures (such as **STRUCT** and **ARRAY**) work best for hierarchical data that is queried as complete records. They minimize billing by scanning a single table, simplify queries that work with related data, and match the structure of JSON and Avro sources. Use them for event data, orders with line items, and user profiles where you typically need the full record.

Star schemas (such as flat normalized tables) work best when dimensions are managed independently, updated frequently, or reused across multiple fact tables. They make sense when you are migrating from traditional warehouses, when different teams own different tables, or when your queries filter dimensions before joining. The trade-off is higher billing due to multiple table scans and more complex SQL with joins.

Wide denormalized tables work best when query speed is the priority and storage cost is acceptable. They eliminate joins and **UNNEST** operations, giving you the fastest execution time for aggregation queries. Use them for materialized views, pre-computed aggregations, and high-concurrency dashboards where every millisecond matters.

In practice, most data warehouses use a hybrid approach–nested structures for transactional data, star schemas for reusable dimensions, and wide tables for performance-critical analytics. The key is understanding the trade-offs and choosing the right structure for each table based on how it is queried.

Partitioning and clustering matter more than the modeling approach for large tables. A well-partitioned nested table will outperform a poorly partitioned star schema, regardless of the theoretical advantages of either approach.

In the next chapter, we will cover details about partitioning, clustering, and other optimizations. We will dig deep into physical optimizations–the techniques that reduce the amount of data BigQuery scans without changing your table structure or queries.

Points to Remember

- BigQuery supports three main modeling approaches: nested (**`STRUCT/ARRAY`**), star schema (flat tables), and wide denormalized tables.
- Nested structures minimize billing by scanning a single table, but can be slower for complex aggregations.
- Star schemas enable independent dimension management but increase billing due to multiple table scans (10 MB minimum per table).
- Wide denormalized tables provide the fastest query execution by eliminating joins, at the cost of increased storage.
- Slot milliseconds (compute time) affects query speed and concurrency–lower is better for high-traffic applications.
- Use nested structures for hierarchical data, event streams, and when you need complete records.
- Use star schemas when dimensions are updated independently, reused across fact tables, or managed by different teams.
- Use wide tables for performance-critical dashboards, materialized views, and when query speed matters more than storage cost.
- Hybrid approaches work best–use different modeling patterns for different tables based on their query patterns.
- Partitioning and clustering have a bigger impact on performance than modeling approach for large tables.
- Schema evolution is easier with star schemas (one table at a time) than nested structures (entire row structure).

Multiple Choice Questions

1. What is the minimum billing amount per table scanned in BigQuery?

   a. 1 MB

   b. 5 MB

   c. 10 MB

   d. 100 MB

2. Which modeling approach processed the least data in the revenue-by-category query?

   a. Nested structure (305 B)

   b. Star schema (545 B)

   c. Wide table (345 B)

   d. All processed the same amount

3. What SQL operation is required to flatten an ARRAY field in a nested structure?

   a. `FLATTEN`

   b. `UNNEST`

   c. `EXPAND`

   d. `EXPLODE`

4. Which approach had the fastest compute time (lowest slot milliseconds) for aggregation queries?

   a. Nested structure

   b. Star schema

   c. Wide denormalized table

   d. They all had the same compute time

5. What is the main advantage of using **`ARRAY_LENGTH`** on a nested structure?

   a. It is faster than **`COUNT(*)`**

   b. You can filter on array size without unnesting

   c. It reduces storage costs

   d. It automatically creates indexes

6. Why did the star schema approach get billed more than the nested approach?

   a. Star schema tables are larger

   b. Star schema queries are slower

   c. Each table scanned adds a 10 MB minimum charge
   d. BigQuery charges extra for JOIN operations
7. When should you use a star schema instead of nested structures?
   a. When you need to update dimension data independently
   b. When you want faster queries
   c. When you want to minimize storage costs
   d. When your data is hierarchical
8. What is the main trade-off of using wide denormalized tables?
   a. Slower query performance
   b. More complex SQL
   c. Increased storage due to data duplication
   d. Cannot use partitioning
9. Which BigQuery feature has the biggest impact on query performance for large tables?
   a. Nested versus flat structure
   b. Partitioning and clustering
   c. Number of columns
   d. Table name length
10. What happens when you add a new field to a `STRUCT` in an existing table?
   a. The operation fails—you must recreate the table
   b. Existing rows get `NULL` for the new field
   c. Existing rows are deleted
   d. The table is automatically partitioned

Answers

1. c
2. a
3. b
4. c

5. b
6. c
7. a
8. c
9. b
10. b

Questions

1. Explain why the nested structure approach resulted in lower billing (10 MB) compared to the star schema approach (20-40 MB) for the same queries, even though both processed similar amounts of actual data.
2. The revenue-by-category query showed that the nested structure used 209 slot-ms while the star schema used only 26 slot-ms, despite the nested structure processing less data. What causes this difference in compute time?
3. Describe a scenario where you would choose a star schema over a nested structure, even though nested structures generally result in lower billing costs.
4. The wide denormalized table had the fastest query execution (17 slot-ms) for aggregation queries. What is the main tradeoff of using this approach, and when is that tradeoff acceptable?
5. How does the UNNEST operation work in BigQuery, and why is it necessary when querying ARRAY fields in nested structures?
6. Explain why partitioning and clustering can have a bigger impact on query performance than the choice between nested and flat table structures.
7. A company has order data where each order can have 1 to 50 line items. They need to frequently update product names and categories. Should they use a nested structure or a star schema? Justify your answer.

Key Terms

- **STRUCT**: A BigQuery data type that represents a nested record with named fields, similar to a JSON object. Used to group related fields together within a single column.
- **ARRAY**: A BigQuery data type that represents an ordered list of values of the same type. Can contain simple types or complex types such as **STRUCT**s.

- `UNNEST`: A SQL operation that flattens an `ARRAY` into multiple rows, creating a cross join between the table and the array elements.
- **Star Schema:** A dimensional modeling approach where fact tables reference dimension tables through foreign keys, creating a star-like structure when visualized.
- **Denormalization:** The process of combining data from multiple normalized tables into a single table, duplicating data to eliminate joins.
- **Bytes Processed:** The amount of data BigQuery reads from storage to execute a query, which determines the query cost.
- **Bytes Billed**: The amount of data BigQuery charges for, which is the maximum of bytes processed or 10 MB per table scanned.
- **Slot Milliseconds**: A measure of compute time used by a query, calculated as the number of slots multiplied by the execution time in milliseconds.
- **Partitioning**: Dividing a table into segments based on a column value (typically a date), allowing queries to scan only relevant segments.
- **Clustering**: Sorting data within partitions based on specified columns, improving performance for queries that filter or aggregate on those columns.
- **Fact Table**: A table in a star schema that contains measurable events or transactions, typically with foreign keys to dimension tables.
- **Dimension Table**: A table in a star schema that contains descriptive attributes used to filter and group fact data.
- **Wide Table**: A fully denormalized table where all the related data is stored in a single row, eliminating the need for joins.
- `ARRAY_LENGTH`: A BigQuery function that returns the number of elements in an `ARRAY` without requiring `UNNEST`.
- **Schema Evolution**: The process of modifying table structures over time by adding, removing, or changing columns and fields.

CHAPTER 5
Partitioning, Clustering, and Optimization

Introduction

The previous chapter showed you how to model data—nested structures, star schemas, and wide tables. You learned how table structure affects query performance and costs. However, even with the right model, queries can still scan more data than necessary and cost more than they should.

This chapter focuses on physical optimizations—the techniques that reduce the amount of data BigQuery scans without changing your table structure or queries. Partitioning divides tables into segments so that queries only read relevant data. Clustering sorts data within those segments in order to skip even more blocks. Column pruning ensures that you only scan the columns you need.

These are not optional nice-to-haves. On a table with a year of data, a query filtering by one day can scan 1/365th of the table with partitioning, or scan the entire table without it. That is the difference between processing 100 MB and processing 36 GB, and paying for it.

The techniques in this chapter apply anyhow whether you use nested structures, star schemas, or wide tables. They work on top of your modeling choices to make queries faster and cheaper. By the end, you will know when to partition, how to choose clustering keys, and which optimizations have the biggest impact.

Structure

In this chapter, we will cover the following topics:

- Understanding Partitioning

- Hands-on: Partitioning Impact
- Clustering Explained
- Column-Level Optimizations
- Table Sharding Anti-Pattern
- Practical Optimization Guidelines

Understanding Partitioning

Partitioning divides a table into segments based on a column value. When you query with a filter on that column, BigQuery only scans the relevant segments instead of the entire table.

Partitioning

Without partitioning, every query scans the entire table:

```
-- Without partitioning: scans all 365 days of data
SELECT country, SUM(amount) AS revenue
FROM orders
WHERE order_date = '2023-06-15'
GROUP BY country;
```

BigQuery reads every row, checks **`order_date = '2023-06-15`**', and keeps only matching rows. If the table has a year of data, you are scanning 364 days of irrelevant data.

With partitioning by **`order_date`**, BigQuery organizes the table into date-based segments in the following manner:

```
CREATE TABLE orders
PARTITION BY order_date
AS SELECT ...;
```

Now, the same query only scans the June 15th partition. BigQuery knows which partition contains that date and skips all others—with no wasted scanning.

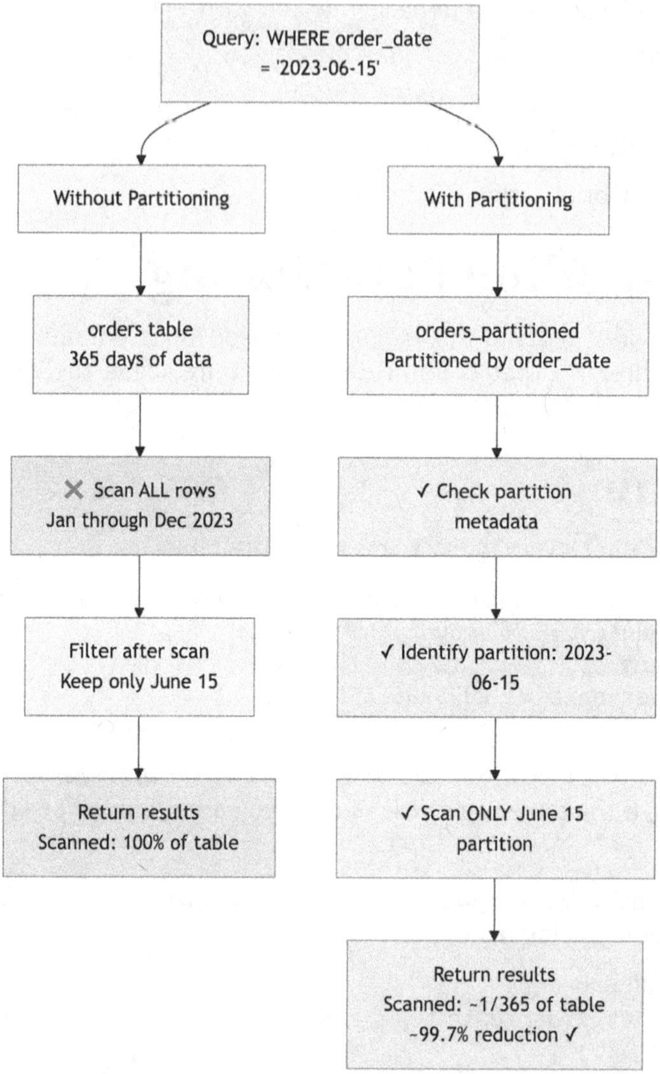

Figure 5.1: *Partition Pruning Comparison—without versus with Partitioning*

Figure 5.1 shows the key difference: without partitioning, BigQuery scans all data, then filters. With partitioning, BigQuery checks partition metadata first, identifies the relevant partition, and only scans that particular segment.

Partition Types

BigQuery supports the following three partition types:

Type 1: Date/Timestamp Partitioning (Most Common)

Partition by a **DATE** or **TIMESTAMP** column in the following way:

```
CREATE TABLE events
PARTITION BY DATE(event_timestamp)
AS SELECT ...;
```

Each day gets its own partition. Queries filtering by date only scan relevant days.

Type 2: Ingestion-Time Partitioning

Partition by when data was loaded into BigQuery in the following manner:

```
CREATE TABLE events
PARTITION BY _PARTITIONTIME
AS SELECT ...;
```

_PARTITIONTIME is a pseudo-column that BigQuery automatically maintains. It does not appear in your data or in **SELECT *** results—you must explicitly select it if you want to see it as follows:

```
-- Pseudo-column must be explicitly selected
SELECT _PARTITIONTIME, event_id, event_type
FROM events
WHERE _PARTITIONTIME = '2023-06-15';
```

Useful when you do not have a date column in your data, but you want to query the recent data efficiently based on when it was loaded.

Type 3: Integer Range Partitioning

Partition by an integer column (such as **customer_id** or **region_id**) in the following way:

```
CREATE TABLE customers
PARTITION BY RANGE_BUCKET(customer_id, GENERATE_ARRAY(0, 100000,
1000))
AS SELECT ...;
```

This is less common, but useful for evenly distributed integer keys.

For most analytical workloads, date partitioning is the right choice. Time-based queries are the most common pattern in data warehouses.

Hands-on: Measuring Partitioning Impact

To see how partitioning affects query performance, let us compare the same query on partitioned and non-partitioned tables in this section.

The Test Setup

Create a table with 5,000 orders spanning one year (for instance, from 2023-01-01 to 2023-12-31). This is small enough to run quickly yet large enough to show clear patterns.

Generate synthetic data with SQL in the following manner:

```
CREATE TABLE orders_raw AS
SELECT
  ROW_NUMBER() OVER() AS order_id,
  DATE_ADD('2023-01-01', INTERVAL CAST(RAND() * 365 AS INT64) DAY)
AS order_date,
  CASE
    WHEN RAND() < 0.3 THEN 'USA'
    WHEN RAND() < 0.6 THEN 'Canada'
    ELSE 'UK'
  END AS country,
  CASE
    WHEN RAND() < 0.25 THEN 'Electronics'
    WHEN RAND() < 0.5 THEN 'Clothing'
    ELSE 'Books'
  END AS category,
  ROUND(RAND() * 500 + 10, 2) AS amount
FROM UNNEST(GENERATE_ARRAY(1, 5000)) AS n;
```

This creates orders that are distributed randomly across the year. No CSV files are needed–BigQuery generates the data.

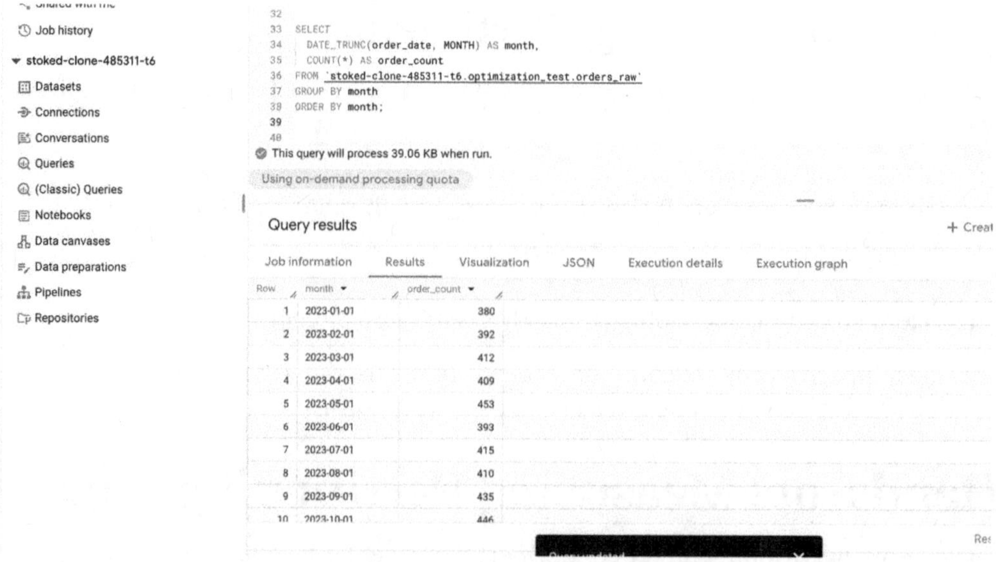

Figure 5.2: *Order Count by Month Showing Data Distribution across 2023*

Non-Partitioned Table

Create a standard table with no partitioning in the following way:

```
CREATE TABLE orders_no_partition AS
SELECT * FROM orders_raw;
```

Query for one month of data:

```
SELECT
  country,
  category,
  COUNT(*) AS order_count,
  SUM(amount) AS total_revenue
FROM orders_no_partition
WHERE order_date BETWEEN '2023-06-01' AND '2023-06-30'
GROUP BY country, category;
```

Results from This Test:

- Bytes processed: 156 KB
- Bytes billed: 10 MB
- Slot-ms: 25

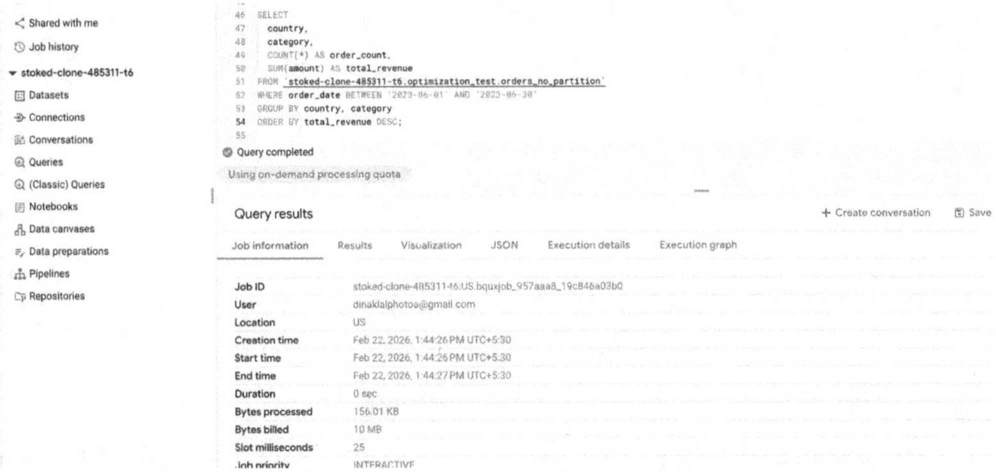

***Figure 5.3:** Non-Partitioned Query Execution Details Showing 156 KB Processed*

BigQuery scanned the entire table (5,000 rows) even though the query only needed the data from June (roughly 1/12 of the table). The **`WHERE`** clause was filtered after scanning, not before.

Partitioned Table

Create the same table with date partitioning in the following way:

```
CREATE TABLE orders_partitioned
```

```
PARTITION BY order_date
AS SELECT * FROM orders_raw;
```

Run the exact same query:

```
SELECT
  country,
  category,
  COUNT(*) AS order_count,
  SUM(amount) AS total_revenue
FROM orders_partitioned
WHERE order_date BETWEEN '2023-06-01' AND '2023-06-30'
GROUP BY country, category;
```

Results from This Test:

- Bytes processed: 12.2 KB
- Bytes billed: 10 MB
- Slot-ms: 186

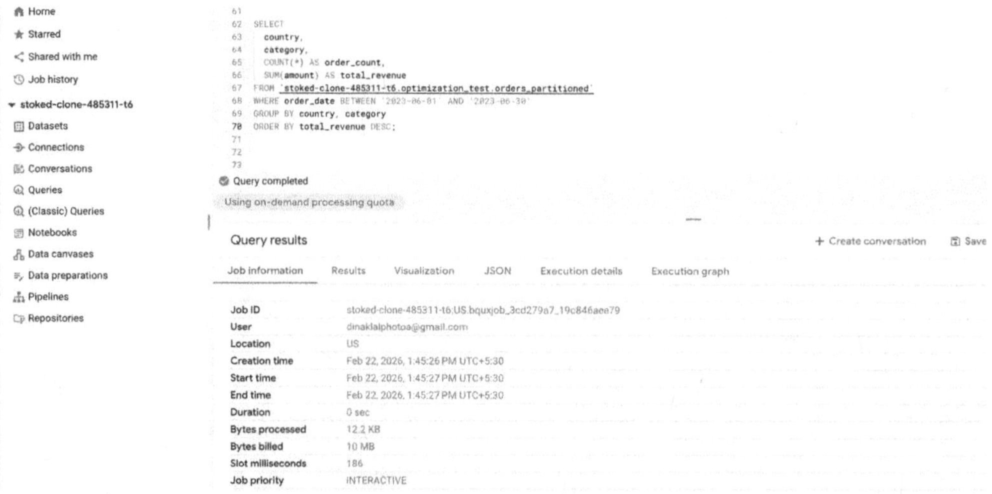

Figure 5.4: *Partitioned Query Execution Details Showing 12.2 KB Processed*

BigQuery scanned only the June partitions–about 1/12 of the table. The bytes processed dropped from 156 KB to 12.2 KB, leading to a 92% reduction.

The Pattern Scales: On a table with 100 GB of data that is evenly distributed across a year, querying one day with partitioning scans ~274 MB instead of 100 GB. On a table with 10 TB, it scans ~27 GB instead of 10 TB. The reduction ratio stays consistent, assuming relatively even data distribution across partitions.

Why Does Slot Time Increase?

Notice that slot-ms went up (that is, 25 → 186) even though bytes processed went down. This is normal for small datasets. The overhead of partition pruning–that is, checking which partitions to scan—is more visible when the actual data scan is tiny. At scale, with gigabytes or terabytes of data, the partition pruning overhead becomes negligible compared to the scan time saved.

Tip: *Partitioning reduces bytes scanned dramatically. On small test datasets, you might not see slot-ms improvements, but on production data, both bytes scanned and query time improve significantly.*

Clustering Explained

Clustering sorts data within partitions based on specified columns. This allows BigQuery to skip blocks of data that do not match your query filters.

Clustering

After partitioning divides your table by date, clustering sorts the data within each partition. When you filter on a clustered column, BigQuery can skip the entire blocks without scanning them in the following way:

```
CREATE TABLE orders_partitioned_clustered
PARTITION BY order_date
CLUSTER BY country, category
AS SELECT * FROM orders_raw;
```

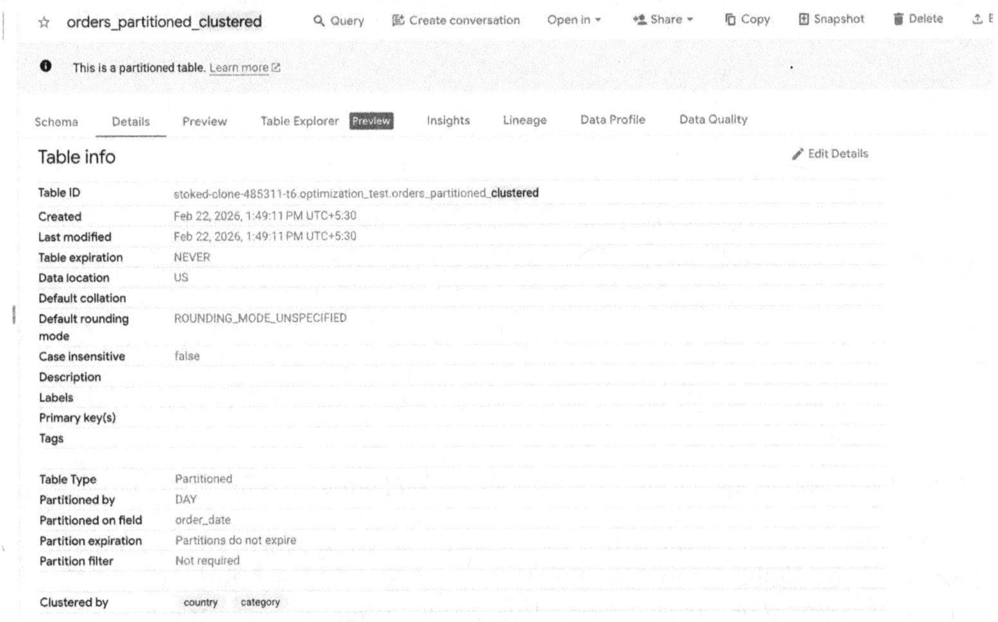

Figure 5.5: *Table Schema Showing Partitioning by order_date and Clustering by Country or Category*

This table is partitioned by date and clustered by country and category. Within each day's partition, both USA orders and Canada orders are two groups; and within each country, orders are sorted by category.

Use Cases for Clustering

Query with both partition and cluster filters in the following manner:

```
SELECT
  Country, category, COUNT(*) AS order_count, SUM(amount)
AS total_revenue
FROM orders_partitioned_clustered
WHERE order_date BETWEEN '2023-06-01' AND '2023-06-30'
  AND country = 'USA'
  AND category = 'Electronics'
GROUP BY country, category;
```

Results from This Test:

- Bytes processed: 12.04 KB
- Bytes billed: 10 MB
- Slot-ms: 224

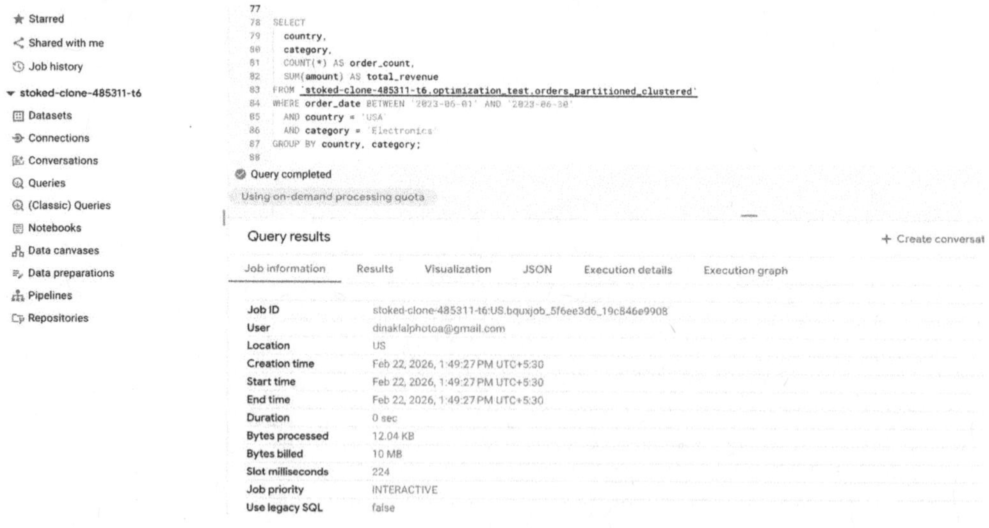

Figure 5.6: *Partitioned and Clustered Query Execution Details Showing 12.04 KB Processed*

Compared to partitioned-only (12.2 KB), clustering saved 160 bytes. On a 5,000-row table, this is negligible. However, the pattern matters: clustering reduces the data scanned by skipping blocks that do not contain USA/Electronics orders.

At scale, clustering makes a bigger difference. On a table with millions of rows per day, clustering by country could reduce a single-country query from scanning gigabytes to scanning megabytes. The benefit grows with data size.

Choosing Clustering Keys

You can cluster by up to 4 columns. BigQuery sorts by the first column, then by the second within each group of the first, and so on.

Guidelines:

- **First Column**: Your most common filter (for example, **`country`**, **`status`**, or **`user_id`**)
- **Second Column**: Your second most common filter (for example, category or **`event_type`**)
- **Order Matters**: Cluster by columns in the order you filter them

Good Clustering:

```
CLUSTER BY country, category, status
```

This works well for queries filtering by country, or country + category, or all the three.

Bad Clustering:

```
CLUSTER BY status, category, country
```

This does not help queries filtering only by country—you would need to scan all status groups.

Avoiding Cluster Scenarios

Clustering adds overhead during data ingestion as BigQuery has to sort the data. Skip clustering in the following cases:

- Your table is small (< 1 GB).
- You do not have common filter patterns.
- Your queries scan most of the table anyway.
- Data changes frequently, as clustering degrades over time and requires re-clustering.

Partitioning is almost always worth it. Clustering is worth it when you have clear and repetitive filter patterns.

Column-Level Optimizations

BigQuery is columnar—it stores each column separately. This means you only pay for the columns you query, and not the entire row.

SELECT * versus Specific Columns

Compare these two queries on the same partitioned table:

Query All Columns:

```
SELECT *
FROM orders_partitioned
WHERE order_date BETWEEN '2023-06-01' AND '2023-06-30';
```

Results from This Test:

- Bytes processed: 26.15 KB

***Figure* 5.7:** *Query Execution Details for SELECT * Showing 26.15 KB Processed*

Query Only Needed Columns:

```
SELECT order_id, order_date, country, amount
FROM orders_partitioned
WHERE order_date BETWEEN '2023-06-01' AND '2023-06-30';
```

Results from This Test:

- Bytes processed: 11.56 KB

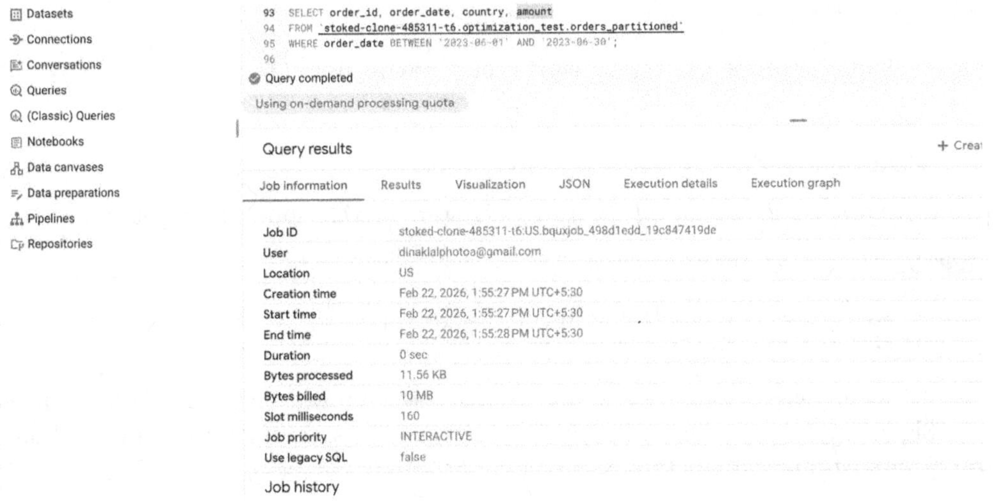

Figure 5.8: *Query Execution Details for Specific Columns Showing 11.56 KB Processed*

Selecting 4 columns instead of 8 reduced bytes scanned by 56%. The pattern holds at any scale: if you select half the columns, you scan roughly half the data.

Why Does This Matter?

On small tables, the difference between 26 KB and 11 KB is trivial. However, on production tables:

- A table with 100 columns where you need 10: scanning 10% of the data instead of 100%.
- A 1 TB table: scanning 100 GB instead of 1 TB.
- A query running 1,000 times per day: 100 TB scanned instead of 1 PB.

The cost difference is real. BigQuery charges $6.25 per TB scanned (on-demand pricing, as of 2026–Check the official pricing page for the latest rates). Scanning 1 PB instead of 100 TB costs $6,250 instead of $625.

Common Column Mistakes

Mistake 1: `SELECT *` in production queries.

```
-- Bad: Scans all columns even if you only use a few
SELECT * FROM orders WHERE order_date = '2023-06-15';
```

Fix: Select only what you need:

```
-- Good: Scans only the columns you use
SELECT order_id, country, amount FROM orders WHERE order_date
= '2023-06-15';
```

Mistake 2: Selecting columns you do not use

```
-- Bad: Selects customer_email but never uses it
SELECT order_id, customer_email, amount
FROM orders
WHERE order_date = '2023-06-15';
```

If you are not displaying or filtering by **`customer_email`**, do not select it.

Mistake 3: Using **`LIMIT`** to save money

```
-- Bad: Still scans the entire table
SELECT * FROM orders LIMIT 10;
```

Every new BigQuery user tries this, thinking **`LIMIT 10`** will only scan 10 rows. It does not. BigQuery scans the entire table, retrieves all rows, then returns only 10. You are billed for scanning the full table.

Why: BigQuery is a columnar, distributed system. It does not know which 10 rows to return until it scans all partitions and sorts/filters the data. **`LIMIT`** happens after the scan, not before.

Fix: Combine **`LIMIT`** with partition filters in the following way:

```
-- Good: Scans only one day, then limits
SELECT * FROM orders
WHERE order_date = '2023-06-15'
LIMIT 10;
```

Now, you are only scanning one day's partition, then limiting to 10 rows. The partition filter reduces bytes scanned; **`LIMIT`** reduces rows returned.

Mistake 4: Joining before filtering

-- Bad: Joins all data, then filters

```
SELECT o.order_id, c.name, o.amount FROM orders o
JOIN customers c ON o.customer_id = c.customer_id
WHERE o.order_date = '2023-06-15';
```

Better: Filter first, then join:

```
-- Good: Filters orders first, then joins only matching rows
SELECT o.order_id, c.name, o.amount
FROM (
  SELECT order_id, customer_id, amount  FROM orders
  WHERE order_date = '2023-06-15'
) o JOIN customers c ON o.customer_id = c.customer_id;
```

BigQuery's optimizer often does this automatically, but being explicit helps on complex queries.

Table Sharding Anti-Pattern

Before BigQuery had partitioning, teams created separate tables for each time period—a pattern called table sharding. However, this is almost always the wrong approach now.

Table Sharding

Instead of one partitioned table, you can create multiple tables in the following way:

```
CREATE TABLE orders_2023_01 AS SELECT * FROM orders WHERE ...;
CREATE TABLE orders_2023_02 AS SELECT * FROM orders WHERE ...;
CREATE TABLE orders_2023_03 AS SELECT * FROM orders WHERE ...;
-- ... 12 tables total
```

To query across months, you need UNION ALL:

```
SELECT country, COUNT(*) AS order_count FROM (
  SELECT * FROM orders_2023_01
  UNION ALL
  SELECT * FROM orders_2023_02
  UNION ALL
  SELECT * FROM orders_2023_03
) WHERE country = 'USA' GROUP BY country;
```

Sharding is Expensive

Results from This Test (3 Sharded Tables):

- Bytes processed: 7.3 KB
- Bytes billed: 30 MB (10 MB × 3 tables)
- Slot-ms: 50

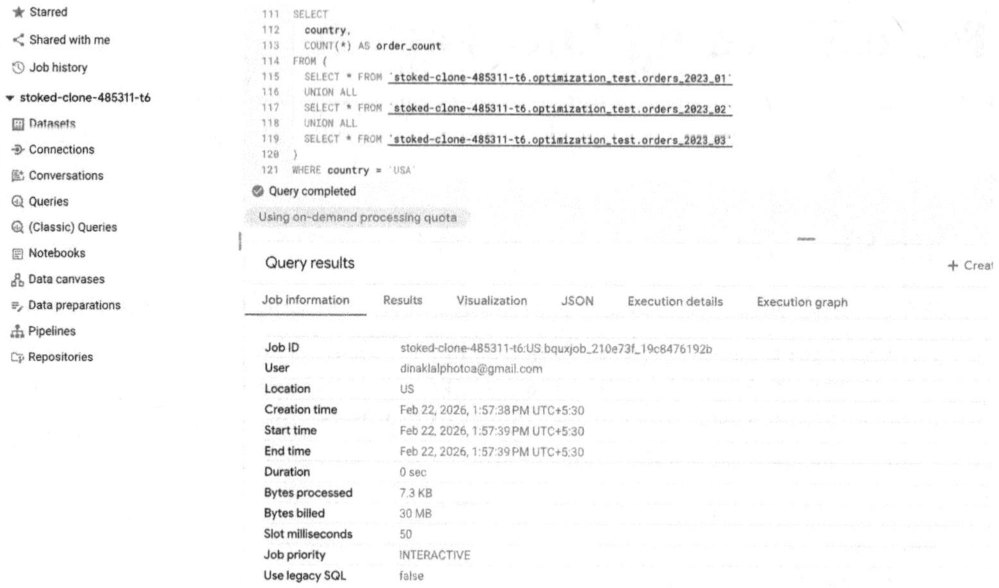

Figure 5.9: *Sharded Tables Query Execution Showing 30 MB Billed across 3 Tables*

Compare to Partitioned Table (3 Months):

- Bytes processed: 16.55 KB
- Bytes billed: 10 MB (single table)
- Slot-ms: 473

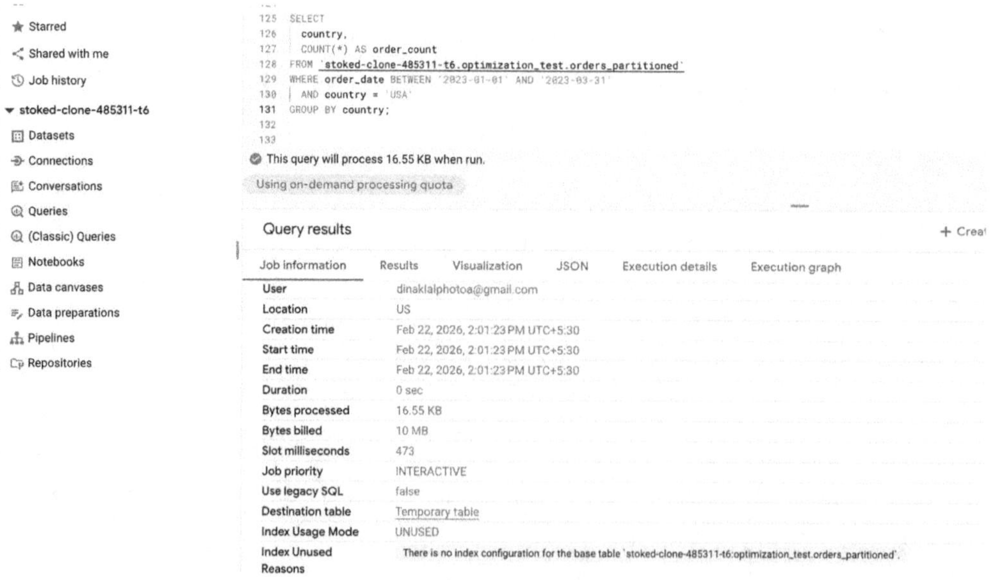

Figure 5.10: *Partitioned Table Query Execution Showing 10 MB Billed for Single Table*

The sharded approach costs 3x more in billing (30 MB versus 10 MB), as BigQuery charges a 10 MB minimum per table scanned–the same penalty we saw in *Chapter 4: Modeling for Scale* while comparing star schemas to wide tables. While the sharded query processed less data (7.3 KB versus 16.55 KB), it hits the minimum charge three times.

At scale, this gets worse. Query 12 months of sharded data: 120 MB billed (12 × 10 MB). Query 12 months of partitioned data: 10 MB billed. That is a 12x cost difference for the same query.

Other Problems with Sharding

There are a few other issues that are associated with sharding, including:

- **Query Complexity**: Every query needs **`UNION ALL`** across all relevant tables. Querying a year of data means listing 12 or 365 tables. Queries become unreadable and error-prone.
- **Schema Changes are Painful**: Adding a column requires altering every table. With 365 sharded tables, that is 365 ALTER TABLE statements.
- **No Automatic Partition Pruning**: You have to manually specify which tables to query. With partitioning, BigQuery automatically determines which partitions to scan based on your **`WHERE`** clause.
- **Metadata Overhead**: Each table has its own metadata. With thousands of sharded tables, even listing tables becomes slow.

Historical Context of Sharding

Before 2016, BigQuery did not have partitioning. Table sharding was the only way to avoid full table scans. Teams created date-based tables because it was better than scanning everything.

Now, partitioning solves the same problem in a better way. The only valid reason to use sharding today is if you need to completely delete old data for compliance (for instance, dropping a table is faster than deleting rows). Even then, partitioned tables support partition expiration, which handles this automatically.

Use partitioning, not sharding, as it is simpler, cheaper, and more maintainable.

Practical Optimization Guidelines

When you are optimizing a BigQuery table or query, focus on the techniques with the biggest impact first.

Optimization Priority Order

Most people are confused about the preferences we need to give to each optimization. In this section, we will check the priority order of optimizations, which is as follows:

Step 1: Add Partitioning (Highest Impact)

If your table grows over time and queries filter by date, partition it. This typically reduces the bytes scanned by 90%+ for time-filtered queries.

Partition When:

- Table is larger than 1 GB.
- Queries filter by date, timestamp, or time range.
- Data arrives continuously (for instance, events, logs, or transactions).

Skip When:

- Table is small (< 1 GB) and will not grow much.
- Queries always scan the entire table.
- No clear date/time column to partition by.

Step 2: Select Only Needed Columns (Medium Impact)

Replace `SELECT *` with explicit column lists. This typically reduces the bytes scanned by 30–70% depending on how many columns are actually needed.

When It Matters Most:

- Wide tables with many columns
- Queries that only need a few columns
- High-frequency queries (run thousands of times per day)

Step 3: Add Clustering (Medium Impact at Scale)

If you have common filter patterns beyond the partition key, add clustering. This typically reduces the bytes scanned by 10-50% for filtered queries.

Cluster When:

- Table is larger than 10 GB.
- Queries frequently filter by specific columns (for example, **`country`**, **`status`**, or **`user_id`**).
- Filter patterns are consistent and predictable.

Skip When:

- Table is small (< 1 GB).
- No consistent filter patterns.
- Data changes frequently (for instance, clustering degrades and requires maintenance).

Step 4: Optimize Query Structure (Variable Impact)

Filter before joining, avoid subqueries in `SELECT` clauses, and use approximate aggregation functions when exact counts are not needed.

When It Matters Most:

- Complex queries with multiple joins
- Queries with correlated subqueries
- Aggregations over billions of rows

Measuring Impact

Before and after any optimization, check the query's job information:

- Bytes Processed: Did it go down?
- Bytes Billed: Did the cost decrease?
- Slot-ms: Did execution time improve?

For production queries, also track:

- Query Frequency: How often does this run?
- Total Cost: Bytes billed × frequency × $6.25 per TB

A query that scans 100 GB and runs once per day costs $0.625/day (~$228/year). The same query running every minute costs $900/day ($328,500/year). Optimization priority depends on both scan size and frequency.

Common Scenarios

The following are some common scenarios that we can potentially face while handling real-world scenarios.

Scenario 1: Event/Log Table Growing Daily

- Solution: Partition by date, cluster by event_type or user_id
- Expected Impact: 90%+ reduction in bytes scanned for time-filtered queries

Scenario 2: Wide Fact Table with 50+ Columns

- Solution: Create curated views with only commonly used columns
- Expected Impact: 50–80% reduction in bytes scanned

Scenario 3: Dashboard Queries Running Every 5 Minutes

- Solution: Partition + cluster + materialized view
- Expected Impact: 95%+ reduction in bytes scanned + sub-second query time

Scenario 4: Ad-Hoc Analysis on Historical Data

- Solution: Partition by date, no clustering needed
- Expected Impact: 90%+ reduction when filtering by date ranges

Partition and Cluster Maintenance

Partitioning and clustering are not set and then forgotten. They require occasional maintenance to stay effective.

Partition Expiration

Old partitions can be automatically deleted after a specified time in the following way:

```
CREATE TABLE events
PARTITION BY DATE(event_timestamp)
OPTIONS(
  partition_expiration_days=90
)
AS SELECT ...;
```

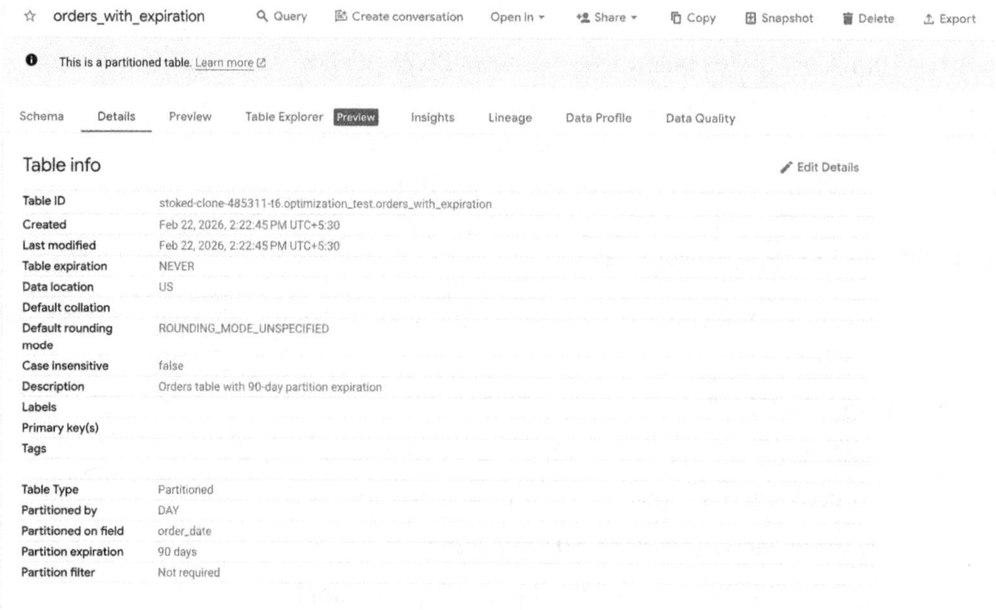

Figure 5.11: *Table Details Showing Partition Expiration Set to 90 Days*

After 90 days, partitions are automatically dropped. This is useful for:

- Compliance requirements (for instance, deleting data after retention period),
- Cost control (for instance, do not pay to store old data you do not query), and
- Performance (for instance, fewer partitions to manage).

Clustering Degradation

As data is inserted, updated, or streamed into a table, clustering can degrade. Rows are no longer perfectly sorted by the cluster keys.

BigQuery automatically re-clusters tables in the background, but you can manually trigger it in the following manner:

```
-- Check clustering quality
SELECT
  table_name,
  clustering_ordinal_position,
  clustering_field
FROM `project.dataset.INFORMATION_SCHEMA.CLUSTERING_FIELDS`
WHERE table_name = 'orders_partitioned_clustered';
```

If queries start scanning more data than expected, re-clustering might help. However, BigQuery's automatic re-clustering usually handles this without any manual intervention.

Partition Limits

BigQuery has the following limits on partitions:

- Maximum Partitions per Table: 4,000
- Maximum Partitions Queried: 4,000

For daily partitions, 4,000 days is about 11 years. For hourly partitions, 4,000 hours is only about 166 days—which is a common trap for teams that partition high-frequency event tables by hour without setting partition expiration. If you need more, consider the following:

- Using monthly or yearly partitions instead of daily.
- Archiving old data to separate tables.
- Using ingestion-time partitioning with partition expiration.

Modifying Partition/Cluster Settings

You cannot change partition or cluster keys on an existing table. To change them, you need to recreate the table in the following way:

```
-- Create new table with different partitioning
CREATE TABLE orders_new
PARTITION BY DATE_TRUNC(order_date, MONTH)  -- Monthly instead of
daily
CLUSTER BY country
AS SELECT * FROM orders_old;
-- Drop old table
DROP TABLE orders_old;
-- Rename new table
ALTER TABLE orders_new RENAME TO orders;
```

This is expensive on large tables, as you are copying all the data, so choose your partition and cluster keys carefully upfront.

Conclusion

Physical optimizations—such as partitioning, clustering, and column pruning—reduce the amount of data BigQuery scans without changing your table structure or query logic. These techniques work on top of your modeling choices, and they can reduce query costs by 90% or more.

Partitioning divides tables into segments based on a column value—typically a date. Queries that filter on the partition key only scan relevant segments rather than the entire table. This is the single most impactful optimization for time-series data. On a table with a year of data, querying one day with partitioning scans 1/365th of the table.

Clustering sorts data within partitions based on specified columns. When queries filter on clustered columns, BigQuery can skip blocks of data without scanning them. Clustering provides additional reduction beyond partitioning, typically 10-50% for queries with consistent filter patterns. The benefit grows with table size—clustering matters more on tables with millions or billions of rows.

Column pruning takes advantage of BigQuery's columnar storage. Selecting specific columns instead of **`SELECT *`** reduces bytes scanned proportionally. If you select 10 columns out of 100, you scan roughly 10% of the data. This applies to every query, regardless of partitioning or clustering.

Table sharding—that is, creating separate tables for each time period—is an anti-pattern in modern BigQuery. It costs more due to the 10 MB minimum billing per table, creates complex UNION queries, and makes schema changes painful. Partitioning solves the same problem better in every way.

The optimization priority is clear: partition first (90%+ impact), select specific columns (30-70% impact), then add clustering if you have consistent filter patterns (10-50% additional impact). Measure the impact of each optimization by checking bytes processed before and after changes.

These techniques apply whether you are using nested structures, star schemas, or wide tables. They are physical optimizations that work on top of your logical model. A well-partitioned nested table outperforms a poorly partitioned star schema, and vice versa. Focus on partitioning and column selection first–they provide the biggest return for the least effort.

In the next chapter, we will cover the performance and cost side of BigQuery. This gives an idea about monitoring compute usage, choosing between exact and approximate functions, and using caching and materialization to make repetitive queries nearly instantaneous.

Points to Remember

- Partitioning is the highest-impact optimization for time-series data, typically reducing bytes scanned by 90%+ for time-filtered queries.
- Date partitioning is the most common and useful partition type for analytical workloads.
- Clustering provides additional pruning beyond partitioning, most effective on large tables (> 10 GB) with consistent filter patterns.
- Cluster keys should be ordered by filter frequency–most common filter first, second most common second.
- Column pruning–that is, selecting specific columns instead of **SELECT ***–reduces bytes scanned proportionally to columns selected.
- BigQuery's columnar storage means that you only pay for columns you query, and not entire rows.
- Table sharding costs more than partitioning due to a 10 MB minimum billing per table scanned.
- Partitioning is simpler, cheaper, and more maintainable than table sharding in every scenario.
- Optimization priority: partition first (biggest impact), select specific columns (medium impact), and then add clustering (additional benefit at scale).
- Measure optimization impact by comparing bytes processed, bytes billed, and slot-ms before and after changes.
- Partition expiration automatically deletes old data after a specified retention period.
- You cannot change partition or cluster keys on the existing tables–choose carefully upfront.
- BigQuery automatically re-clusters tables in the background as data changes.
- A maximum of 4,000 partitions per table is about 11 years of daily partitions.

- Partitioning and clustering work on top of your modeling choices—they apply to nested, star schema, and wide tables equally.

Multiple Choice Questions

1. What is the primary benefit of partitioning a table by date?
   a. It makes queries run faster by using more slots.
   b. It reduces bytes scanned by only reading relevant partitions.
   c. It automatically creates indexes on the partition column.
   d. It compresses data more efficiently.
2. How many columns can you cluster in BigQuery?
   a. 1
   b. 2
   c. 4
   d. Unlimited
3. Which partition type is most common for analytical workloads?
   a. Integer range partitioning
   b. Ingestion-time partitioning
   c. Date/timestamp partitioning
   d. String partitioning
4. Why does table sharding cost more than partitioning?
   a. Sharded tables use more storage
   b. Each table scanned incurs a 10 MB minimum charge
   c. `UNION ALL` operations are expensive
   d. Sharded tables cannot be compressed
5. What happens when you `SELECT *` instead of specific columns?
   a. BigQuery scans all columns, increasing bytes processed.
   b. The query fails with an error.
   c. BigQuery automatically optimizes to only scan the needed columns.
   d. It has no impact on bytes scanned.

6. In what order should clustering keys be specified?
   a. Alphabetically by column name
   b. By data type (strings first, then numbers)
   c. By filter frequency (most common filter first)
   d. Random order doesn't matter
7. What is the maximum number of partitions allowed per table?
   a. 365
   b. 1,000
   c. 4,000
   d. 10,000
8. When does clustering provide the most benefit?
   a. On small tables (< 1 GB)
   b. On large tables (> 10 GB) with consistent filter patterns
   c. On tables that are never queried
   d. On tables with no `WHERE` clauses
9. Can you change the partition key on an existing table?
   a. Yes, using `ALTER TABLE`
   b. Yes, but only within 24 hours of creation
   c. No, you must recreate the table
   d. Yes, but it requires downtime
10. What does partition expiration do?
    a. Marks old partitions as read-only
    b. Automatically deletes partitions after a specified time
    c. Compresses old partitions to save storage
    d. Moves old partitions to cheaper storage

Answers

1. b
2. c
3. c
4. b
5. a
6. c
7. c
8. b
9. c
10. b

Questions

1. Explain why partitioning reduced bytes scanned from 156 KB to 12.2 KB in the test, and how this pattern would scale to a table with 100 GB of data queried for one day.
2. The test showed that clustering provided minimal benefit (160 bytes saved) on a 5,000-row table. Explain why clustering becomes more valuable as table size increases.
3. Describe a scenario where you would choose to cluster by two columns instead of one, and explain the order you would specify them.
4. Why did the table sharding approach cost 30 MB in billing while processing only 7.3 KB of data, when the partitioned approach cost 10 MB while processing 16.55 KB?
5. A dashboard query runs every 5 minutes and scans 50 GB each time using `SELECT *`. The table has 100 columns, but the dashboard only displays 10. Calculate the potential cost savings from selecting only needed columns, and explain your reasoning.
6. Explain why you cannot change partition keys on an existing table, and describe the process you would follow to change partitioning on a production table with 5 TB of data.

7. A table receives 10,000 new rows every hour, and queries typically filter by the last 24 hours of data. Should you partition by day or by hour? Explain the tradeoffs of each approach.

Key Terms

- **Partitioning:** Dividing a table into segments based on a column value, allowing queries to scan only relevant segments instead of the entire table.
- **Partition Key:** The column used to divide a table into partitions, typically a `DATE` or `TIMESTAMP` column.
- **Partition Pruning:** BigQuery's process of determining which partitions to scan based on query filters, skipping irrelevant partitions.
- **Clustering:** Sorting data within partitions based on specified columns, allowing BigQuery to skip blocks of data that do not match query filters.
- **Cluster Key:** The columns used to sort data within partitions, specified in order of filter frequency.
- **Column Pruning:** Selecting only needed columns instead of `SELECT *`, reducing bytes scanned by leveraging BigQuery's columnar storage.
- **Columnar Storage:** A storage format where each column is stored separately, allowing queries to read only the columns they need.
- **Table Sharding:** An anti-pattern of creating separate tables for each time period instead of using partitioning.
- **Partition Expiration:** Automatic deletion of partitions after a specified retention period, useful for compliance and cost control.
- **Ingestion-Time Partitioning:** Partitioning based on when data was loaded into BigQuery rather than a column value in the data.
- **Integer Range Partitioning:** Partitioning based on ranges of integer values, less common than date partitioning.
- **Clustering Degradation:** The gradual loss of clustering effectiveness as data is inserted, updated, or streamed, requiring re-clustering.
- **Block:** A unit of storage in BigQuery, typically a few MB, used for organizing and skipping data during query execution.
- **Partition Limit:** The maximum number of partitions allowed per table (4,000) or queried in a single query (4,000).
- **Re-clustering:** The process of re-sorting data by cluster keys to restore clustering effectiveness after degradation.

CHAPTER 6

Performance and Cost Engineering

Introduction

The previous chapter showed you how partitioning, clustering, and column pruning reduce the amount of data BigQuery scans. Those are storage-side optimizations–they shrink the input before BigQuery's compute engine processes it. However, reducing bytes scanned is only half the story.

This chapter will focus on the compute side–how BigQuery allocates resources to your queries, what drives performance beyond data size, and how to control both speed and cost. You will discover that two queries scanning identical amounts of data can have vastly different performance profiles and costs, depending on how much computation they require.

The key insight is understanding the difference between bytes processed (what you scan from storage) and slot-ms (how much compute you consume). On-demand pricing cares about bytes processed. Query performance cares about slot-ms. Optimizing for one does not automatically optimize for the other.

Through hands-on testing, you will see how BigQuery's query cache can make repeated queries free, how Materialized Views (MVs) can accelerate aggregations by 200x, and how query patterns affect compute consumption. You will also learn practical cost-control techniques and optimization patterns that reduce both scan time and compute time.

By the end of this chapter, you will understand how to monitor compute usage, choose between exact and approximate functions, and use caching and materialization to make repetitive queries nearly instantaneous.

Structure

This chapter will cover the following topics:

- Understanding Slots and Compute
- Hands-on: Measuring Slot Usage
- Understanding BigQuery Pricing Models
- Reservations and Workload Isolation
- BI Engine for Dashboard Acceleration
- Query Caching in Action
- Materialized Views (MVs) Performance
- Cost Control and Query Optimization
- Additional Query Optimization Patterns

Understanding Slots and Compute

In *Chapter 2, Inside BigQuery Storage, Compute, and Execution*, you learned that BigQuery executes queries using slots–compute units that provide CPU, memory, and network resources. Each query consumes slot-ms based on its complexity. This chapter will put that concept into practice by measuring real slot consumption across different query patterns.

Monitoring Query Performance

The most important tool for understanding compute consumption is **INFORMATION_SCHEMA.JOBS**. This system view contains detailed execution history for all your queries, which is as follows:

```
SELECT
  job_id,
  user_email,
  query,
  total_bytes_processed / POW(1024, 3) AS gb_processed,
  total_slot_ms / 1000 AS slot_seconds,
  TIMESTAMP_DIFF(end_time, start_time, SECOND) AS duration_seconds,
  creation_time
FROM `region-us`.INFORMATION_SCHEMA.JOBS
WHERE creation_time > TIMESTAMP_SUB(CURRENT_TIMESTAMP(), INTERVAL 24
HOUR)
```

```
  AND job_type = 'QUERY'
  AND state = 'DONE'
ORDER BY total_slot_ms DESC
LIMIT 20;
```

This shows your 20 most compute-intensive queries from the last 24 hours. The **`total_slot_ms`** column reveals exactly how much compute each query consumed, identifying optimization opportunities.

You can also see slot-ms in the "**`Job information`**" tab after running any query. This metric is your primary tool for understanding compute consumption and optimizing query performance.

Hands-on: Measuring Slot Usage

To understand how different query patterns affect compute consumption, let us run identical tests and measure the results in this section.

Simple Aggregation Query

Start with a basic aggregation query, which is as follows:

```
SELECT
  country,
  category,
  COUNT(*) AS order_count,
  SUM(amount) AS total_revenue
FROM `your-project-id.optimization_test.orders_partitioned`
WHERE order_date BETWEEN '2023-06-01' AND '2023-06-30'
GROUP BY country, category
ORDER BY total_revenue DESC;
```

Results from This Test:

- Bytes processed: 12.2 KB
- Bytes billed: 10 MB
- Slot-ms: 102
- Elapsed time: 507 ms

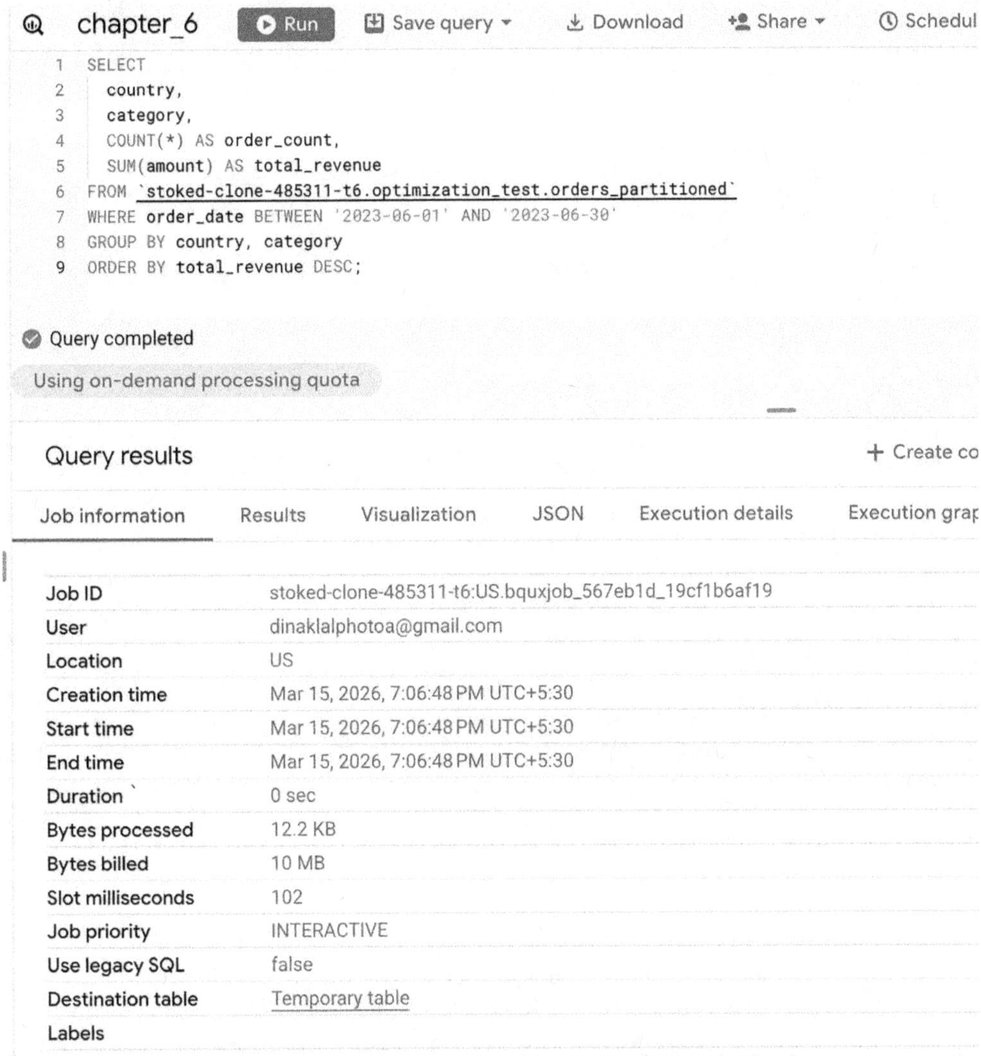

***Figure 6.1:** Simple Aggregation Query Job Information, Showing 12.2 KB Processed and 102 slot-ms*

The "**`Execution Details`**" tab provides a further breakdown of the query work, as shown in *Figure 6.2*:

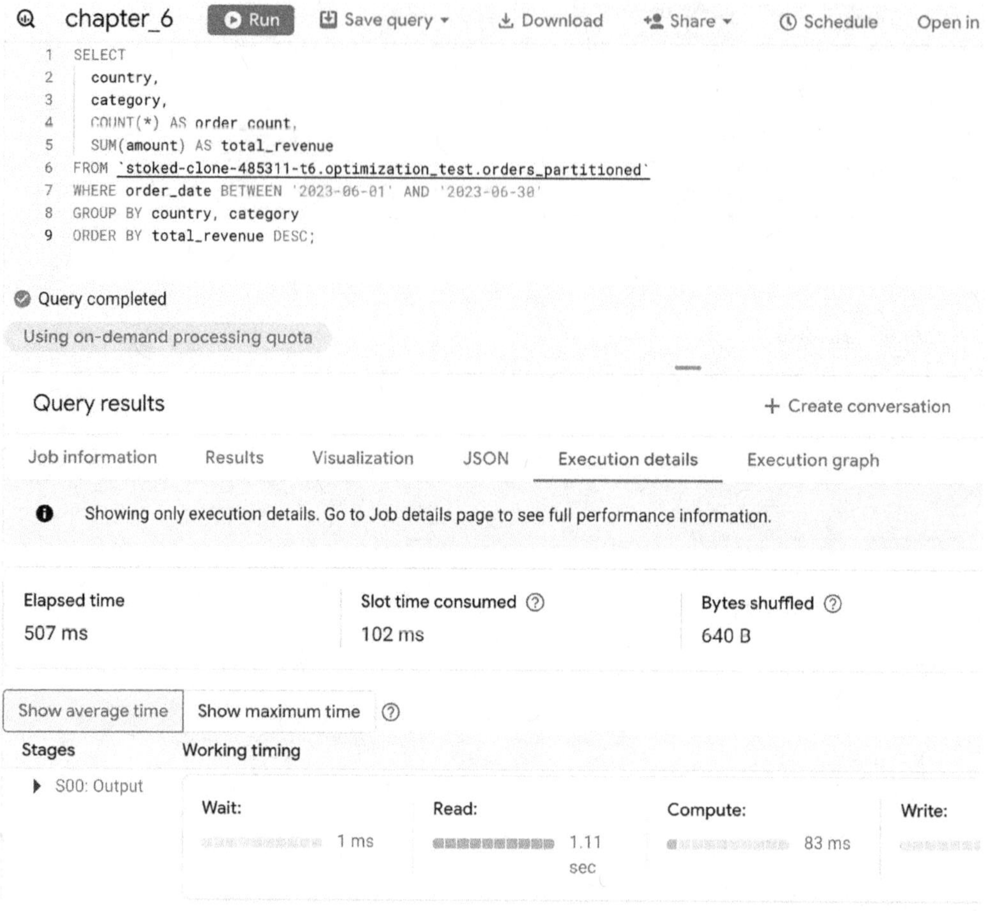

Figure 6.2: *Simple Aggregation Query Execution Details, Showing Elapsed Time 507 ms and Slot Time 102 ms*

This query scans one month of partitioned data (12.2 KB) and performs basic aggregations. The 102 slot-ms represents the compute needed for the **`GROUP BY`** and **`ORDER BY`** operations.

Query with `JOIN`

Now, add a JOIN to see how compute changes in the following manner:

```
SELECT
  o.country,
  o.category,
  COUNT(*) AS order_count,
  SUM(o.amount) AS total_revenue,
  p.commission_rate,
```

```
  SUM(o.amount * p.commission_rate) AS commission
FROM `your-project-id.optimization_test.orders_partitioned` o
JOIN `your-project-id.optimization_test.products_ref` p
  ON o.category = p.category
WHERE o.order_date BETWEEN '2023-06-01' AND '2023-06-30'
GROUP BY o.country, o.category, p.commission_rate
ORDER BY total_revenue DESC;
```

Results from This Test:

- Bytes processed: 12.27 KB (similar to simple query)
- Bytes billed: 20 MB (2 tables scanned)
- Slot-ms: 145
- Elapsed time: 239 ms

***Figure 6.3:** JOIN Query Job Information, Showing 12.27 KB Processed and 145 slot-ms*

The JOIN increased slot-ms by 42% (that is, 102 → 145) while scanning nearly identical data. The additional compute comes from the following:

- Hash table creation for the `JOIN`
- Additional aggregation calculations (commission)
- More complex execution plan coordination

Key Insight: Query complexity affects compute consumption independently of data size. The JOIN added minimal data scanning, but also significant compute overhead.

Understanding the Execution Plan

In the execution details, you can see how BigQuery broke down the work in the following stages:

Simple Query Stages:

- S00: Output stage (102 ms slot time)
- Records read: 393, Records written: 16

JOIN Query Stages:

- S00: Output stage (145 ms slot time)
- Records read: 397, Records written: 16

The stage breakdown shows where compute time is spent. Most slot-ms proceeds to the output stage, which handles the "`GROUP BY`" aggregation and sorting.

Wait times in the execution details indicate resource contention. In this test, wait times were minimal (such as 1-2 ms), showing that the queries had adequate slot allocation.

Understanding BigQuery Pricing Models

BigQuery offers two fundamentally different pricing approaches that affect how you optimize for cost and performance, which are discussed in this section.

On-Demand Pricing

This is the default model where you pay per byte scanned, with the following details:

- **Cost**: $6.25 per TB scanned (as of 2026)
- **Minimum**: 10 MB per table scanned
- **Free Tier**: First 1 TB per month is free

- **Slot Allocation**: Shared pool, no guarantees

When On-Demand Works Well:

- Workloads under ~30 TB scanned per month
- Irregular or unpredictable query volumes
- Development and testing environments
- Teams getting started with BigQuery

Capacity Pricing (BigQuery Editions)

Instead of paying per byte scanned, you pay for dedicated compute capacity:

Edition	Baseline Slots	Autoscaling	Key Features
Standard	100	Up to 1,600	Basic capacity pricing
Enterprise	100	Up to 1,600	+ BI Engine, MV savings
Enterprise Plus	100	Up to 1,600	+ Advanced security, disaster recovery

***Table 6.1**: BigQuery Pricing*

Key Differences:

- **Predictable Costs**: Fixed monthly bill regardless of bytes scanned.
- **Guaranteed Slots**: Dedicated compute, and no sharing with other users.
- **Workload Isolation**: Create separate slot pools for different workloads.
- **Autoscaling**: Automatically scales between baseline and maximum slots.

Choosing the Right Model

The break-even point depends on your usage patterns, as demonstrated by the following examples:

On-Demand Example:

- Monthly Scan: 100 TB
- Cost: 100 × $6.25 = $625/month

Capacity Example (Standard Edition):

- 100-Slot Baseline: ~$2,920/month
- Break-Even: ~450-500 TB/month

Beyond Cost Considerations:

- **Performance Predictability**: Capacity provides guaranteed slots.

- **Workload Isolation**: Separate ETL from dashboard queries.
- **Query Concurrency**: Higher limits with dedicated capacity.
- **BI Engine**:Available on On-Demand pricing (100 GB free tier), Enterprise, and Enterprise+ editions.

Most teams start with on-demand and switch to capacity as workloads grow, requiring predictable performance.

Reservations and Workload Isolation

Once you are on capacity pricing, reservations allow you to create isolated slot pools for different workloads.

The Problem Reservations Solve

Without reservations, all users share the same slot pool, with the following consequences:

- Heavy ETL jobs can consume all slots, slowing dashboards.
- Ad-hoc queries can delay production pipelines.
- No way to prioritize critical workloads.

Common Reservation Patterns

Idle slots are shared by default–if ETL is not using its 300 slots, analytics can temporarily borrow them.

ETL versus Analytics Isolation:

```
Total: 500 slots
├── etl_reservation: 300 slots (batch processing)
├── analytics_reservation: 150 slots (dashboards)
└── adhoc_reservation: 50 slots (exploration)
```

Production versus Development:

```
Total: 400 slots
├── prod_reservation: 300 slots (production workloads)
└── dev_reservation: 100 slots (development, testing)
```

Creating Reservations

We can create reservations using the query window in the following way:

```
-- Create reservations (requires capacity pricing)
CREATE RESERVATION `project.region-us.etl_reservation`
```

```
OPTIONS (slot_capacity = 300, edition = 'ENTERPRISE');

-- Assign projects to reservations
CREATE ASSIGNMENT `project.region-us.etl_reservation.etl_assignment`
OPTIONS (assignee = 'projects/my-etl-project', job_type = 'QUERY');
```

Note: *Reservations require capacity pricing* (Editions). *Through on-demand pricing, all queries share BigQuery's global slot pool.*

BI Engine for Dashboard Acceleration

BI Engine is BigQuery's in-memory analysis service that caches frequently accessed data for sub-second dashboard performance.

BI Engine's Functionality

BI Engine allocates memory (RAM) and caches columns that dashboards query frequently. Queries served from cache return in 50–200 milliseconds instead of 1–10 seconds.

```
-- Create BI Engine reservation (requires On-Demand, Enterprise or
Enterprise
-- pricing)
CREATE CAPACITY `project.region-us.bi_engine`
AS JSON '{"size_gb": 2}';
-- Alter existing BI Engine reservation
ALTER BI_CAPACITY `project.region-us.bi_engine`
SET OPTIONS(size_gb = 2);
```

Use Cases for BI Engine

There are several scenarios where BI Engine helps, but it is not recommended in all cases.

Best for:

- Looker Studio dashboards with filters and date ranges.
- Repeated queries on the same tables and columns.
- Interactive exploration requiring sub-second response.
- High-concurrency dashboard usage.

Limitations:

- Only works with supported functions–some advanced functions bypass BI Engine.

- Cache size limits; if the working dataset exceeds the reservation, queries fall back.
- Requires On-Demand, Enterprise or Enterprise+ pricing, leading to additional cost.

BI Engine versus Materialized Views (MVs)

Table 6.2 shows the comparison between BI Engine and MVs on the basis of their features:

Factor	**BI Engine**	**Materialized Views (MVs)**
Speed	50-200 ms (in-memory)	Fast but not sub-second
Data freshness	Real-time	Near real-time (auto-refresh)
Cost	BI Engine capacity fee	Storage cost for MV
Query patterns	Any supported pattern	Simple aggregations only
Setup	Just create reservation	Create MV + maintain

Table 6.2: *BI Engine and MV*

- Use BI Engine when dashboards need real-time data with sub-second response times.
- Use MVs when you need dramatic compute reduction (for instance, 224x improvement) for specific aggregation patterns.

Query Caching in Action

BigQuery automatically caches query results for 24 hours. When you run the same query twice, the second execution returns cached results with zero cost and near-instant response time.

Perfect Cache Hit

Run the same simple aggregation query from the previous section, which is as follows:

```
SELECT
  country,
  category,
  COUNT(*) AS order_count,
  SUM(amount) AS total_revenue
FROM `your-project-id.optimization_test.orders_partitioned`
WHERE order_date BETWEEN '2023-06-01' AND '2023-06-30'
GROUP BY country, category
ORDER BY total_revenue DESC;
```

Results from This Test (Second Execution):

- Bytes Processed: 0 B (results cached)
- Bytes Billed: 0 B
- Slot-ms: No compute needed
- Elapsed time: Instant

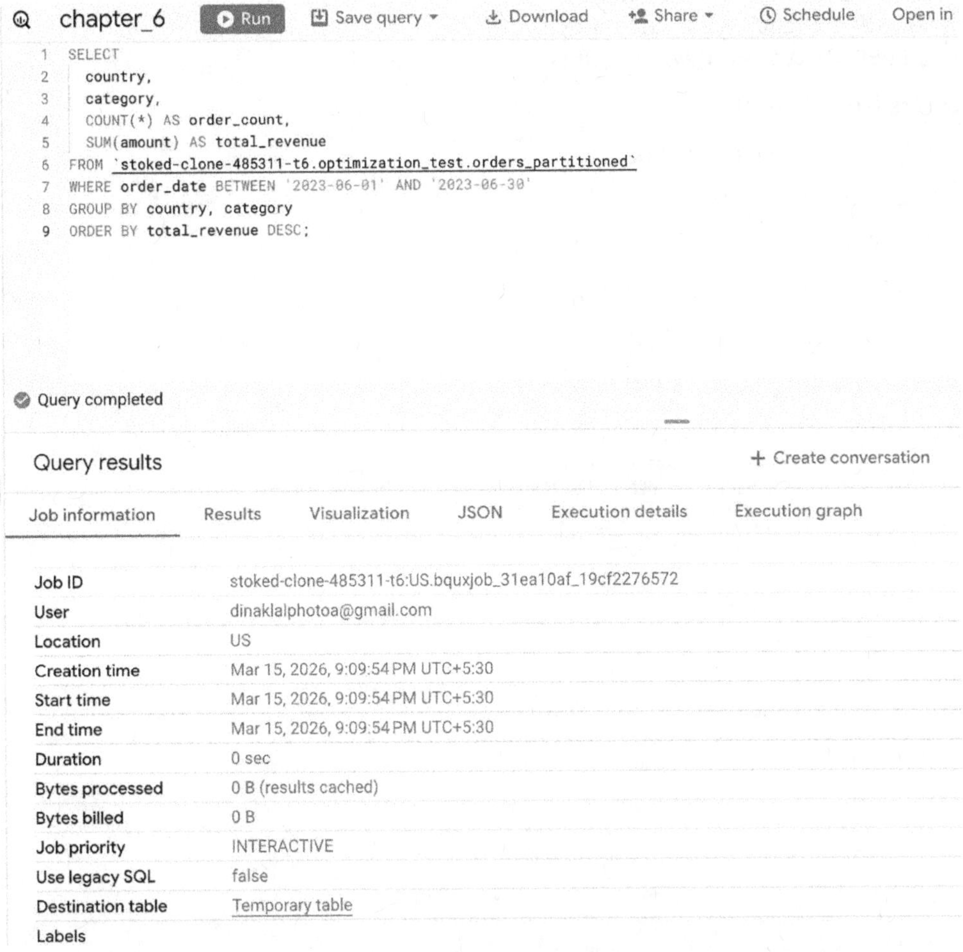

Figure 6.4: *Cache Hit Job Information, Showing 0 Bytes Processed (Results Cached)*

The query returned identical results but consumed zero resources. BigQuery recognized the same SQL text and returned the cached results instead of re-executing the query.

Cache Miss with Minor Change

Now, modify the query slightly by changing the date range in the following manner:

```
SELECT
  country,
  category,
  COUNT(*) AS order_count,
  SUM(amount) AS total_revenue
FROM `your-project-id.optimization_test.orders_partitioned`
WHERE order_date BETWEEN '2023-06-01' AND '2023-07-01'  -- Changed
end date
GROUP BY country, category
ORDER BY total_revenue DESC;
```

Results from This Test:

- Bytes Processed: 12.68 KB
- Bytes Billed: 10 MB
- Slot-ms: 167

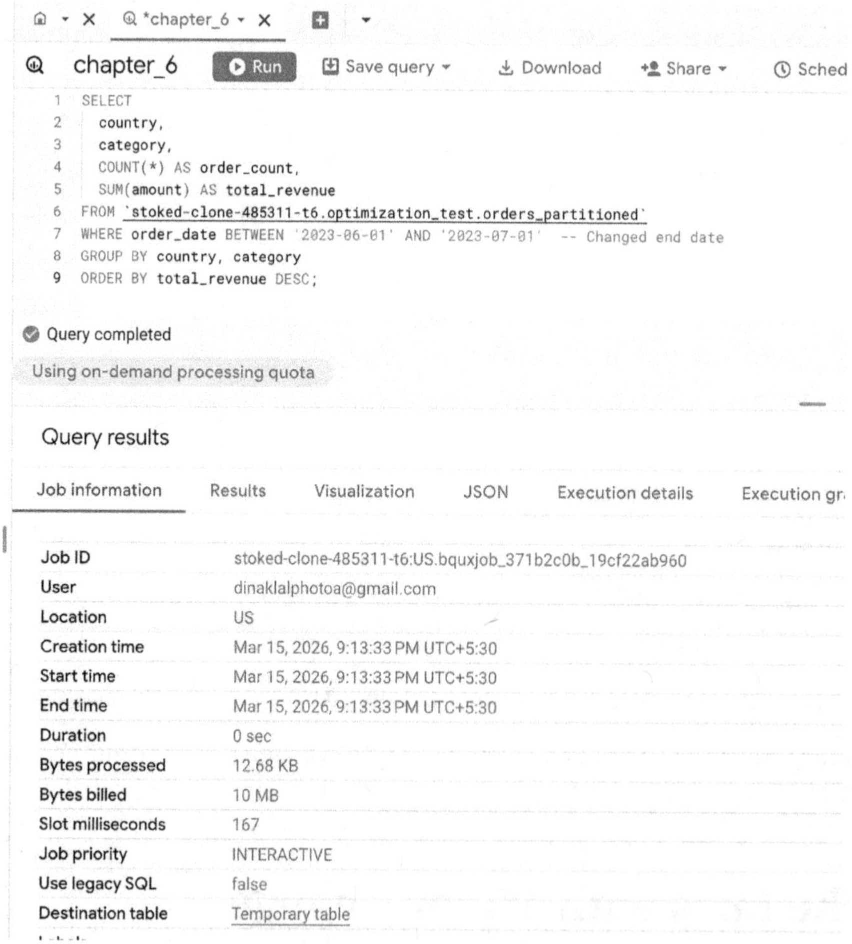

Figure 6.5: *Cache Miss Job Information, Showing 12.68 KB Processed and 167 slot-ms*

Changing one character in the "**WHERE**" clause broke the cache. BigQuery treats this as a completely different query and executes it normally.

Cache Behavior Rules

From this testing, the cache behavior is clear in the following ways:

Cache Hits When:

- Exact same SQL text (including whitespace)
- Same user account
- Underlying data has not changed
- Within a 24-hour window

Cache Misses When:

- Any character changes in the SQL
- Different user runs the query
- Base table receives new data
- More than 24 hours have passed

Practical Implications:

- Dashboard queries with identical SQL benefit from caching.
- Parameterized queries (such as different date ranges) do not share cache.
- Streaming tables rarely benefit from caching due to constant data changes.
- Query formatting matters—extra spaces break the cache.

The cache is automatic and free. You do not need to configure anything, but understanding when it works can explain why some queries are suddenly free and instant.

Materialized Views (MVs) Performance

MVs pre-compute query results, providing dramatic performance improvements for repetitive aggregation patterns.

Creating the MV

Create an MV for monthly revenue aggregations in the following manner:

```
CREATE MATERIALIZED VIEW `your-project-id.optimization_test.monthly_
revenue_mv`
AS
SELECT
  DATE_TRUNC(order_date, MONTH) AS month,
  country,
  category,
  COUNT(*) AS order_count,
  SUM(amount) AS total_revenue
FROM `your-project-id.optimization_test.orders_partitioned`
GROUP BY month, country, category;
```

This pre-computes monthly aggregations by country and category. BigQuery will automatically maintain this view as new data arrives in the base table.

Querying the MV

Query the MV directly in the following manner:

```
SELECT
  month,
  country,
  SUM(total_revenue) AS revenue
FROM `your-project-id.optimization_test.monthly_revenue_mv`
WHERE month BETWEEN '2023-06-01' AND '2023-08-31'
GROUP BY month, country
ORDER BY month, revenue DESC;
```

Results from This Test:

- Bytes Processed: 4.32 KB
- Bytes Billed: 10 MB
- Slot-ms: 11
- Elapsed Time: 370 ms

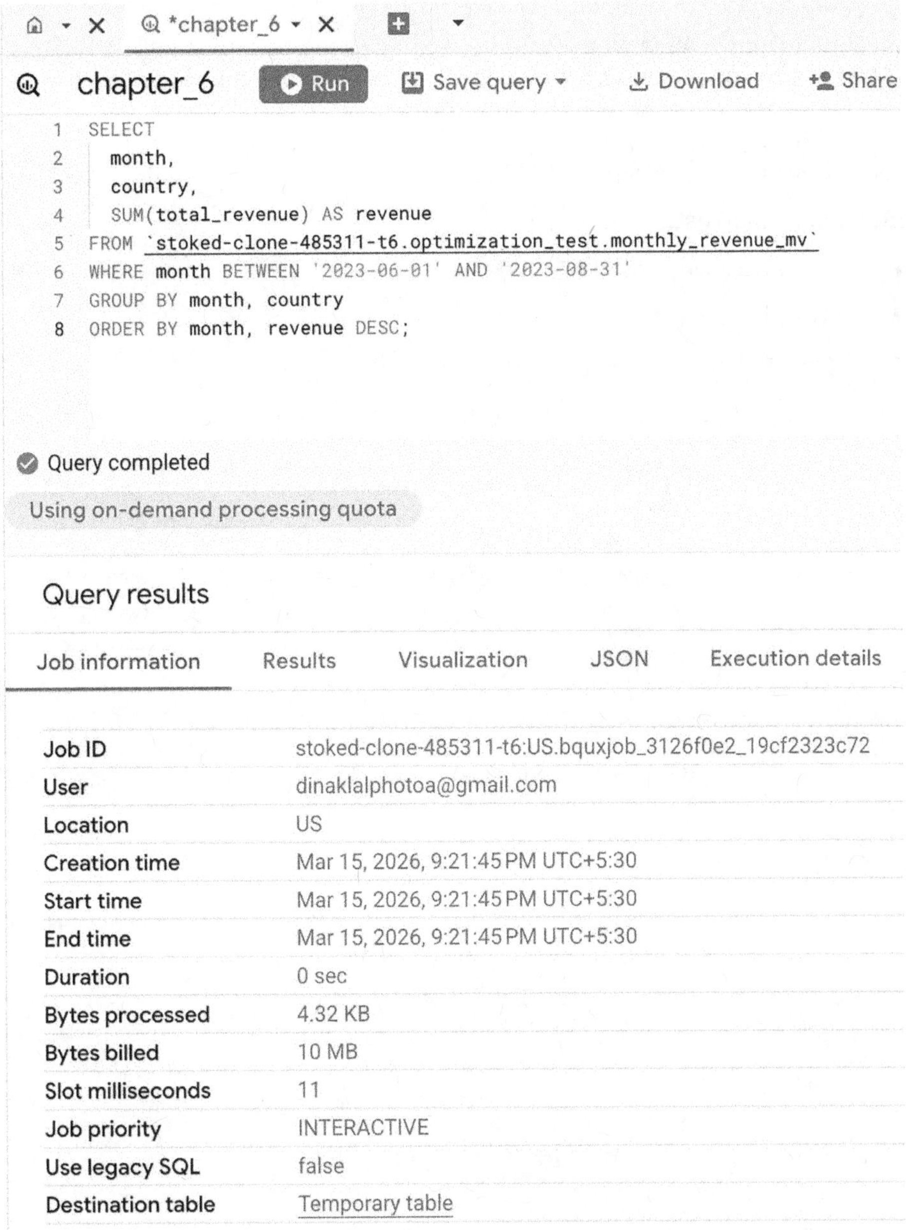

***Figure 6.6:** MV Query Job Information, Showing 4.32 KB Processed and 11 slot-ms*

Equivalent Query on Base Table

Run the same logic against the base table in the following way:

```
SELECT
  DATE_TRUNC(order_date, MONTH) AS month,
```

```
    country,
    SUM(amount) AS revenue
  FROM `your-project-id.optimization_test.orders_partitioned`
  WHERE order_date BETWEEN '2023-06-01' AND '2023-08-31'
  GROUP BY month, country
  ORDER BY month, revenue DESC;
```

Results from This Test:

- Bytes Processed: 26.41 KB
- Bytes Billed: 10 MB
- Slot-ms: 2,467

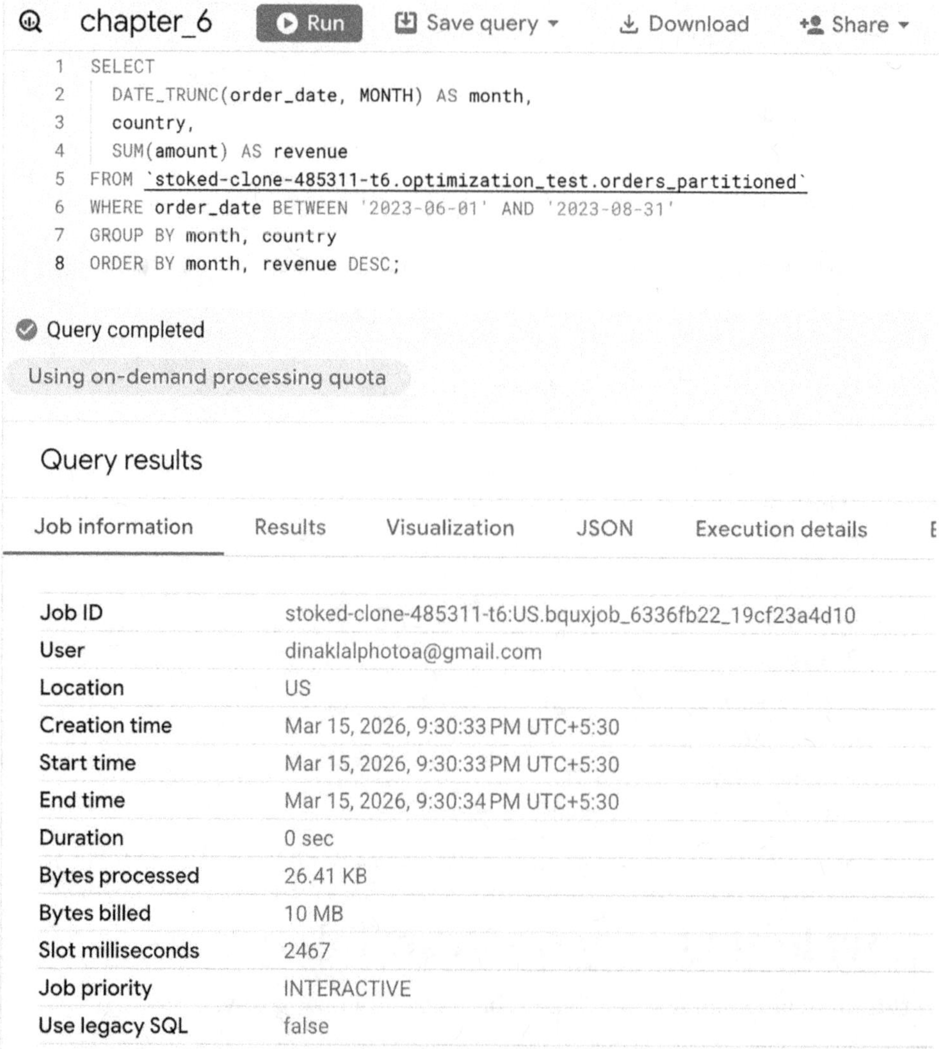

Figure 6.7: *Base Table Query Job Information, Showing 26.41 KB Processed and 2,467 slot-ms*

The Performance Impact

The MV provided dramatic improvements in the following way:

Metric	Base Table	Materialized View (MV)	Improvement
Bytes processed	26.41 KB	4.32 KB	84% reduction
Slot-ms	2,467	11	224x faster
Elapsed time	519 ms	370 ms	29% faster

Table 6.3: *Performance Comparison*

The slot-ms improvement is remarkable–224x less compute for the same results. This happens because:

- The aggregation work is already done (pre-computed).
- BigQuery only needs to read and sum the pre-aggregated values.
- No GROUP BY computation on the raw data.

Key Insight: MVs excel at reducing compute (slot-ms) more than reducing data scanning. The 84% scan reduction is massive, but the 224x compute reduction is the real game-changer.

Scaling Considerations: These tests use a small dataset (for example, 5,000 rows) for demonstrating clarity, but the patterns scale to production workloads. On a 500-GB production table, MV improvements are typically 50-200x rather than 224x, as absolute compute time increases for both approaches. However, the fundamental benefit–eliminating redundant aggregation work–holds regardless of scale. The larger your base table and the more complex your aggregations, the more dramatic the MV performance gains become.

Automatic Query Rewriting

Test whether BigQuery automatically uses the MV in the following manner:

```
SELECT
  DATE_TRUNC(order_date, MONTH) AS month,
  country,
  category,
  COUNT(*) AS order_count,
  SUM(amount) AS total_revenue
FROM `your-project-id.optimization_test.orders_partitioned`
WHERE order_date BETWEEN '2023-06-01' AND '2023-08-31'
GROUP BY DATE_TRUNC(order_date, MONTH), country, category
ORDER BY month, total_revenue DESC;
```

Results from This Test:

- Bytes Processed: 37.9 KB
- Bytes Billed: 10 MB
- Slot-ms: 1,777

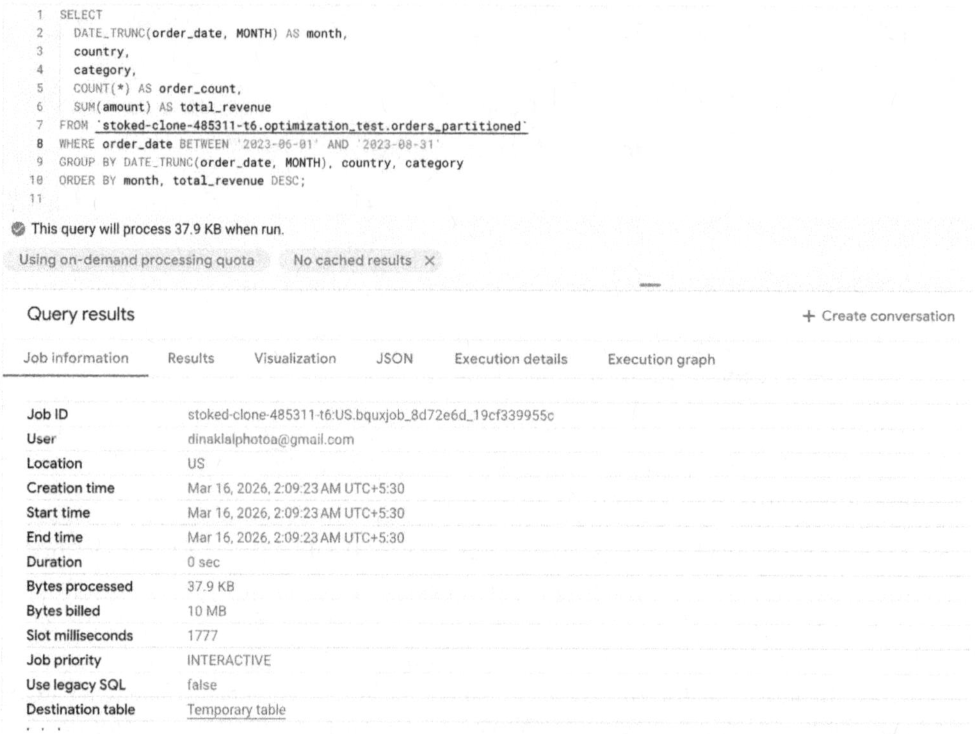

Figure 6.8: *Base Table Query That Could Use MV but Did Not–Job Information, Showing* 37.9 KB

BigQuery did not automatically rewrite this query to use the MV, even though it contains exactly the needed aggregations. This shows that automatic query rewriting has limitations and is not always triggered.

When Automatic Rewriting Works:

- Simple aggregation patterns that exactly match the MV structure
- Queries that are subsets of the MV's "**`GROUP BY`**" columns
- No complex "**`WHERE`**" clauses or functions

When It Does Not Work:

- Complex queries with additional logic
- Queries with different column aliases
- Queries that do not exactly match the MV pattern

For guaranteed MV usage, query the MV directly rather than relying on automatic rewriting.

Cost Control and Query Optimization

Beyond caching and materialization, several query-level techniques can reduce both cost and compute consumption, which will be covered in this section.

Approximate versus Exact Aggregation

For large datasets, approximate functions can provide significant performance improvements with minimal loss of accuracy.

Exact Count (Distinct):

```
SELECT
  country,
  COUNT(DISTINCT order_id) AS exact_distinct_orders
FROM `your-project-id.optimization_test.orders_partitioned`
GROUP BY country;
```

Results from This Test:

- Bytes Processed: 69.69 KB
- Bytes Billed: 10 MB
- Slot-ms: 9,535

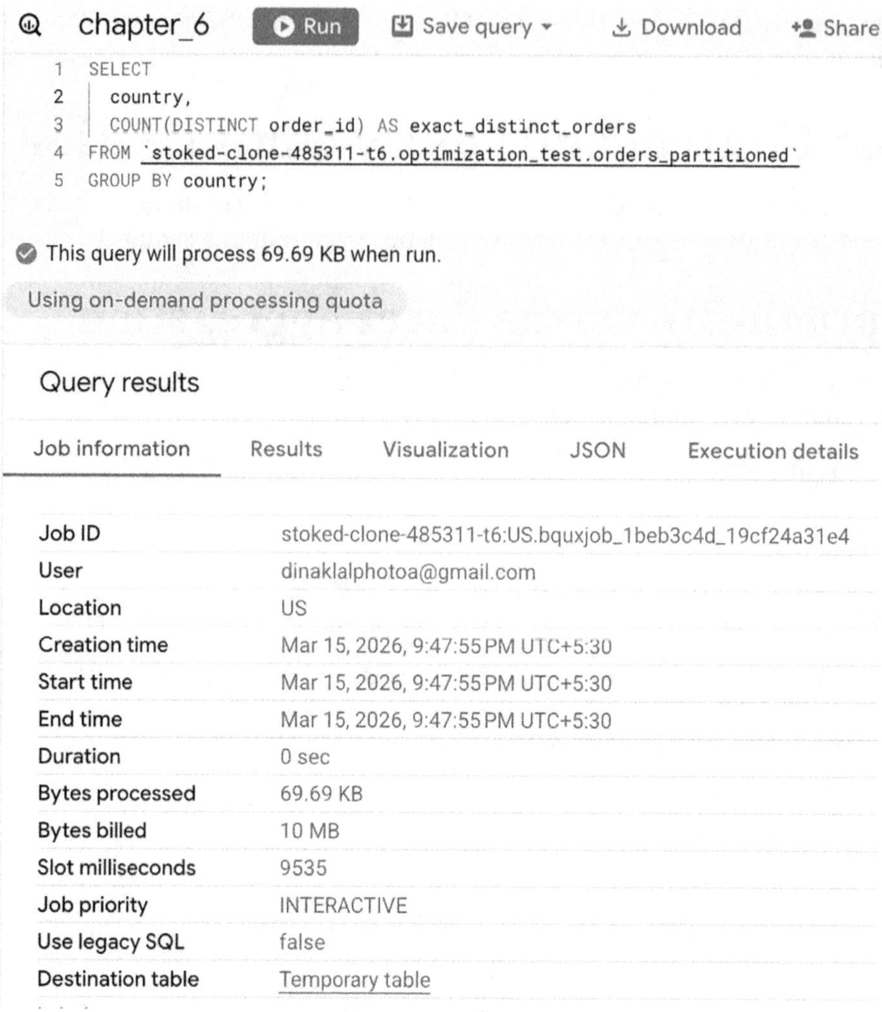

Figure 6.9: *Exact COUNT(DISTINCT) Job Information, Showing 69.69 KB Processed and 9,535 slot-ms*

Approximate Count (Distinct):

```
SELECT
  country,
  APPROX_COUNT_DISTINCT(order_id) AS approx_distinct_orders
FROM `your-project-id.optimization_test.orders_partitioned`
GROUP BY country;
```

Results from This Test:

- Bytes Processed: 69.69 KB (same as exact)
- Bytes Billed: 10 MB
- Slot-ms: Reduced

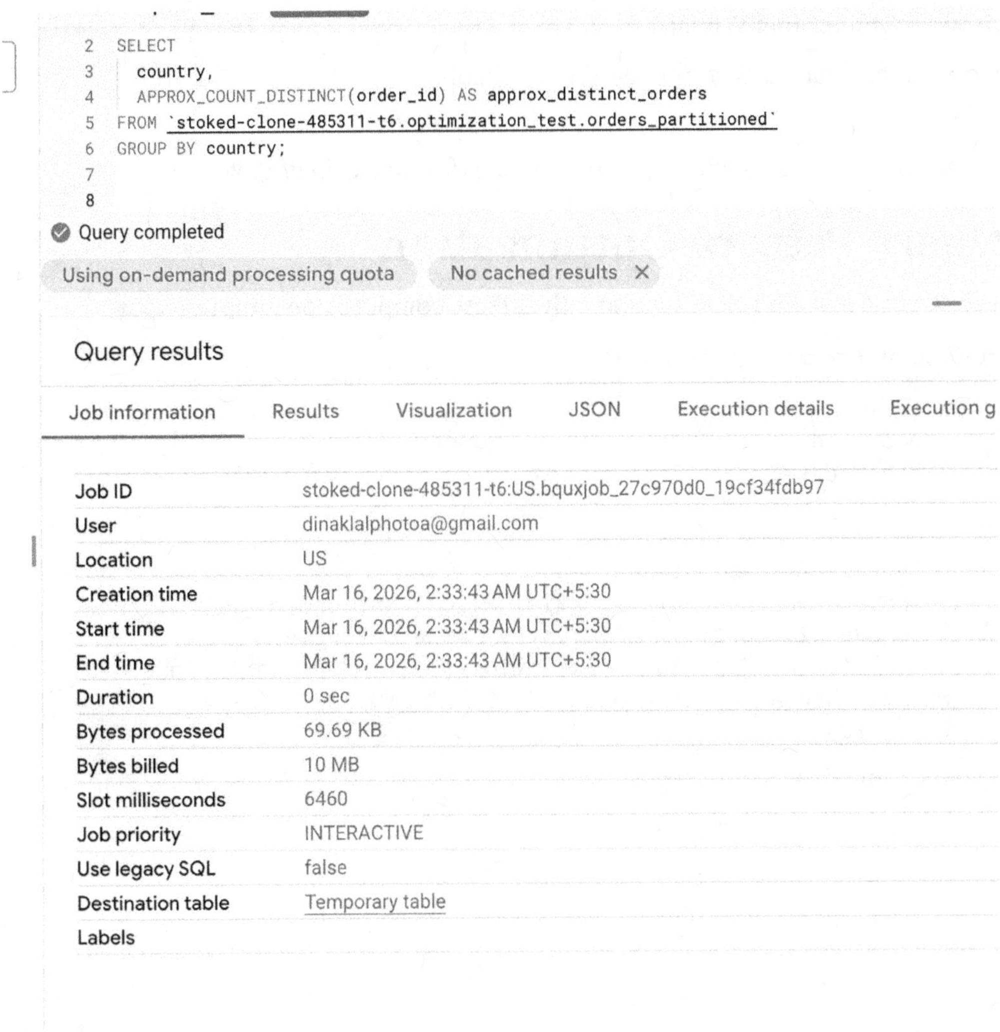

Figure 6.10: APPROX_COUNT_DISTINCT *Job Information, Showing* 69.69 KB *Processed*

The approximate function noticeably reduced the compute while scanning identical data. The results were identical in this test (both showed the same distinct counts), but **APPROX_COUNT_DISTINCT** typically has ~2% error margin.

Use Approximate Functions When:

- Dashboard queries where exact precision is not critical.
- Large datasets where compute savings are significant.
- Trend analysis and monitoring, ensuring that small errors do not affect insights.

Use Exact Functions When:

- Financial calculations require precision.
- Compliance reporting with audit requirements arises.
- Small datasets where performance difference is negligible.

Query Pattern Optimization

The structure of your SQL significantly affects compute consumption.

Inefficient: Correlated Subquery

```
SELECT
  order_id,
  order_date,
  country,
  amount,
  (SELECT AVG(amount)
   FROM `your-project-id.optimization_test.orders_partitioned` o2
   WHERE o2.country = o1.country) AS country_avg
FROM `your-project-id.optimization_test.orders_partitioned` o1
WHERE order_date BETWEEN '2023-06-01' AND '2023-06-30'
LIMIT 100;
```

Results from This Test:

- Bytes Processed: 147.82 KB
- Bytes Billed: 10 MB
- Slot-ms: 17,164

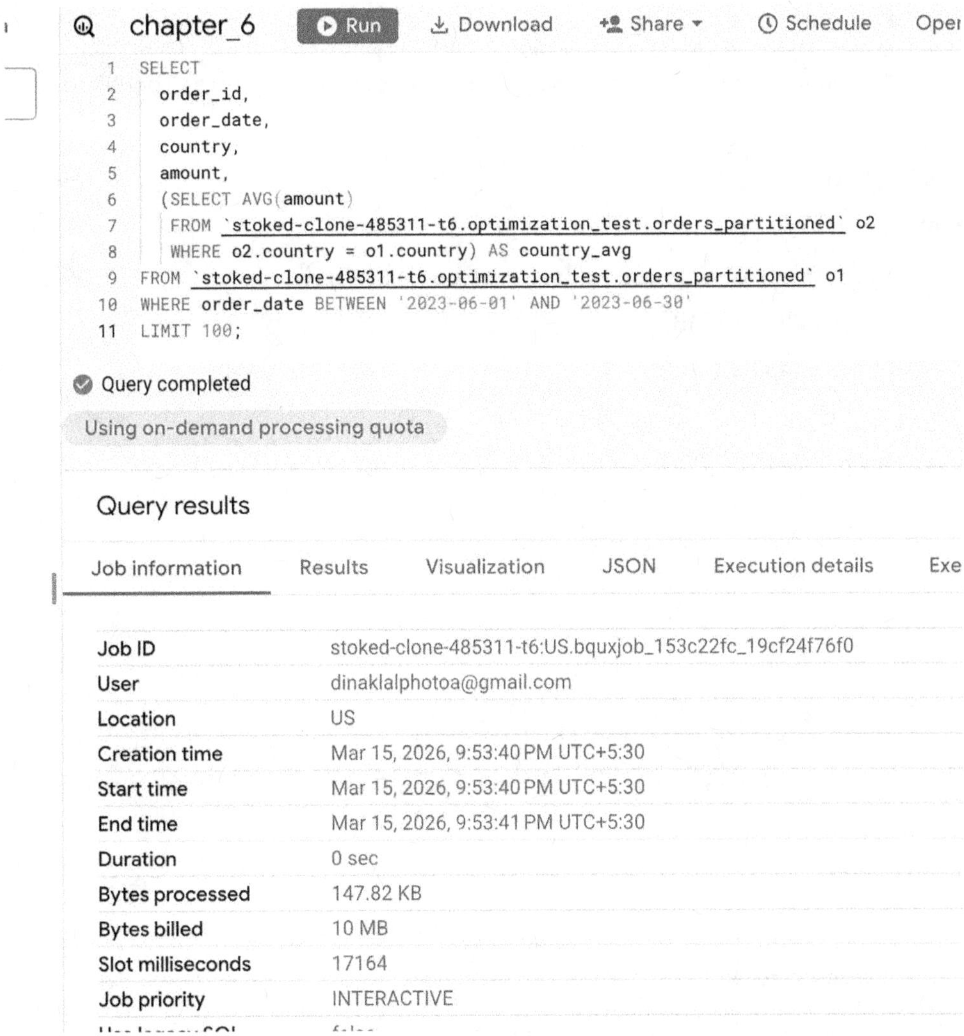

Figure 6.11: *Correlated Subquery Job Information, Showing 147.82 KB Processed and 17,164 slot-ms*

Efficient: CTE with `JOIN`

```
WITH country_avg AS (
  SELECT
    country,
    AVG(amount) AS avg_amount
  FROM `your-project-id.optimization_test.orders_partitioned`
  GROUP BY country
)
SELECT
  o.order_id,
  o.order_date,
  o.country,
```

```
    o.amount,
    ca.avg_amount AS country_avg
  FROM `your-project-id.optimization_test.orders_partitioned` o
  JOIN country_avg ca ON o.country = ca.country
  WHERE o.order_date BETWEEN '2023-06-01' AND '2023-06-30'
  LIMIT 100;
```

Results from This Test:

- Bytes Processed: 147.82 KB (same as correlated)
- Bytes Billed: 10 MB
- Slot-ms: 13,622

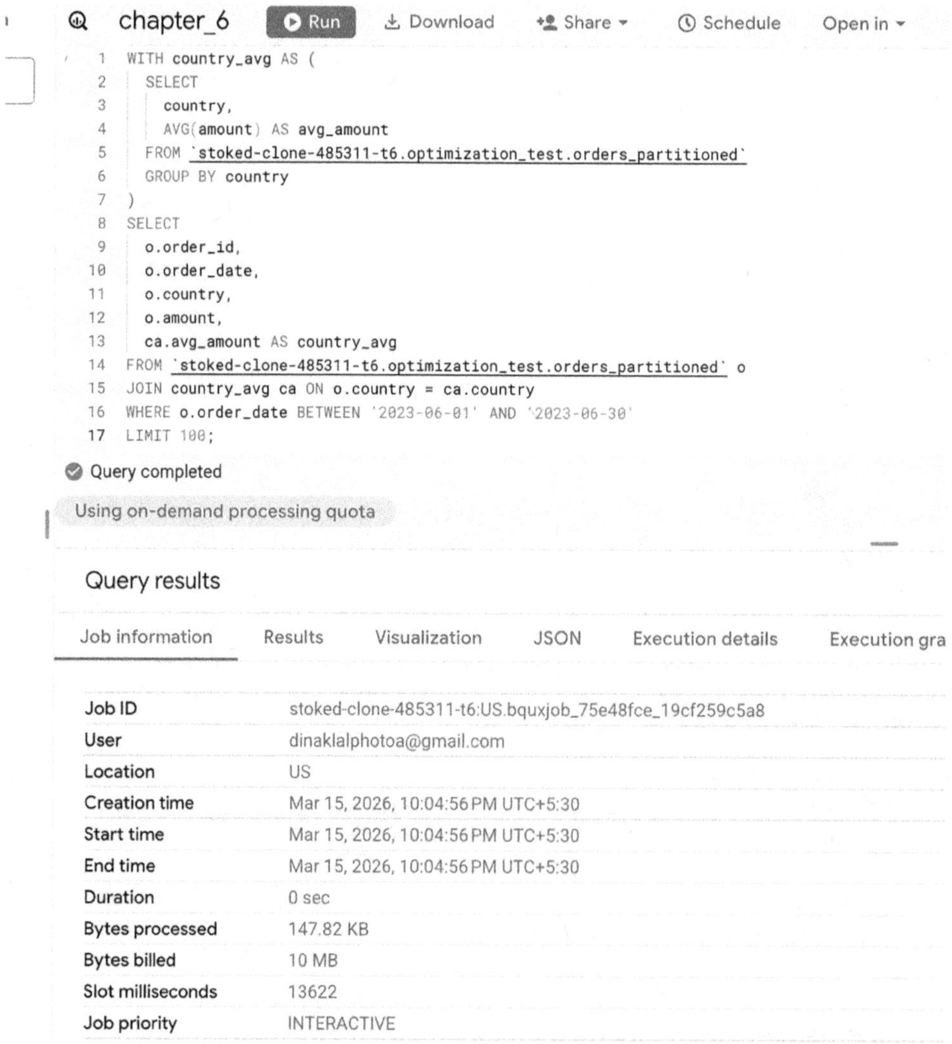

Figure 6.12: *Optimized CTE + JOIN Job Information, Showing 147.82 KB Processed and 13,622 slot-ms*

The Optimization Impact

The CTE approach provided measurable compute savings, as demonstrated in *Table 6.4*:

Metric	Correlated Subquery	CTE + JOIN	Improvement
Bytes processed	147.82 KB	147.82 KB	No change
Slot-ms	17,164	13,622	21% reduction

Table 6.4: *Correlated Subquery versus CTE + JOIN Performance Comparison*

The CTE approach reduced the compute by 21% while scanning identical data. The correlated subquery forces BigQuery to execute the subquery for every row in the outer query. The CTE computes the country averages once and JOINs the results.

Why the Elapsed Time Increased: The CTE approach used fewer slot-ms but took slightly longer wall-clock time. This can happen when BigQuery allocates fewer slots to the optimized query, trading parallelism for efficiency.

Practical Cost Control Techniques

Beyond query optimization, these practical controls prevent cost overruns in the following ways:

1. **Set Maximum Bytes Billed Limits:** The most important cost guardrail is preventing accidental expensive queries. While the BigQuery UI for setting query-level limits has changed, you can set project-level controls in the following manner:

   Project-Level Quotas (Cloud Console → BigQuery → Admin → Quotas):

   - Daily query usage limit per user (for example, 1 TB per day)
   - Project-level daily scan limit (for example, 10 TB per day)
   - Concurrent query limits

   Why This Matters: One `SELECT *` on a 10 TB table costs $62.50. Setting limits prevents accidental expensive queries from junior developers or runaway scripts.

   Note: *Query-level* ***`maximum_bytes_billed`*** *options have limited support in current BigQuery interfaces, so project-level quotas are the most reliable approach.*

2. **Monitor Expensive Queries:** Use `INFORMATION_SCHEMA.JOBS` to find your most expensive queries in the following way:

```
SELECT
  user_email,
  query,
  total_bytes_processed / POW(1024, 3) AS gb_processed,
  total_slot_ms / 1000 AS slot_seconds,
  creation_time
FROM `region-us`.INFORMATION_SCHEMA.JOBS
WHERE creation_time > TIMESTAMP_SUB(CURRENT_TIMESTAMP(), INTERVAL
7 DAY)
  AND job_type = 'QUERY'
  AND state = 'DONE'
ORDER BY total_bytes_processed DESC
LIMIT 10;
```

3. **Set Project-Level Quotas**

   In **`Cloud Console`** → **`BigQuery`** → **`Admin`** → **`Quotas`**, set the following:

   - Daily query usage limit per user
   - Project-level daily scan limit
   - Concurrent query limits

4. **Use Approximate Functions for Dashboards**

   Replace exact aggregations with approximate ones, such as:

   - `COUNT(DISTINCT x) → APPROX_COUNT_DISTINCT(x)`
   - `PERCENTILE_CONT(x, 0.5)→APPROX_QUANTILES(x, 100)[OFFSET(50)]`

5. **Optimize Query Patterns**

   - Replace correlated subqueries with CTEs and JOINs
   - Use **`NOT EXISTS`** instead of **`NOT IN`**
   - Combine multiple aggregations into single queries
   - Filter before joining whenever possible

Additional Query Patterns for Compute Optimization

Beyond the tested patterns, these query structures also reduce slot-ms consumption in the following manner:

Replace `NOT IN` with `NOT EXISTS`:

```
-- Higher slot-ms: NOT IN forces full evaluation
WHERE customer_id NOT IN (SELECT customer_id FROM banned_customers)
```

```
-- Lower slot-ms: NOT EXISTS allows early termination
WHERE NOT EXISTS (SELECT 1 FROM banned_customers b WHERE b.custom-
er_id = o.customer_id)
```

Combine Multiple Aggregations:

```
-- Higher slot-ms: 3 separate table scans
SELECT 'orders' AS metric, COUNT(*) FROM orders
UNION ALL SELECT 'revenue', SUM(amount) FROM orders
UNION ALL SELECT 'avg_order', AVG(amount) FROM orders

-- Lower slot-ms: Single scan with multiple aggregations
SELECT COUNT(*) AS orders, SUM(amount) AS revenue, AVG(amount) AS
avg_order FROM orders
```

Filter before Joining (When Optimizer Does Not Do It Automatically):

```
-- Potentially higher slot-ms: Join then filter
SELECT o.order_id, c.name FROM orders o
JOIN customers c ON o.customer_id = c.customer_id
WHERE o.order_date = '2024-01-15'

-- Lower slot-ms: Filter then join
SELECT o.order_id, c.name FROM (
  SELECT order_id, customer_id FROM orders WHERE order_date
= '2024-01-15'
) o JOIN customers c ON o.customer_id = c.customer_id
```

These patterns complement the tested optimizations (such as MVs, caching, or approximate functions) to create a comprehensive compute optimization strategy.

Conclusion

Performance and cost engineering in BigQuery requires understanding the distinction between data scanning (bytes processed) and computation (slot-ms). While the previous chapter detailed reducing bytes scanned through partitioning and clustering, this chapter focused on reducing compute consumption and leveraging BigQuery's acceleration features.

Now, you have a complete compute optimization toolkit. You know how to leverage MVs to mathematically skip redundant aggregations, how to format your dashboard queries to guarantee free cache hits, when to trade perfect accuracy for massive speedups using approximate functions, and why CTEs run circles around correlated subqueries. By keeping a close eye on "**`INFORMATION_SCHEMA.JOBS`**," you can spot the quiet slot-ms hogs in your own projects and apply these exact patterns to permanently tame them.

In the next chapter, we will explore how to build production-grade data pipelines by using a data build tool (dbt) with BigQuery, applying the partitioning, clustering, and optimization techniques you have learned to real-world ELT workflows.

Points to Remember

- Slots are BigQuery's compute units; slot-ms measures total compute consumed by a query.
- Bytes processed (storage) and slot-ms (compute) are independent–optimizing one does not automatically optimize the other.
- On-demand pricing charges per TB scanned; capacity pricing (Editions) provides dedicated slots with predictable costs.
- Reservations enable workload isolation by creating dedicated slot pools for different teams or use cases.
- BI Engine provides in-memory acceleration for dashboard queries, delivering sub-second response times.
- Query caching provides 100% cost reduction for identical SQL but breaks with any text changes.
- Materialized Views (MVs) can reduce slot-ms by 200x+ for matching aggregation patterns.
- Automatic query rewriting to use MVs has limitations; query the MV directly for guaranteed usage.
- Correlated subqueries consume significantly more compute than equivalent CTEs with JOINs.
- Query structure affects compute consumption independently of data size.
- `"INFORMATION_SCHEMA.JOBS"` is the primary tool for monitoring compute usage and identifying expensive queries.
- Project-level quotas in Cloud Console provide spending controls when query-level limits are not available.
- Cache hits show 0 bytes processed and 0 bytes billed in job details.
- MVs excel at reducing compute (slot-ms) more than reducing data scanning.
- The same query can have different slot-ms consumption based on BigQuery's slot allocation and parallelism.
- Wait times in execution details indicate resource contention and potential slot limitations.
- Elapsed time and slot-ms do not always correlate–higher parallelism can reduce wall-clock time while using more total compute.

Multiple Choice Questions

1. What does slot-ms measure in BigQuery?
   a. The amount of data scanned from storage
   b. The total compute resources consumed by a query
   c. The number of parallel connections
   d. The query execution time in milliseconds
2. When does BigQuery's query cache provide a cache hit?
   a. When any user runs a similar query
   b. When the same user runs the same SQL text and the underlying data has not changed
   c. When queries scan the same amount of data
   d. When queries use the same tables
3. What happened when the query date range was changed from "2023-06-30" to "2023-07-01"?
   a. The query cache still worked
   b. The query cache was invalidated and the query executed normally
   c. BigQuery automatically used a Materialized View (MV)
   d. The query failed with an error
4. Which query pattern consumed more slot-ms in the test?
   a. CTE with `JOIN`
   b. Correlated subquery
   c. Both consumed the same slot-ms
   d. The test results were inconclusive
5. What was the primary benefit of using `APPROX_COUNT_DISTINCT` over `COUNT (DISTINCT)`?
   a. It scanned less data.
   b. It reduced slot-ms with minimal accuracy loss.
   c. It provided more accurate results.
   d. It worked better with Materialized Views (MVs).

6. Why did BigQuery not automatically use the Materialized View (MV) for the base table query?
   a. The Materialized View (MV) was corrupted.
   b. Automatic query rewriting has limitations and does not always trigger.
   c. The query was too complex.
   d. The Materialized View (MV) was not refreshed.
7. What is the relationship between bytes processed and slot-ms?
   a. They are always proportional.
   b. Higher bytes processed always means higher slot-ms.
   c. They are independent metrics–queries can scan identical data but use different compute.
   d. Slot-ms is always 10% of bytes processed.
8. What is the main advantage of BigQuery capacity pricing (Editions) over on-demand pricing?
   a. Lower cost per TB scanned
   b. Predictable monthly costs and dedicated compute capacity
   c. Faster query execution for all queries
   d. Automatic query optimization
9. What is the primary purpose of reservations in BigQuery?
   a. To cache query results for faster access
   b. To create isolated slot pools for different workloads
   c. To automatically partition large tables
   d. To compress data for storage savings

Answers

1. b
2. b
3. b
4. b
5. b

6. b
7. c
8. b
9. b

Questions

1. Explain why the Materialized View (MV) provided great improvement in slot-ms, but less improvement in bytes processed. What does this tell you about where Materialized Views (MVs) provide the most value?

2. The query cache broke when changing "2023-06-30" to "2023-07-01" in the `"WHERE"` clause. Describe three practical strategies for maximizing cache hit rates in a dashboard environment.

3. Compare the trade-offs between using Materialized Views (MVs) versus query caching for a dashboard that refreshes every 5 minutes with the same SQL queries.

4. The correlated subquery used more slot-ms than the CTE + JOIN approach, while scanning identical data. Explain why query structure affects compute consumption and provide two other examples of query patterns that would increase slot-ms.

5. `APPROX_COUNT_DISTINCT` reduced slot-ms compared to exact `COUNT(DISTINCT)`. In what scenarios would you choose the approximate function, and when would you require the exact function despite the performance cost?

6. The test showed that bytes processed and slot-ms are independent metrics. Describe a scenario where a query would have high bytes processed but low slot-ms, and another scenario with low bytes processed but high slot-ms.

7. BigQuery did not automatically rewrite the base table query to use the Materialized View (MV). Design a strategy that ensures that your team gets the performance benefits of Materialized Views (MVs) without relying on automatic query rewriting.

Key Terms

- **Slot:** BigQuery's unit of compute, providing CPU, memory, and network resources for query execution. Queries are executed across multiple slots in parallel.

- **Slot-ms (Slot Milliseconds):** A measure of total compute consumed by a query, calculated as the number of slots multiplied by execution time in milliseconds.
- **On-Demand Pricing:** BigQuery's default pricing model where you pay $6.25 per TB scanned, with a 10 MB minimum per table.
- **Capacity Pricing (BigQuery Editions):** A pricing model where you pay for dedicated compute capacity (slot-hours) rather than bytes scanned, available in Standard, Enterprise, and Enterprise Plus tiers.
- **Reservation:** A dedicated pool of slots assigned to specific projects or workloads, providing guaranteed compute capacity and workload isolation (requires capacity pricing).
- **Autoscaling:** A BigQuery Editions feature that automatically adjusts slot allocation between a configured baseline and maximum based on workload demand.
- **BI Engine:** BigQuery's in-memory analysis service that caches frequently accessed data for sub-second query performance, included with Enterprise+ editions.
- **Query Cache:** BigQuery's automatic 24-hour cache of query results. Identical queries from the same user return cached results at zero cost unless the underlying data has changed.
- **Cache Hit:** When BigQuery returns results from the query cache instead of re-executing the query, resulting in 0 bytes processed and 0 bytes billed.
- **Cache Miss:** When the query cache cannot be used due to SQL text changes, different users, data changes, or cache expiration, requiring normal query execution.
- **Materialized View (MV):** A pre-computed query result that BigQuery stores, automatically refreshes, and can use to accelerate queries with matching aggregation patterns.
- **Automatic Query Rewriting:** BigQuery's optimizer feature that can transparently redirect queries to read from Materialized Views (MVs) instead of base tables when patterns match.
- **Correlated Subquery:** A subquery that references columns from the outer query, forcing execution for each row in the outer query and typically consuming more compute resources.
- **Common Table Expression (CTE):** A named temporary result set defined within a query using the WITH clause, often more efficient than correlated subqueries for complex logic.
- **`APPROX_COUNT_DISTINCT`:** An approximate aggregation function that estimates distinct counts using HyperLogLog++ algorithm, significantly faster than exact `COUNT(DISTINCT)` with ~2% error margin.

- **Bytes Processed:** The amount of data BigQuery reads from storage to execute a query, which determines cost under on-demand pricing.
- **Execution Details:** The BigQuery console tab showing detailed query performance metrics including slot-ms, stages, wait times, and data shuffling information.
- **`INFORMATION_SCHEMA.JOBS`:** A system view containing detailed execution history for all BigQuery jobs, including performance metrics and resource consumption data.
- **Maximum Bytes Billed:** A cost control mechanism that prevents queries from scanning more than a specified amount of data, available through project-level quotas.
- **Wait Time:** Time spent waiting for compute resources during query execution, visible in execution details and indicating potential slot contention.

CHAPTER 7
ELT with dbt and BigQuery

Introduction

As data teams mature and their BigQuery environments grow, scheduling standard SQL queries quickly becomes unmanageable. What begins as a handful of "`CREATE TABLE`" and "`INSERT INTO`" scripts often turns into a tangled web of interdependent, hard-coded procedures. When an upstream schema changes, downstream dashboards can break, and untangling the execution order to fix the failure can take hours.

To solve this, modern data engineering relies on the Extract, Load, Transform (ELT) pattern. Traditionally, teams used an ETL pattern, in which data was extracted, transformed in external processing servers, and finally loaded into the database. In the ELT model, raw data is loaded directly into BigQuery first, and transformations are executed natively using BigQuery's massive compute power.

To manage this SQL complexity, modern teams use a data build tool (dbt).

dbt is a framework that allows you to treat SQL as software. It brings modularity, version control, automated testing, and Continuous Integration (CI) directly to data analytics. In this chapter, you will learn how to transition away from fragile scheduled queries and build robust, automatically documented, and fully tested dbt pipelines.

Structure

In this chapter, we will cover the following topics:

- The Case for dbt in BigQuery
- Setting up dbt with BigQuery
- Building Modular Transformation Models
- Data Modeling Layers
- Writing Tests and Validating Data Quality

- Managing Lineage and Documentation
- Deployment and Automation Strategies
- Hands-on Lab

The Case for dbt in BigQuery

Before dbt, data transformation in BigQuery relied heavily on Data Definition Language (DDL) and Data Manipulation Language (DML). A typical pipeline script might appear in the following manner:

```
-- Legacy approach: Hardcoded DDL and DML
CREATE OR REPLACE TABLE `my-project.analytics.daily_revenue` AS
SELECT
  DATE(order_timestamp) as order_date,
  SUM(amount) as revenue
FROM `my-project.raw_data.orders`
WHERE status = 'completed';
```

While functional, this approach scales poorly owing to the following reasons:

- **Hardcoded Dependencies:** If the **`raw_data.orders`** table name changes, or if you want to test this logic in a **`dev`** dataset, you have to manually find-and-replace the project and dataset strings.
- **Execution Ordering:** If **`daily_revenue`** depends on **`orders`**, and another table **`monthly_revenue`** depends on **`daily_revenue`**, you must manually orchestrate the exact order in which these scripts run—often using complex Airflow DAGs.
- **Lack of Testing:** There is no built-in way to ensure that **`revenue`** is never negative, or that **`order_date`** is strictly unique.
- **Boilerplate:** You are forced to write **`CREATE OR REPLACE TABLE`** in every script.

The dbt Philosophy

`dbt` solves these problems by treating your transformations purely as "**`SELECT`**" statements. You can never write DDL or DML. Instead, you write the business logic, and dbt compiles your SQL and handles the physical creation of tables or views in BigQuery behind the scenes.

By defining dependencies dynamically, **`dbt`** automatically constructs a Directed Acyclic Graph (DAG) and executes your queries in the correct topological order. It acts as the orchestration, testing, and documentation compiler for your BigQuery data warehouse.

Setting up dbt with BigQuery

dbt comes in two primary flavors: dbt Core (a free, open-source command-line tool written in Python) and dbt Cloud (a managed, browser-based IDE and scheduler). Regardless of the version you use, the fundamental project structure remains the same.

The dbt Project Structure

A standard dbt project is a directory of folders containing SQL and YAML files. The heart of the project is the **`dbt_project.yml`** file, which configures the project settings:

```
my_dbt_project/
├── dbt_project.yml         # Primary configuration file
├── models/                 # The actual SQL transformations
│   ├── sources.yml         # Source table definitions
│   ├── staging/            # Clean, standardized raw data
│   ├── intermediate/       # Business logic and joins
│   └── marts/              # Final analytics tables
├── tests/                  # Custom data tests (singular tests)
├── macros/                 # Reusable Jinja functions
└── seeds/                  # Static CSV files loaded into BigQuery
```

Connecting to BigQuery

To connect dbt to BigQuery, you need to configure a **`profiles.yml`** file. This tells dbt exactly which Google Cloud Project to target, which dataset to write into, and how to authenticate.

BigQuery securely integrates with dbt via the following two primary authentication methods:

1. **OAuth (for Development):** Individual analysts authenticate via their personal Google Workspace accounts (**`gcloud auth application-default login`**). Their models are written to personal development datasets (for example, **`dbt_demo_dev`**).
2. **Service Accounts (for Production):** Automated deployment servers (such as GitHub Actions or DBT Cloud) use a Google Cloud Service Account JSON key to authenticate and build models directly into the production datasets.

Example `profiles.yml` Configuration:

```
dbt_elt_lab:
  target: dev
  outputs:
```

```
    dev:
      type: bigquery
      method: oauth
      project: your-project-id
      dataset: dbt_demo_dev
      threads: 4            # Number of concurrent queries BigQuery
can run
      location: US
      priority: interactive
```

Installing dbt Core

The installation process is straightforward but requires attention to Python version compatibility. As of this writing, **`dbt-bigquery`** works best with Python 3.11 or 3.12:

```
# Create virtual environment with Python 3.11
python3.11 -m venv dbt-env

# Activate it
source dbt-env/bin/activate

# Install dbt-bigquery
pip install --upgrade pip
pip install dbt-bigquery

# Verify installation
dbt -version
```

After installation, authenticate with Google Cloud:

```
gcloud auth application-default login
gcloud config set project your-project-id
```

Test your connection:

```
dbt debug
```

If all checks pass (with green checkmarks), you are ready to build models.

Building Modular Transformation Models

In **`dbt`**, a model is simply a **`.sql`** file containing a single "**`SELECT`**" statement.

The Magic of `{{ ref() }}` and Jinja

dbt utilizes Jinja, that is, a pythonic templating language embedded directly inside your SQL code. The most important Jinja function in dbt is the **`{{ ref() }}`** function.

Suppose that you have a model named "**stg_customers.sql.**" If you want to build a downstream model that reads from **stg_customers**, you do not hardcode the BigQuery **project.dataset.table** name. Instead, you use **ref()** in the following manner:

```
-- models/marts/mart_customer_analytics.sql
WITH customers AS (
    SELECT * FROM {{ ref('stg_customers') }}
),

metrics AS (
    SELECT * FROM {{ ref('int_customer_order_metrics') }}
),

final AS (
    SELECT
        c.customer_id,
        c.customer_name,
        c.email,
        c.country,
        COALESCE(m.total_orders, 0) AS total_orders,
        COALESCE(m.total_revenue, 0) AS lifetime_value
    FROM customers c
    LEFT JOIN metrics m ON c.customer_id = m.customer_id
)
SELECT * FROM final
```

The Power of ref()

1. **Environment Awareness:** When you run "**dbt run**" on your laptop, dbt compiles that **ref()** into **`your_schema.dbt_demo_dev.stg_customers`**. When the production server runs it, it compiles into **`your_schema.analytics_prod.stg_customers`**. Code promotion across environments requires zero code changes.

2. **Dependency Inference:** As **dbt** parses the text of your files looking for **ref()** functions, it automatically knows that **mart_customer_analytics** depends on both **stg_customers** and **int_customer_order_metrics**. BigQuery will not attempt to build **mart_customer_analytics** until both dependencies finish successfully.

Defining Sources with {{ source() }}

For raw tables that exist outside of **dbt**–loaded via Fivetran, Data Transfer Service, or manual ingestion–you can define them in a **sources.yml** file in the following manner:

```
version: 2
sources:
  - name: raw_data
    database: your-project-id
    schema: dbt_demo
    description: Raw e-commerce data
    tables:
      - name: raw_orders
        description: Raw order transactions
      - name: raw_customers
        description: Raw customer information
      - name: raw_products
        description: Raw product catalog
```

Then, reference them in your staging models using **`{{ source() }}`** in the following way:

```
-- models/staging/stg_orders.sql
WITH source AS (
    SELECT * FROM {{ source('raw_data', 'raw_orders') }}
),
cleaned AS (
    SELECT
        order_id,
        customer_id,
        order_date,
        LOWER(TRIM(status)) AS status,
        amount,
        CURRENT_TIMESTAMP() AS loaded_at
    FROM source
    WHERE order_date IS NOT NULL
      AND amount > 0
)
SELECT * FROM cleaned
```

This approach provides the following two benefits:

1. **Centralized Source Definitions:** All raw table references live in one YAML file.
2. **Lineage Tracking: `dbt`** knows that these are external sources and displays them differently in the DAG.

BigQuery Materializations

`dbt` allows you to dictate how BigQuery physically materializes a model by using a configuration block at the top of the **`.sql`** file in the following manner:

```
{{ config(
    materialized='table',
    partition_by={
      "field": "order_date",
      "data_type": "date",
      "granularity": "day"
    },
    cluster_by=["country", "status"]
) }}
SELECT * FROM ...
```

There are the following four core materializations in dbt for BigQuery, which are as follows:

1. **`view`:** dbt executes a "**`CREATE OR REPLACE VIEW`**" statement. Views do not store data, making them perfect for lightweight transformations and simple renaming, where you always want real-time underlying data. This is the default materialization.

2. **`table`:** dbt executes a "**`CREATE OR REPLACE TABLE`**" statement. Tables are physically built and stored. This is ideal for heavy aggregations or complex joins that would consume too much slot-ms if queried dynamically.

3. **`incremental`:** This is the most powerful and complex materialization. On the first run, it builds a full table. On subsequent runs, dbt dynamically generates a "**`MERGE`**" or "**`INSERT`**" statement to append only new records to the existing table. This saves enormous amounts of bytes processed and drastically reduces BigQuery costs for multi-terabyte datasets.

   ```
   {{ config(materialized='incremental') }}
   SELECT *
   FROM {{ ref('stg_events') }}
   {% if is_incremental() %}
    -- This filter only runs on subsequent executions
    WHERE event_timestamp > (SELECT max(event_timestamp) FROM {{
   this }})
   {% endif %}
   ```

   Cost Awareness: The choice of materialization directly impacts your BigQuery bill. Using a table or view on a 10 TB dataset means that BigQuery scans the entire 10 TB every time the model or downstream dashboard runs. By switching to incremental, the model might only scan the 500 MB of new data that arrived today, drastically reducing the processed bytes and saving massive compute costs over time.

4. **ephemeral:** The model is not built in BigQuery at all. Instead, anytime it is referenced downstream via **ref()**, **dbt** physically injects the model's SQL as a Common Table Expression (CTE).

Data Modeling Layers

To prevent messy logic, experienced analytics engineers organize their BigQuery dbt projects into strictly defined layers. The most widely adopted structure is the Staging, Intermediate, and Mart methodology.

Layer 1: Staging Layer (stg_)

The staging layer serves as the front door to your **dbt** project. These models read directly from raw tables (for example, ingested via Fivetran or BigQuery Data Transfer Service).

The Rules for Staging Models:

- 1:1 relationship with the raw tables, with no joins.
- Focus strictly on renaming columns to standard conventions, casting data types (for example, **STRING** to **TIMESTAMP**), and basic JSON extraction.
- Provide a clean foundation, so that downstream models never touch the raw data directly.

The following is a real staging model from our e-commerce pipeline:

```
-- models/staging/stg_customers.sql
WITH source AS (
    SELECT * FROM {{ source('raw_data', 'raw_customers') }}
),
cleaned AS (
    SELECT
        customer_id,
        TRIM(customer_name) AS customer_name,
        LOWER(TRIM(email)) AS email,
        UPPER(TRIM(country)) AS country,
        signup_date,
        CURRENT_TIMESTAMP() AS loaded_at
    FROM source
    WHERE email IS NOT NULL
      AND signup_date IS NOT NULL
)
SELECT * FROM cleaned
```

The preceding model does the following:

- Standardizes string casing and trims whitespace.

- Filters out invalid records (such as missing email or **signup_date**).
- No joins, no aggregations, and no complex business logic.

Layer 2: Intermediate Layer (int_)

The intermediate layer is where complex business logic lives. If you need to join a customer table with a transaction table to calculate lifetime value, you do it in this layer.

The Rules for Intermediate Models:

- Designed to be referenced by other models, rarely intended to be queried directly by end-users.
- Materialized as "**view**" or "**ephemeral**" to save BigQuery storage, unless the logic is so heavy that it requires a **table**.

The following is an intermediate model that calculates customer order metrics:

```
-- models/intermediate/int_customer_order_metrics.sql
WITH orders AS (
    SELECT * FROM {{ ref('stg_orders') }}
),
customer_metrics AS (
    SELECT
        customer_id,
        COUNT(*) AS total_orders,
        COUNT(CASE WHEN status = 'completed' THEN 1 END)
AS completed_orders,
        COUNT(CASE WHEN status = 'cancelled' THEN 1 END)
AS cancelled_orders,
        SUM(CASE WHEN status = 'completed' THEN amount ELSE 0 END)
AS total_revenue,
        AVG(CASE WHEN status = 'completed' THEN amount END)
AS avg_order_value,
        MIN(order_date) AS first_order_date,
        MAX(order_date) AS last_order_date,
        DATE_DIFF(MAX(order_date), MIN(order_date), DAY)
AS customer_lifetime_days
    FROM orders
    GROUP BY customer_id
)
SELECT * FROM customer_metrics
```

This model performs the following tasks:

- Reads from the staging layer (**stg_orders**).
- Performs aggregations to calculate metrics per customer.

- Handles conditional logic (such as completed versus cancelled orders).
- Calculates derived metrics (such as customer lifetime days).
- Produces a reusable dataset for downstream marts.

Layer 3: Mart Layer (`mart_`, `dim_`, `fct_`)

The mart layer consists of the final, polished tables that are exposed to your BI tools (such as Looker and Tableau). These are typically structured using dimensional modeling concepts (Kimball methodology), such as:

- **Fact Tables (`fct_`):** Narrow, deep tables recording immutable events and metrics (for example, **`fct_orders`** and **`fct_page_views`**).
- **Dimension Tables (`dim_`):** Wide, shallow tables providing descriptive context (for example, **`dim_customers`** and **`dim_products`**).
- **Mart Tables (`mart_`):** Denormalized, wide tables combining facts and dimensions for specific analytical use cases.

The following is a complete mart model that combines customer profiles with order metrics and adds segmentation logic:

```
-- models/marts/mart_customer_analytics.sql
WITH customers AS (
    SELECT * FROM {{ ref('stg_customers') }}
),
metrics AS (
    SELECT * FROM {{ ref('int_customer_order_metrics') }}
),
final AS (
    SELECT
        c.customer_id,
        c.customer_name,
        c.email,
        c.country,
        c.signup_date,
        COALESCE(m.total_orders, 0) AS total_orders,
        COALESCE(m.completed_orders, 0) AS completed_orders,
        COALESCE(m.cancelled_orders, 0) AS cancelled_orders,
        COALESCE(m.total_revenue, 0) AS lifetime_value,
        COALESCE(m.avg_order_value, 0) AS avg_order_value,
        m.first_order_date,
        m.last_order_date,
        CASE
            WHEN m.last_order_date >= DATE_SUB(CURRENT_DATE(),
INTERVAL 30 DAY) THEN 'Active'
```

```
            WHEN m.last_order_date >= DATE_SUB(CURRENT_DATE(),
INTERVAL 90 DAY) THEN 'At Risk'
            WHEN m.last_order_date IS NOT NULL THEN 'Churned'
            ELSE 'Never Ordered'
        END AS customer_segment
    FROM customers c
    LEFT JOIN metrics m ON c.customer_id = m.customer_id
)
SELECT * FROM final
```

This mart model performs the following tasks:

- Joins staging and intermediate layers.
- Uses "**COALESCE**" to handle customers with no orders.
- Adds business logic (such as customer segmentation based on recency).
- Produces a wide, denormalized table that is ready for BI tools.
- Materialized as a **table** with clustering on **country** and **customer_segment**.

When you run **dbt run**, dbt automatically determines the correct execution order, which is as follows:

1. **stg_orders** and **stg_customers** (no dependencies)
2. **int_customer_order_metrics** (depends on **stg_orders**)
3. **mart_customer_analytics** (depends on **stg_customers** and **int_customer_order_metrics**)

Writing Tests and Validating Data Quality

One of the biggest flaws with legacy SQL pipelines is the silent propagation of bad data. If a bug in a source system suddenly generates duplicate **order_id**s, an untested pipeline will blindly process those duplicates, inflating downstream revenue dashboards.

By design, BigQuery does not support or enforce primary keys or foreign keys. It relies entirely on the developer to ensure data uniqueness. dbt brings automated testing to BigQuery to serve as a firewall against bad data.

Generic Tests Configured in schema.yml

Tests in dbt are assertions about the state of your data. You can define them alongside your model declarations in YAML files in the following manner:

```
version: 2
models:
  - name: stg_orders
```

```
        description: Cleaned and standardized orders
        columns:
          - name: order_id
            description: Unique order identifier
            tests:
              - unique
              - not_null
          - name: customer_id
            tests:
              - not_null
          - name: amount
            tests:
              - not_null
          - name: status
            tests:
              - accepted_values:
                  values: ['completed', 'pending', 'cancelled']
      - name: stg_customers
        description: Cleaned customer information
        columns:
          - name: customer_id
            tests:
              - unique
              - not_null
          - name: email
            tests:
              - unique
              - not_null
```

When you execute the **dbt test** command, dbt compiles these YAML assertions into SQL queries and runs them against BigQuery. For example, the **unique** test compiles to something resembling the following:

```
SELECT customer_id, count(*)
FROM `your-project-id.dbt_demo_dev.stg_customers`
GROUP BY customer_id
HAVING count(*) > 1
```

If the query returns any rows, the test fails, immediately surfacing the corruption before business stakeholders notice anomalies on a dashboard.

Running **dbt test** on our e-commerce pipeline produces output in the following manner:

```
10:45:23  Running with dbt=1.11.7
10:45:25  Found 7 models, 8 tests, 3 sources
10:45:25
10:45:25  Concurrency: 4 threads (target='dev')
10:45:25
```

```
10:45:27  1 of 8 START test not_null_stg_customers_customer_id ................ [RUN]
10:45:27  2 of 8 START test not_null_stg_customers_email ........................ [RUN]
10:45:27  3 of 8 START test not_null_stg_orders_amount .......................... [RUN]
10:45:27  4 of 8 START test not_null_stg_orders_customer_id ..................... [RUN]
10:45:29  1 of 8 PASS not_null_stg_customers_customer_id ........................ [PASS
in 1.82s]
10:45:29  2 of 8 PASS not_null_stg_customers_email .............................. [PASS
in 1.79s]
10:45:29  3 of 8 PASS not_null_stg_orders_amount ................................ [PASS
in 1.84s]
10:45:29  4 of 8 PASS not_null_stg_orders_customer_id ........................... [PASS
in 1.81s]
10:45:29  5 of 8 START test unique_stg_customers_customer_id .................... [RUN]
10:45:29  6 of 8 START test unique_stg_customers_email .......................... [RUN]
10:45:29  7 of 8 START test unique_stg_orders_order_id .......................... [RUN]
10:45:29  8 of 8 START test accepted_values_stg_orders_status ................... [RUN]
10:45:31  5 of 8 PASS unique_stg_customers_customer_id .......................... [PASS
in 1.76s]
10:45:31  6 of 8 PASS unique_stg_customers_email ................................ [PASS
in 1.73s]
10:45:31  7 of 8 PASS unique_stg_orders_order_id ................................ [PASS
in 1.78s]
10:45:31  8 of 8 PASS accepted_values_stg_orders_status ......................... [PASS
in 1.75s]
10:45:31
10:45:31  Finished running 8 tests in 0 hours 0 minutes and 6.42 seconds (6.42s).
```

All 8 tests passed, giving us confidence that our data quality is intact.

Singular Tests

If you have extremely specific business logic that a generic test cannot cover—for instance, ensuring that a **return_date** is always strictly after an **order_date**—you can write a Singular Test.

A Singular Test is simply a **.sql** file in your **tests/** directory. The rule is simple: if the query returns rows, the test fails, as demonstrated:

```
-- tests/assert_return_date_after_order.sql
SELECT
  order_id,
  order_date,
  return_date
FROM {{ ref('fct_orders') }}
WHERE return_date < order_date
```

Relationships Tests

dbt also supports referential integrity tests. Since BigQuery does not enforce foreign keys, you can use the **relationships** test to ensure that every **customer_id** in **stg_orders** exists in **stg_customers** in the following way:

```
- name: stg_orders
  columns:
    - name: customer_id
      tests:
        - relationships:
            to: ref('stg_customers')
            field: customer_id
```

This compiles to a query that finds orphaned records, which is as follows:

```
SELECT customer_id
FROM `my-project.dbt_demo_dev.stg_orders`
WHERE customer_id NOT IN (
  SELECT customer_id
  FROM `your_project.dbt_demo_dev.stg_customers`)
```

Managing Lineage and Documentation

Documentation in data engineering is notoriously prone to rotting. A wiki page written three years ago describing a table's schema is rarely updated when columns naturally shift over time.

dbt solves this by keeping the documentation "as code", right alongside your SQL models.

`schema.yml` and Data Dictionaries

By utilizing the **description** fields in the **schema.yml** (as seen in the previous sections), you ensure that the context surrounding a specific metric lives natively in the repository. These descriptions are invaluable for onboarding new analysts. However, dbt goes a step further: by configuring **persist_docs** in **dbt_project.yml**, dbt can actually push these column and table descriptions directly into BigQuery. If a user opens the BigQuery UI and clicks on **mart_customer_analytics**, your YAML descriptions will be visible right in the BigQuery Schema tab.

To enable this, add the following configuration to your **dbt_project.yml**:

```
models:
  dbt_elt_lab:
    +persist_docs:
      relation: true
      columns: true
```

Example documentation in **schema.yml**:

```
version: 2
models:
  - name: mart_customer_analytics
    description: >
      Customer analytics mart combining customer profile data with
      order metrics and segmentation. Primary table for customer
analysis.
    columns:
      - name: customer_id
        description: Unique customer identifier
      - name: customer_segment
        description: >
          Customer lifecycle segment:
          - Active: Ordered in last 30 days
          - At Risk: Ordered 30-90 days ago
          - Churned: No orders in 90+ days
          - Never Ordered: Signed up but never purchased
      - name: lifetime_value
        description: Total revenue from completed orders
```

Generating and Serving Docs

Executing the command **dbt docs generate** triggers dbt to parse your entire project, evaluate all **ref()** functions, and construct a robust metadata artifact, with the following output:

```
dbt docs generate
Output:
10:52:15  Running with dbt=1.11.7
10:52:17  Found 7 models, 8 tests, 3 sources
10:52:17  Building catalog
10:52:19  Catalog written to target/catalog.json
```

Using **dbt docs serve** launches an interactive yet static HTML website hosted locally (or via dbt Cloud). This site contains a searchable data dictionary of every model, column, test, and macro in your environment.

```
dbt docs serve
```

This opens **http://localhost:8080** in your browser, displaying the following:

- A searchable list of all models,
- Column-level descriptions,
- Test coverage for each column,
- Source freshness checks, and

- Macro documentation.

Auto-Generated Lineage Graphs (DAG)

The most powerful feature of the dbt documentation suite is the interactive DAG. As you relied entirely on **`ref()`** rather than hard-coded table names, dbt intimately understands the relationship between every piece of data.

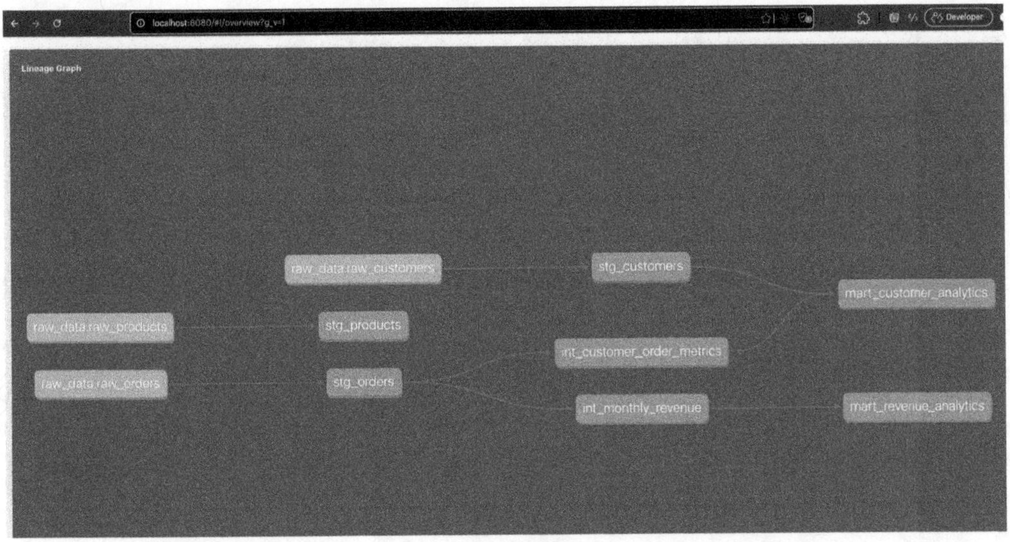

***Figure 7.1:** dbt Lineage Graph Showing the Complete Data Flow from Raw Sources through Staging, Intermediate, and Mart Layers*

The visual Lineage Graph allows data engineers to instantly trace the metric upstream path to its source or accurately gauge the "blast radius" downstream when a specific intermediate table needs to be deprecated.

For our e-commerce pipeline, the DAG shows the following:

- 3 raw sources (for example, **`raw_orders`**, **`raw_customers`**, and **`raw_products`**)
- 3 staging models (for example, **`stg_orders`**, **`stg_customers`**, and **`stg_products`**)
- 2 intermediate models (for example, **`int_customer_order_metrics`** and **`int_monthly_revenue`**)
- 2 mart models (for example, **`mart_customer_analytics`** and **`mart_revenue_analytics`**)

You can click on any node to see:

- The compiled SQL,
- Column descriptions,
- Tests applied, and

- Upstream and downstream dependencies.

Deployment and Automation Strategies

Transforming data on a laptop is only the first step. To build an enterprise-grade ELT workflow, you must implement continuous deployment, separating development environments from production.

Environment Separation in BigQuery

In a dbt workflow, environments are dictated by the target BigQuery datasets, including:

- **Development Environment:** Analysts branch off from the main Git repository and use **`dbt run`** locally. Their profiles are configured to write to isolated sandbox datasets (for example, **`dbt_demo_dev`**). They can freely test schema changes and break tests here without impacting the business.
- **Production Environment:** Once the code is merged into the **`main`** branch, a CI/CD orchestration tool (such as GitHub Actions, GitLab CI, or DBT Cloud) triggers the production job. It connects via a Service Account and runs the command targeting the production datasets (for example, **`analytics_prod`**).

Example `profiles.yml` with Multiple Targets:

```
dbt_elt_lab:
  target: dev
  outputs:
    dev:
      type: bigquery
      method: oauth
      project: your-project-id
      dataset: dbt_demo_dev
      threads: 4
      location: US

    prod:
      type: bigquery
      method: service-account
      project: your-project-id
      dataset: analytics_prod
      threads: 8
      location: US
      keyfile: /path/to/service-account.json
```

To run against production, try the following:

```
dbt run --target prod
```

Continuous Integration (CI) and Pull Request (PR) Checks

Before the code is allowed to merge into the **`main`** branch, it must pass a rigorous CI check. When an analyst opens a PR, an automated bot wakes up and executes a test build of the proposed code against a temporary and isolated schema (for example, **`dbt_pr_1234`**).

The bot runs the following steps:

1. **`dbt build`**—which sequentially creates the models and executes their tests.
2. If any model fails to compile, or if a **`not_null`** test catches a data anomaly, the CI job crashes and restricts the code from being merged.

Example GitHub Actions Workflow:

```
name: dbt CI
on:
  pull_request:
    branches: [main]
jobs:
  test:
    runs-on: ubuntu-latest
    steps:
      - uses: actions/checkout@v2
      - uses: actions/setup-python@v2
        with:
          python-version: '3.11'
      - run: pip install dbt-bigquery
      - run: dbt deps
      - run: dbt build --target ci
```

Slim CI (State-Based Execution)

In a massive project with 500+ models, running a complete **`dbt build`** from start to finish on every PR can rack up massive slot-ms bills and take hours to complete.

To solve this, dbt introduces "Slim CI". By storing a **`manifest.json`** file representing the current state of production, the CI runner can compare the PR's code against production's state. Using the flag **`dbt build --select state:modified+`**, dbt smartly determines exactly which models were changed by the PR and builds only those affected models and their immediate downstream children in the following manner:

```
# Download production manifest
gcloud storage cp gs://my-bucket/manifest.json ./
# Run only modified models and their children
dbt build --select state:modified+ --state ./
```

This highly advanced technique ensures data quality while preserving compute resources, enabling remarkably fast iteration cycles.

Troubleshooting and Handling Failures

In a production environment, models and tests will inevitably fail due to upstream schema changes, bad data, or logic errors. When a failure occurs during dbt run or dbt test, dbt automatically halts downstream dependencies to prevent corrupt data from cascading into the mart layer.

How to Debug:

- **Check the Compiled SQL:** dbt generates plain BigQuery SQL for every model. When a model fails, navigate to the `target/compiled/` directory, copy the generated SQL, and run it directly in the BigQuery console to isolate the syntax or data error.
- **Review Test Failures:** If a test fails, check `target/compiled/` for the test's SQL. Running it in BigQuery will return the exact rows, violating your assertion.
- **Run from the Point of Failure:** Once you fix the bug, you do not need to rebuild the whole project. Run `dbt build --select <failed_model>+` to resume the build from the failed model and its downstream dependencies.

Hands-on Lab: Building a Complete ELT Pipeline

To solidify these concepts, let us walk through building a complete dbt project from scratch. This lab demonstrates the full workflow: from raw data ingestion to tested, documented analytics tables.

Lab Overview

We will build an e-commerce analytics pipeline with the following:

- 3 raw source tables (such as orders, customers, and products)
- 3 staging models (such as data cleaning and standardization)

- 2 intermediate models (such as business logic and aggregations)
- 2 mart models (such as final analytics tables)
- 8 data quality tests
- Full documentation with lineage graph

Step 1: Create Raw Data in BigQuery

First, we will create a dataset and populate it with synthetic e-commerce data in the following manner:

```
-- Create dataset
CREATE SCHEMA `your_project.dbt_demo`
OPTIONS (
  location = 'US',
  description = 'dbt ELT lab dataset'
);

-- Create raw_orders (5,000 rows)
CREATE OR REPLACE TABLE `your_project.dbt_demo.raw_orders` AS
SELECT
  GENERATE_UUID() AS order_id, customer_id, order_date, status, amount
FROM (
  SELECT
    CONCAT('CUST', CAST(CAST(RAND() * 1000 AS INT64) AS STRING)) AS
customer_id,
    DATE_ADD('2023-01-01', INTERVAL CAST(RAND() * 365 AS INT64) DAY)
AS order_date,
    CASE
      WHEN RAND() < 0.7 THEN 'completed'
      WHEN RAND() < 0.9 THEN 'pending'
      ELSE 'cancelled'
    END AS status, ROUND(RAND() * 500 + 10, 2) AS amount
  FROM UNNEST(GENERATE_ARRAY(1, 5000))
);
-- Create Raw Customers Table (1,000 rows)
CREATE OR REPLACE TABLE `your_project.dbt_demo.raw_customers` AS
SELECT
  Customer_id, Customer_name, email, country, signup_date
FROM (
  SELECT
    CONCAT('CUST', CAST(number AS STRING)) AS customer_id,
    CONCAT('Customer ', CAST(number AS STRING)) AS customer_name,
    CONCAT('customer', CAST(number AS STRING), '@example.com') AS email,
    CASE
      WHEN MOD(number, 4) = 0 THEN 'USA'
```

```
      WHEN MOD(number, 4) = 1 THEN 'UK'
      WHEN MOD(number, 4) = 2 THEN 'Canada'
      ELSE 'Australia'
    END AS country,
    DATE_ADD('2022-01-01', INTERVAL CAST(RAND() * 500 AS INT64) DAY)
AS signup_date
  FROM UNNEST(GENERATE_ARRAY(1, 1000)) AS number
);
-- Create Raw Products Table (100 rows)
CREATE OR REPLACE TABLE `your_project.dbt_demo.raw_products` AS
SELECT
  Product_id, product_name, category, price
FROM (
  SELECT
    CONCAT('PROD', CAST(number AS STRING)) AS product_id,
    CONCAT('Product ', CAST(number AS STRING)) AS product_name,
    CASE
      WHEN MOD(number, 3) = 0 THEN 'Electronics'
      WHEN MOD(number, 3) = 1 THEN 'Clothing'
      ELSE 'Home & Garden'
    END AS category,
    ROUND(RAND() * 200 + 10, 2) AS price
  FROM UNNEST(GENERATE_ARRAY(1, 100)) AS number );
```

This will create the tables as mentioned in the UI in the following way:

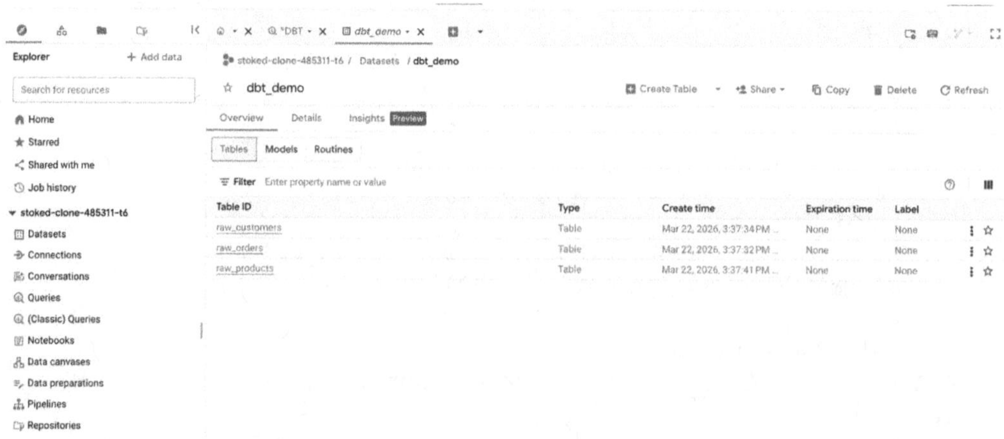

Figure 7.2: *BigQuery Explorer Showing dbt_demo Dataset with 3 Raw Tables*

Verify that the tables were created in the following manner:

```
SELECT 'raw_orders' AS table_name, COUNT(*) AS row_count
FROM `your_project.dbt_demo.raw_orders`
UNION ALL
SELECT 'raw_customers', COUNT(*)
```

```
FROM `your_project.dbt_demo.raw_customers`
UNION ALL
SELECT 'raw_products', COUNT(*)
FROM `your_project.dbt_demo.raw_products`;
```

This will give us the record counts in our tables in the following way:

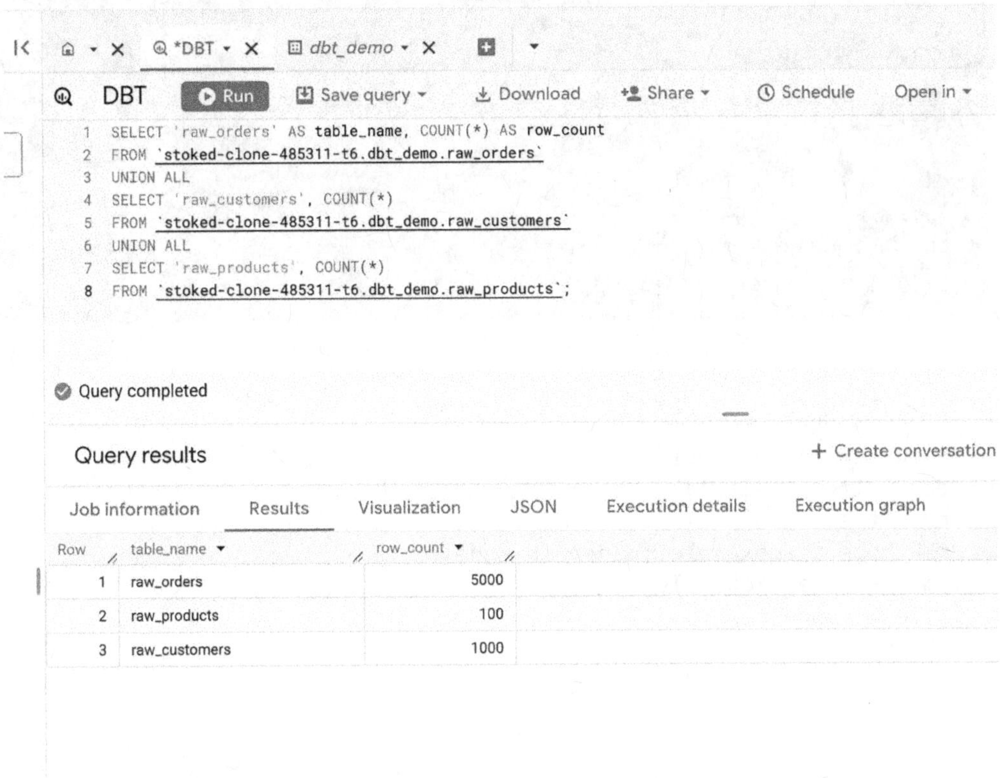

Figure 7.3: *Verification Query Results Showing Row Counts: 5,000 Orders, 1,000 Customers, 100 Products*

Step 2: Initialize dbt Project

Now, we have to create the DBT project in our local environment. We will connect to this with the preceding created schema in the later sections.

```
# Create virtual environment
python3.11 -m venv dbt-env
source dbt-env/bin/activate
# Install dbt
pip install dbt-bigquery
```

Let us check the installed **dbt**. We can verify its version in the following way:

Figure 7.4: *Terminal Showing dbt-Version Output*

Next, the steps are to use **dbt** to create our project:

```
# Initialize project
dbt init dbt_elt_lab
cd dbt_elt_lab
# Remove the example folder in models
rm -rf models/example
# Test connection
dbt debug
```

The **debug** command will check the connection for us.

***Figure** 7.5: Terminal Showing Successful dbt Debug Output with All Checks Passing*

Step 3: Define Sources

Next, we will start with these dbt code changes. Create **`models/sources.yml`**:

```
version: 2
sources:
  - name: raw_data
    database: your_project
    schema: dbt_demo
    description: Raw e-commerce data
    tables:
      - name: raw_orders
```

```
        - name: raw_customers
        - name: raw_products
```

From now on, our staging models will reference these via **`{{ source('raw_data', 'raw_orders') }}`** rather than hardcoding the project and dataset.

Step 4: Build Staging Models

Staging models have one job: clean and standardize the raw data. One staging model per source table, with no joins and business logic. Create the **`models/staging/`** folder and add three files:

models/staging/stg_orders.sql :

```
WITH source AS (
    SELECT * FROM {{ source('raw_data', 'raw_orders') }}
),
cleaned AS (
  SELECT
        order_id,customer_id, order_date, LOWER(TRIM(status)) AS
status,
        amount, CURRENT_TIMESTAMP() AS loaded_at
    FROM source WHERE order_date IS NOT NULL AND amount > 0
)
SELECT * FROM cleaned
```

models/staging/stg_customers.sql :

```
WITH source AS (
    SELECT * FROM {{ source('raw_data', 'raw_customers') }}
),
cleaned AS (
    SELECT
        customer_id,  TRIM(customer_name) AS customer_name,
 LOWER(TRIM(email)) AS email, UPPER(TRIM(country)) AS country,
signup_date, CURRENT_TIMESTAMP() AS loaded_at
    FROM source WHERE email IS NOT NULL  AND signup_date IS NOT NULL
)
SELECT * FROM cleaned
```

models/staging/stg_products.sql :

```
WITH source AS (
    SELECT * FROM {{ source('raw_data', 'raw_products') }} ),
cleaned AS (
    SELECT
        product_id, TRIM(product_name) AS product_name,
TRIM(category) AS category,
        price, CURRENT_TIMESTAMP() AS loaded_at
    FROM source  WHERE price > 0
)
```

```
SELECT * FROM cleaned

Run the staging models:
dbt run --select staging
```

Output: You will see 3 models complete successfully.

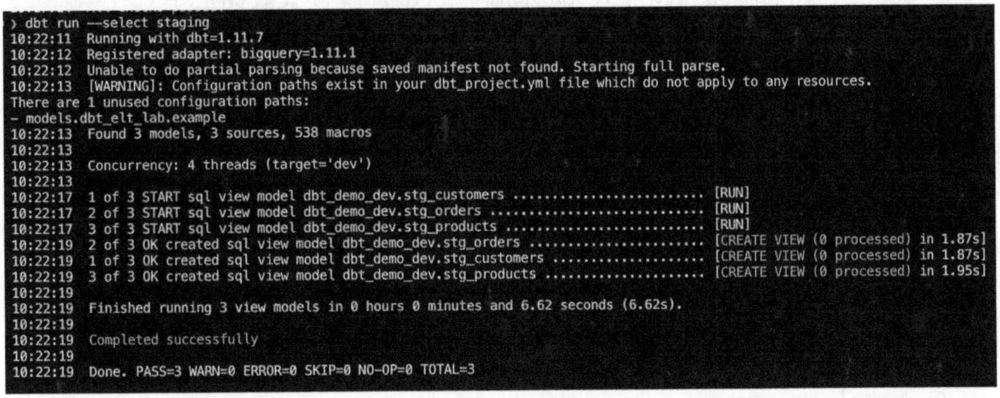

***Figure 7.6:** Terminal Showing Staging Models Built Successfully*

Query one of the staging tables in the following way:

```
SELECT * FROM `your_project.dbt_demo_dev.stg_orders`
ORDER BY order_date DESC
LIMIT 10;
```

We can also check this BigQuery UI in the following manner:

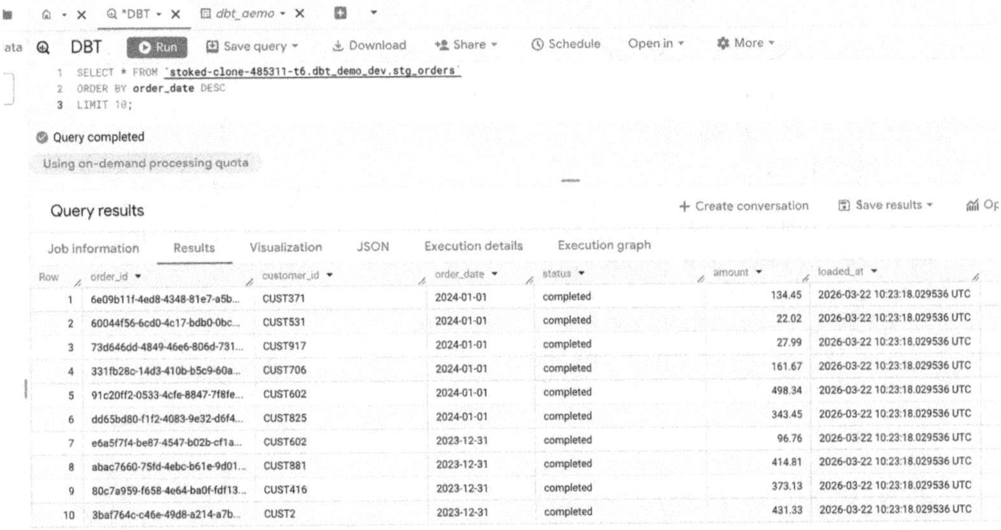

***Figure 7.7:** BigQuery Results Showing Staging Table Data with Cleaned Columns (Such as Lowercase Status or Trimmed Values)*

Step 5: Build Intermediate Models

The intermediate layer is where business logic lives–joins, aggregations, and derived metrics. These models read from the staging layer, and are consumed by marts.

Create **models/intermediate/int_customer_order_metrics.sql:**

```
WITH orders AS (
    SELECT * FROM {{ ref('stg_orders') }}
),
customer_metrics AS (
    SELECT
        Customer_id, COUNT(*) AS total_orders,
        COUNT(CASE WHEN status = 'completed' THEN 1 END)
AS completed_orders,
        COUNT(CASE WHEN status = 'cancelled' THEN 1 END)
AS cancelled_orders,
        SUM(CASE WHEN status = 'completed' THEN amount ELSE 0 END)
AS total_revenue,
        AVG(CASE WHEN status = 'completed' THEN amount END)
AS avg_order_value,
        MIN(order_date) AS first_order_date,  MAX(order_date)
AS last_order_date,
        DATE_DIFF(MAX(order_date), MIN(order_date), DAY)
AS customer_lifetime_days
    FROM orders
    GROUP BY customer_id )
SELECT * FROM customer_metrics
```

Create **models/intermediate/int_monthly_revenue.sql:**

```
WITH orders AS (  SELECT * FROM {{ ref('stg_orders') }}),
monthly_revenue AS (
    SELECT
        DATE_TRUNC(order_date, MONTH) AS month, status,
        COUNT(*) AS order_count,SUM(amount) AS total_amount,
 AVG(amount) AS avg_amount, COUNT(DISTINCT customer_id)
AS unique_customers
    FROM orders GROUP BY month, status
) SELECT * FROM monthly_revenue
ORDER BY month DESC, status
```

Run the intermediate models: **dbt run --select intermediate**

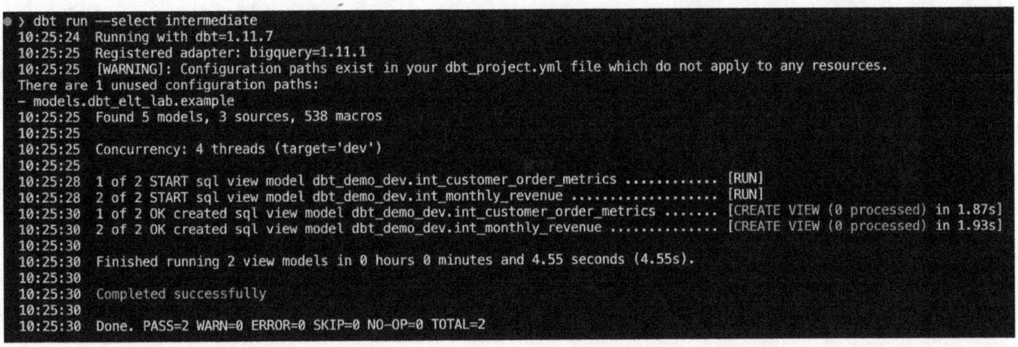

***Figure 7.8**: Terminal Showing Intermediate Models Built Successfully*

Query the results in the following way:

```
SELECT
    customer_id,
    total_orders,
    completed_orders,
    total_revenue,
    avg_order_value
FROM `your_project.dbt_demo_dev.int_customer_order_metrics`
ORDER BY total_revenue DESC
LIMIT 10;
```

The output in the UI will look as follows:

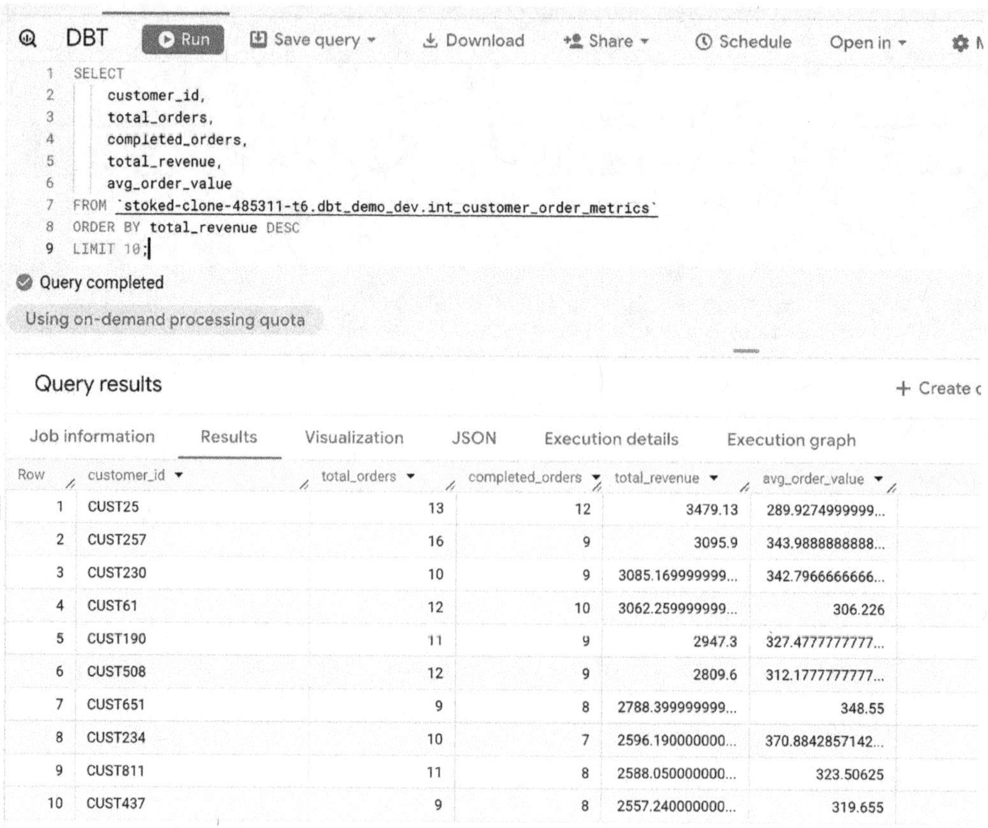

Figure 7.9: *Top 10 Customers by Revenue Showing Real Aggregated Metrics*

Step 6: Build Mart Models

Marts are final, polished tables that BI tools and analysts consume. They join staging and intermediate models and add the last bit of presentation logic. Create **models/marts/mart_customer_analytics.sql**:

```
WITH customers AS (
    SELECT * FROM {{ ref('stg_customers') }}
),
metrics AS (  SELECT * FROM {{ ref('int_customer_order_metrics') }} ),
final AS (
    SELECT
        c.customer_id, c.customer_name, c.email, c.country,
        c.signup_date,COALESCE(m.total_orders, 0) AS total_orders,
        COALESCE(m.completed_orders, 0) AS completed_orders,
        COALESCE(m.cancelled_orders, 0) AS cancelled_orders,
        COALESCE(m.total_revenue, 0) AS lifetime_value,
        COALESCE(m.avg_order_value, 0) AS avg_order_value,
```

```
        m.first_order_date, m.last_order_date,
        CASE
            WHEN m.last_order_date >= DATE_SUB(CURRENT_DATE(),
INTERVAL 30 DAY) THEN 'Active'
            WHEN m.last_order_date >= DATE_SUB(CURRENT_DATE(),
INTERVAL 90 DAY) THEN 'At Risk'
            WHEN m.last_order_date IS NOT NULL THEN 'Churned'
            ELSE 'Never Ordered'
        END AS customer_segment
    FROM customers c  LEFT JOIN metrics m ON c.customer_id
= m.customer_id
)
SELECT * FROM final
```

Create **models/marts/mart_revenue_analytics.sql**:

```
WITH monthly_data AS (
    SELECT
        month, status, order_count, total_amount, avg_amount,
unique_customers
    FROM {{ ref('int_monthly_revenue') }}
),
revenue_summary AS (
    SELECT  month,
        SUM(CASE WHEN status = 'completed' THEN total_amount ELSE 0
END) AS completed_revenue,
        SUM(CASE WHEN status = 'completed' THEN order_count ELSE 0
END) AS completed_orders,
        SUM(CASE WHEN status = 'cancelled' THEN total_amount ELSE 0
END) AS cancelled_revenue,
        SUM(CASE WHEN status = 'cancelled' THEN order_count ELSE 0
END) AS cancelled_orders,
        SUM(CASE WHEN status = 'completed' THEN unique_customers
ELSE 0 END) AS active_customers
    FROM monthly_data GROUP BY month
),
with_previous AS (
    SELECT
        month, completed_revenue, completed_orders, cancelled_revenue,
        cancelled_orders, active_customers,
        LAG(completed_revenue) OVER (ORDER BY month) AS prev_month_
revenue
    FROM revenue_summary
),
with_growth AS (
    SELECT
        month, completed_revenue, completed_orders,
        cancelled_revenue, cancelled_orders, active_customers,
```

```
        prev_month_revenue, ROUND(
            (completed_revenue - prev_month_revenue)
            / NULLIF(prev_month_revenue, 0) * 100,
            2
        ) AS revenue_growth_pct   FROM with_previous
)
SELECT
    month, completed_revenue, completed_orders,  cancelled_revenue,
    cancelled_orders, active_customers, prev_month_revenue, reve-
nue_growth_pct
FROM with_growth ORDER BY month DESC
```

Run the mart models: `dbt run --select marts`

Output is as follows:

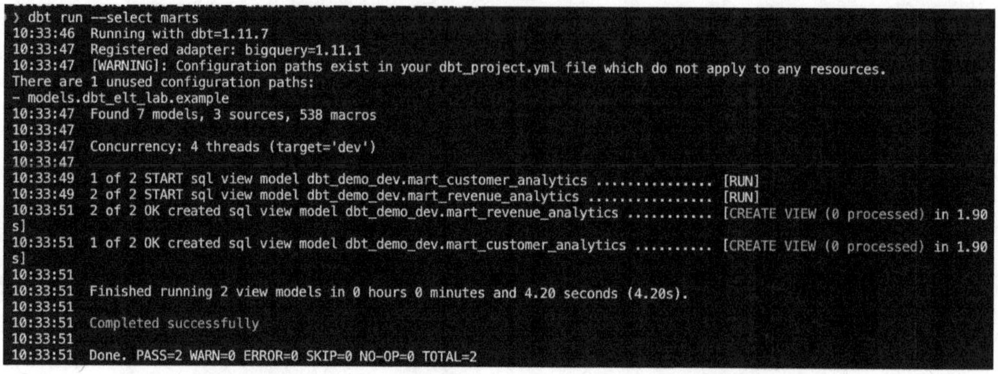

```
) dbt run --select marts
10:33:46  Running with dbt=1.11.7
10:33:47  Registered adapter: bigquery=1.11.1
10:33:47  [WARNING]: Configuration paths exist in your dbt_project.yml file which do not apply to any resources.
There are 1 unused configuration paths:
- models.dbt_elt_lab.example
10:33:47  Found 7 models, 3 sources, 538 macros
10:33:47
10:33:47  Concurrency: 4 threads (target='dev')
10:33:47
10:33:49  1 of 2 START sql view model dbt_demo_dev.mart_customer_analytics ............... [RUN]
10:33:49  2 of 2 START sql view model dbt_demo_dev.mart_revenue_analytics ................ [RUN]
10:33:51  2 of 2 OK created sql view model dbt_demo_dev.mart_revenue_analytics ........... [CREATE VIEW (0 processed) in 1.90
s]
10:33:51  1 of 2 OK created sql view model dbt_demo_dev.mart_customer_analytics .......... [CREATE VIEW (0 processed) in 1.90
s]
10:33:51
10:33:51  Finished running 2 view models in 0 hours 0 minutes and 4.20 seconds (4.20s).
10:33:51
10:33:51  Completed successfully
10:33:51
10:33:51  Done. PASS=2 WARN=0 ERROR=0 SKIP=0 NO-OP=0 TOTAL=2
```

***Figure 7.10**: Terminal Showing Mart Models Built Successfully*

Query customer segmentation: **SELECT**

```
    customer_segment,
    COUNT(*) AS customer_count,
    SUM(lifetime_value) AS total_ltv,
    ROUND(AVG(lifetime_value), 2) AS avg_ltv
FROM `your_project.dbt_demo_dev.mart_customer_analytics`
GROUP BY customer_segment
ORDER BY total_ltv DESC;
```

Output in BigQuery UI:

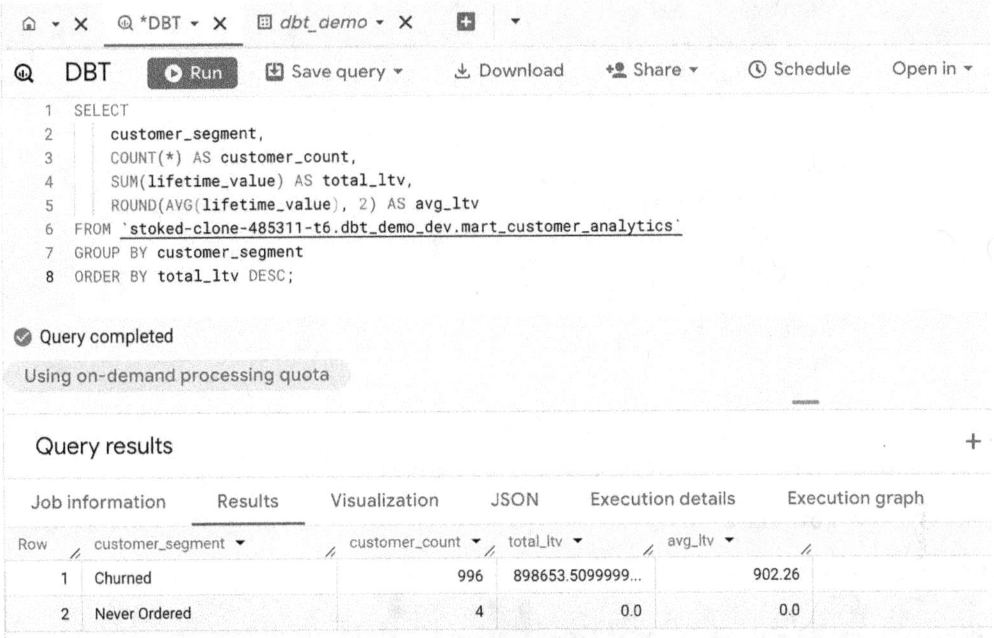

Figure 7.11: *Customer Segmentation Results Showing Active, at Risk, Churned, and Never Ordered Segments*

Step 7: Add Data Quality Tests

Tests are dbt's firewall against bad data. We will add a schema.yml for staging and one for the marts containing tests.

Create **`models/staging/schema.yml`** with tests:

```
version: 2
models:
  - name: stg_orders
    description: Cleaned and standardized orders
    columns:
      - name: order_id
        description: Unique order identifier
        tests:
          - unique
          - not_null
      - name: customer_id
        tests:
          - not_null
      - name: amount
        tests:
          - not_null
      - name: status
```

```
          tests:
            - accepted_values:
                values: ['completed', 'pending', 'cancelled']
    - name: stg_customers
      description: Cleaned customer information
      columns:
        - name: customer_id
          tests:
            - unique
            - not_null
        - name: email
          tests:
            - unique
            - not_null
```

That is 9 tests in total: 5 on orders and 4 on customers.

Run all tests: **`dbt test`**

Terminal Output:

```
> dbt test
10:35:47  Running with dbt=1.11.7
10:35:47  Registered adapter: bigquery=1.11.1
10:35:48  [WARNING][MissingArgumentsPropertyInGenericTestDeprecation]: Deprecated
functionality
Found top-level arguments to test `accepted_values` defined on 'stg_orders' in
package 'dbt_elt_lab' (models/staging/schema.yml). Arguments to generic tests
should be nested under the `arguments` property.
10:35:48  [WARNING]: Configuration paths exist in your dbt_project.yml file which do not apply to any resourc
There are 1 unused configuration paths:
- models.dbt_elt_lab.example
10:35:48  Found 7 models, 9 data tests, 3 sources, 538 macros
10:35:48
10:35:48  Concurrency: 4 threads (target='dev')
10:35:48
10:35:50  1 of 9 START test accepted_values_stg_orders_status__completed__pending__cancelled  [RUN]
10:35:50  2 of 9 START test not_null_stg_customers_customer_id .......................... [RUN]
10:35:50  3 of 9 START test not_null_stg_customers_email ................................ [RUN]
10:35:50  4 of 9 START test not_null_stg_orders_amount .................................. [RUN]
10:35:52  4 of 9 PASS not_null_stg_orders_amount ........................................ [PASS in 2.45s]
10:35:52  5 of 9 START test not_null_stg_orders_customer_id ............................. [RUN]
10:35:53  1 of 9 PASS accepted_values_stg_orders_status__completed__pending__cancelled ... [PASS in 2.88s]
10:35:53  6 of 9 START test not_null_stg_orders_order_id ................................ [RUN]
10:35:53  3 of 9 PASS not_null_stg_customers_email ...................................... [PASS in 2.96s]
10:35:53  7 of 9 START test unique_stg_customers_customer_id ............................ [RUN]
10:35:53  2 of 9 PASS not_null_stg_customers_customer_id ................................ [PASS in 3.37s]
10:35:53  8 of 9 START test unique_stg_customers_email .................................. [RUN]
10:35:55  5 of 9 PASS not_null_stg_orders_customer_id ................................... [PASS in 2.36s]
10:35:55  9 of 9 START test unique_stg_orders_order_id .................................. [RUN]
10:35:55  6 of 9 PASS not_null_stg_orders_order_id ...................................... [PASS in 2.34s]
10:35:55  7 of 9 PASS unique_stg_customers_customer_id .................................. [PASS in 2.54s]
10:35:56  8 of 9 PASS unique_stg_customers_email ........................................ [PASS in 2.45s]
10:35:57  9 of 9 PASS unique_stg_orders_order_id ........................................ [PASS in 2.51s]
10:35:57
10:35:57  Finished running 9 data tests in 0 hours 0 minutes and 9.27 seconds (9.27s).
10:35:57
10:35:57  Completed successfully
10:35:57
10:35:57  Done. PASS=9 WARN=0 ERROR=0 SKIP=0 NO-OP=0 TOTAL=9
10:35:57  [WARNING][DeprecationsSummary]: Deprecated functionality
Summary of encountered deprecations:
- MissingArgumentsPropertyInGenericTestDeprecation: 1 occurrence
To see all deprecation instances instead of just the first occurrence of each,
run command again with the `--show-all-deprecations` flag. You may also need to
run with `--no-partial-parse` as some deprecations are only encountered during
parsing.
```

Figure 7.12: *Terminal Showing All 9 Tests Passing*

Create **models/marts/schema.yml**–adds documentation that our dbt docs step will render:

```
version: 2
models:
  - name: mart_customer_analytics
    description: >
      Customer analytics mart combining customer profile data with
      order metrics and segmentation. Primary table for customer
analysis.
    columns:
      - name: customer_id
        description: Unique customer identifier
      - name: customer_segment
        description: >
          Customer lifecycle segment:
          - Active: Ordered in last 30 days
          - At Risk: Ordered 30-90 days ago
          - Churned: No orders in 90+ days
          - Never Ordered: Signed up but never purchased
      - name: lifetime_value
        description: Total revenue from completed orders
  - name: mart_revenue_analytics
    description: Monthly revenue trends with growth calculations
```

Step 8: Generate Documentation

We can generate documentation and lineage by using the following commands, as discussed in the preceding section:

```
dbt docs generate
dbt docs serve
```

dbt Service Home Page:

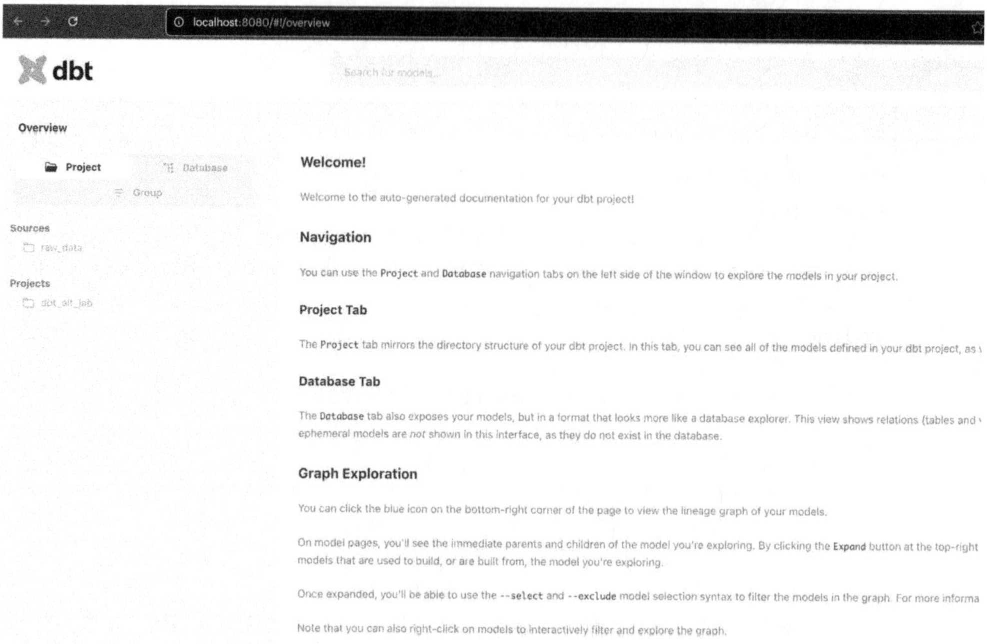

Figure 7.13: *dbt Docs Homepage Showing Project Overview with 7 Models and 3 Sources*

Click the lineage icon (bottom-right of any model page) to see the full DAG. You will see raw sources flowing into staging, staging to intermediate, and intermediate to marts.

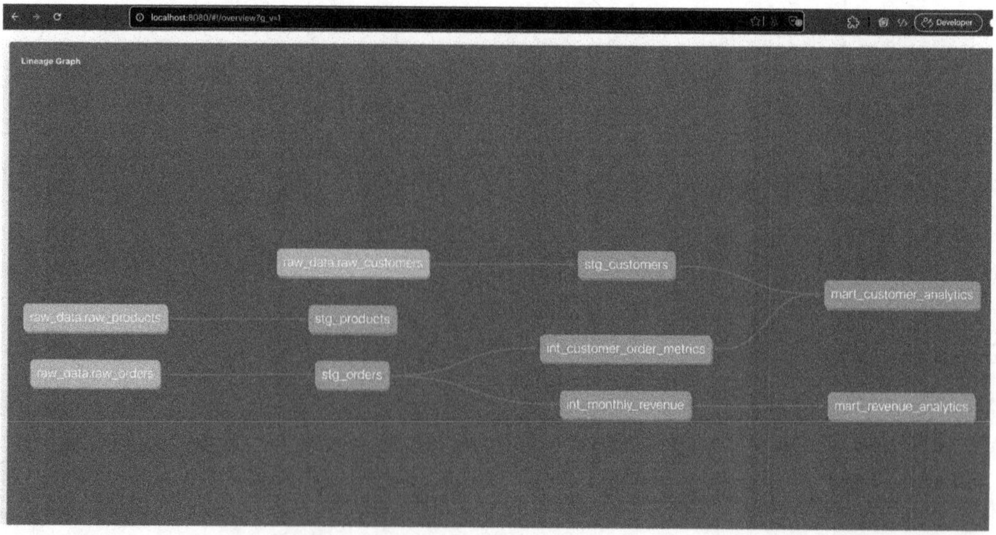

Figure 7.14: *Lineage Graph (DAG) Showing Complete Data Flow from Sources through All Layers*

Documentation Page for a Specific Mart Table:

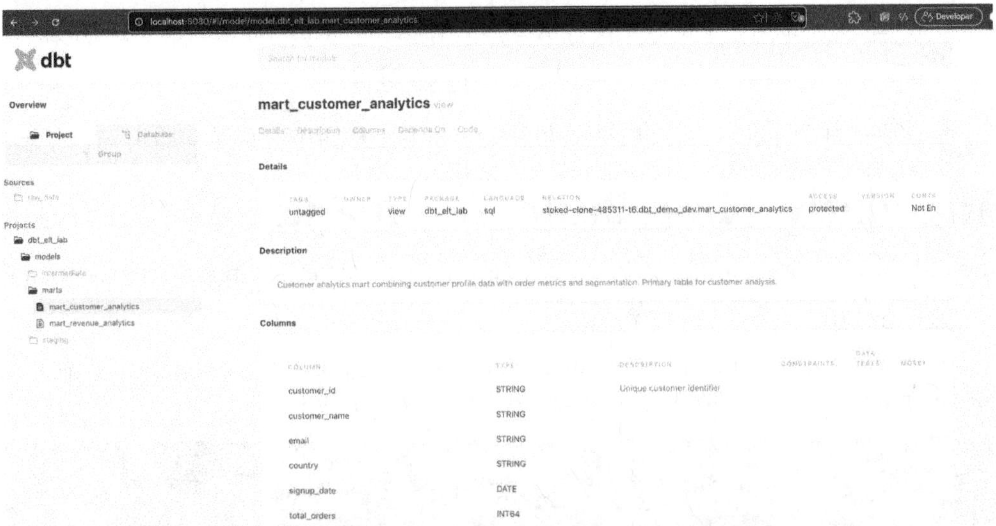

Figure 7.15: *Model Documentation Page for mart_customer_analytics Showing Column Descriptions and Tests*

Step 9: Run Complete Pipeline

Finally, run the entire pipeline in dependency order:

```
dbt run
```

This will run all the models.

```
dbt run
10:39:52  Running with dbt=1.11.7
10:39:53  Registered adapter: bigquery=1.11.1
10:39:53  [WARNING]: Configuration paths exist in your dbt_project.yml file which do not apply to any resources.
There are 1 unused configuration paths:
- models.dbt_elt_lab.example
10:39:53  Found 7 models, 9 data tests, 3 sources, 538 macros
10:39:53
10:39:53  Concurrency: 4 threads (target='dev')
10:39:53
10:39:55  1 of 7 START sql view model dbt_demo_dev.stg_customers ......................... [RUN]
10:39:55  2 of 7 START sql view model dbt_demo_dev.stg_orders ............................ [RUN]
10:39:55  3 of 7 START sql view model dbt_demo_dev.stg_products .......................... [RUN]
10:39:57  2 of 7 OK created sql view model dbt_demo_dev.stg_orders ....................... [CREATE VIEW (0 processed) in 1.73s]
10:39:57  4 of 7 START sql view model dbt_demo_dev.int_customer_order_metrics ............ [RUN]
10:39:57  5 of 7 START sql view model dbt_demo_dev.int_monthly_revenue ................... [RUN]
10:39:57  1 of 7 OK created sql view model dbt_demo_dev.stg_customers .................... [CREATE VIEW (0 processed) in 1.74s]
10:39:57  3 of 7 OK created sql view model dbt_demo_dev.stg_products ..................... [CREATE VIEW (0 processed) in 1.75s]
10:39:59  5 of 7 OK created sql view model dbt_demo_dev.int_monthly_revenue .............. [CREATE VIEW (0 processed) in 1.74s]
10:39:59  6 of 7 START sql view model dbt_demo_dev.mart_revenue_analytics ................ [RUN]
10:39:59  4 of 7 OK created sql view model dbt_demo_dev.int_customer_order_metrics ....... [CREATE VIEW (0 processed) in 2.09s]
10:39:59  7 of 7 START sql view model dbt_demo_dev.mart_customer_analytics ............... [RUN]
10:40:00  6 of 7 OK created sql view model dbt_demo_dev.mart_revenue_analytics ........... [CREATE VIEW (0 processed) in 1.75s]
10:40:01  7 of 7 OK created sql view model dbt_demo_dev.mart_customer_analytics .......... [CREATE VIEW (0 processed) in 1.80s]
10:40:01
10:40:01  Finished running 7 view models in 0 hours 0 minutes and 7.95 seconds (7.95s).
10:40:01
10:40:01  Completed successfully
10:40:01
10:40:01  Done. PASS=7 WARN=0 ERROR=0 SKIP=0 NO-OP=0 TOTAL=7
```

Figure 7.16: *Terminal Showing Full dbt Run with All 7 Models Completed in Correct Dependency Order*

Notice how dbt automatically determined the following execution order:

1. The 3 staging models ran in parallel (no dependencies).
2. Then, the 2 intermediate models ran in parallel (both depend only on staging).
3. Finally, the 2 mart models ran in parallel (depend on staging and intermediate).

Alternative: Run Build Command

The **`dbt build`** command runs both models and tests together in a single command:

```
dbt build
```

This is more efficient than running **`dbt run`** followed by **`dbt test`** separately, as it can fail fast if a model does not build correctly before running tests.

```
dbt build
10:41:01  Running with dbt=1.11.7
10:41:02  Registered adapter: bigquery=1.11.1
10:41:02  [WARNING]: Configuration paths exist in your dbt_project.yml file which do not apply to any resources.
There are 1 unused configuration paths:
- models.dbt_elt_lab.example
10:41:02  Found 7 models, 9 data tests, 3 sources, 538 macros
10:41:02
10:41:02  Concurrency: 4 threads (target='dev')
10:41:02
10:41:05  1 of 16 START sql view model dbt_demo_dev.stg_customers ........................ [RUN]
10:41:05  2 of 16 START sql view model dbt_demo_dev.stg_orders ........................... [RUN]
10:41:05  3 of 16 START sql view model dbt_demo_dev.stg_products ......................... [RUN]
10:41:06  1 of 16 OK created sql view model dbt_demo_dev.stg_customers ................... [CREATE VIEW (0 processed) in 1.78s]
10:41:06  3 of 16 OK created sql view model dbt_demo_dev.stg_products .................... [CREATE VIEW (0 processed) in 1.78s]
10:41:06  2 of 16 OK created sql view model dbt_demo_dev.stg_orders ...................... [CREATE VIEW (0 processed) in 1.78s]
10:41:06  4 of 16 START test not_null_stg_customers_customer_id .......................... [RUN]
10:41:06  5 of 16 START test not_null_stg_customers_email ................................ [RUN]
10:41:06  6 of 16 START test unique_stg_customers_customer_id ............................ [RUN]
10:41:06  7 of 16 START test unique_stg_customers_email .................................. [RUN]
10:41:09  6 of 16 PASS unique_stg_customers_customer_id .................................. [PASS in 2.26s]
10:41:09  8 of 16 START test accepted_values_stg_orders_status__completed__pending__cancelled  [RUN]
10:41:09  7 of 16 PASS unique_stg_customers_email ........................................ [PASS in 2.31s]
10:41:09  9 of 16 START test not_null_stg_orders_amount .................................. [RUN]
10:41:09  4 of 16 PASS not_null_stg_customers_customer_id ................................ [PASS in 2.33s]
10:41:09  10 of 16 START test not_null_stg_orders_customer_id ............................ [RUN]
10:41:09  5 of 16 PASS not_null_stg_customers_email ...................................... [PASS in 2.37s]
10:41:09  11 of 16 START test not_null_stg_orders_order_id ............................... [RUN]
10:41:11  11 of 16 PASS not_null_stg_orders_order_id ..................................... [PASS in 2.35s]
10:41:11  12 of 16 START test unique_stg_orders_order_id ................................. [RUN]
10:41:11  8 of 16 PASS accepted_values_stg_orders_status__completed__pending__cancelled .. [PASS in 2.46s]
10:41:11  10 of 16 PASS not_null_stg_orders_customer_id .................................. [PASS in 2.41s]
10:41:11  9 of 16 PASS not_null_stg_orders_amount ........................................ [PASS in 2.46s]
10:41:13  12 of 16 PASS unique_stg_orders_order_id ....................................... [PASS in 2.23s]
10:41:13  13 of 16 START sql view model dbt_demo_dev.int_customer_order_metrics .......... [RUN]
10:41:13  14 of 16 START sql view model dbt_demo_dev.int_monthly_revenue ................. [RUN]
10:41:15  13 of 16 OK created sql view model dbt_demo_dev.int_customer_order_metrics ..... [CREATE VIEW (0 processed) in 1.65s]
10:41:15  15 of 16 START sql view model dbt_demo_dev.mart_customer_analytics ............. [RUN]
10:41:15  14 of 16 OK created sql view model dbt_demo_dev.int_monthly_revenue ............ [CREATE VIEW (0 processed) in 1.72s]
10:41:15  16 of 16 START sql view model dbt_demo_dev.mart_revenue_analytics .............. [RUN]
10:41:17  16 of 16 OK created sql view model dbt_demo_dev.mart_revenue_analytics ......... [CREATE VIEW (0 processed) in 1.61s]
10:41:17  15 of 16 OK created sql view model dbt_demo_dev.mart_customer_analytics ........ [CREATE VIEW (0 processed) in 1.89s]
10:41:17
10:41:17  Finished running 9 data tests, 7 view models in 0 hours 0 minutes and 14.57 seconds (14.57s).
10:41:17
10:41:17  Completed successfully
10:41:17
10:41:17  Done. PASS=16 WARN=0 ERROR=0 SKIP=0 NO-OP=0 TOTAL=16
```

Figure 7.17: *Terminal Showing dbt Build Output with Models and Tests Running Together*

Lab Insights

This hands-on lab demonstrates the following key advantages of DBT:

- **Automatic Dependency Resolution:** We never specified execution order. dbt figured it out from **`ref()`** calls.

- **Parallel Execution:** Models with no dependencies ran simultaneously, maximizing BigQuery's concurrency.
- **Environment Isolation:** All models were created in `dbt_demo_dev`, keeping our work separate from production.
- **Data Quality Enforcement:** 9 tests ensure that our data meets business requirements.
- **Self-Documenting Code:** The lineage graph and column descriptions provide instant understanding.

Conclusion

Building scalable analytics pipelines inside BigQuery does not require thousands of lines of hard-coded DML scripts or brittle Airflow operators. With dbt, data transformation is treated as software engineering.

Analysts can modularize complex SQL logic into layered components and link them automatically using the `ref()` function. Rather than blindly pushing data, dbt's generic tests provide a practical workaround for BigQuery's lack of primary key constraints, ensuring data quality even before it reaches production dashboards.

Adopting a structured ELT workflow simplifies your warehouse architecture. It generates your DAG automatically, standardizes your environment promotion, enables incremental loading, and brings the safety of standard CI/CD practices to your analytics team.

In the next chapter, we will move from batch ELT into the streaming world: building real-time pipelines with Apache Beam and Dataflow that ingest events directly into BigQuery.

Points to Remember

- **ELT over ETL:** BigQuery is fast enough to handle transformations natively using SQL, eliminating the need to process data externally.
- **dbt Workflow:** Manage your transformations exclusively by writing simple "`SELECT`" statements; dbt handles the DDL and execution order.
- **Environment Management:** The `ref()` function automatically builds your execution DAG and resolves dev/prod schemas dynamically without code changes.
- **Materialization Efficiency:** Choose materializations wisely–use "`incremental`" for large rolling datasets and "`ephemeral`" to inject CTEs without writing tables.

- **Data Layers:** Organize models into Staging (raw passthrough), Intermediate (business logic), and Marts (end-user consumption).
- **Automated Testing:** Use `schema.yml` generic tests to enforce the "`unique`" and "`not_null`" constraints that BigQuery lacks natively.
- **Documentation:** dbt automatically renders your YAML descriptions into a searchable, visual lineage web interface and pushes column descriptions to BigQuery's UI.
- **Slim CI:** Use `state:modified+` to build and test only the files changed in a PR, saving significant slot-ms and compilation time.
- **Version Compatibility:** Run dbt-bigquery with Python 3.11 or 3.12 to avoid dependency conflicts.
- **External Dependencies:** Always use the `source()` function to reference raw tables, ensuring proper dependency tracking from non-dbt sources.

Multiple Choice Questions

1. What does the acronym ELT stand for in a modern BigQuery stack?
   a. Execute, Load, Template
   b. Extract, Load, Transform
   c. Encrypt, Log, Transfer
   d. Evaluate, Link, Test
2. Which of the following is NOT an advantage of using dbt over traditional BigQuery Scheduled Queries?
   a. Automated lineage and DAG inference
   b. Built-in data modeling testing (for example, `unique` or `not_null`)
   c. Allowing users to write transformations using Python Pandas rather than SQL
   d. Dynamic targeting of different datasets for development and production
3. What is the fundamental building block of a dbt project?
   a. Deeply nested JSON configuration blobs
   b. A Python script utilizing the `google-cloud-bigquery` library
   c. A `.sql` file executing DDL commands such as `CREATE OR REPLACE TABLE`
   d. A `.sql` file containing a singular `SELECT` statement

4. Why is the **{{ ref() }}** function preferred over explicitly writing **my_project.my_dataset.my_table** inside a dbt model?

   a. It actively reduces the amount of bytes processed by the query.

   b. It prevents BigQuery from cache-missing between environments.

   c. It automatically orders execution graphs and dynamically adjusts dataset references between dev and prod targets.

   d. It provides a 2x performance optimization on analytical queries.

5. If a **dbt** model has minimal complex logic and needs to provide entirely real-time throughput from underlying tables, what materialization should be utilized?

   a. `view`

   b. `table`

   c. `incremental`

   d. `ephemeral`

6. What is the primary purpose of the staging (**stg_**) layer in **dbt**?

   a. To perform heavy, computationally expensive multi-table JOINs

   b. To serve wide, denormalized facts to BI dashboards

   c. To extract JSON payloads, cast specific data types, and enforce basic naming conventions directly against raw sources

   d. To temporarily cache data using BigQuery BI Engine

7. How does a developer implement a test ensuring that an **order_id** column contains no duplicate values or NULLs?

   a. Utilizing a **UNIQUE NOT NULL** constraint in a **CREATE TABLE** query

   b. Writing a Python script that pulls the data using a cursor and asserts conditions

   c. Configuring **unique** and **not_null** generic tests targeting the column under the **models:** configuration block in **schema.yml**

   d. Creating a dbt macro that deletes offending rows before job execution

8. When configuring **dbt** Docs, how can column descriptions entered into your **schema.yml** be pushed into the Native BigQuery Web UI?

   a. Ensuring **persist_docs** is enabled in **dbt_project.yml**

   b. Contacting Google Cloud support to synchronize APIs

   c. Writing a scheduled Cloud Function that pings the dbt metadata API
   d. This feature is not possible; dbt docs only exist as standalone HTML files

9. What is Slim CI?
   a. A method to compress analytical data before testing
   b. An optimization flag explicitly for the **`incremental`** materialization
   c. Running **`dbt build --select state:modified+`** to evaluate only models whose files have been actively updated (and their downstream dependencies) rather than the entire project
   d. A specialized BigQuery slot reservation strictly limited to low-compute queries

10. What type of test is configured using a custom **`.sql`** file located directly in the **`tests/`** directory?
    a. A Generic Validation Test
    b. A Singular Test
    c. An Ephemeral Test
    d. A Syntax Assertion Test

Answers

1. b
2. c
3. d
4. c
5. a
6. c
7. c
8. a
9. c
10. b

Questions

1. Describe the key conceptual difference between standard BigQuery Scheduled Queries and a managed dbt pipeline, focusing closely on DML/DDL writing overhead and dynamic promotion across environments.
2. In your own words, break down the functional difference between the **`incremental`** and **`ephemeral`** materializations in dbt Core. Detail a scenario where each would be appropriately used.
3. Compare the Staging and Mart modeling layers. What are the strict rules dictating what interactions are permitted at the Staging layer, and what is the primary structural expectation of the Mart layer?
4. BigQuery distinctly lacks physical primary key and foreign key constraints. How does an analytics engineer overcome this limitation by practically using dbt?
5. Outline a robust CI/CD workflow for deploying a dbt project. Explain what should fundamentally happen chronologically from an analyst attempting to merge a GitHub Pull Request through to models updating in the production dataset.
6. A developer needs to ensure that the **`delivery_date`** in **`fct_orders`** is strictly equal to or sequentially after the **`order_date`**. What mechanism in dbt accommodates this logic? Explain what is required for the test to pass or fail.
7. Explain the benefit of utilizing Slim CI. How exactly does using **`state:modified+`** impact total compute waste (slot-ms) across an enterprise team merging five distinct tracking PRs simultaneously?
8. Walk through the execution order when running **`dbt run`** on a project with the following models: **`stg_orders`**, **`stg_customers`**, **`int_customer_metrics`** (depends on **`stg_orders`**), and **`mart_customer_analytics`** (depends on **`stg_customers`** and **`int_customer_metrics`**). Explain how dbt determines this order.

Key Terms

- **data build tool (dbt):** A data transformation framework that brings software engineering best practices such as modularity, version control, and testing, to data analytics.
- **dbt Core:** The open-source command-line version of dbt used to compile, test, and execute data projects.

- **Extract, Load, Transform (ELT):** A paradigm where raw data is extracted and loaded directly into a warehouse, followed by transformations performed natively within the database engine using SQL.
- **Jinja:** A templating language embedded within dbt SQL files, allowing for dynamic queries using loops, conditionals, and variables.
- **`ref()`:** A dbt function that references other models, enabling automatic dependency resolution and environment-aware compilation without hardcoding table names.
- **`source()`:** A dbt function used to reference external raw tables, establishing centralized source definitions and tracking external lineage.
- **Directed Acyclic Graph (DAG):** A visual network displaying the precise mathematical execution order of data models, inferred entirely from **`ref()`** function calls.
- **Materialization:** The explicit configuration determining how a compiled query is materialized within BigQuery (for example, **`table`**, **`view`**, **`incremental`**, or **`ephemeral`**).
- **Ephemeral Materialization:** A configuration where the model is not physically stored, but its SQL is compiled dynamically as a Common Table Expression (CTE) in downstream models.
- **Incremental Materialization:** A highly efficient build pattern that uses **`MERGE`** statements to incrementally append only new records, saving massive compute costs on large datasets.
- **Staging Layer:** The foundational data modeling layer strictly dedicated to 1:1 mapping of raw source tables, primarily handling standard renaming and data type casting.
- **Intermediate Layer:** The middle data modeling layer where complex joins and business logic live, preventing redundant transformations in downstream analytics.
- **Mart Layer:** The final polished modeling layer consisting of wide, denormalized dimension and fact tables explicitly built for business intelligence dashboards.
- **Generic Test:** Built-in parameters configured via YAML files that automatically assert data constraints such as uniqueness or not null.
- **Singular Test:** Custom SQL validation queries stored in the **`tests/`** directory designed to fail the pipeline if they return any active rows.
- **Slim CI:** An optimized CI process that uses **`state:modified+`** to build and test only the specific models that were altered in a Pull Request, avoiding a full project rebuild.

- **dbt Docs:** Highly interactive, self-generating HTML documentation that renders complete schema definitions and lineage graphs directly from codebase annotations.
- **Lineage Graph:** A visual map of data flow showing how downstream analytical models logically depend on upstream data sources across all transformation layers.
- **Schema Test:** Another term for generic tests defined in `schema.yml` files, primarily used to establish data constraints BigQuery lacks natively.

CHAPTER 8

Apache Beam and Dataflow

Introduction

The previous chapter introduced the data build tool (**`dbt`**) as a way to manage SQL-based transformations inside BigQuery. That model works well when your data already sits in BigQuery tables. However, what happens when the data has not arrived yet? When you need to read millions of CSV rows from Cloud Storage, parse and filter them, and land the results into BigQuery? Or when you need to process a continuous stream of events from Pub/Sub and aggregate them in real-time?

These are data pipeline problems, and they require a different tool. Google Cloud Dataflow is a fully managed service for executing data processing pipelines at scale. The programming model behind Dataflow is Apache Beam, which is an open-source Software Development Kit (SDK) that defines both batch and streaming pipelines using the same code.

This chapter will walk through the core concepts of Apache Beam, explain how Dataflow executes those pipelines on Google Cloud, and cover the critical differences between batch and streaming processing. You will then build both pipelines from scratch in the hands-on lab.

By the end of this chapter, you will have a solid understanding of how to architect both real-time stream processing and massive batch workflows using Apache Beam. You will learn to seamlessly ingest, transform, and land continuous data streams directly into BigQuery. More broadly, mastering these patterns carries significant implications for your data engineering career, as it empowers you to evolve traditional, static data warehouses into resilient and event-driven platforms capable of delivering fresh insights at any scale.

Structure

In this chapter, we will cover the following topics:

- The Apache Beam Programming Model
- Batch versus Streaming Pipelines
- Core Beam Transforms
- Windowing and Triggers
- Handling Failures and Late Data
- Google Cloud Dataflow
- Connecting Beam to BigQuery
- Hands-on Lab

The Apache Beam Programming Model

Apache Beam is a unified programming model for defining data processing pipelines. The keyword is "unified"–the same code can run as a batch job over a finite dataset or as a streaming job over a continuous data feed. You write the pipeline once, and the execution engine (called a "runner") handles the rest.

Core Abstractions

Beam pipelines are built from the following three fundamental building blocks:

1. **`Pipeline`:** The top-level container. A pipeline encapsulates the entire data processing workflow–from reading input to writing output.
2. **`PCollection`:** A distributed dataset. Think of it as a parallel collection of elements. A PCollection can be bounded (a finite file) or unbounded (a continuous stream). Elements in a PCollection are immutable–once created, they cannot be modified in place. Every transform produces a new PCollection.
3. **`PTransform`:** An operation applied to a PCollection. Transforms include reading data, mapping functions across elements, filtering, grouping, and writing output. Transforms are chained together using the pipe operator (|), forming a Directed Acyclic Graph (DAG).

The following is a minimal Beam Pipeline that reads a text file, counts the words, and prints the results:

```
import apache_beam as beam

with beam.Pipeline() as p:
```

```
(p
 | 'Read' >> beam.io.ReadFromText('input.txt')
 | 'Split' >> beam.FlatMap(lambda line: line.split())
 | 'Count' >> beam.combiners.Count.PerElement()
 | 'Print' >> beam.Map(print)
)
```

The Pipe Operator

The | (pipe) operator is how you chain transforms together. Each step takes a PCollection as input and produces a new PCollection as output. The string before >> (for example, **`'Read'`**) is a label that names the transform—it appears in the Dataflow job graph and is required to be unique within the pipeline.

Runners

A runner is the execution engine that processes your pipeline. The Beam supports multiple runners, such as:

- **`DirectRunner`:** Runs locally on your machine. Useful for development and testing with small datasets.
- **`DataflowRunner`:** Submits your pipeline to Google Cloud Dataflow for distributed execution.
- **`FlinkRunner` / `SparkRunner`:** Runs on Apache Flink or Apache Spark clusters.

The runner is configured via pipeline options. Switching from local testing to cloud execution is a single configuration change—your pipeline code stays identical.

Batch versus Streaming Pipelines

The distinction between batch and streaming is fundamental to understanding the Beam.

Batch Processing

A batch pipeline operates on a bounded dataset. The input has a defined beginning and end—such as a CSV file, a database export, or a BigQuery table. The pipeline reads all the data, processes it, writes the output, and terminates. Batch jobs are finite.

Typical batch use cases include:

- Loading historical data from Cloud Storage into BigQuery.
- Running daily ETL jobs that process the previous day's transactions.
- Backfilling data after schema changes.

Streaming Processing

A streaming pipeline operates on an unbounded dataset. The input has no defined end–messages arrive continuously from sources such as Pub/Sub, Kafka, or IoT devices. The pipeline runs indefinitely, processing new elements as they arrive.

Typical streaming use cases include:

- Real-time fraud detection on payment transactions.
- Live dashboards aggregating user activity metrics.
- IoT sensor data ingestion and alerting.

The Unified Model

Beam's key innovation is that you write the same transforms regardless of whether the data is bounded or unbounded. A `Map` transform works identically on a CSV file and on a Pub/Sub stream. The difference lies in the source (where data comes from) and the windowing strategy (how you group unbounded data into finite chunks for aggregation).

Core Beam Transforms

Every Beam Pipeline is a sequence of transforms applied to PCollections. The transforms that you will use most frequently are listed in this section.

Map

`beam.Map` applies a function to every element in the PCollection, producing exactly one output element per input element.

```
# Convert each line to uppercase
lines | 'ToUpper' >> beam.Map(str.upper)
```

FlatMap

`beam.FlatMap` applies a function that can return zero, one, or many output elements per input element. It flattens the results into a single PCollection.

```
# Split each line into individual words
lines | 'Split' >> beam.FlatMap(lambda line: line.split())
```

Filter

`beam.Filter` keeps only elements that satisfy a predicate function.

```
# Keep only completed transactions
records | 'FilterCompleted' >> beam.Filter(lambda r: r['status'] ==
'completed')
```

GroupByKey

`beam.GroupByKey` takes a PCollection of key-value pairs and groups all values sharing the same key. This is the Beam equivalent of a SQL `GROUP BY`.

```
# Input: [('alice', 10), ('bob', 20), ('alice', 30)]
# Output: [('alice', [10, 30]), ('bob', [20])]
pairs | 'GroupByCustomer' >> beam.GroupByKey()
```

`CombinePerKey` and `CombineGlobally`

`CombinePerKey` applies a combining function (such as **`sum`**, **`count`**, and **`average`**) to grouped values. **`CombineGlobally`** applies the combination across the entire **`PCollection`**.

```
# Sum amounts per customer
pairs | 'SumPerCustomer' >> beam.CombinePerKey(sum)
```

For more complex aggregations, you can extend **`beam.CombineFn`** to create custom combiners with explicit accumulator logic.

ParDo

`beam.ParDo` is the most general transform. It applies a **`DoFn`** (a user-defined function class) to every element. Unlike **`Map`**, a **`DoFn`** can produce zero or multiple output elements, access side inputs, and maintain state.

```
class FilterAndTag(beam.DoFn):
    def process(self, record):
        if record['amount'] > 100:
            yield {'tag': 'high_value', **record}

records | 'TagHighValue' >> beam.ParDo(FilterAndTag())
```

Windowing and Triggers

When processing unbounded (streaming) data, you need a way to group elements into finite chunks for aggregation. Without windowing, operations such as **`GroupByKey`** cannot complete – there is no end to the data. Windows solve this by assigning each element to a time-based bucket.

Fixed Windows

Fixed windows divide time into non-overlapping intervals of a fixed duration. Every element is assigned to exactly one window.

```
from apache_beam.transforms.window import FixedWindows

# 60-second fixed windows
data | 'Window' >> beam.WindowInto(FixedWindows(60))
```

A 60-second fixed window means that all elements with timestamps between 12:00:00 and 12:00:59 are grouped together, all elements between 12:01:00 and 12:01:59 are in the next window, and so on.

Sliding Windows

Sliding windows have a fixed duration but overlap by a defined period. An element can belong to multiple windows. These are useful for computing moving averages.

```
from apache_beam.transforms.window import SlidingWindows

# 5-minute windows, sliding every 1 minute
data | 'Window' >> beam.WindowInto(SlidingWindows(300, 60))
```

Session Windows

Session windows group elements that arrive within a specified gap duration. If no new element arrives within the gap, the window closes. These are useful for user session analysis.

Watermarks

A watermark tracks the progress of event time in a streaming pipeline. It answers the question: "At what point can we be reasonably confident that all data up to time T has arrived?" When the watermark passes the end of a window, Beam fires that window's aggregation.

Triggers

Triggers control when windowed results are emitted. The default trigger fires once, when the watermark passes the window boundary. You can configure early triggers (to emit partial results before the window closes) and late triggers (to handle late-arriving data).

```
from apache_beam.transforms.trigger import AfterWatermark,
AfterProcessingTime, AccumulationMode
```

```
beam.WindowInto(
    FixedWindows(60),
    trigger=AfterWatermark(early=AfterProcessingTime(30)),
    accumulation_mode=AccumulationMode.DISCARDING
)
```

This configuration creates 60-second windows with early results emitted every 30 seconds. The **DISCARDING** accumulation mode means each firing includes only new elements since the last firing – not the cumulative total.

Handling Failures and Late Data

Production pipelines must handle three categories of problems: malformed records, late-arriving data, and transient infrastructure failures.

Dead-Letter Queues

Not every record in a pipeline will parse correctly. A malformed JSON message, an unexpected null field, or a type conversion error will cause a transform to throw an exception. If unhandled, a single bad record can crash the entire pipeline.

The standard pattern is a Dead-Letter Queue (DLQ): route failed records to a separate output instead of letting them kill the pipeline.

```
class ParseWithDLQ(beam.DoFn):
    def process(self, element):
        try:
            record = json.loads(element.decode('utf-8'))
            yield record
        except Exception as e:
            yield beam.pvalue.TaggedOutput('dead_letter',
                {'raw': element, 'error': str(e)})

parsed, dead = (messages
    | 'Parse' >> beam.ParDo(ParseWithDLQ())
        .with_outputs('dead_letter', main='parsed'))
```

The **dead_letter** output can be written to a separate BigQuery table or Cloud Storage bucket for later analysis and reprocessing. This ensures that the main pipeline continues processing valid records while bad records are safely captured.

Late Data Handling

In streaming systems, data frequently arrives after its window has closed. A mobile app might batch events and upload them minutes later, or a network outage might delay message delivery. Beam handles this through its watermark and trigger mechanisms.

By default, Beam drops late data once the watermark passes the window boundary. To retain late arrivals, configure an allowed lateness in the following manner:

```
beam.WindowInto(
    FixedWindows(60),
    trigger=AfterWatermark(
        early=AfterProcessingTime(30),
        late=AfterProcessingTime(60)),
    accumulation_mode=AccumulationMode.ACCUMULATING,
    allowed_lateness=Duration(seconds=300)
)
```

This configuration keeps windows open for an additional 5 minutes (300 seconds) after the watermark passes. Late-arriving elements trigger a re-emission of the updated window results.

Retry Behavior

Dataflow automatically retries failed work items. If a worker crashes or a transform throws a transient error (for example, a BigQuery API timeout), the affected bundle of elements is retried on another worker. This is built into the Dataflow runner – you do not need to implement retry logic yourself.

For persistent failures (for example, a consistently malformed record), the DLQ pattern prevents infinite retry loops. Without a DLQ, Dataflow would retry the same failing record repeatedly, eventually stalling the pipeline.

Google Cloud Dataflow

Dataflow is a fully managed service that executes Apache Beam pipelines on Google Cloud. You submit a pipeline, and Dataflow handles provisioning workers, distributing work, scaling up or down, and cleaning up resources when the job finishes.

Dataflow Functioning

When you submit a Beam pipeline with **`DataflowRunner`**, the following steps take place:

1. The SDK serializes your pipeline into a JSON execution graph and uploads it to Dataflow.
2. Staging files are uploaded to Cloud Storage (such as your compiled code and dependencies).

3. Dataflow provisions worker VMs in the specified region.
4. Workers pull tasks from the execution graph and process data in parallel.
5. Autoscaling adjusts the number of workers based on backlog and throughput.
6. For batch jobs, workers shut down after all the data is processed.
7. For streaming jobs, workers run continuously until you stop the job.

Pipeline Options

Pipeline options can configure how and where your pipeline runs in the following way:

```
from apache_beam.options.pipeline_options import PipelineOptions,
GoogleCloudOptions, StandardOptions

pipeline_options = PipelineOptions()
pipeline_options.view_as(GoogleCloudOptions).project
= 'your-project-id'
pipeline_options.view_as(GoogleCloudOptions).region = 'us-east1'
pipeline_options.view_as(GoogleCloudOptions).temp_location
= 'gs://your-bucket/temp'
pipeline_options.view_as(GoogleCloudOptions).staging_location
= 'gs://your-bucket/staging'
pipeline_options.view_as(StandardOptions).runner = 'DataflowRunner'
```

Autoscaling

Dataflow automatically scales the number of workers based on the pipeline's needs. For batch jobs, it scales up when processing large file reads and scales down during lighter transforms. For streaming jobs, it scales based on system lag–if the pipeline falls behind the incoming data rate, more workers are added.

You can control this with the **--max_num_workers** flag to cap costs in the following manner:

```
--max_num_workers=2
```

Job Lifecycle

Dataflow jobs have the following distinct states:

- **Pending:** The job is being prepared, and workers are starting up.
- **Running:** Workers are actively processing data.
- **Succeeded (Batch Only):** All data has been processed, and the job is complete.

- **Draining (Streaming Only):** The job stops reading new data but finishes processing in-flight elements.
- **Cancelled:** The job is immediately terminated; in-flight data may be lost.

For streaming jobs, always use "`Drain`" instead of "`Cancel`" for a clean shutdown. "`Drain`" ensures that all buffered data is flushed to the sink before workers shut down.

Monitoring

The Dataflow console provides the following three critical views:

- **Job Graph:** A visual DAG of your pipeline showing each transform step, element counts, and processing time.
- **Job Metrics:** Throughput charts, system lag, data freshness, and autoscaling activity.
- **Worker Logs:** Standard output and error logs from individual worker VMs.

Connecting Beam to BigQuery

Apache Beam has native connectors for reading from and writing to BigQuery.

Writing to BigQuery

`beam.io.WriteToBigQuery` is the primary sink for landing pipeline results into BigQuery tables. It supports the following two write dispositions:

- **`WRITE_TRUNCATE`:** Overwrites the destination table. Used in batch pipelines where you recompute the full result set.
- **`WRITE_APPEND`:** Appends new rows. Used in streaming pipelines where new windowed results arrive continuously.

The table schema is defined as a dictionary in the following way:

```
table_schema = {
    'fields': [
        {'name': 'customer_id', 'type': 'STRING', 'mode':
'REQUIRED'},
        {'name': 'total_revenue', 'type': 'FLOAT', 'mode':
'REQUIRED'},
        {'name': 'transaction_count', 'type': 'INTEGER', 'mode':
'REQUIRED'}
    ]
}
```

```
results | 'WriteBQ' >> beam.io.WriteToBigQuery(
    'project:dataset.table',
    schema=table_schema,
    write_disposition=beam.io.BigQueryDisposition.WRITE_TRUNCATE,
    create_disposition=beam.io.BigQueryDisposition.CREATE_IF_NEEDED
)
```

Reading from BigQuery

`beam.io.ReadFromBigQuery` reads data from a BigQuery table or query result into a PCollection of dictionaries in the following manner:

```
rows = p | 'ReadBQ' >> beam.io.ReadFromBigQuery(
    query='SELECT * FROM `project.dataset.table` WHERE date >
"2024-01-01"',
    use_standard_sql=True
)
```

Streaming Writes

For streaming pipelines, BigQuery uses the Storage Write API to insert rows with low latency. The pipeline continuously appends new windowed results as they are emitted.

Hands-on Lab: Building Batch and Streaming Pipelines

In this lab, you will build two data pipelines: a batch pipeline that reads CSV data from Cloud Storage and aggregates it into BigQuery, and a streaming pipeline that processes real-time messages from Pub/Sub as well as writes windowed aggregations to BigQuery.

Prerequisites

- Google Cloud Project with billing enabled
- APIs enabled: Dataflow, Pub/Sub, BigQuery, Cloud Storage
- Python 3.12 installed (Beam supports 3.9-3.13 as of 2026)
- `gcloud` CLI installed and authenticated

Step 1: Set up the Environment

Start by enabling the required APIs and creating the infrastructure:

```
# Set your project
export PROJECT_ID="your-project-id"
gcloud config set project $PROJECT_ID

# Enable APIs
gcloud services enable dataflow.googleapis.com
gcloud services enable pubsub.googleapis.com
gcloud services enable bigquery.googleapis.com
gcloud services enable storage-api.googleapis.com

Create a Cloud Storage bucket for Dataflow's staging and temporary
files:
export BUCKET_NAME="${PROJECT_ID}-dataflow-lab"
gcloud storage buckets create gs://${BUCKET_NAME} --location=US
```

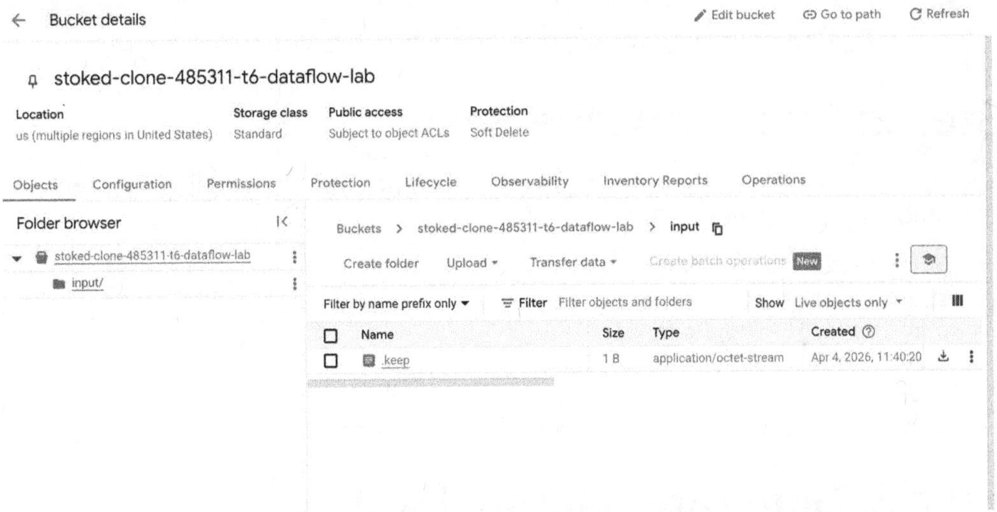

Figure 8.1: *Cloud Storage Console Showing the Dataflow Lab Bucket*

Create a BigQuery dataset to receive the pipeline output in the following way:

```
CREATE SCHEMA `your-project-id.dataflow_lab`
OPTIONS (
  location = 'US',
  description = 'Apache Beam & Dataflow lab dataset'
);
```

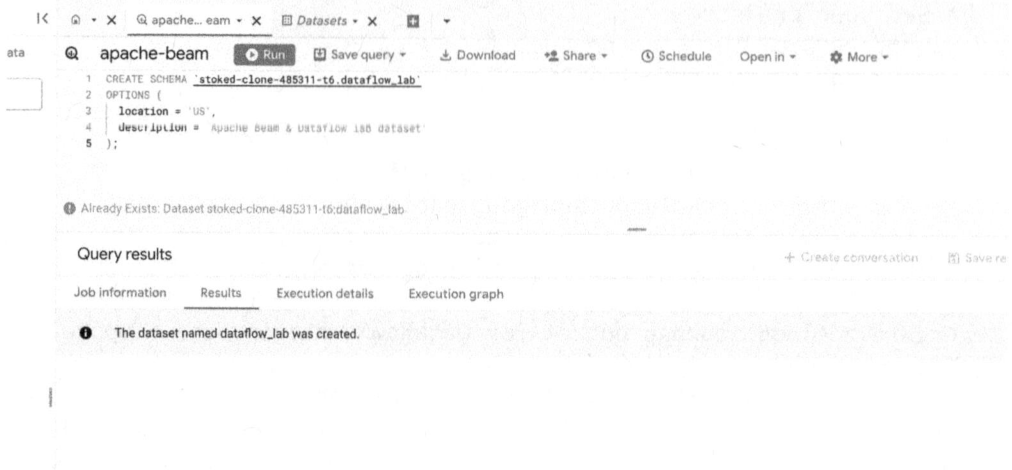

Figure 8.2: *BigQuery Console Showing the dataflow_lab Dataset Created*

Step 2: Install Apache Beam

Apache Beam requires a Python virtual environment. Create one using Python 3.12 or later in the following way:

```
python3.12 -m venv beam-env
source beam-env/bin/activate
pip install --upgrade pip
pip install 'apache-beam[gcp]'
# Verify
python -c "import apache_beam as beam; print(beam.__version__)"
```

Step 3: Generate Sample Data

Create a script to generate 10,000 synthetic transactions:

```
import csv
import random
from datetime import datetime, timedelta
transactions = []
start_date = datetime(2024, 1, 1)
statuses = ['completed', 'pending', 'failed']
status_weights = [0.7, 0.2, 0.1]

for i in range(10000):
    transaction = {
        'transaction_id': f'TXN{i:06d}',
        'customer_id': f'CUST{random.randint(1, 1000):04d}',
        'product_id': f'PROD{random.randint(1, 100):03d}',
```

```
        'amount': round(random.uniform(10, 500), 2),
        'timestamp': (start_date + timedelta(minutes=i)).isoformat(),
        'status': random.choices(statuses, weights=status_weights)
[0]
    }
    transactions.append(transaction)

with open('transactions.csv', 'w', newline='') as f:
    writer = csv.DictWriter(f, fieldnames=transactions[0].keys())
    writer.writeheader()
    writer.writerows(transactions)
 print(f"Generated {len(transactions)} transactions")
```

Run the script and upload the CSV to Cloud Storage:

```
python generate_sample_data.py
gcloud storage cp transactions.csv gs://${BUCKET_NAME}/input/
```

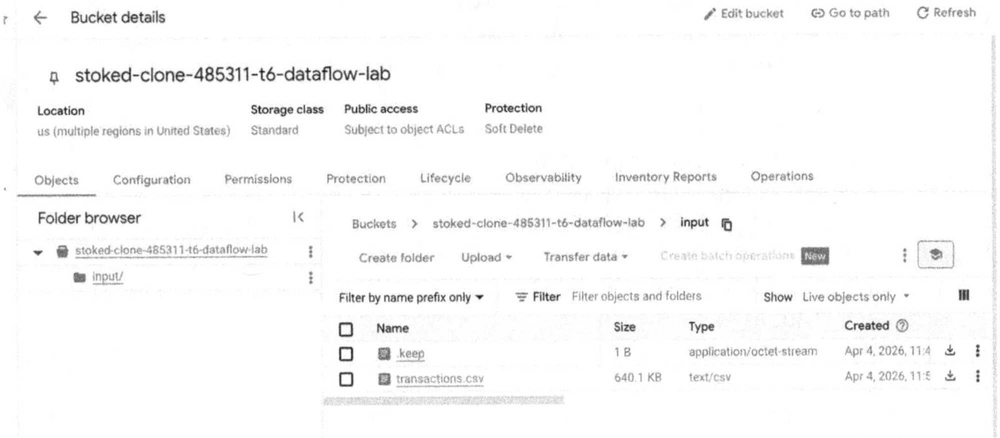

Figure 8.3: *Cloud Storage Console Showing the Uploaded transactions.csv File*

Step 4: Build the Batch Pipeline

This pipeline reads the CSV from Cloud Storage, filters completed transactions, groups by customer, and writes the aggregated revenue per customer into BigQuery.

```
import apache_beam as beam
from apache_beam.options.pipeline_options import PipelineOptions,
GoogleCloudOptions, StandardOptions
import argparse

def parse_csv(line):
    """Parse CSV line into dictionary"""
    fields = ['transaction_id', 'customer_id', 'product_id',
              'amount', 'timestamp', 'status']
```

```
        values = line.split(',')
        return dict(zip(fields, values))

    def filter_completed(record):
        """Filter only completed transactions"""
        return record['status'] == 'completed'

    def calculate_revenue(record):
        """Extract customer_id and amount as key-value pair"""
        return (record['customer_id'], float(record['amount']))

    def sum_amounts(customer_amounts):
        """Sum amounts per customer"""
        customer_id, amounts = customer_amounts
        amounts_list = list(amounts)
        return {
            'customer_id': customer_id,
            'total_revenue': sum(amounts_list),
            'transaction_count': len(amounts_list)
        }

    def run_batch_pipeline(argv=None):
        parser = argparse.ArgumentParser()
        parser.add_argument('--input', required=True, help='Input file
    pattern')
        parser.add_argument('--output', required=True, help='Output
    BigQuery table')
        parser.add_argument('--project', required=True, help='GCP Project
    ID')
        parser.add_argument('--region', default='us-east1', help='GCP
    Region')
        parser.add_argument('--temp_location', required=True)
        parser.add_argument('--staging_location', required=True)

        known_args, pipeline_args = parser.parse_known_args(argv)

        pipeline_options = PipelineOptions(pipeline_args)
        pipeline_options.view_as(GoogleCloudOptions).project
    = known_args.project
        pipeline_options.view_as(GoogleCloudOptions).region
    = known_args.region
        pipeline_options.view_as(GoogleCloudOptions).temp_location
    = known_args.temp_location
        pipeline_options.view_as(GoogleCloudOptions).staging_location
    = known_args.staging_location
        pipeline_options.view_as(StandardOptions).runner = 'DataflowRunner'
```

```
    table_schema = {
        'fields': [
            {'name': 'customer_id', 'type': 'STRING', 'mode':
'REQUIRED'},
            {'name': 'total_revenue', 'type': 'FLOAT', 'mode':
'REQUIRED'},
            {'name': 'transaction_count', 'type': 'INTEGER', 'mode':
'REQUIRED'}
        ]
    }

    with beam.Pipeline(options=pipeline_options) as p:
        (p
         | 'Read CSV' >> beam.io.ReadFromText(
             known_args.input, skip_header_lines=1)
         | 'Parse CSV' >> beam.Map(parse_csv)
         | 'Filter Completed' >> beam.Filter(filter_completed)
         | 'Extract Revenue' >> beam.Map(calculate_revenue)
         | 'Group By Customer' >> beam.GroupByKey()
         | 'Sum Revenue' >> beam.Map(sum_amounts)
         | 'Write to BigQuery' >> beam.io.WriteToBigQuery(
             known_args.output,
             schema=table_schema,
             write_disposition=beam.io.BigQueryDisposition.WRITE_
TRUNCATE,
             create_disposition=beam.io.BigQueryDisposition.CREATE_
IF_NEEDED
         )
        )

if __name__ == '__main__':
    run_batch_pipeline()
```

Step 5: Run the Batch Pipeline on Dataflow

Submit the pipeline to Dataflow:

```
python batch_pipeline.py \
  --input gs://${BUCKET_NAME}/input/transactions.csv \
  --output ${PROJECT_ID}:dataflow_lab.customer_revenue \
  --project ${PROJECT_ID} \
  --region us-east1 \
  --temp_location gs://${BUCKET_NAME}/temp \
  --staging_location gs://${BUCKET_NAME}/staging \
  --runner DataflowRunner \
  --max_num_workers=2
```

Once submitted, open the Dataflow console to monitor the job. The Job Graph tab shows a visual DAG of your pipeline–each box represents a transform step, and you can see element counts flowing between them.

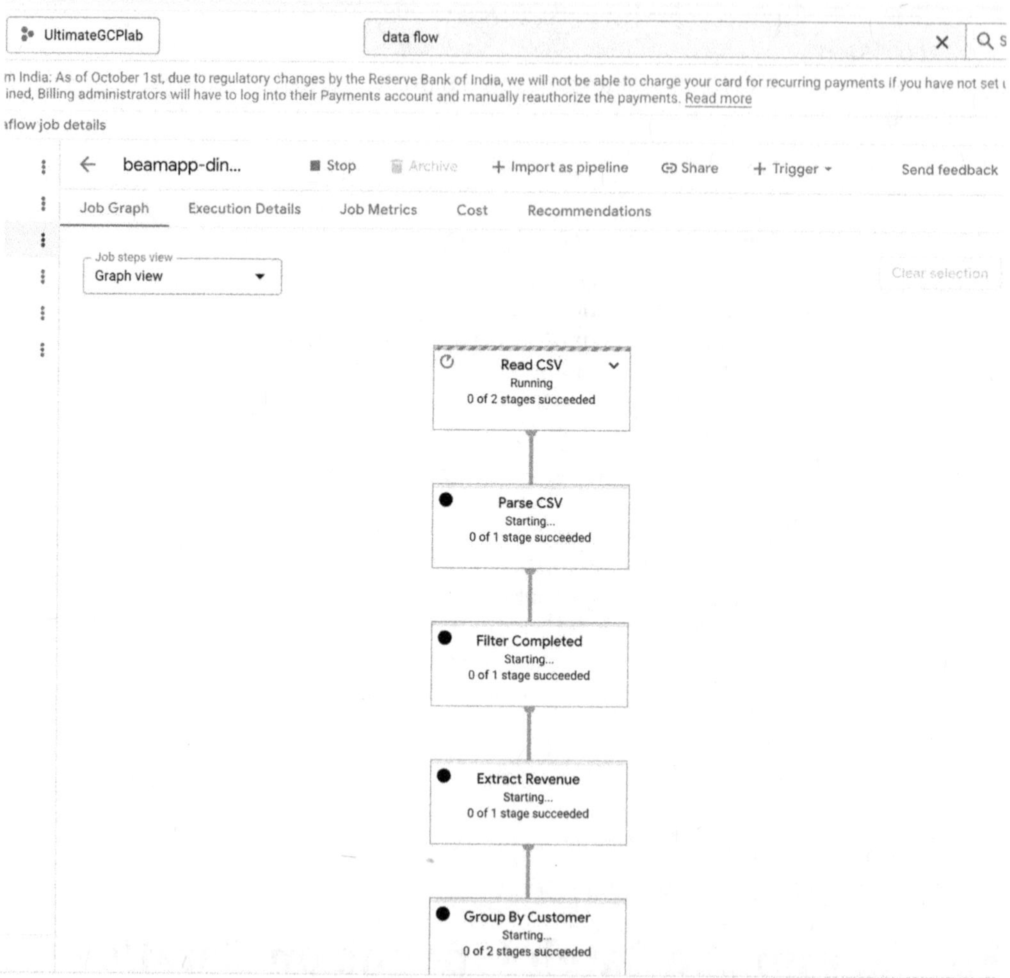

Figure 8.4: *Dataflow Console Showing the Batch Pipeline Execution Graph*

The Job Metrics tab shows autoscaling behavior and throughput. For a 10,000-row dataset, the job typically completes in 3-5 minutes with a single worker.

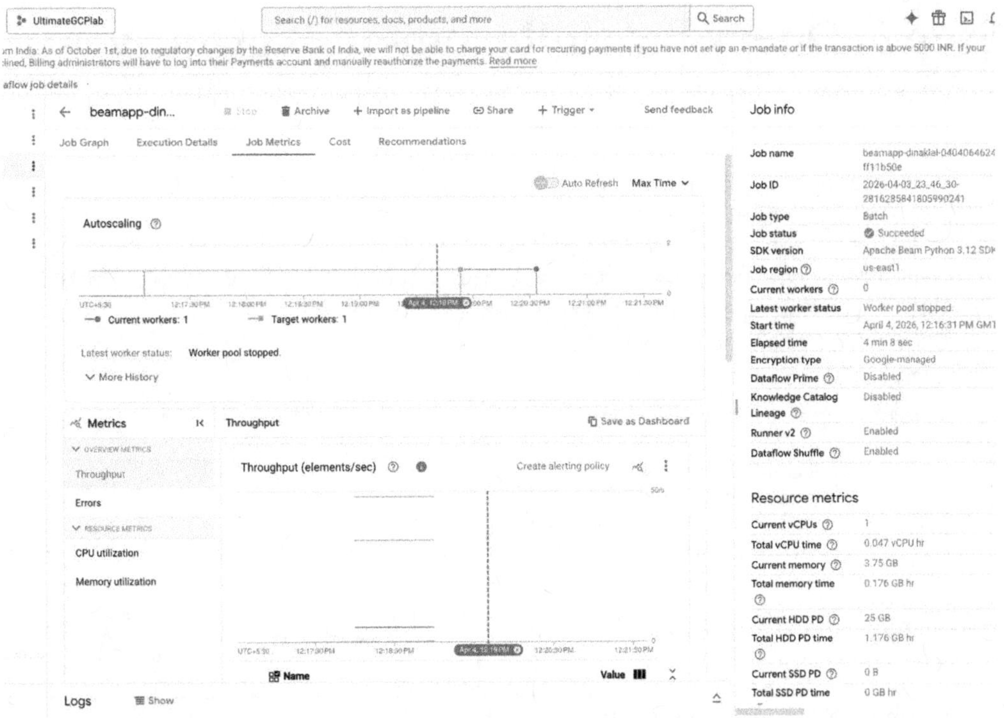

Figure 8.5: *Dataflow Job Metrics Showing Autoscaling and Throughput for the Batch Job*

We can see that the graph section is also completed.

Figure 8.6: *Dataflow Console Showing the Batch Job Completed Successfully*

Step 6: Query Batch Results in BigQuery

With the batch job complete, query the results in the following way:

```
SELECT
  customer_id,
  total_revenue,
  transaction_count,
  ROUND(total_revenue / transaction_count, 2) AS avg_transaction
FROM `your-project-id.dataflow_lab.customer_revenue`
ORDER BY total_revenue DESC
LIMIT 10;
```

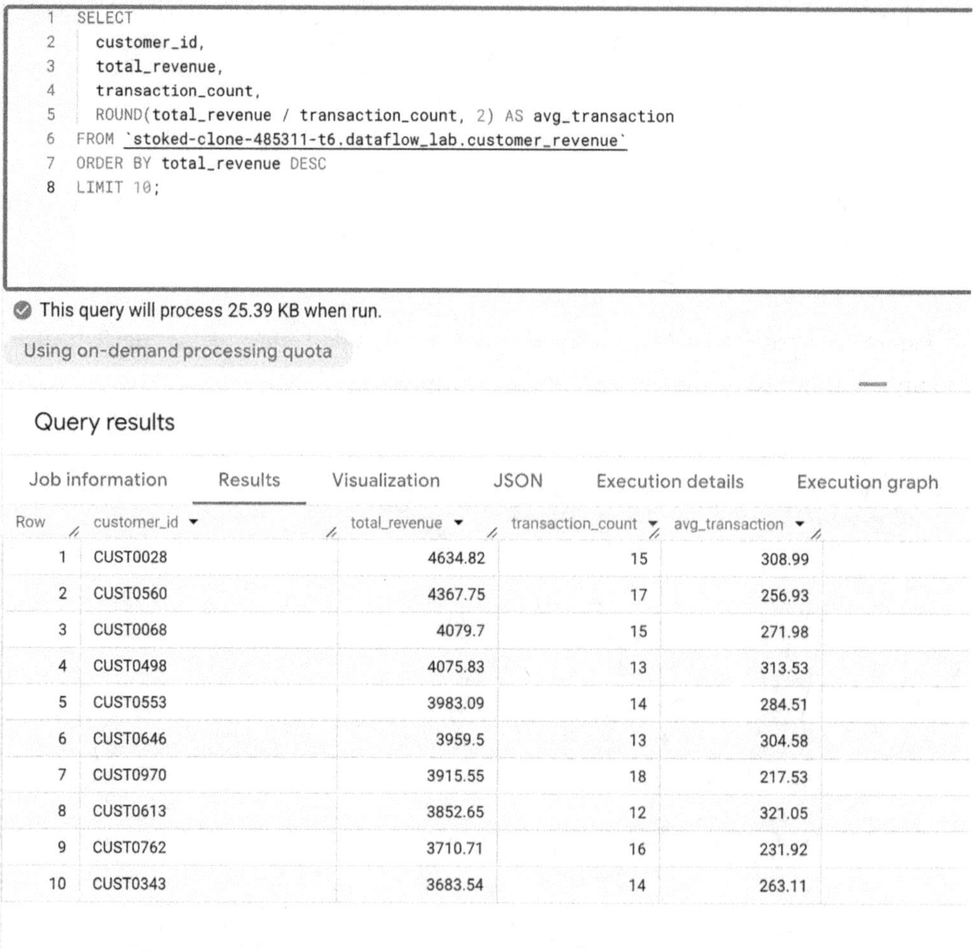

Figure 8.7: *BigQuery Results Showing the Top 10 Customers by Total Revenue*

Step 7: Set up Pub/Sub for Streaming

Create a Pub/Sub topic and subscription. The topic receives incoming messages, and the subscription is what the streaming pipeline reads from:

```
gcloud pubsub topics create transactions-stream

gcloud pubsub subscriptions create transactions-sub \
  --topic transactions-stream \
  --ack-deadline=60
```

This will show subscriptions in pub/sub console in the following manner:

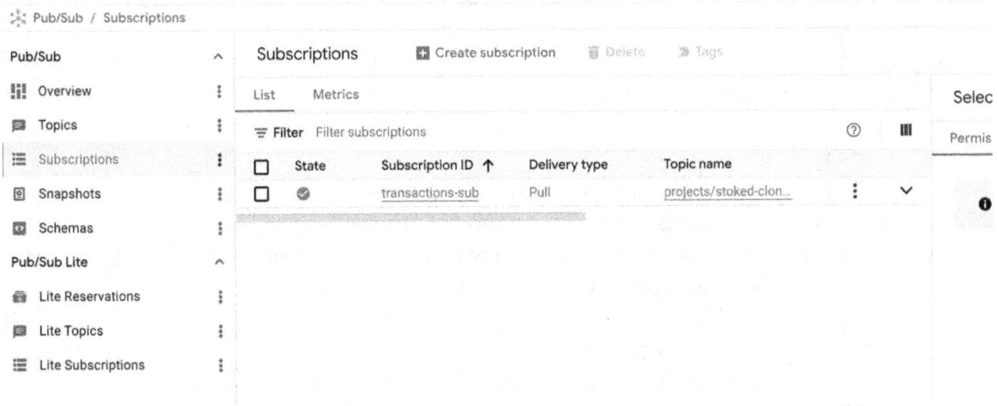

Figure 8.8a: *Pub/Sub Console Showing the Transactions-Sub Subscription*

In the same console, you can check the topic created using the preceding commands:

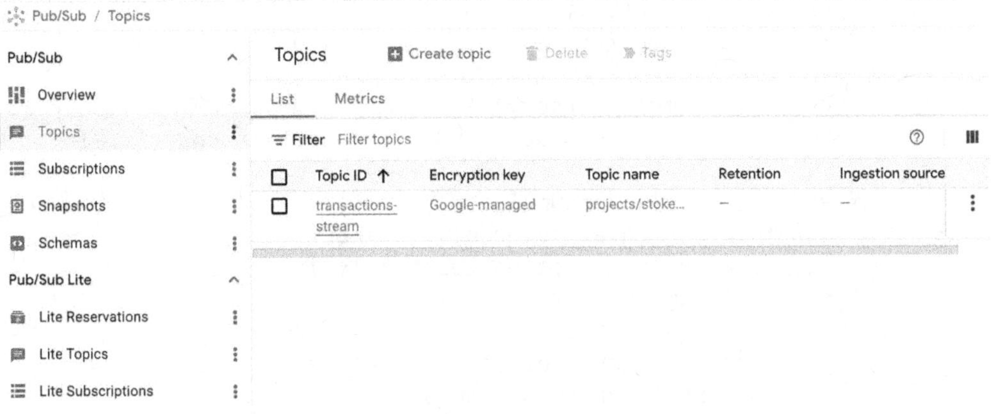

Figure 8.8b: *Pub/Sub Console Showing the Transactions-Stream Topic*

Step 8: Build the Streaming Pipeline

The streaming pipeline reads JSON messages from Pub/Sub, assigns event-time timestamps, applies 60-second fixed windows, aggregates revenue per window, and writes the results to BigQuery in the following way:

```
import apache_beam as beam
from apache_beam.options.pipeline_options import (
    PipelineOptions, GoogleCloudOptions, StandardOptions)
from apache_beam.transforms.window import FixedWindows, Timestamped-
Value
from apache_beam.transforms.trigger import (
    AfterWatermark, AfterProcessingTime, AccumulationMode)
import argparse
import json
from datetime import datetime

def parse_json(message):
    """Parse Pub/Sub message and assign event timestamp"""
    data = json.loads(message.decode('utf-8'))
    timestamp = datetime.fromisoformat(data['timestamp']).timestamp()
    return TimestampedValue(data, timestamp)

def extract_amount(record):
    """Extract transaction amount for completed orders"""
    if record['status'] == 'completed':
        return float(record['amount'])
    return 0.0

class AggregateRevenue(beam.CombineFn):
    """Custom combiner for revenue aggregation"""

    def create_accumulator(self):
        return {'total_revenue': 0.0, 'transaction_count': 0}

    def add_input(self, accumulator, input):
        accumulator['total_revenue'] += input
        accumulator['transaction_count'] += 1
        return accumulator

    def merge_accumulators(self, accumulators):
        merged = self.create_accumulator()
        for acc in accumulators:
            merged['total_revenue'] += acc['total_revenue']
            merged['transaction_count'] += acc['transaction_count']
        return merged
```

```
    def extract_output(self, accumulator):
        return accumulator
def format_output(element):
    """Format the windowed aggregation for BigQuery"""
    return {
        'total_revenue': element['total_revenue'],
        'transaction_count': element['transaction_count']
    }
```

The pipeline definition chains these transforms together in the following way:

```
with beam.Pipeline(options=pipeline_options) as p:
    (p
      | 'Read from Pub/Sub' >> beam.io.ReadFromPubSub(
          subscription=known_args.input_subscription)
      | 'Parse JSON' >> beam.Map(parse_json)
      | 'Extract Amount' >> beam.Map(extract_amount)
      | 'Window into 1min' >> beam.WindowInto(
          FixedWindows(60),
          trigger=AfterWatermark(early=AfterProcessingTime(30)),
          accumulation_mode=AccumulationMode.DISCARDING
      )
      | 'Aggregate Revenue' >> beam.CombineGlobally(
          AggregateRevenue()).without_defaults()
      | 'Format Output' >> beam.Map(format_output)
      | 'Write to BigQuery' >> beam.io.WriteToBigQuery(
          known_args.output,
          schema=table_schema,
          write_disposition=beam.io.BigQueryDisposition.WRITE_APPEND,
          create_disposition=beam.io.BigQueryDisposition.CREATE_IF_
NEEDED
      )
    )
```

The critical differences from the batch pipeline include:

- **`ReadFromPubSub`** instead of **`ReadFromText`**—the source is unbounded.
- **`WindowInto(FixedWindows(60))`**—groups elements into 1-minute windows.
- **`AfterWatermark(early=AfterProcessingTime(30))`**—emits partial results every 30 seconds.
- **`WRITE_APPEND`** instead of **`WRITE_TRUNCATE`**—each window's result is appended as a new row.
- **`streaming = True`** is set on pipeline options to signal Dataflow this is a streaming job.

Step 9: Run the Streaming Pipeline

Submit the streaming pipeline in the following way:

```
python streaming_pipeline.py \
  --input_subscription projects/${PROJECT_ID}/subscriptions/transac-
tions-sub \
  --output ${PROJECT_ID}:dataflow_lab.streaming_revenue \
  --project ${PROJECT_ID} \
  --region us-east1 \
  --temp_location gs://${BUCKET_NAME}/temp \
  --staging_location gs://${BUCKET_NAME}/staging \
  --runner DataflowRunner \
  --max_num_workers=2
```

Unlike the batch job, a streaming pipeline runs indefinitely. The terminal output will eventually time out, or you can press *Ctrl+C*—the job runs on Dataflow regardless.

Figure 8.9: *Dataflow Console Showing the Streaming Pipeline Running with Its Execution Graph*

Step 10: Publish Test Messages

With the streaming pipeline running, publish test messages to the Pub/Sub topic in the following way:

```
from google.cloud import pubsub_v1
import json, time, random
from datetime import datetime
```

```
project_id = "your-project-id"
topic_id = "transactions-stream"

publisher = pubsub_v1.PublisherClient()
topic_path = publisher.topic_path(project_id, topic_id)

for i in range(100):
    message = {
        'transaction_id': f'STREAM{i:06d}',
        'customer_id': f'CUST{random.randint(1, 100):04d}',
        'product_id': f'PROD{random.randint(1, 50):03d}',
        'amount': round(random.uniform(10, 500), 2),
        'timestamp': datetime.utcnow().isoformat(),
        'status': random.choice(['completed', 'pending', 'failed'])
    }

    data = json.dumps(message).encode('utf-8')
    future = publisher.publish(topic_path, data)
    print(f"Published message {i}: {future.result()}")
    time.sleep(0.5)

print("Finished publishing messages")

After 1-2 minutes, windowed results start appearing in BigQuery:
SELECT
  window_start,
  window_end,
  total_revenue,
  transaction_count,
  avg_amount
FROM `your-project-id.dataflow_lab.streaming_revenue`
ORDER BY window_start DESC
LIMIT 10;
```

Through these messages, we can observe in the console as well:

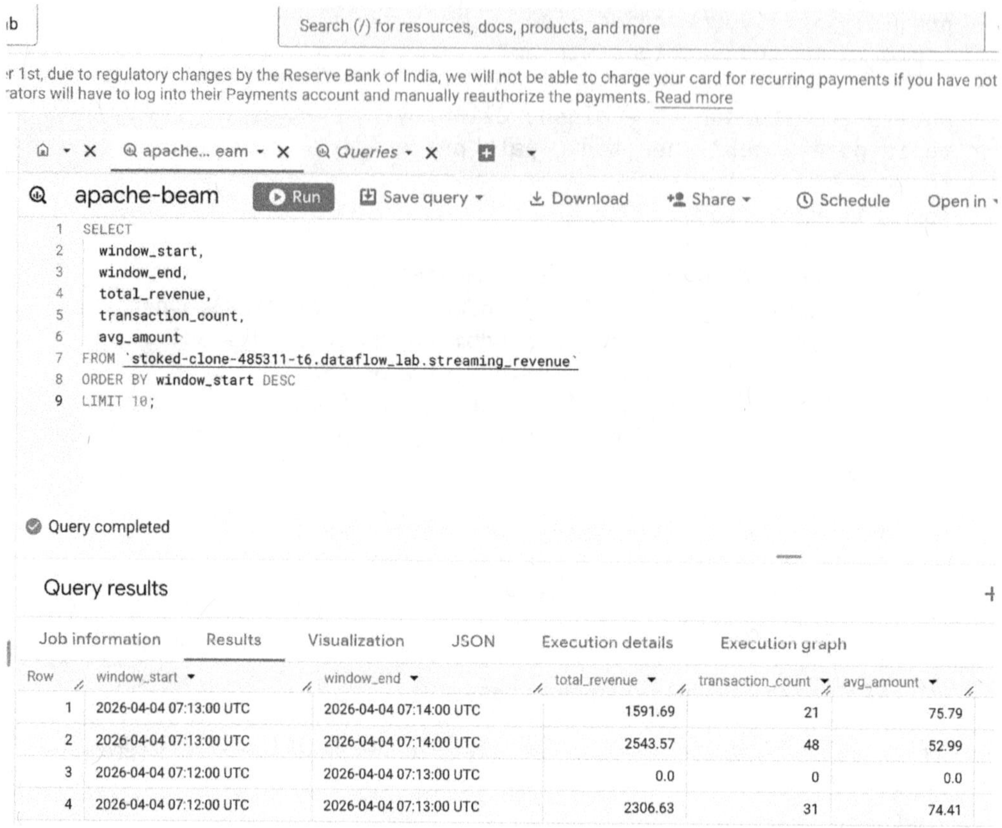

***Figure 8.10:** BigQuery Results Showing Windowed Streaming Revenue Aggregations*

Step 11: Compare Batch versus Streaming Results

Run a comparison query to see both pipeline outputs side by side in the following way:

```
SELECT
  'batch' AS pipeline_type,
  COUNT(*) AS total_rows,
  SUM(total_revenue) AS total_revenue,
  ROUND(AVG(total_revenue), 2) AS avg_revenue
FROM `your-project-id.dataflow_lab.customer_revenue`

UNION ALL

SELECT
  'streaming' AS pipeline_type,
```

```
    COUNT(*) AS total_rows,
    SUM(total_revenue) AS total_revenue,
    ROUND(AVG(total_revenue), 2) AS avg_revenue
FROM `your-project-id.dataflow_lab.streaming_revenue`;
```

Results view as per our data, are as follows:

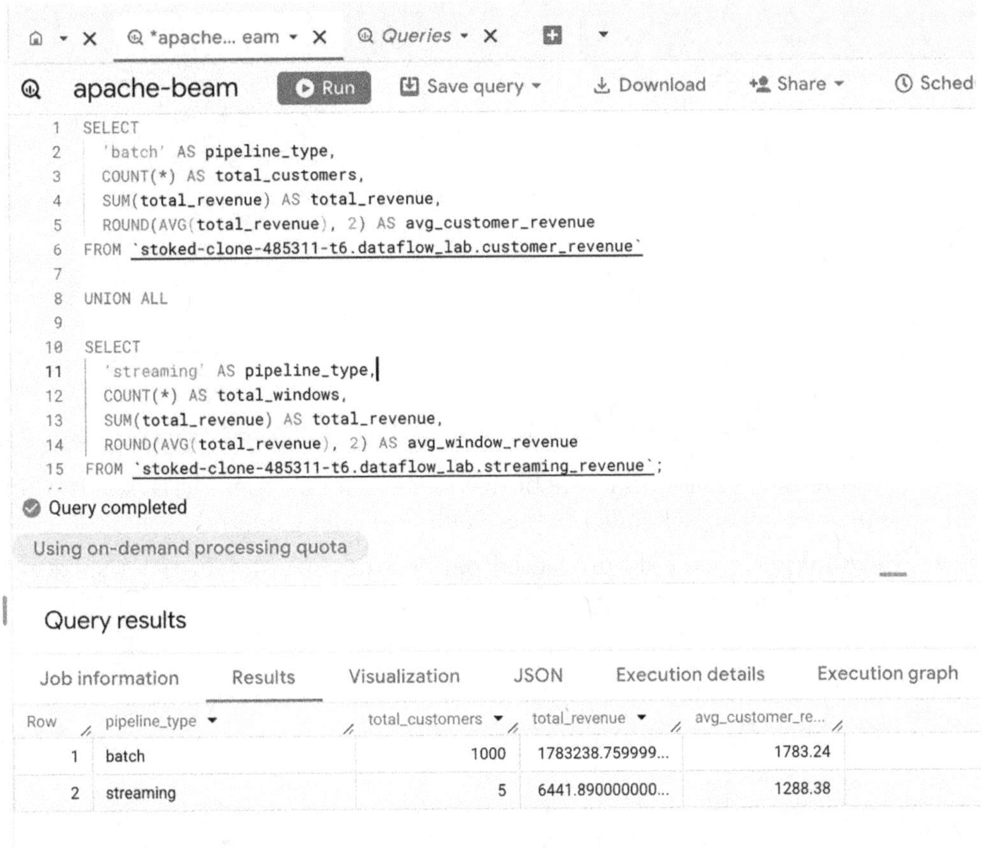

***Figure 8.11:** BigQuery Comparison Showing Batch versus Streaming Pipeline Results*

The batch pipeline produced one row per customer (aggregated across all transactions), while the streaming pipeline produced one row per 1-minute window (aggregated across all transactions in that window). Same data, different granularity—and that is the fundamental difference between batch and streaming processing.

Step 12: Monitor Streaming Metrics

In the Dataflow console, the Job Metrics tab shows the following streaming-specific metrics:

- **Data Freshness:** How old the most recent processed element is. Lower values mean the pipeline is keeping up with the incoming data.

Figure 8.12a: *Dataflow Console Showing Streaming Data Freshness*

- **System Lag:** Time difference between when an element arrives and when it is processed. Spikes indicate the pipeline is falling behind.
- **Throughput:** Elements processed per second. You should see a spike when the **`publish_messages.py`** script runs.

Figure 8.12b: *Dataflow Console Showing Streaming Throughput Metrics*

Step 13: Clean up

Stop the streaming job by clicking "`Stop`" in the Dataflow console and selecting "`Drain`." This ensures that all buffered data is flushed to BigQuery before workers shut down.

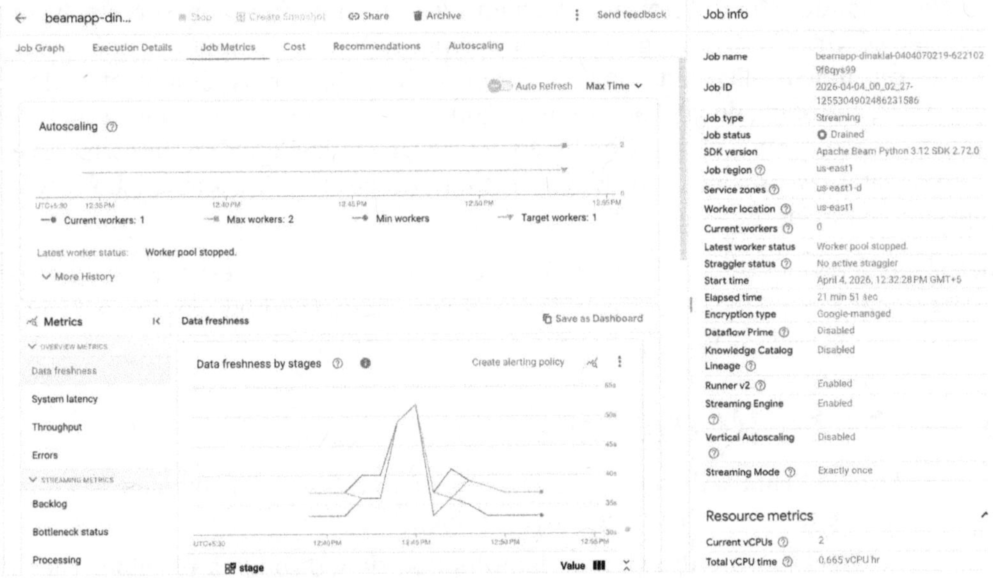

Figure 8.13: *Dataflow Console Showing the Streaming Job in Drained Status*

Delete the Pub/Sub and Cloud Storage resources in the following way:

```
gcloud pubsub subscriptions delete transactions-sub
gcloud pubsub topics delete transactions-stream
gcloud storage rm --recursive gs://${BUCKET_NAME}
```

Conclusion

Apache Beam and Dataflow extend BigQuery's capabilities beyond SQL transformations. Where dbt handles structured, table-to-table transformations inside BigQuery, Beam handles the data movement layer–getting data into BigQuery from external sources such as Cloud Storage files and Pub/Sub streams.

The distinction between dbt and Beam is architectural, not competitive. Use dbt when your data is already inside BigQuery, and you need to build layered transformations with testing and documentation. Use Beam when you need to ingest, parse, and reshape data before it reaches BigQuery–whether that data arrives as flat files in Cloud Storage or as real-time event streams from Pub/Sub. In many production environments, both tools coexist: Beam pipelines land raw data into BigQuery, and dbt models transform that raw data into analytics-ready tables.

The batch pipeline demonstrated a straightforward pattern: read a file, apply transforms, write to BigQuery. The streaming pipeline introduced the added complexity of windowing and triggers, but the core transform operations remained identical. That is Beam's unified model in practice.

Dataflow handles the operational burden. You do not provision servers, manage clusters, or write autoscaling logic. You submit a pipeline definition, and Dataflow figures out how to distribute and execute it efficiently. For batch jobs, it scales up, processes, and shuts down. For streaming jobs, it runs continuously, adjusting worker counts based on data volume. Combined with the DLQ and late data patterns covered earlier, Dataflow provides a production-grade execution environment for any data pipeline that feeds into BigQuery.

In the next chapter, we will shift our focus to hybrid architectures: how Apache Spark on **`Dataproc`** complements BigQuery, when to use each, and how the Spark-BigQuery connector lets them work together.

Points to Remember

- **Apache Beam** is the programming model; **Dataflow** is the managed execution engine that runs Beam pipelines on Google Cloud.
- **PCollections** are distributed datasets that flow through a pipeline. They can be bounded (batch) or unbounded (streaming).
- **`PTransforms`** (such as `Map`, `Filter`, `GroupByKey`, and `CombineGlobally`) are chained using the pipe operator (|) to form a processing DAG.
- **Batch versus Streaming:** Batch processes finite data and terminates. Streaming processes continuous data and runs indefinitely.
- **Windowing** is required for streaming aggregations. Fixed windows divide time into non-overlapping buckets; triggers control when results are emitted.
- **Runners** are interchangeable. Use `DirectRunner` for local testing and `DataflowRunner` for cloud execution–pipeline code stays the same.
- **`WriteToBigQuery`** supports `WRITE_TRUNCATE` for batch (overwrite) and `WRITE_APPEND` for streaming (incremental).
- **Autoscaling** in Dataflow adjusts worker count automatically. Use `--max_num_workers` to cap costs.
- **Drain** a streaming job instead of cancelling it. Drain flushes buffered data to the sink before shutting down workers.
- **Cost Awareness:** Batch jobs cost per run ($0.50-$1.00 for small datasets). Streaming jobs cost per hour (~$2-3/h) because workers run continuously.

Multiple Choice Questions

1. What is the relationship between Apache Beam and Google Cloud Dataflow?
   a. They are the same product with different names
   b. Beam is a programming model; Dataflow is a managed runner that executes Beam pipelines
   c. Dataflow is an open-source alternative to Beam
   d. Beam is a GCP-exclusive SDK that only runs on Dataflow
2. What is a `PCollection` in Apache Beam?
   a. A Python collection type such as a list or dictionary
   b. A configuration object for pipeline settings
   c. A distributed dataset of elements flowing through the pipeline
   d. A BigQuery table reference
3. How does a batch pipeline differ from a streaming pipeline?
   a. Batch pipelines use Python; streaming pipelines use Java
   b. Batch pipelines process bounded data and terminate; streaming pipelines process unbounded data continuously
   c. Batch pipelines cannot write to BigQuery
   d. Streaming pipelines are always faster than batch pipelines
4. Why is windowing required for streaming aggregations?
   a. To improve query performance in BigQuery
   b. To limit the number of workers Dataflow provisions
   c. Because GroupByKey cannot operate on unbounded data without finite grouping boundaries
   d. To encrypt data in transit between Pub/Sub and BigQuery
5. What does the **`AfterWatermark(early=AfterProcessingTime(30))`** trigger configuration do?
   a. Delays all processing for 30 seconds
   b. Emits partial windowed results every 30 seconds before the window closes

   c. Limits the pipeline to processing 30 elements per second

   d. Restarts failed workers every 30 seconds

6. What is the correct write disposition for a streaming pipeline writing to BigQuery?

   a. `WRITE_TRUNCATE`: overwrite the table on each window

   b. `WRITE_EMPTY`: only write if the table is empty

   c. `WRITE_APPEND`: append new windowed results as additional rows

   d. `WRITE_REPLACE`: replace matching rows based on primary key

7. What happens when you choose "**`Drain`**" instead of "**`Cancel`**" to stop a streaming Dataflow job?

   a. The job immediately terminates, and all data is lost.

   b. The job stops reading new input but finishes processing in-flight data before shutting down.

   c. The job pauses and can be resumed later.

   d. The job switches from streaming to batch mode to finish processing.

8. Which transform would you use to apply a function that returns multiple output elements per input element?

   a. `beam.Map`

   b. `beam.Filter`

   c. `beam.FlatMap`

   d. `beam.GroupByKey`

9. What is the purpose of `` `CombineFn` `` in Apache Beam?

   a. To merge multiple pipelines into one

   b. To define custom aggregation logic with explicit accumulator, merge, and extract operations

   c. To combine different data sources into a single PCollection

   d. To join two PCollections on a common key

10. How does Dataflow autoscaling work for streaming jobs?

   a. You must manually specify the exact number of workers.

   b. Dataflow adds or removes workers based on system lag and data backlog.

c. Workers are fixed at the number specified by `--num_workers`.

d. Autoscaling only works for batch jobs, not streaming.

Answers

1. b
2. c
3. b
4. c
5. b
6. c
7. b
8. c
9. b
10. b

Questions

1. Explain the three core abstractions in Apache Beam (Pipeline, PCollection, PTransform). How do they relate to each other, and what role does the pipe operator (|) play in connecting them?

2. A data engineer needs to process both a nightly CSV export (2 million rows) and a live Pub/Sub event stream using the same transformation logic. How does Beam's unified model allow this without duplicating code?

3. Compare Fixed Windows and Session Windows. Provide a concrete use case where each would be appropriate, and explain why the wrong choice would produce misleading results.

4. Describe the Dataflow job lifecycle for a streaming pipeline, from submission to draining. What happens to in-flight data at each stage, and why should you never use "`Cancel`" on a production streaming job?

5. Walk through the execution of the batch pipeline from this chapter. For each transform step (`Read CSV` → `Parse` → `Filter` → `Extract` → `GroupByKey` → `Sum` → `Write`), explain what the input `PCollection` and the output `PCollection` look like.

6. A streaming pipeline is showing increasing system lag in the Dataflow console. List three potential causes and the corresponding remediation steps.
7. Explain the difference between `WRITE_TRUNCATE` and `WRITE_APPEND` in `WriteToBigQuery`. Why would using `WRITE_TRUNCATE` in a streaming pipeline cause data loss?
8. Your streaming pipeline uses 60-second fixed windows with an early trigger firing every 30 seconds. If 50 messages arrive in the first 30 seconds and 30 more arrive in the remaining 30 seconds, how many early and final firings occur, and what does each contain under `DISCARDING` accumulation mode?

Key Terms

- **Apache Beam:** An open-source programming model for defining both batch and streaming data processing pipelines using a single API.
- **Pipeline:** The top-level Beam object that encapsulates an entire data processing workflow from source to sink.
- **PCollection:** A distributed, immutable collection of elements that flows through a Beam pipeline. Can be bounded (batch) or unbounded (streaming).
- **PTransform:** An operation applied to a PCollection, such as `Map`, `Filter`, `GroupByKey`, or `CombineGlobally`.
- **Runner:** The execution engine that processes a Beam pipeline. Examples include DirectRunner (local), DataflowRunner (Google Cloud), and FlinkRunner (Apache Flink).
- **DirectRunner:** A local runner used for development and testing. Executes the pipeline on a single machine without cloud infrastructure.
- **DataflowRunner:** Google Cloud's managed runner that distributes pipeline execution across autoscaling worker VMs.
- **Google Cloud Dataflow:** A fully managed service for executing Apache Beam pipelines at scale on Google Cloud.
- **Bounded PCollection:** A finite dataset with a defined beginning and end. Processed by batch pipelines.
- **Unbounded PCollection:** A continuous data stream with no defined end. Processed by streaming pipelines.
- **Fixed Window:** A windowing strategy that divides time into non-overlapping intervals of a fixed duration.
- **Sliding Window:** A windowing strategy with overlapping intervals, allowing an element to belong to multiple windows.

- **Session Window:** A windowing strategy that groups elements arriving within a gap duration, closing the window after inactivity.
- **Watermark:** A system-generated timestamp that tracks event-time progress in a streaming pipeline, indicating when it is safe to emit windowed results.
- **Trigger:** A mechanism that controls when windowed aggregation results are emitted. Supports early firing (partial results) and late firing (updated results for late data).
- **Accumulation Mode:** Determines how multiple firings for the same window are combined. `DISCARDING` emits only new elements; `ACCUMULATING` emits the full cumulative result.
- **CombineFn:** A Beam class for defining custom aggregation logic with explicit methods for creating accumulators, adding inputs, merging partial results, and extracting output.
- **Pub/Sub:** Google Cloud's messaging service for real-time event ingestion. Used as the source for streaming Beam pipelines.
- **Drain:** A clean shutdown mechanism for streaming Dataflow jobs. Stops reading new input but finishes processing buffered data before terminating.
- **Autoscaling:** Dataflow's automatic adjustment of worker count based on pipeline backlog and system lag.
- **System Lag:** A streaming metric measuring the delay between when data arrives and when it is processed. High lag indicates the pipeline is falling behind.
- **Data Freshness:** A streaming metric indicating the age of the most recently processed element. Lower values mean the pipeline is processing near-real-time.

CHAPTER 9
Spark and BigQuery Integration

Introduction

Apache Spark is the standard for open-source distributed data processing. For over a decade, it has been the foundation of big data engineering, powering massive Extract, Transform, and Load (ETL) pipelines, complex Machine Learning (ML) workloads, and streaming applications. While BigQuery provides unparalleled serverless SQL analytics, many organizations already have substantial investments in Spark–whether in on-premises Hadoop clusters or cloud-native Dataproc environments.

The good news is that you do not have to choose between Spark and BigQuery. In fact, they are highly complementary. This chapter will explore how Spark workloads running on Google Cloud Dataproc can work together with BigQuery. We will examine the Spark–BigQuery connector, compare when to use Spark versus BigQuery's native SQL, and walk through the architectural patterns for designing hybrid ETL and Extract, Load, and Transform (ELT) pipelines that leverage the strengths of both engines.

By the end of this chapter, you will learn to use the Spark–BigQuery connector for high-throughput data transfer, differentiate between workloads best suited for Spark versus BigQuery native SQL, provision and manage ephemeral Google Cloud Dataproc clusters, and design as well as execute practical Hybrid ETL and ELT pipelines.

Structure

In this chapter, we will cover the following topics:

- Spark versus BigQuery
- The Spark–BigQuery Connector
- Dataproc: Managed Spark on Google Cloud

- Designing Hybrid ETL and ELT Pipelines
- Hands-on Lab

Spark versus BigQuery

A common dilemma in modern data architecture is deciding where a transformation should run. Should the pipeline execute in Spark, or should the raw data be loaded directly into BigQuery for SQL-based transformations–as we saw with `dbt` in *Chapter 7, ELT with dbt and BigQuery*?

The answer depends entirely on the nature of the transformation workload.

Strengths of BigQuery (SQL)

BigQuery is optimized for structured data, fast aggregations, and analytical queries. You should push transformations into BigQuery SQL whenever possible, especially for:

- Filtering, joining, and aggregating structured tables.
- Table-to-table ELT workflows where the data safely resides within BigQuery.
- Reporting layer views and ad-hoc analytics.

Using BigQuery native SQL minimizes data movement, avoids the overhead of managing distributed compute clusters, and provides a much lower barrier to entry for analysts.

Strengths of Apache Spark

Spark shines where declarative SQL struggles. As Spark operates using general-purpose programming languages such as Python, Scala, and Java, it also provides complete flexibility over how data is processed. You should utilize Spark for:

- **Complex Graph Analysis**: Algorithms such as PageRank or deep connection network mapping–such as finding products frequently bought together across millions of shopping carts–are notoriously difficult and inefficient in pure SQL.
- **Iterative ML**: Preparing heavy feature engineering pipelines or training custom machine learning models using MLlib.
- **Complex Data Ingestion**: Parsing deeply nested JSON, malformed XML, or unstructured log files before they reach the clean and structured realm of the data warehouse.
- **Legacy Code Migrations**: Moving the existing on-premises Hadoop/Spark

workloads to the cloud without rewriting tens of thousands of lines of code into SQL.

- **Differing Design Choices in Practice:** To understand why you might choose one over the other, consider parsing a deeply nested, irregular JSON file. If you force this into BigQuery SQL, you will write extremely complex `JSON_EXTRACT` and `UNNEST` queries that are hard to maintain and expensive to run on unstructured text.

If you choose `Spark,` Spark's programmatic nature makes this trivial:

```
# Spark elegantly infers complex JSON schemas
df = spark.read.json("gs://bucket/raw_logs/*.json")
# Flatten and write clean tabular data to BigQuery
df.write.format("bigquery").option("table", "dataset.clean_logs").
save()
```

This is why the hybrid pattern is so prevalent: use Spark to programmatically clean the chaotic data, and then use BigQuery to analyze the structured results.

The Hybrid Approach

Effective enterprise data platform architectures utilize both. A typical hybrid pattern involves using Spark for complex, programmatic heavy lifting (such as the Extract and Transform phase) to prepare data, and then landing that semi-processed data into BigQuery. Once in BigQuery, further downstream transformations, aggregations, and business logic are applied using SQL (such as the final Load and Transform phase).

The Spark–BigQuery Connector

To facilitate this hybrid architecture, Google maintains the Spark–BigQuery connector. This open-source connector allows Spark to read and write data from and write data to BigQuery using the standard Spark SQL DataFrame API.

Behind the scenes, the connector is highly optimized in the following manner:

- **Reading Data**: It uses the BigQuery Storage Read API. Instead of executing a slow query and paginating through the results, the Storage Read API streams data directly from BigQuery's underlying Colossus storage into the memory of your Spark workers in parallel using gRPC. Furthermore, it supports "predicate pushdown"–which means that if you add a `.filter()` to your Spark DataFrame, that filter is passed down to BigQuery, so that only the necessary rows are transmitted over the network.
- **Writing Data**: To write data to BigQuery, the connector temporarily writes the Spark DataFrame partitions as Apache Parquet files to a designated Cloud

Storage bucket. It then triggers a high-speed BigQuery Load Job to ingest those Parquet files into the target table, and finally cleans up the temporary bucket.

Owing to this architecture, moving large datasets between a Spark cluster and BigQuery takes minutes, not hours.

Dataproc: Managed Spark on Google Cloud

To run Apache Spark, you need a cluster of compute nodes. Google Cloud Dataproc is a fully managed service that provisions, configures, and manages Hadoop and Spark clusters.

In traditional on-premises Hadoop environments, setting up a cluster takes weeks of hardware procurement and software configuration. Furthermore, as those clusters store data permanently on the nodes' local hard drives (HDFS), the clusters must remain running 24/7, resulting in high operational costs.

Dataproc changes this operational model by separating compute from storage in the following ways:

1. **Ephemeral Compute**: You spin up a Dataproc cluster in 90 seconds.
2. **Cloud Storage Integration**: The cluster reads its required data from BigQuery or Cloud Storage, avoiding the need for permanent HDFS storage.
3. **Delete on Completion**: Once the Spark job finishes, the cluster is immediately deleted.

As Dataproc scales easily and charges by the second, keeping clusters ephemeral ensures that you only pay for compute when data is actively being processed.

Designing Hybrid ETL and ELT Pipelines

The integration between Spark and BigQuery enables distinct architectural patterns depending on your goals.

The Spark ETL Pattern

In the classic ETL pattern, Spark acts as the processing engine outside the warehouse. Spark reads data from a source (such as Cloud Storage logs or BigQuery raw tables), uses its distributed memory to execute complex DataFrame transformations, and writes the final, clean analytical tables directly to BigQuery. The data enters BigQuery only when it is fully prepared for analysts to consume.

The Hybrid ELT Pattern

In the hybrid ELT approach, Spark is used specifically for the transformations that SQL handles poorly. For example, Spark might ingest raw logs, run a complex sessionization algorithm over user web clicks, and write those raw sessions to BigQuery. Once the sessions are in BigQuery, native SQL (often orchestrated by tools such as dbt) takes over to build the daily aggregates, marketing funnels, and executive dashboards.

Hands-on Lab: Building Hybrid Data Pipelines with Dataproc and BigQuery

In this lab, we will provision a Dataproc cluster and use PySpark to execute both a classic ETL pipeline and a Hybrid ELT pipeline. We will use the Spark–BigQuery connector to calculate customer segmentations, product affinity (which products are bought together), and Recency, Frequency, Monetary (RFM) scores from simulated e-commerce data.

Part 1: Environment Setup

First, let us configure the Google Cloud environment by enabling the required APIs for Dataproc, BigQuery, and Cloud Storage in the following manner:

```
# Set your project configuration
export PROJECT_ID="your-project-id"
export REGION="us-central1"
export ZONE="us-central1-a"
gcloud config set project $PROJECT_ID

# Enable requisite APIs
gcloud services enable dataproc.googleapis.com bigquery.googleapis.
com storage-api.googleapis.com compute.googleapis.com
```

Dataproc requires a Cloud Storage bucket to cleanly orchestrate Spark job scripts and hold temporary Parquet data as it transitions between Spark memory and BigQuery storage.

```
# Create a GCS bucket for Dataproc staging and scripts
export BUCKET_NAME="${PROJECT_ID}-dataproc-lab"
gcloud storage buckets create gs://${BUCKET_NAME} --location=US

# Create logical folder paths
echo "" | gcloud storage cp - gs://${BUCKET_NAME}/staging/.keep
```

```
echo "" | gcloud storage cp - gs://${BUCKET_NAME}/temp/.keep
echo "" | gcloud storage cp - gs://${BUCKET_NAME}/scripts/.keep
```

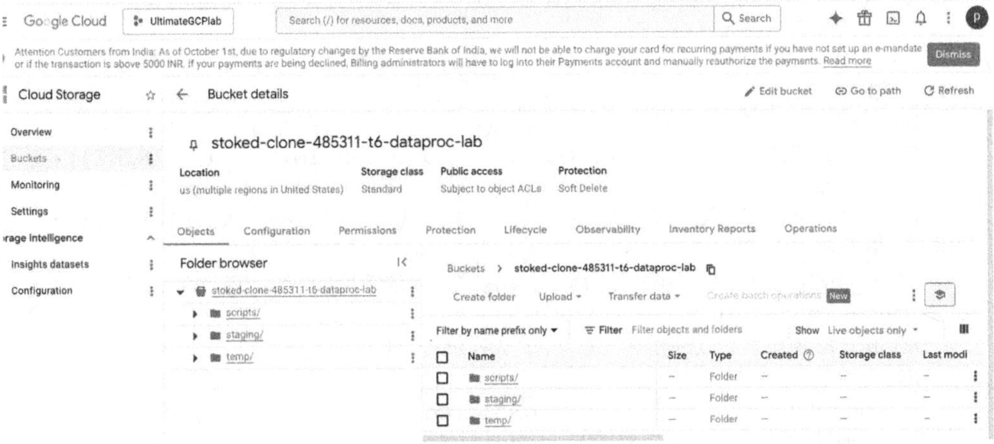

Figure 9.1: *Cloud Storage Browser Showing Created Bucket and Folders*

Next, we will establish our landing zone in BigQuery by creating a dataset and generating 100,000 synthetic e-commerce orders and 5,000 customer profiles:

```
CREATE SCHEMA `your-project-id.spark_lab`
OPTIONS (
  location = 'US',
  description = 'Spark & BigQuery integration lab dataset'
);
```

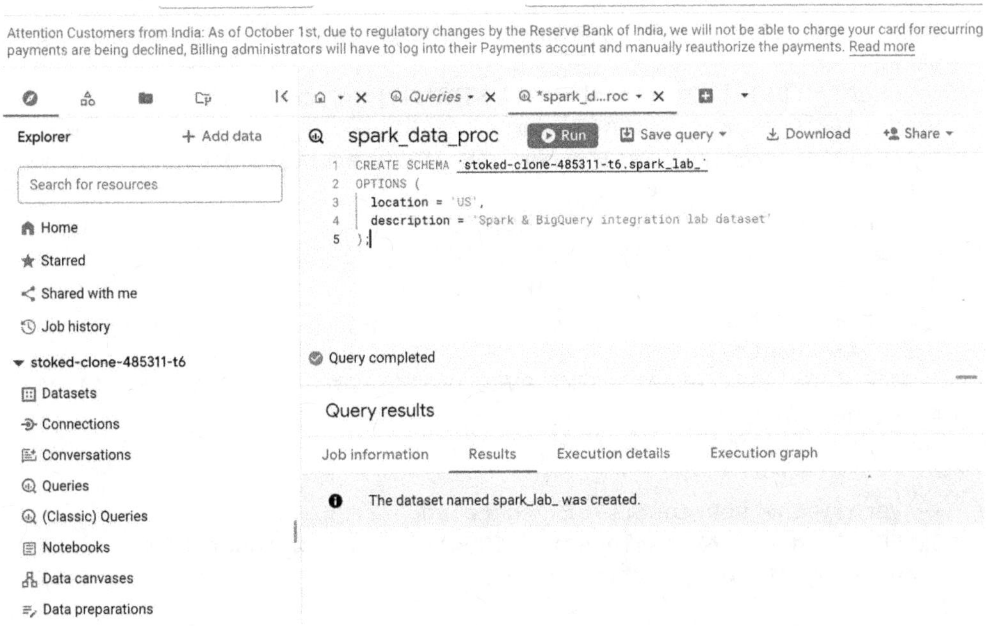

Figure 9.2: *BigQuery Showing spark_lab Dataset Created*

Run the following SQL in the BigQuery UI to generate the randomized sample data in the following way:

```
-- Create orders table
CREATE OR REPLACE TABLE `your-project-id.spark_lab.orders` AS
SELECT
  GENERATE_UUID() AS order_id,
  CONCAT('CUST', CAST(CAST(RAND() * 5000 AS INT64) AS STRING))
AS customer_id,
  CONCAT('PROD', CAST(CAST(RAND() * 500 AS INT64) AS STRING))
AS product_id,
  DATE_ADD('2023-01-01', INTERVAL CAST(RAND() * 365 AS INT64) DAY)
AS order_date,
  ROUND(RAND() * 1000 + 10, 2) AS amount,
  CASE
    WHEN RAND() < 0.7 THEN 'completed'
    WHEN RAND() < 0.9 THEN 'pending'
    ELSE 'cancelled'
  END AS status,
  CASE
    WHEN RAND() < 0.3 THEN 'Electronics'
    WHEN RAND() < 0.6 THEN 'Clothing'
    ELSE 'Home & Garden'
  END AS category
FROM UNNEST(GENERATE_ARRAY(1, 100000));

-- Create customers table
CREATE OR REPLACE TABLE `your-project-id.spark_lab.customers` AS
SELECT
  CONCAT('CUST', CAST(number AS STRING)) AS customer_id,
  CONCAT('Customer ', CAST(number AS STRING)) AS customer_name,
  CONCAT('customer', CAST(number AS STRING), '@example.com') AS email,
  CASE
    WHEN MOD(number, 4) = 0 THEN 'USA'
    WHEN MOD(number, 4) = 1 THEN 'UK'
    WHEN MOD(number, 4) = 2 THEN 'Canada'
    ELSE 'Australia'
  END AS country,
  DATE_ADD('2022-01-01', INTERVAL CAST(RAND() * 500 AS INT64) DAY)
AS signup_date
FROM UNNEST(GENERATE_ARRAY(1, 5000)) AS number;

-- Verify the row counts of generated data
SELECT 'orders' AS table_name, COUNT(*) AS row_count FROM
`your-project-id.spark_lab.orders`
```

```
UNION ALL
SELECT 'customers', COUNT(*) FROM `your-project-id.spark_lab.
customers`;
```

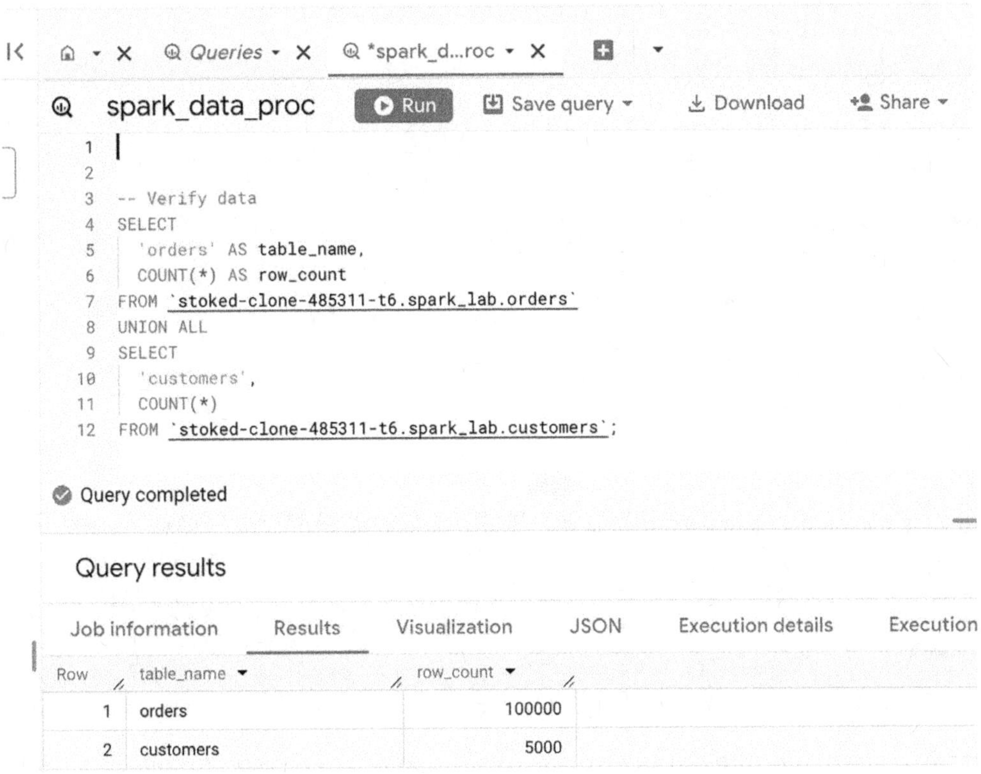

Figure 9.3: *BigQuery Output Showing Sample Data Loaded with Row Counts*

With the data staged, we provision the Dataproc cluster. Notice the following **--properties** flag in the command; it explicitly maps the open-source Spark BigQuery connector **jar** package into the cluster's distributed environment:

```
gcloud dataproc clusters create spark-bq-cluster \
  --region=${REGION} \
  --zone=${ZONE} \
  --master-machine-type=n1-standard-4 \
  --master-boot-disk-size=50GB \
  --num-workers=2 \
  --worker-machine-type=n1-standard-4 \
  --worker-boot-disk-size=50GB \
  --image-version=2.1-debian11 \
  --optional-components=JUPYTER \
  --enable-component-gateway \
  --metadata='PIP_PACKAGES=google-cloud-bigquery pandas' \
```

```
  --initialization-actions=gs://goog-dataproc-initialization-
actions-${REGION}/python/pip-install.sh \
  --properties=spark:spark.jars.packages=com.google.cloud.
spark:spark-bigquery-with-dependencies_2.12:0.32.2 \
  --max-idle=3600s
```

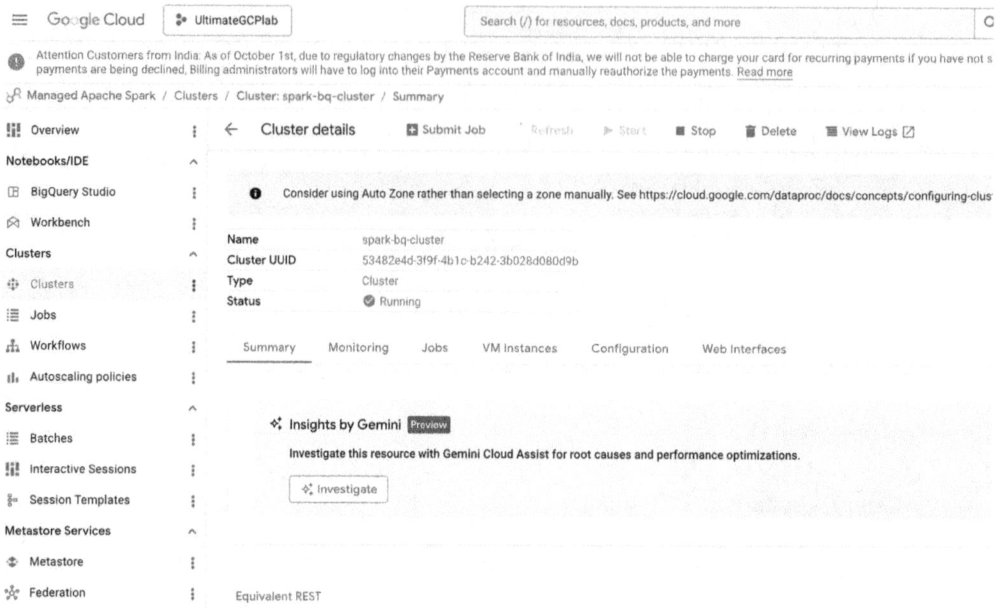

Figure 9.4: *Dataproc Console Showing Cluster Running with Component Gateway Enabled*

To verify that the integration works, we SSH into the cluster's master node and launch the PySpark shell to execute an interactive read in the following manner:

```
gcloud compute ssh spark-bq-cluster-m --zone=${ZONE}
--project=${PROJECT_ID}

# Once logged into the master node, launch the shell
pyspark

df = spark.read \
  .format("bigquery") \
  .option("table", "your-project-id.spark_lab.orders") \
  .load()

print(f"Loaded {df.count()} rows from BigQuery")
df.show(5)
```

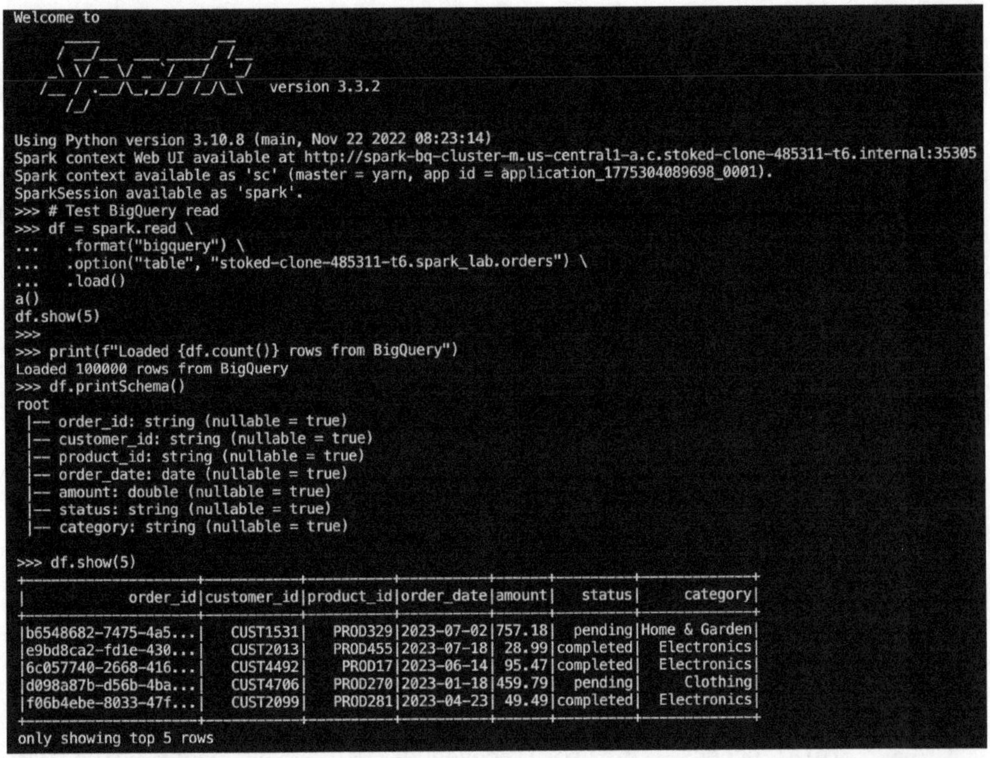

```
Welcome to
                                        version 3.3.2

Using Python version 3.10.8 (main, Nov 22 2022 08:23:14)
Spark context Web UI available at http://spark-bq-cluster-m.us-central1-a.c.stoked-clone-485311-t6.internal:35305
Spark context available as 'sc' (master = yarn, app id = application_1775304089698_0001).
SparkSession available as 'spark'.
>>> # Test BigQuery read
>>> df = spark.read \
...     .format("bigquery") \
...     .option("table", "stoked-clone-485311-t6.spark_lab.orders") \
...     .load()
a()
df.show(5)
>>>
>>> print(f"Loaded {df.count()} rows from BigQuery")
Loaded 100000 rows from BigQuery
>>> df.printSchema()
root
 |-- order_id: string (nullable = true)
 |-- customer_id: string (nullable = true)
 |-- product_id: string (nullable = true)
 |-- order_date: date (nullable = true)
 |-- amount: double (nullable = true)
 |-- status: string (nullable = true)
 |-- category: string (nullable = true)

>>> df.show(5)
+--------------------+-----------+----------+----------+------+---------+-------------+
|            order_id|customer_id|product_id|order_date|amount|   status|     category|
+--------------------+-----------+----------+----------+------+---------+-------------+
|b6548682-7475-4a5...|   CUST1531|   PROD329|2023-07-02|757.18|  pending|Home & Garden|
|e9bd8ca2-fd1e-430...|   CUST2013|   PROD455|2023-07-18| 28.99|completed|  Electronics|
|6c057740-2668-416...|   CUST4492|    PROD17|2023-06-14| 95.47|completed|  Electronics|
|d098a87b-d56b-4ba...|   CUST4706|   PROD270|2023-01-18|459.79|  pending|     Clothing|
|f06b4ebe-8033-47f...|   CUST2099|   PROD281|2023-04-23| 49.49|completed|  Electronics|
+--------------------+-----------+----------+----------+------+---------+-------------+
only showing top 5 rows
```

Figure 9.5: *PySpark Shell Showing Successful BigQuery Read with Schema and Sample Rows*

Part 2: ETL Pipeline with Spark

In this first pipeline, Spark does all the analytical work. The following script reads the raw orders and customers tables, joins them in distributed memory, calculates lifetime value metrics (such as **days_since_last_order** and **avg_order_value**), and writes the final curated table directly to BigQuery.

```
#!/usr/bin/env python3
from pyspark.sql import SparkSession
from pyspark.sql.functions import col, sum, count, avg, round, max,
min, datediff, current_date, when
import os
import sys

PROJECT_ID = os.getenv("PROJECT_ID", "your-project-id")

def main():
    spark = SparkSession.builder.appName("Customer Metrics ETL").
getOrCreate()

    # Extract
```

```
    orders_df = spark.read.format("bigquery").option("table",
f"{PROJECT_ID}.spark_lab.orders").load()
    customers_df = spark.read.format("bigquery").option("table",
f"{PROJECT_ID}.spark_lab.customers").load()

    # Transform
    completed_orders = orders_df.filter(col("status") == "completed")

    customer_metrics = completed_orders.groupBy("customer_id").agg(
        count("order_id").alias("total_orders"),
        sum("amount").alias("total_revenue"),
        avg("amount").alias("avg_order_value"),
        max("order_date").alias("last_order_date"),
        min("order_date").alias("first_order_date")
    )

    customer_metrics = customer_metrics.withColumn(
        "days_since_last_order", datediff(current_date(),
col("last_order_date"))
    )

    result = customers_df.join(customer_metrics, on="customer_id",
how="left").fillna({
        "total_orders": 0, "total_revenue": 0.0, "avg_order_value": 0.0
    })

    result = result.withColumn(
        "customer_segment",
        when(col("days_since_last_order").isNull(), "Never Ordered")
        .when(col("days_since_last_order") <= 30, "Active")
        .when(col("days_since_last_order") <= 90, "At Risk")
        .otherwise("Churned")
    )

    result = result.withColumn("total_revenue",
round(col("total_revenue"), 2))

    # Load
    result.write \
        .format("bigquery") \
        .option("table", f"{PROJECT_ID}.spark_lab.customer_metrics_
spark") \
        .option("temporaryGcsBucket", f"{PROJECT_ID}-dataproc-
lab/temp") \
        .mode("overwrite") \
        .save()
```

```
    spark.stop()

if __name__ == "__main__":
    main()
```

Save this as "**etl_pipeline.py**." To execute it, upload the file to Cloud Storage and submit the job to Dataproc via the following **gcloud** command-line:

```
gcloud storage cp etl_pipeline.py gs://${BUCKET_NAME}/scripts/

gcloud dataproc jobs submit pyspark \
  gs://${BUCKET_NAME}/scripts/etl_pipeline.py \
  --cluster=spark-bq-cluster \
  --region=${REGION}
```

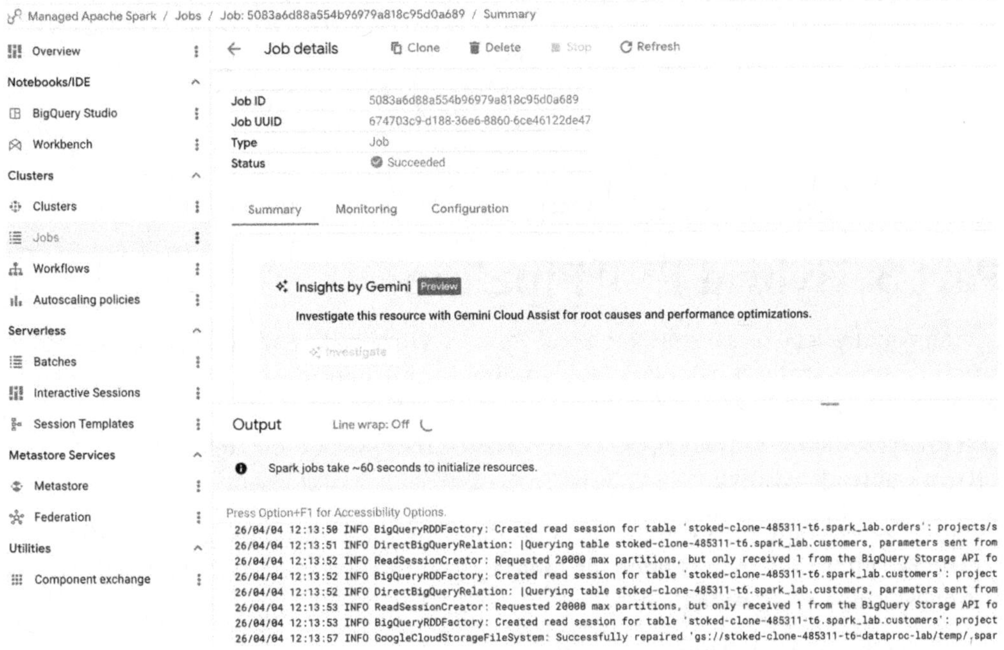

Figure 9.6: *Dataproc Console Showing Job Completed Successfully*

As Spark writes the metrics back directly as a polished table, an analyst can query the Spark-generated segments in BigQuery immediately in the following way:

```
SELECT
  customer_segment,
  COUNT(*) AS customer_count,
  SUM(total_revenue) AS segment_revenue,
  ROUND(AVG(total_orders), 1) AS avg_orders_per_customer
FROM `your-project-id.spark_lab.customer_metrics_spark`
GROUP BY customer_segment
ORDER BY segment_revenue DESC;
```

***Figure 9.7**: BigQuery Customer Segmentation Results from Spark ETL*

Part 3: Hybrid ELT Pipeline

Certain analytical patterns–such as graph traversal and complex windowing functions–can strain BigQuery's SQL engine. In this hybrid pipeline, we can leverage Spark's programmatic capabilities to perform a "Product Affinity" calculation. We find every combination of products that customers purchased together and map the network of transactions.

Once PySpark completes the heavy combinatorial math, it lands the raw affinities in BigQuery schemas (such as **`product_affinity`** and **`rfm_scores`**), allowing SQL analysts to finalize the aggregations.

```
#!/usr/bin/env python3
from pyspark.sql import SparkSession
from pyspark.sql.functions import col, collect_list, size, array_
distinct, explode, count, datediff, current_date, ntile, sum, max, when
from pyspark.sql.window import Window
import os

PROJECT_ID = os.getenv("PROJECT_ID", "your-project-id")
BUCKET = f"{PROJECT_ID}-dataproc-lab"

def main():
    spark = SparkSession.builder.appName("Hybrid ELT Pipeline")
.getOrCreate()
```

```
    orders_df = spark.read.format("bigquery").option
("table", f"{PROJECT_ID}.spark_lab.orders").load()

    # 1. Product Affinity (Graph Math)
    customer_products = orders_df.filter(col("status") == "completed") \
        .groupBy("customer_id") \
        .agg(array_distinct(collect_list("product_id")).alias
("products"))

    multi_product = customer_products.filter(size(col("products")) > 1)

    product_pairs = multi_product.alias("a") \
        .join(multi_product.alias("b"), col("a.customer_id")
== col("b.customer_id")) \
        .select(explode(col("a.products")).alias("product_a"),
col("b.products").alias("products_b")) \
        .select(col("product_a"), explode(col("products_b")).
alias("product_b")) \
        .filter(col("product_a") < col("product_b"))

    affinity = product_pairs.groupBy("product_a", "product_b") \
        .agg(count("*").alias("co_purchase_count")) \
        .filter(col("co_purchase_count") >= 5)

    # 2. RFM Windowing
    rfm_metrics = orders_df.filter(col("status") == "completed").
groupBy("customer_id").agg(
        datediff(current_date(), max("order_date")).alias("recency"),
        count("order_id").alias("frequency"),
        sum("amount").alias("monetary")
    )

    r_window = Window.orderBy(col("recency").desc())
    f_window = Window.orderBy(col("frequency"))

    rfm_scores = rfm_metrics.withColumn("r_score", ntile(5).over
(r_window)) \
                             .withColumn("f_score", ntile(5).over
(f_window)) \
                             .withColumn("rfm_score", col("r_score")
+ col("f_score"))

    # Write intermediate outputs to BQ
    affinity.write.format("bigquery").option("table", f"{PROJECT_ID}.
spark_lab.product_affinity")\
        .option("temporaryGcsBucket", f"{BUCKET}/temp").mode
("overwrite").save()
```

```
    rfm_scores.write.format("bigquery").option("table",
f"{PROJECT_ID}.spark_lab.rfm_scores")\
        .option("temporaryGcsBucket", f"{BUCKET}/temp").mode
("overwrite").save()

    spark.stop()

if __name__ == "__main__":
    main()
```

Submit this hybrid processing script similarly in the following way:

```
gcloud storage cp hybrid_elt_pipeline.py gs://${BUCKET_NAME}/scripts/

gcloud dataproc jobs submit pyspark gs://${BUCKET_NAME}/scripts/hybrid_
elt_pipeline.py --cluster=spark-bq-cluster --region=${REGION}
```

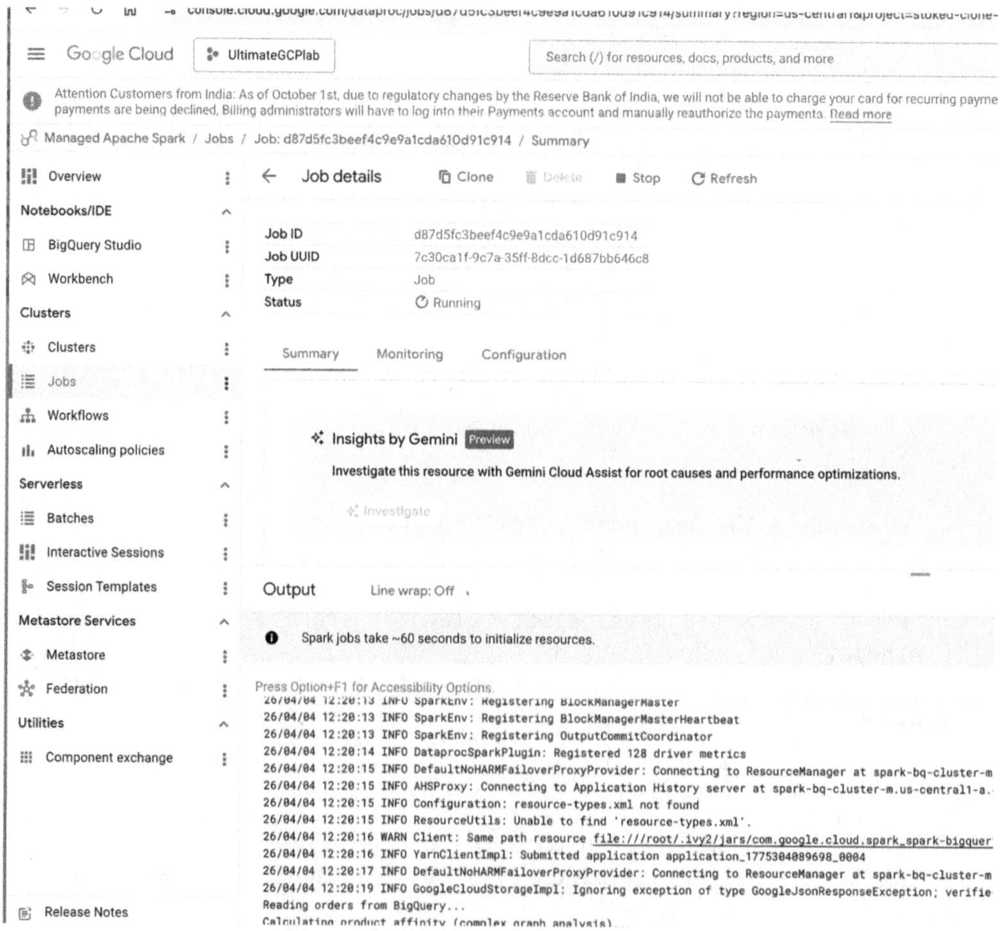

Figure 9.8: *Dataproc Hybrid ELT Job Running*

We can check the job section to see the detailed info, as demonstrated in *Figure* 9.9:

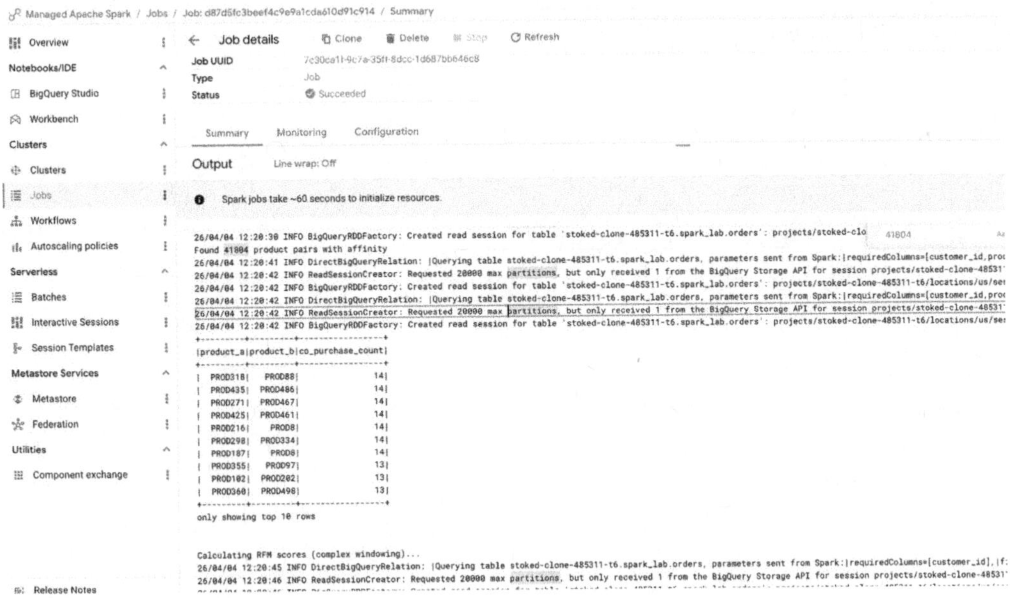

Figure 9.9: *Dataproc Job Logs Showing Calculations*

With the complex mathematics by PySpark, the results now safely reside inside BigQuery. We can execute the final "L" layer of the ELT pipeline by entirely using standard SQL to discover which product pairs are dominating the sales.

```
SELECT
  product_a,
  product_b,
  co_purchase_count,
  ROUND(co_purchase_count * 100.0 / (
    SELECT COUNT(DISTINCT customer_id)
    FROM `your-project-id.spark_lab.orders`
  ), 2) AS affinity_percentage
FROM `your-project-id.spark_lab.product_affinity`
ORDER BY co_purchase_count DESC
LIMIT 10;
```

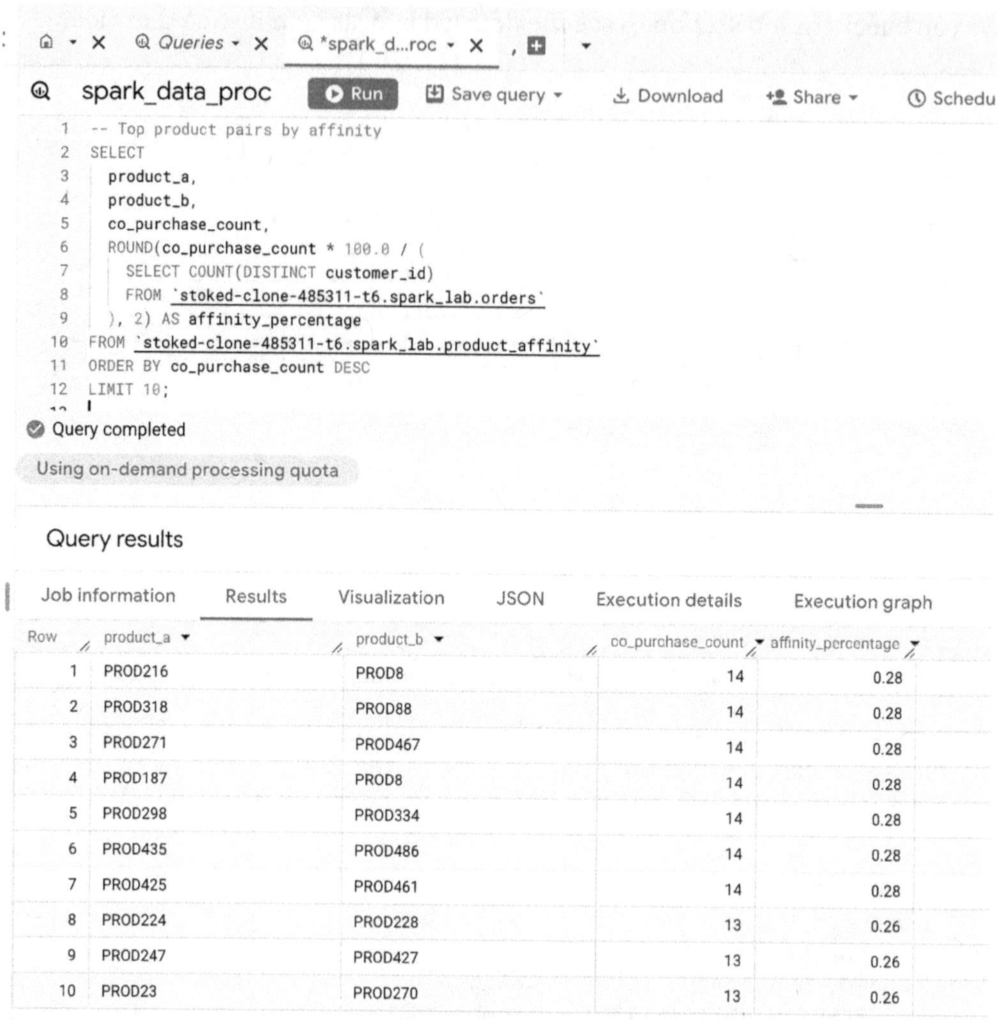

Figure 9.10: *BigQuery Product Affinity Results*

RFM segment distribution is demonstrated in *Figure 9.11*:

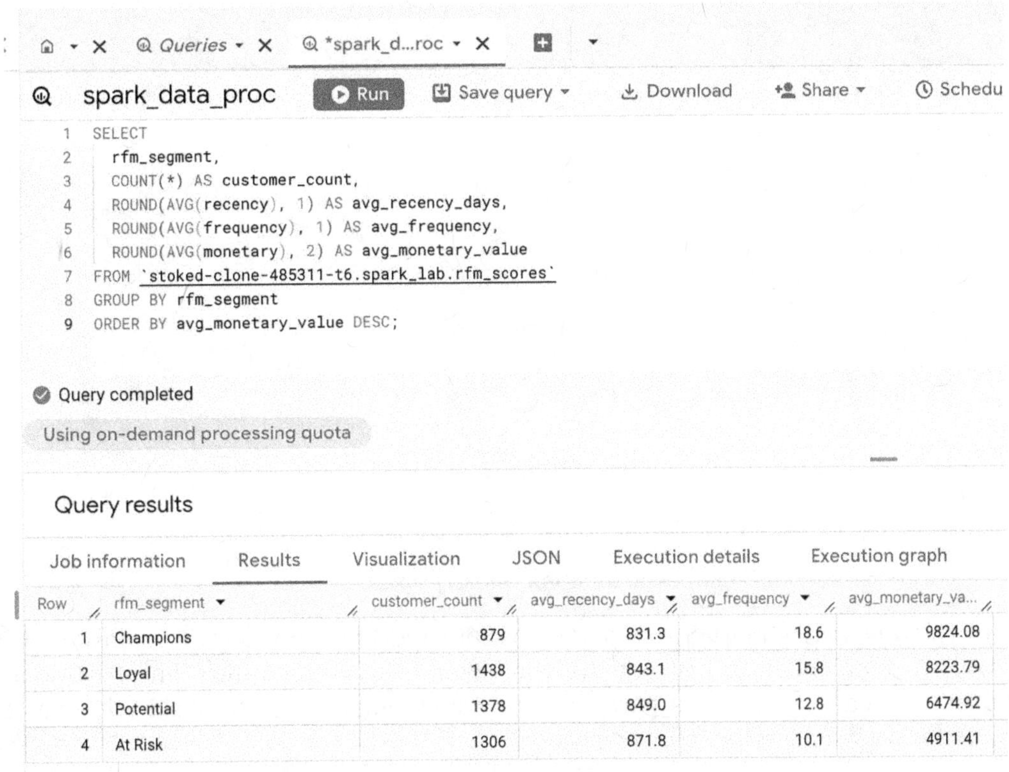

Figure 9.11: *BigQuery RFM Segment Distribution Results*

Part 4: Performance Optimization

As Spark distributes workloads across multiple machines, you can evaluate the actual performance profile inside the Dataproc interface under the "**`Monitoring`**" tab. Reviewing execution time, data processed, and shuffle bytes is critical to optimizing cluster sizing for enterprise workloads.

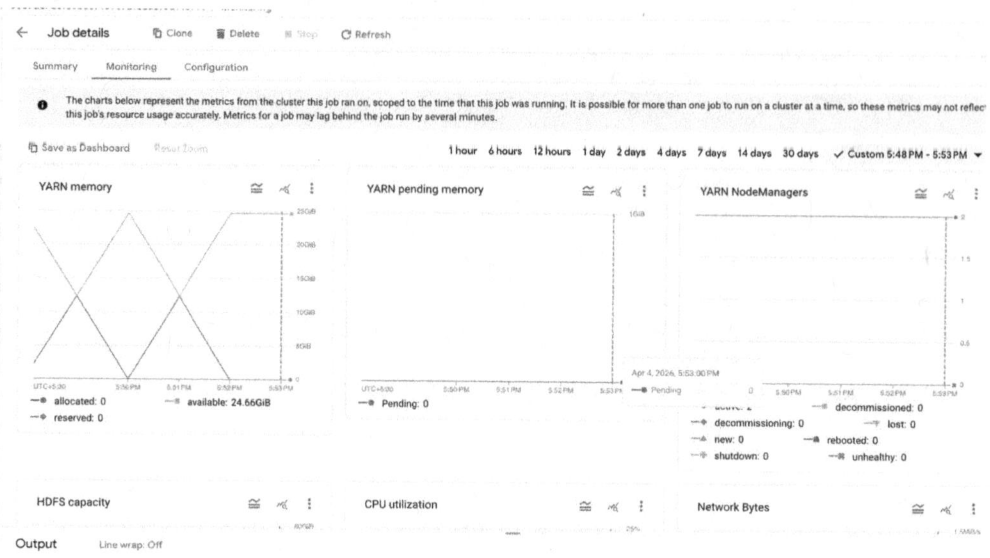

Figure 9.12: *Dataproc Job Performance Metrics*

Finally, to cleanly export Spark partitions into BigQuery on massive datasets, it is highly recommended to instruct the connector to write data into time-partitioned tables. You can execute this partitioned write command directly inside the master node PySpark shell in the following way:

```
df = spark.read.format("bigquery").option("table", "your-project-id.
spark_lab.orders").load()

# Write with partitioning explicit mapping
df.write \
    .format("bigquery") \
    .option("table", "your-project-id.spark_lab.orders_partitioned") \
    .option("partitionField", "order_date") \
    .option("partitionType", "DAY") \
    .option("temporaryGcsBucket", "your-project-id-dataproc-lab/
temp") \
    .mode("overwrite") \
    .save()
```

If we observe the BigQuery interface, we will now see our complete integration architecture materialized natively.

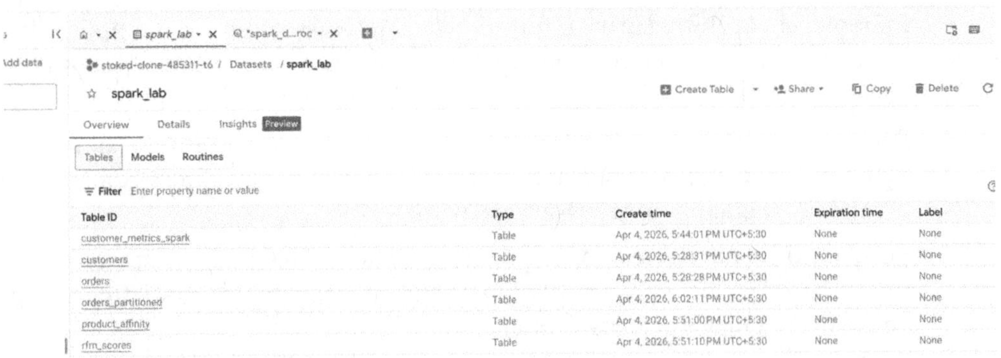

Figure 9.13: *Final BigQuery Dataset Tables*

Once the workloads are complete, standard practice dictates deleting the ephemeral Dataproc cluster immediately to stop compute costs from accruing in the following manner:

```
gcloud dataproc clusters delete spark-bq-cluster --region=${REGION}
--quiet
```

Conclusion

Apache Spark and BigQuery do not compete; rather, they complement each other. The open-source Spark–BigQuery connector binds the world's most popular distributed computing engine directly to the world's most powerful data warehouse.

By separating compute from storage, Dataproc allows organizations to orchestrate ephemeral Spark clusters exclusively when required. Whether replacing legacy Hadoop infrastructure, scaling complex graph algorithms, or cleaning chaotic upstream datasets before loading them into BigQuery, integrating Spark is a foundational skill for modern data engineers. By deliberately isolating where complex logic lives, you can build a more adaptable and cost-efficient enterprise data architecture.

In the next chapter, we will cover Cloud Composer orchestration, where we will learn to automate and orchestrate complex pipelines using Apache Airflow.

Points to Remember

- **Complementary Tools**: BigQuery is designed for fast SQL aggregates on structured data, whereas Spark handles complex programmatic transformations, algorithm-heavy jobs, and unstructured file parsing.
- **Connector Efficiency**: The Spark–BigQuery connector leverages the BigQuery Storage Read API and gRPC streams to read and write directly to and from Spark executor memory blazingly fast.

- **Ephemeral Architecture**: Dataproc facilitates separating compute from storage, allowing you to spin up Spark clusters only when data requires processing and immediately dismissing them upon completion.
- **Predicate Pushdown**: The Spark-BigQuery integration intelligently maps PySpark **`.filter()`** operations directly down into BigQuery table scans, drastically reducing unnecessary network traffic.
- **Parquet Intermediaries**: When Spark writes to BigQuery, it stages data as temporary Apache Parquet files in Cloud Storage before initiating a high-performance BigQuery Load Job.
- **Partitioning**: By explicitly declaring `partitionField` properties during a Spark write, large tables are natively partitioned inside BigQuery upon creation, significantly optimizing downstream SQL costs.
- **Hybrid Architectures**: "Spark for the T, BigQuery for the L" translates to executing complex tasks (such as product affinity graph building) on Spark clusters, and relying on native SQL for the final, clean analytics.

Multiple Choice Questions

1. Why is the Spark-BigQuery connector highly optimized for reading massive amounts of data from BigQuery?
   a. It issues paginated `SELECT` statements over `REST`.
   b. It uses the BigQuery Storage Read API with gRPC.
   c. It downloads the data entirely as CSV files onto the master node.
   d. It bypasses IAM permissions.
2. Which architecture concept makes Google Cloud Dataproc vastly more cost-efficient than legacy on-premises Hadoop deployments?
   a. Columnar sharding
   b. Predicate pushdown
   c. Separation of compute from storage
   d. Graph traversal
3. According to hybrid ELT best practices, which transformation is best executed in Spark rather than pure BigQuery SQL?
   a. `SUM()` and `GROUP BY` an established dimension table
   b. Parsing unstructured binary logs and navigating complex product-affinity graphs

   c. Finding the maximum value in an integer column

   d. Creating an authorized reporting view

4. How does Spark physically move data when submitting a `.save()` command to write a DataFrame into BigQuery?

   a. It writes rows one-by-one via the `BigQuery insertAll` Streaming API.

   b. It creates temporary Apache Parquet files in Cloud Storage and triggers a Load Job.

   c. It executes thousands of parallel SQL INSERT statements.

   d. It modifies BigQuery's internal proprietary storage binaries directly.

5. What Dataproc parameter ensures that you are not running up high costs when the Spark cluster finishes processing data?

   a. `--master-machine-type`

   b. `--optional-components`

   c. `--max-idle`

   d. `--image-version`

Answers

1. b
2. c
3. b
4. b
5. c

Questions

1. Describe the primary differences between workloads inherently optimized for BigQuery SQL versus Apache PySpark.
2. Explain the data movement pathway when a Spark cluster reads and writes from BigQuery using the official Connector.
3. Why do modern cloud architectures encourage shutting down Hadoop/Spark clusters (such as Dataproc) immediately after job completion, and how does this contrast with traditional data lake patterns?

Key Terms

- **Apache Spark:** An open-source distributed and unified analytics engine for large-scale data processing in memory.
- **Dataproc:** Google Cloud's fully managed service for provisioning and orchestrating Hadoop and Spark clusters quickly.
- **Spark-BigQuery Connector:** A native JAR library facilitating high-throughput, parallel data transfer directly between Spark dataframes and BigQuery storage APIs.
- **Predicate Pushdown:** An optimization engine capability where filters defined in Spark are evaluated directly at the database source (BigQuery), minimizing network data transfer.
- **Graph Analysis:** A programmatic analytical field designed to evaluate complex multi-node relationships, such as tracing which e-commerce products share the most purchasing affinity paths.

CHAPTER 10
Orchestration with Cloud Composer

Introduction

Over the last three chapters, you have built increasingly sophisticated data pipelines. *Chapter 7, ELT with dbt and BigQuery* introduced the data build tool (dbt) for modular Extract, Load, and Transform (ELT) transformations inside BigQuery. *Chapter 8, Apache Beam and Dataflow* showed how Apache Beam and Dataflow handle batch and streaming ingestion. *Chapter 9, Spark and BigQuery Integration* demonstrated hybrid Spark pipelines running on Dataproc that push results into BigQuery. Each of these tools solves a specific problem. However, in a real production environment, none of them run in isolation.

A typical daily data workflow might involve triggering a Dataflow batch job at midnight to ingest fresh files from Cloud Storage, followed by a series of dbt models that transform the ingested data into analytics-ready tables, followed by a Spark job that builds Machine Learning (ML) features, and finally a quality check that confirms that everything landed correctly before the morning dashboards refresh. Each step depends on the previous one completing successfully. If the Dataflow job fails, the dbt models should not run. If the dbt models produce zero rows, the downstream Spark job should not proceed.

This is the orchestration problem, solved by Cloud Composer.

Cloud Composer is Google Cloud's fully managed orchestration service, built on top of Apache Airflow–the most widely adopted open-source workflow scheduler in the data engineering ecosystem. In this chapter, you will learn how Airflow works, how Cloud Composer provisions and manages the infrastructure behind it, and how to design Directed Acyclic Graphs (DAGs) that reliably coordinate BigQuery, Dataflow, and Cloud Storage operations. Rather than treating orchestration as a theoretical exercise, we will build and deploy real DAGs into a running Composer environment, observing exactly how Airflow executes, retries, and monitors your pipelines.

Structure

In this chapter, we will cover the following topics:

- Orchestration Matters
- Apache Airflow Fundamentals
- Cloud Composer Architecture
- DAG Design Principles
- Integrating BigQuery, Dataflow, and Cloud Storage
- Reliability Patterns
- Monitoring and Operational Visibility

Orchestration Matters

If you have been following along with the previous chapters, you may have noticed a pattern. Every pipeline we built was triggered manually—by running a command in the terminal, submitting a job through the console, or clicking a button in the Dataproc UI. Manual execution works fine for learning and development. However, it does not work for production.

Production data systems require automation. Data needs to flow through the system on a daily schedule without human intervention. However, automation alone is not enough. You also need the following elements:

- **Dependency Management:** Step B must not start until Step A completes successfully.
- **Failure Handling:** If Step A fails, the system should retry it automatically; and if it keeps failing, it should alert someone instead of silently running Step B on incomplete data.
- **Backfill Capability:** If the pipeline was down for three days, you need to reprocess those three days of data in the correct order.
- **Visibility:** When someone asks "Did yesterday's pipeline run successfully?", you need a clear answer—not merely a log search.

Cron jobs on a virtual machine can handle basic scheduling, but they do not provide these capabilities. You get a timer, and that is all. There is no dependency graph, built-in retry logic, or visual UI to inspect execution history, and no mechanism for backfilling historical data. As soon as your pipeline has more than two or three steps, cron becomes a liability.

This is exactly why Apache Airflow was created.

Apache Airflow Fundamentals

Apache Airflow is an open-source platform for programmatically authoring, scheduling, and monitoring workflows. It was originally developed at Airbnb in 2014 to manage their increasingly complex data pipelines, and it has since become the industry standard for workflow orchestration.

Directed Acyclic Graph (DAG)

The central concept in Airflow is the Directed Acyclic Graph (DAG). A DAG is a Python file that defines a collection of tasks and their dependencies. The word "directed" means that the tasks flow in one direction (from upstream to downstream). The word "acyclic" means there are no circular dependencies–Task A cannot depend on Task B if Task B already depends on Task A.

The following is the simplest possible DAG:

```
from datetime import datetime
from airflow import DAG
from airflow.operators.python import PythonOperator

def say_hello():
    print("Hello from Airflow!")

with DAG(
    dag_id="hello_world",
    start_date=datetime(2024, 1, 1),
    schedule_interval="@daily",
    catchup=False,
) as dag:

    greet = PythonOperator(
        task_id="say_hello",
        python_callable=say_hello,
    )
```

The preceding DAG runs once per day. It contains a single task–that is, **`say_hello`**–that prints a message. In practice, DAGs contain dozens of tasks connected by dependency chains, but the structure is always the same: A Python file that defines the graph.

Tasks and Operators

A task is a single unit of work inside a DAG. Tasks are created by instantiating operators, which are pre-built classes that perform specific operations. Airflow provides hundreds of operators, but the ones most relevant to BigQuery data engineering are as follows:

- **`BigQueryInsertJobOperator`**: Executes a SQL query in BigQuery (such as **CREATE**, **INSERT**, **MERGE**, **SELECT**).
- **`BigQueryCheckOperator`**: Runs a SQL query and fails the task if the result is false (such as zero rows, null, or false). Ideal for data quality gates.
- **`DataflowStartFlexTemplateOperator`**: Launches a Dataflow job by using a Google-provided or custom Flex Template.
- **`GCSToBigQueryOperator`**: Loads files from Cloud Storage directly into a BigQuery table.
- **`PythonOperator`**: Runs any arbitrary Python function.
- **`BashOperator`**: Executes a shell command.

Task Dependencies

Dependencies determine the execution order. You define them using the **>>** operator in the following manner:

```
task_a >> task_b >> task_c          # Sequential: A → B → C
task_a >> [task_b, task_c]          # Fan-out: A → B and C run in
                                      parallel
[task_b, task_c] >> task_d          # Fan-in: D waits for both B and C
```

Airflow will never execute a downstream task until all of its upstream dependencies have completed successfully. This is the fundamental guarantee that makes orchestration reliable.

The Execution Model

When Airflow evaluates a DAG, it creates a **DAG Run**—a specific instance of the DAG tied to a logical execution date. Within each DAG Run, every task becomes a **Task Instance** with its own state: **queued**, **running**, **success**, **failed**, **up_for_retry**, or **skipped**. The Airflow scheduler continuously polls for DAG Runs to be created (based on schedules) and task instances ready to execute (based on dependency resolution).

Cloud Composer Architecture

You could install Airflow on a Compute Engine VM. Many teams have done this, and many have regretted it. Self-managed Airflow requires maintaining a metadata database (PostgreSQL), a message broker (Redis or RabbitMQ), a web server, a scheduler process, and worker nodes–each of which needs monitoring, scaling, and patching independently.

Cloud Composer eliminates this operational burden. When you create a Composer environment, Google provisions and manages the entire Airflow stack, including:

- **Google Kubernetes Engine (GKE) Cluster**: The Airflow scheduler, web server, and workers run as containers on a private GKE cluster.
- **Cloud SQL**: The Airflow metadata database runs as a managed Cloud SQL PostgreSQL instance.
- **Cloud Storage**: A dedicated GCS bucket stores your DAG files, plugins, and logs. Uploading a Python file to the **`dags/`** folder in this bucket automatically registers it with Airflow.
- **Cloud Logging**: All task logs are automatically shipped to Cloud Logging for centralized observability.

The preceding architecture means that deploying a DAG to production is as simple as copying a Python file to a GCS bucket. There are no servers to SSH into, no services to restart, and no deployment scripts to maintain.

Provisioning a Composer Environment

Let us put this into practice. To follow along, enable the required APIs and create a Composer environment in the following way:

```
# Set your project configuration
export PROJECT_ID="your-project-id"
export REGION="us-central1"
gcloud config set project $PROJECT_ID

# Enable APIs
gcloud services enable composer.googleapis.com \
  bigquery.googleapis.com \
  storage-api.googleapis.com \
  dataflow.googleapis.com

# Grant required IAM role to the Composer Service Agent
PROJECT_NUMBER=$(gcloud projects describe $PROJECT_ID
--format="value(projectNumber)")
gcloud iam service-accounts add-iam-policy-binding \
  ${PROJECT_NUMBER}-compute@developer.gserviceaccount.com \
  --member="serviceAccount:service-${PROJECT_NUMBER}@cloudcomposer
-accounts.iam.gserviceaccount.com" \
  --role="roles/composer.ServiceAgentV2Ext"
```

```
# Create the Composer 3 environment
gcloud composer environments create composer-bq-lab \
  --location=${REGION} \
  --image-version=composer-3-airflow-2.10.5-build.1
```

Note: *Composer environments take 15–25 minutes to provision. This is normal. The service provides a GKE cluster, deploys Airflow components, and configures networking.*

Once the environment reaches the **RUNNING** state, retrieve the Airflow web UI URL and the DAGs bucket in the following manner:

```
# Get the Airflow web UI URL
gcloud composer environments describe composer-bq-lab \
  --location=${REGION} \
  --format="value(config.airflowUri)"

# Get the DAGs bucket path
export DAGS_BUCKET=$(gcloud composer environments describe composer
-bq-lab \
  --location=${REGION} \
  --format="value(config.dagGcsPrefix)")
echo "DAGs bucket: ${DAGS_BUCKET}"
```

Before we start building DAGs, we need data to work with. The BigQuery dataset and sample data creation are covered in the next section; *Figure* 10.1 shows what the **composer_lab** dataset looks like after setup:

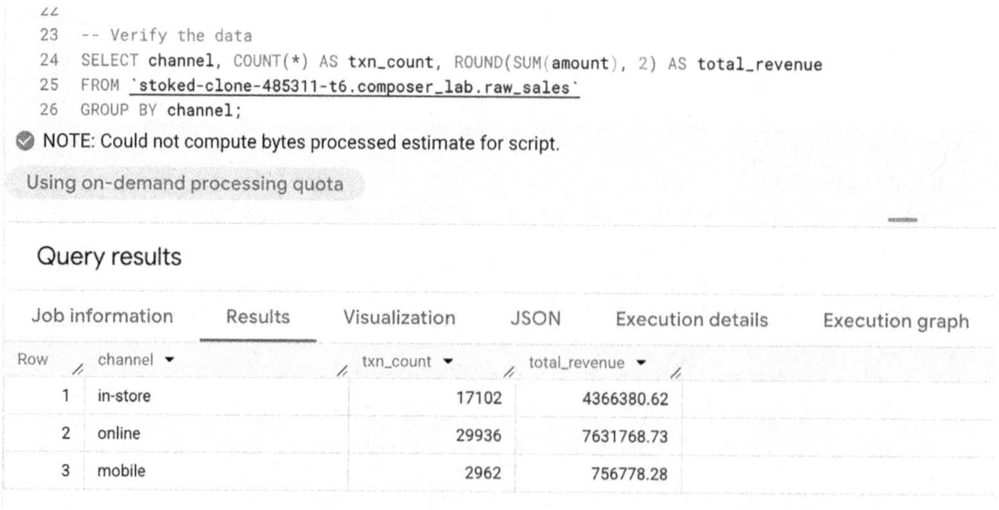

***Figure 10.1:** BigQuery Console Showing `composer_lab` Dataset with `raw_sales` Table and Channel Summary Query Results*

Open the Airflow URL in your browser. You will see the Airflow dashboard—an empty canvas waiting for your first DAG. This is the default view that every new Composer environment presents:

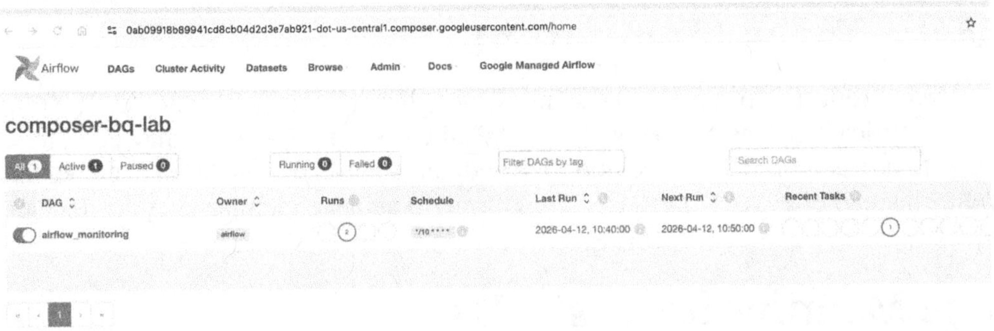

Figure 10.2: *Airflow Web UI Showing the Empty DAGs Dashboard after Initial Login*

Navigate to the **`Cloud Storage`** console to inspect the **`Composer`** bucket. You will find a **`dags/`** folder—this is where you will upload your Python DAG files.

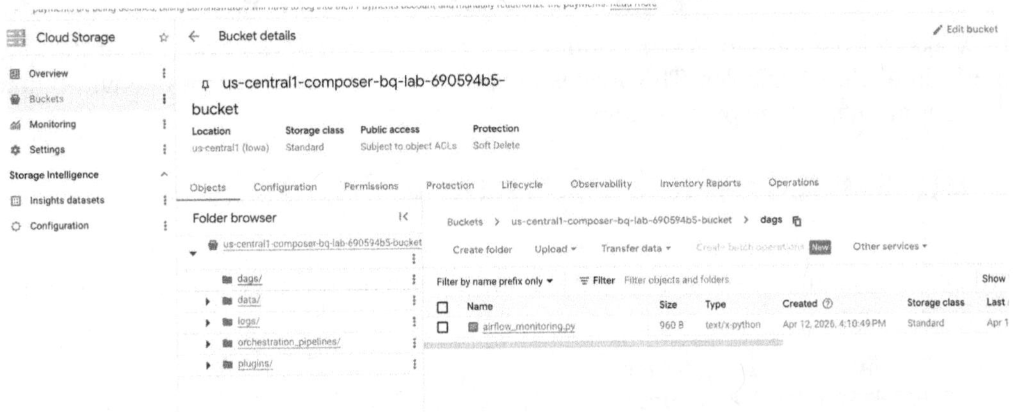

Figure 10.3: *Cloud Storage Browser Showing the Composer DAGs Bucket Structure*

DAG Design Principles

Before writing your first production DAG, it is worth understanding the design principles that separate clean and maintainable pipelines from the fragile ones.

Keep DAGs Declarative

A DAG file should declare the structure of the workflow—including what tasks exist and how they depend on each other. It should not contain heavy business logic. If a task needs to execute a complex transformation, that logic belongs in a BigQuery SQL query, a Dataflow template, or a Python module—not inline in the DAG file.

Make Tasks Idempotent

An idempotent task produces the same result whether you run it once or ten times. This is critical because Airflow will retry failed tasks, and operators may occasionally execute a task more than once due to scheduler restarts. Using **`CREATE OR REPLACE TABLE`** instead of **`INSERT INTO`** is a simple way to achieve idempotency for BigQuery tasks.

Use Meaningful Task IDs

When your DAG has 15 tasks, names such as "**`task_1`**" and "**`task_2`**" are useless in the Airflow UI. Use descriptive names such as "**`stage_raw_data`**," "**`check_row_count`**," and "**`build_customer_metrics`**." Your future self—and your on-call teammates—will thank you.

Separate Configuration from Logic

Keep project IDs, dataset names, and bucket paths as variables at the top of the DAG file or in Airflow Variables. This makes it easy to test DAGs in a staging environment without modifying the pipeline logic.

Your First DAG: A BigQuery Pipeline

Let us build a real DAG that creates and validates a BigQuery summary table. First, create some sample data in BigQuery. Run this SQL in the BigQuery console in the following way:

```
-- Create the lab dataset
CREATE SCHEMA `your-project-id.composer_lab`
OPTIONS (location = 'US', description = 'Cloud Composer
orchestration lab');

-- Generate 500 rows of simulated sales data
CREATE OR REPLACE TABLE `your-project-id.composer_lab.raw_sales` AS
SELECT
  GENERATE_UUID() AS transaction_id,
  CONCAT('CUST', LPAD(CAST(CAST(RAND() * 200 + 1 AS INT64) AS
STRING), 4, '0')) AS customer_id,
  CONCAT('PROD', LPAD(CAST(CAST(RAND() * 50 + 1 AS INT64) AS
STRING), 3, '0')) AS product_id,
  DATE_ADD('2024-01-01', INTERVAL CAST(RAND() * 180 AS INT64) DAY)
AS sale_date,
```

```
  ROUND(RAND() * 500 + 10, 2) AS amount,
  CASE
    WHEN RAND() < 0.5 THEN 'online'
    WHEN RAND() < 0.8 THEN 'in-store'
    ELSE 'mobile'
  END AS channel
FROM UNNEST(GENERATE_ARRAY(1, 500));

-- Quick channel breakdown to verify
SELECT channel, COUNT(*) AS sales, ROUND(SUM(amount), 2) AS revenue
FROM `your-project-id.composer_lab.raw_sales`
GROUP BY channel;
```

Now, create a file called "**bq_daily_summary.py**." This DAG runs two tasks: the first creates a daily sales summary table, and the second validates that the summary contains data.

```
"""
DAG: bq_daily_summary
Runs a daily BigQuery aggregation of sales data by channel and date.
"""
from datetime import datetime, timedelta
from airflow import DAG
from airflow.providers.google.cloud.operators.bigquery import (
    BigQueryInsertJobOperator
)

PROJECT_ID = "your-project-id"
DATASET = "composer_lab"

default_args = {
    "owner": "data-team",
    "depends_on_past": False,
    "email_on_failure": False,
    "retries": 2,
    "retry_delay": timedelta(minutes=2),
}

with DAG(
    dag_id="bq_daily_summary",
    default_args=default_args,
    description="Daily sales summary aggregation in BigQuery",
    schedule_interval="@daily",
    start_date=datetime(2024, 1, 1),
    catchup=False,
    tags=["bigquery", "lab"],
) as dag:
```

```
    create_summary = BigQueryInsertJobOperator(
        task_id="create_daily_summary",
        configuration={
            "query": {
                "query": f"""
                    CREATE OR REPLACE TABLE `{PROJECT_ID}.{DATASET}.
daily_sales_summary` AS
                    SELECT
                        sale_date,
                        channel,
                        COUNT(*) AS total_transactions,
                        ROUND(SUM(amount), 2) AS total_revenue,
                        ROUND(AVG(amount), 2) AS avg_transaction_
value,
                        COUNT(DISTINCT customer_id) AS unique_
customers
                    FROM `{PROJECT_ID}.{DATASET}.raw_sales`
                    GROUP BY sale_date, channel
                    ORDER BY sale_date DESC, total_revenue DESC
                """,
                "useLegacySql": False,
            }
        },
        location="US",
    )

    validate_summary = BigQueryInsertJobOperator(
        task_id="validate_summary_rows",
        configuration={
            "query": {
                "query": f"""
                    SELECT
                        IF(COUNT(*) > 0, 'PASS', 'FAIL')
AS validation_status,
                        COUNT(*) AS row_count,
                        COUNT(DISTINCT sale_date) AS distinct_dates,
                        COUNT(DISTINCT channel) AS distinct_channels
                    FROM `{PROJECT_ID}.{DATASET}.daily_sales_summary`
                """,
                "useLegacySql": False,
            }
        },
        location="US",
    )

    create_summary >> validate_summary
```

The following details in this DAG are worth examining:

- **`default_args`** are applied to every task in the DAG. Setting **`retries=2`** means that if any task fails, Airflow will automatically retry it twice before marking it as permanently failed.
- **`catchup=False`** prevents Airflow from backfilling every day between the **`start_date`** and today. Without this, Airflow would attempt to create hundreds of DAG Runs for historical dates.
- **`CREATE OR REPLACE TABLE`** ensures idempotency. Running this task ten times produces the same result.
- **The `>>` operator** establishes that **`validate_summary_rows`** will only execute after **`create_daily_summary`** succeeds.

Deploying the DAG

To deploy this DAG into your Composer environment, replace the project ID placeholder and upload the file to the DAGs bucket in the following way:

```
# Replace placeholder with your actual project ID and upload
sed -i '' "s/your-project-id/${PROJECT_ID}/g" bq_daily_summary.py
gcloud storage cp bq_daily_summary.py ${DAGS_BUCKET}/
```

Within one to two minutes, Airflow's scheduler will detect the new file and parse the DAG. Open the Airflow web UI, and you should see **`bq_daily_summary`** appear in the DAGs list:

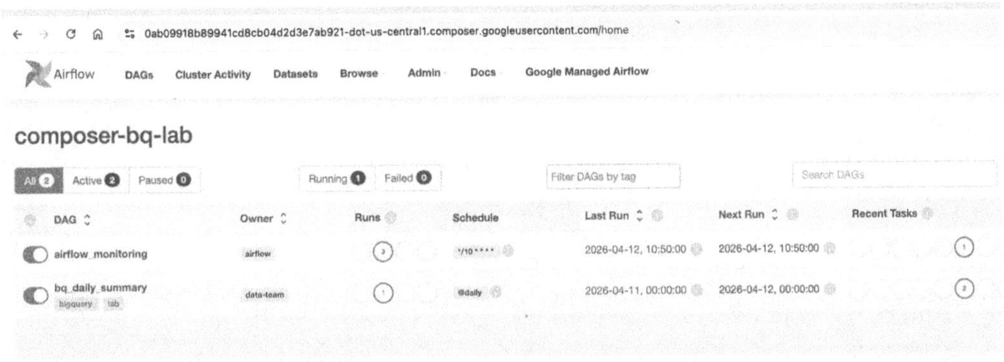

Figure 10.4: *Airflow DAG List Showing `bq_daily_summary` DAG as Registered and Active*

Click the DAG name, then select the "**Graph**" tab to visualize the task dependency chain:

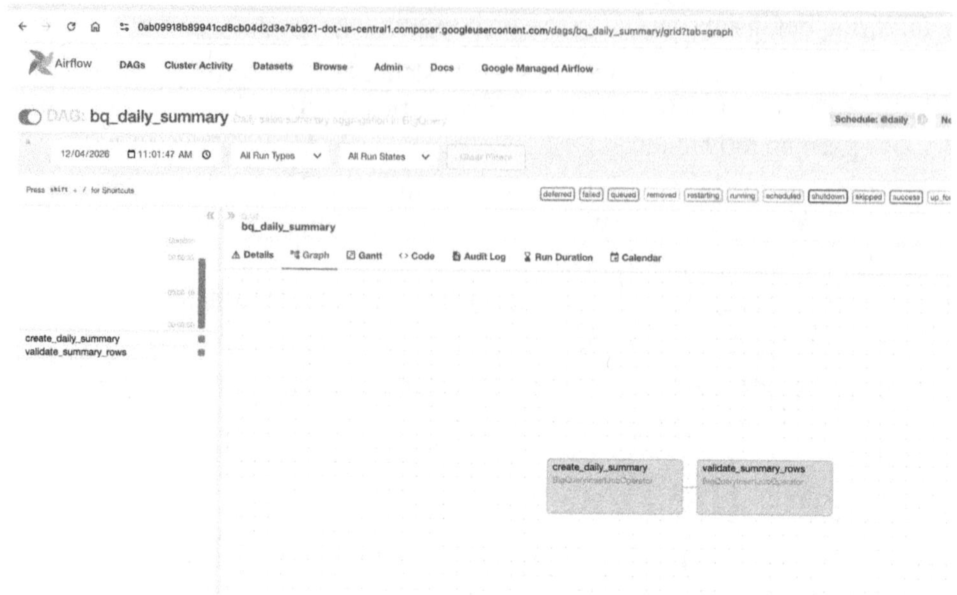

Figure 10.5: *Airflow Graph View Showing `create_daily_summary` → `validate_summary_rows` Task Dependency*

Trigger the DAG manually by clicking the **Play** button (▶) in the top right corner. Watch as each task transitions from **`queued`** to **`running`** to **`success`**. Once both tasks are green, click on "**`create_daily_summary,`**" and open the **`Log`** tab to see the actual BigQuery job ID and execution details.

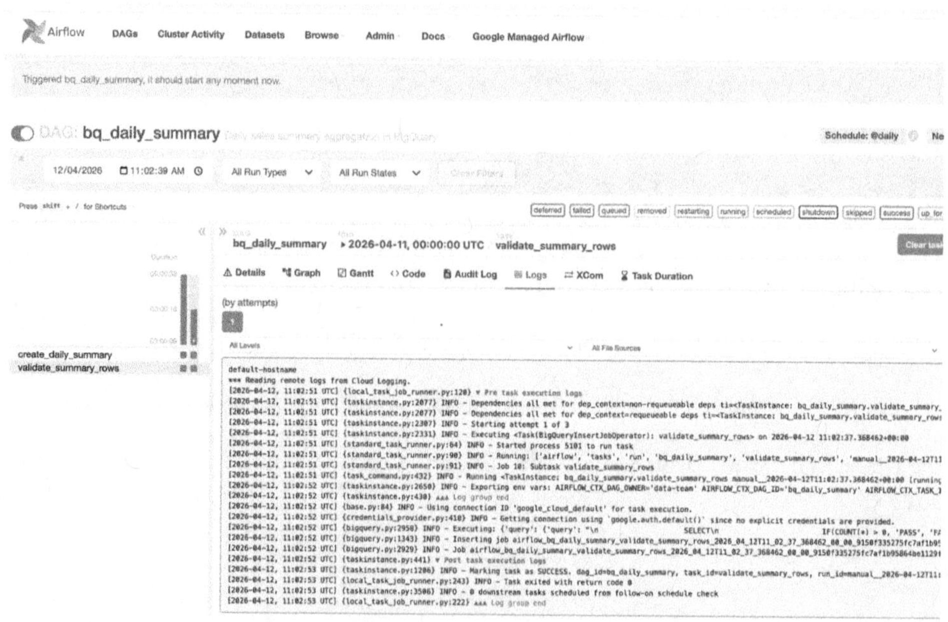

Figure 10.6: *Airflow Task Log Showing Successful BigQuery Job Execution with Query Details*

Verify the results directly in BigQuery in the following way:

```
SELECT * FROM `your-project-id.composer_lab.daily_sales_summary`
ORDER BY sale_date DESC
LIMIT 10;
```

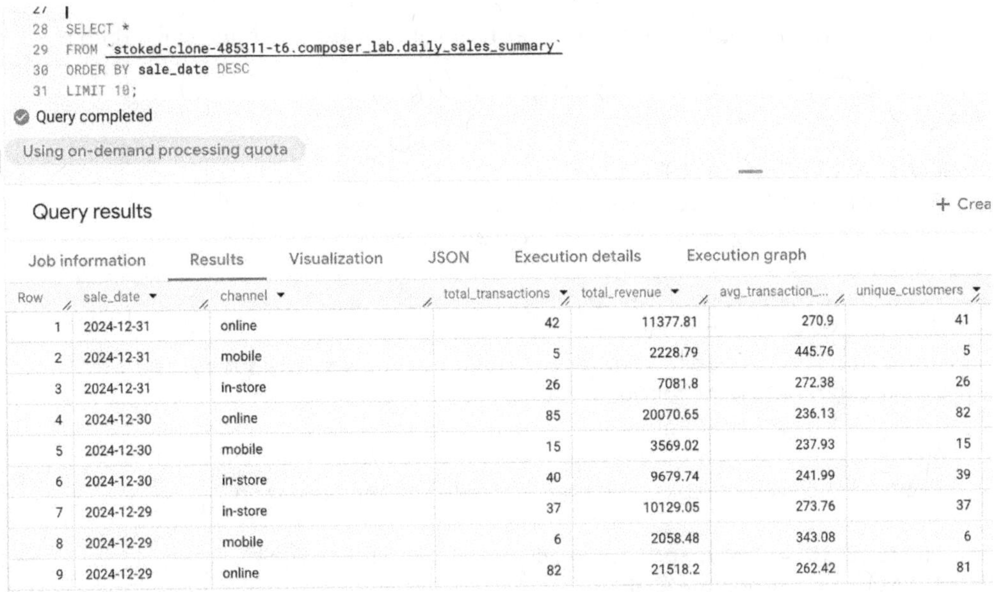

***Figure 10.7:** BigQuery Results Showing `daily_sales_summary` Table with Aggregated Sales Data*

What just happened is significant. You defined a pipeline in Python, uploaded it to a GCS bucket, and Airflow automatically detected, scheduled, executed, and logged the entire workflow. No servers, no cron, and no manual intervention.

Integrating BigQuery, Dataflow, and Cloud Storage

The real power of orchestration emerges when a single DAG coordinates multiple services. In production environments, data rarely flows through just one tool. A realistic pipeline might stage raw data into BigQuery, run quality checks, build parallel analytical tables, and export results to Cloud Storage—all within a single DAG.

Building a Multi-Step ELT Pipeline

The following DAG, **`elt_sales_pipeline`**, demonstrates a production-style ELT pattern with six tasks:

1. **Stage**: Snapshot raw data into a staging table with a timestamp.

2. **Quality Check**: Verify that the staging table has rows using **`BigQueryCheckOperator`**.
3. **Transform (Parallel):** Build **`customer_metrics`** and **`channel_performance`** tables simultaneously.
4. **Final Validation:** Confirm that both output tables exist and have data.
5. **Log Completion:** Record pipeline metadata.

```
"""
DAG: elt_sales_pipeline
Production-style ELT pipeline with staging,
transformation, quality checks, and cleanup.
"""
from datetime import datetime, timedelta
from airflow import DAG
from airflow.providers.google.cloud.operators.bigquery import (
    BigQueryInsertJobOperator,
    BigQueryCheckOperator
)
from airflow.operators.python import PythonOperator

PROJECT_ID = "your-project-id"
DATASET = "composer_lab"

default_args = {
    "owner": "data-team",
    "depends_on_past": False,
    "email_on_failure": False,
    "retries": 3,
    "retry_delay": timedelta(minutes=1),
    "execution_timeout": timedelta(minutes=30),
}

def log_pipeline_status(**context):
    """Log pipeline completion metadata."""
    ti = context["ti"]
    dag_run = context["dag_run"]
    print(f"Pipeline completed successfully!")
    print(f"DAG Run ID: {dag_run.run_id}")
    print(f"Execution Date: {dag_run.execution_date}")
    print(f"Task: {ti.task_id}")

with DAG(
    dag_id="elt_sales_pipeline",
    default_args=default_args,
    description="Multi-step ELT pipeline with quality checks",
```

```
    schedule_interval="@daily",
    start_date=datetime(2024, 1, 1),
    catchup=False,
    tags=["bigquery", "elt", "production"],
) as dag:

    # Step 1: Stage - Create a snapshot of raw data
    stage_data = BigQueryInsertJobOperator(
        task_id="stage_raw_data",
        configuration={
            "query": {
                "query": f"""
                    CREATE OR REPLACE TABLE `{PROJECT_ID}.{DATASET}.
stg_sales` AS
                    SELECT
                        transaction_id, customer_id, product_id,
                        sale_date, amount, channel,
                        CURRENT_TIMESTAMP() AS staged_at
                    FROM `{PROJECT_ID}.{DATASET}.raw_sales`
                    WHERE amount > 0
                """,
                "useLegacySql": False,
            }
        },
        location="US",
    )

    # Step 2: Quality check on staged data
    check_staged_rows = BigQueryCheckOperator(
        task_id="check_staged_data_quality",
        sql=f"""
            SELECT COUNT(*) > 0
            FROM `{PROJECT_ID}.{DATASET}.stg_sales`
        """,
        use_legacy_sql=False,
        location="US",
    )

    # Step 3a: Transform - Build customer metrics
    build_customer_metrics = BigQueryInsertJobOperator(
        task_id="build_customer_metrics",
        configuration={
            "query": {
                "query": f"""
                    CREATE OR REPLACE TABLE `{PROJECT_ID}.{DATASET}.
customer_metrics` AS
                    SELECT
```

```
                        customer_id,
                        COUNT(*) AS total_purchases,
                        ROUND(SUM(amount), 2) AS lifetime_value,
                        ROUND(AVG(amount), 2) AS avg_purchase,
                        MIN(sale_date) AS first_purchase,
                        MAX(sale_date) AS last_purchase,
                       DATE_DIFF(MAX(sale_date), MIN(sale_date), DAY)
                          AS customer_tenure_days,
                        COUNT(DISTINCT channel) AS channels_used
                    FROM `{PROJECT_ID}.{DATASET}.stg_sales`
                    GROUP BY customer_id
                """,
                "useLegacySql": False,
            }
        },
        location="US",
    )

    # Step 3b: Transform - Build channel performance
    build_channel_report = BigQueryInsertJobOperator(
        task_id="build_channel_performance",
        configuration={
            "query": {
                "query": f"""
                    CREATE OR REPLACE TABLE `{PROJECT_ID}.{DATASET}.
channel_performance` AS
                    SELECT
                        channel,
                        COUNT(*) AS total_transactions,
                        COUNT(DISTINCT customer_id) AS unique_cus-
tomers,
                        ROUND(SUM(amount), 2) AS total_revenue,
                        ROUND(AVG(amount), 2) AS avg_order_value,
                        ROUND(SUM(amount) / COUNT(DISTINCT customer
_id), 2)
                          AS revenue_per_customer
                    FROM `{PROJECT_ID}.{DATASET}.stg_sales`
                    GROUP BY channel
                    ORDER BY total_revenue DESC
                """,
                "useLegacySql": False,
            }
        },
        location="US",
    )
```

```
    # Step 4: Final quality check
    check_final_output = BigQueryCheckOperator(
        task_id="check_final_output",
        sql=f"""
            SELECT
                (SELECT COUNT(*) FROM `{PROJECT_ID}.{DATASET}.
customer_metrics`) > 0
                AND
                (SELECT COUNT(*) FROM `{PROJECT_ID}.{DATASET}.
channel_performance`) > 0
        """,
        use_legacy_sql=False,
        location="US",
    )

    # Step 5: Log completion
    log_completion = PythonOperator(
        task_id="log_pipeline_completion",
        python_callable=log_pipeline_status,
    )

    # Define dependencies (the DAG shape)
    stage_data >> check_staged_rows
    check_staged_rows >> [build_customer_metrics, build_channel_
report]
    [build_customer_metrics, build_channel_report] >> check_final_
output
    check_final_output >> log_completion
```

The dependency structure of this DAG is worth studying carefully. After staging and the quality check, the two transform tasks run in parallel—Airflow recognizes that **build_customer_metrics** and **build_channel_performance** have no dependency on each other, and schedules them simultaneously. This parallel execution is a key advantage of declarative orchestration. You do not need to write any threading or multiprocessing code; Airflow handles it naturally from the dependency graph.

Deploy and execute this DAG using the following pattern:

```
sed -i '' "s/your-project-id/${PROJECT_ID}/g" elt_pipeline.py
gcloud storage cp elt_pipeline.py ${DAGS_BUCKET}/
```

Once the DAG appears in the Airflow UI, click on it and open the **Graph** tab. Notice how the dependency declaration at the bottom of the Python file translates into a visual pipeline shape—the diamond pattern where tasks fan out after the quality check and converge before the final validation.

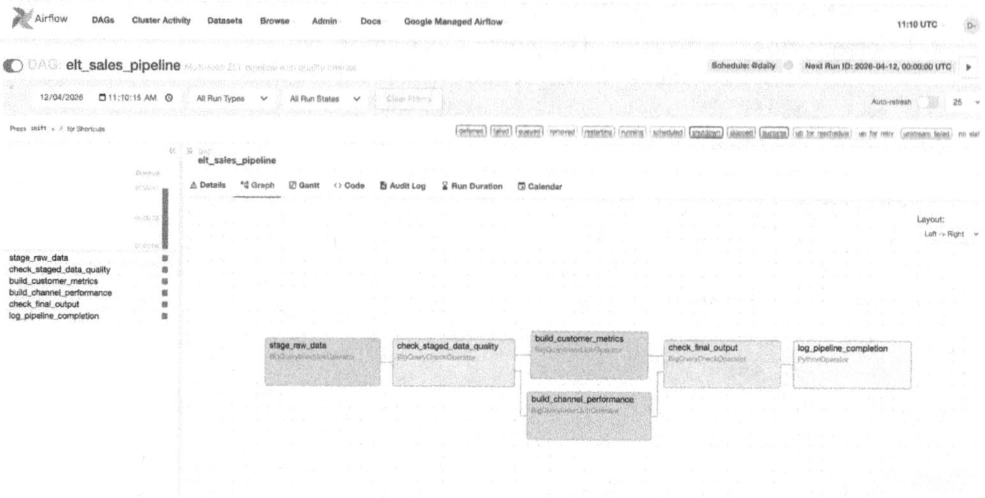

Figure 10.8: *Airflow Graph View Showing the Multi-Step ELT Pipeline with Parallel `build_customer_metrics` and `build_channel_performance` Branches*

Trigger the DAG manually. Watch the Grid view as tasks transition from "**queued**" to "**running**" to "**success**." All six tasks should be completed within a minute or two.

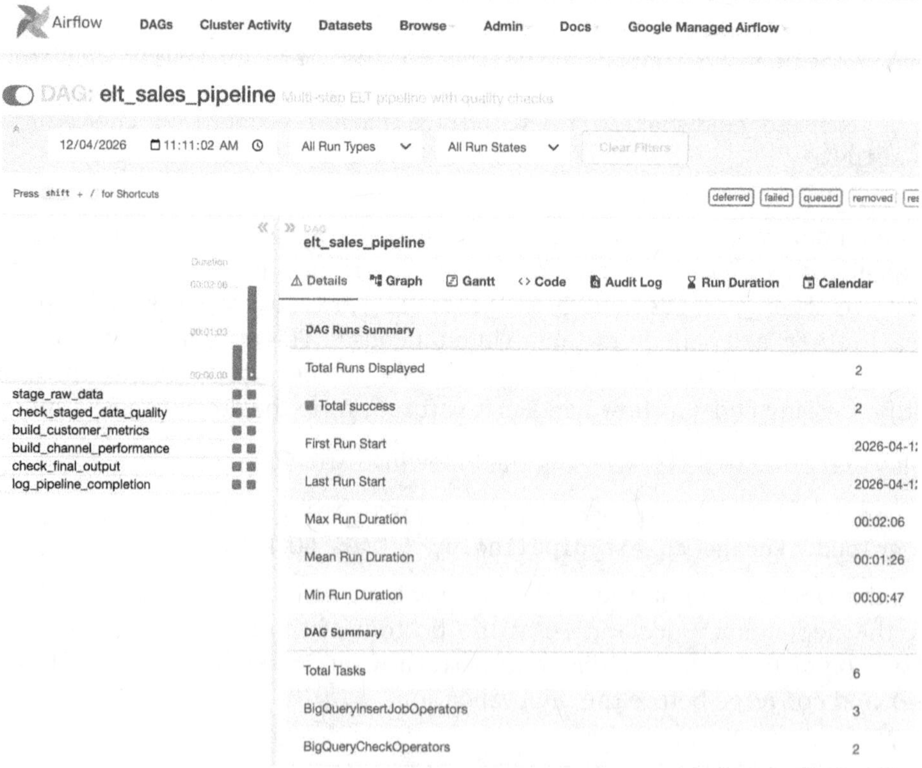

Figure 10.9: *Airflow Grid View Showing All ELT Pipeline Tasks Completed Successfully*

Verify the analytical tables in BigQuery in the following way:

```
-- Customer lifetime metrics
SELECT * FROM `your-project-id.composer_lab.customer_metrics`
ORDER BY lifetime_value DESC
LIMIT 10;

-- Channel performance summary
SELECT * FROM `your-project-id.composer_lab.channel_performance`
ORDER BY total_revenue DESC;
```

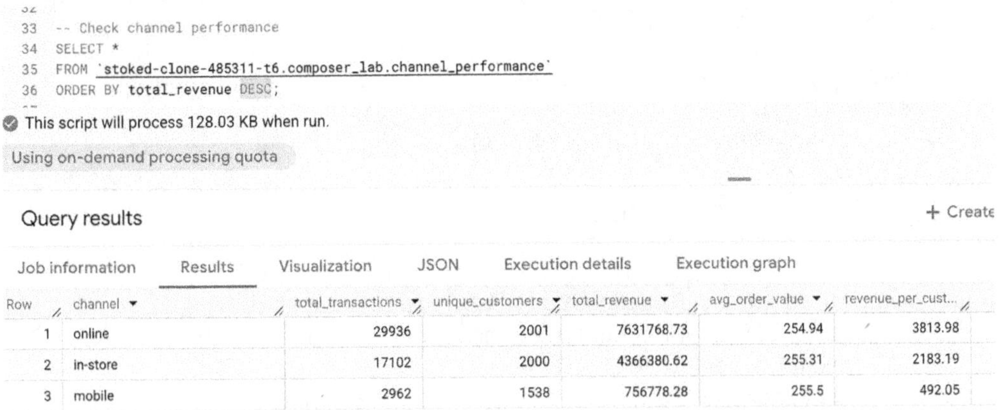

Figure 10.10: *BigQuery Results Showing `customer_metrics` and `channel_performance` Table Outputs*

Orchestrating Dataflow Jobs

In production systems, Airflow often orchestrates Dataflow jobs alongside BigQuery tasks. The **`DataflowStartFlexTemplateOperator`** allows Airflow to launch and monitor Dataflow jobs by using Google-provided Flex Templates. The following DAG exports the **`customer_metrics`** table to Cloud Storage as Parquet files:

```
"""
DAG: dataflow_bq_export
Demonstrates Dataflow operator integration by exporting
BigQuery data to Cloud Storage using a Google-provided Flex Template.
"""
from datetime import datetime, timedelta
from airflow import DAG
from airflow.providers.google.cloud.operators.dataflow import (
    DataflowStartFlexTemplateOperator
)

PROJECT_ID = "your-project-id"
```

```
REGION = "us-central1"
BUCKET = "your-project-id-composer-export"

default_args = {
    "owner": "data-team",
    "retries": 2,
    "retry_delay": timedelta(minutes=2),
}

with DAG(
    dag_id="dataflow_bq_export",
    default_args=default_args,
    description="Export BigQuery table to GCS via Dataflow",
    schedule_interval=None,
    start_date=datetime(2024, 1, 1),
    catchup=False,
    tags=["dataflow", "export"],
) as dag:

    export_to_gcs = DataflowStartFlexTemplateOperator(
        task_id="export_customer_metrics",
        project_id=PROJECT_ID,
        location=REGION,
        body={
            "launchParameter": {
                "jobName": "bq-to-gcs-export",
                "containerSpecGcsPath": f"gs://dataflow-templates-
{REGION}/latest/flex/BigQuery_to_Parquet",
                "parameters": {
                    "tableRef": f"{PROJECT_ID}:composer_lab.customer
_metrics",
                    "bucket": f"gs://{BUCKET}/exports/customer_
metrics/",
                    "numShards": "1",
                },
                "environment": {
                    "tempLocation": f"gs://{BUCKET}/temp/",
                },
            }
        },
    )
```

Note on Dataflow Templates: *Google provides pre-built Flex Templates at* `gs://dataflow-templates-{REGION}/latest/flex/`. *Template names and paths may change over time. Always check the [Dataflow templates documentation] (https://cloud.google.com/dataflow/docs/guides/templates/provided-templates) for the latest available templates.*

Before deploying this DAG, create the export bucket that Dataflow will write the Parquet files into:

```
export EXPORT_BUCKET="${PROJECT_ID}-composer-export"
gcloud storage buckets create gs://${EXPORT_BUCKET} --location=US
```

With the bucket ready, replace the project ID placeholder and upload the DAG to Composer:

```
sed -i '' "s/your-project-id/${PROJECT_ID}/g" dataflow_export.py
gcloud storage cp dataflow_export.py ${DAGS_BUCKET}/
```

Trigger the **dataflow_bq_export** DAG from the Airflow UI. While the job runs, navigate to the **Dataflow** console in GCP to observe the pipeline execution.

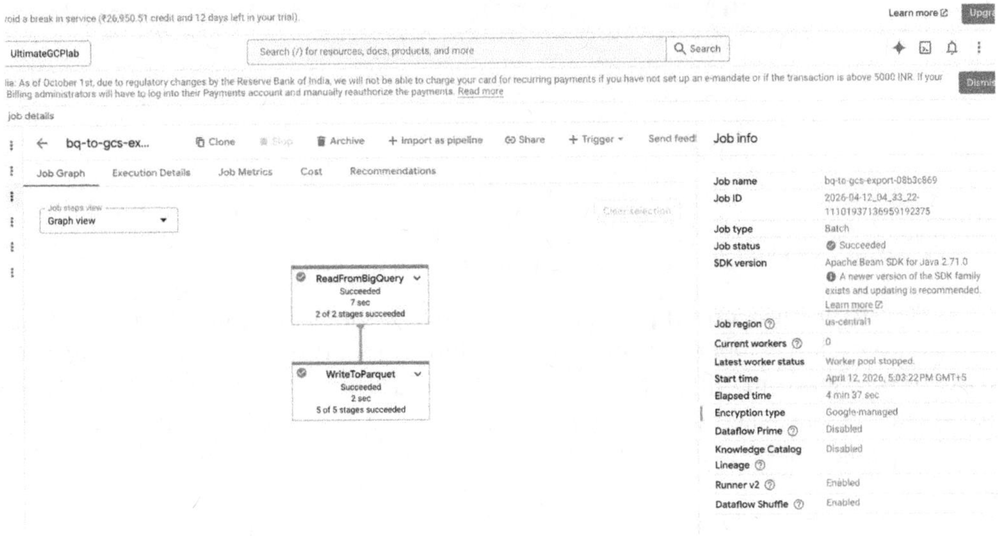

Figure 10.11: *Dataflow Console Showing the BigQuery-to-GCS Parquet Export Job Launched by Airflow*

Once the **Dataflow** job completes, return to the Airflow UI and confirm that the task is marked as successful.

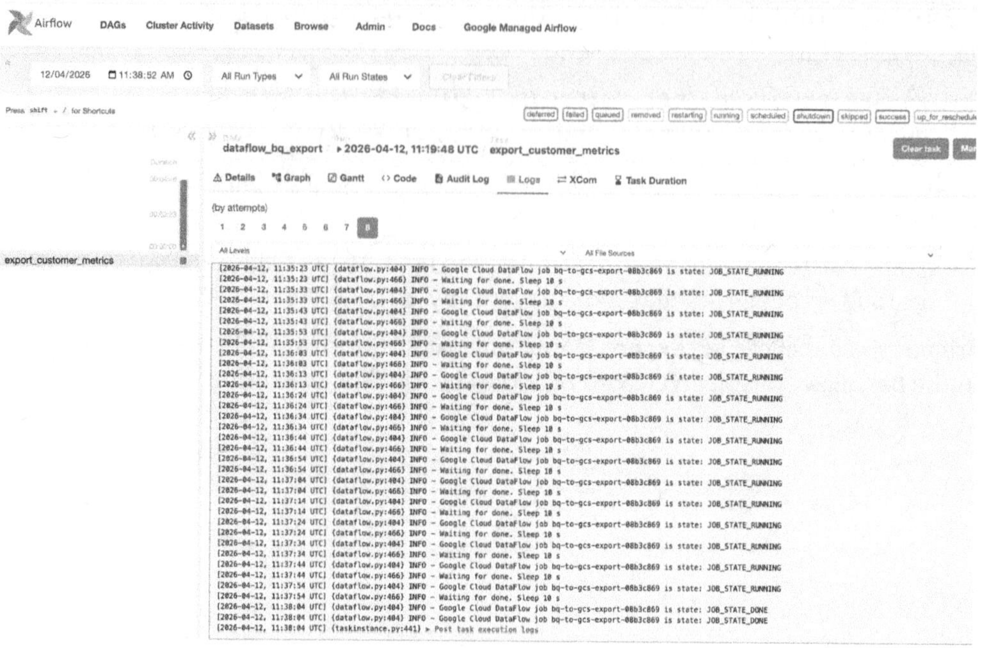

Figure 10.12: *Airflow Task Log Showing Dataflow Job Completed Successfully*

What makes this integration powerful is that Airflow does not simply fire-and-forget the Dataflow job. The operator polls the Dataflow API, waiting for the job to reach **`JOB_STATE_DONE`** before marking the task as successful. If the Dataflow job fails, Airflow marks the task as failed and triggers the retry logic defined in **`default_args`**. This tight coupling between the orchestrator and the execution engine is essential for production reliability.

Reliability Patterns

Production pipelines fail. Network timeouts, transient API errors, BigQuery slot contention, and misconfigured IAM permissions–the list of things that can go wrong is long. The mark of a well-designed pipeline is not that it never fails, but rather, that it handles failure gracefully.

Retries

Every task in Airflow can be configured with automatic retries in the following way:

```
default_args = {
    "retries": 3,                                # Retry up to 3 times
    "retry_delay": timedelta(minutes=1),         # Wait 1 minute between
                                                   retries
```

```
        "execution_timeout": timedelta(minutes=30),  # Kill the task
                                                       after 30 min
    }
```

When a task fails, Airflow marks it as **up_for_retry** and waits the specified delay before attempting again. Only after all retries are exhausted does the task transition to **failed**. For BigQuery workloads, setting retries to 2 or 3 with a 1-2 minute delay handles the vast majority of transient errors.

Demonstrating Retry Behavior

To see retries in action, create a deliberate failure DAG. The following **retry_demo** DAG has two tasks: one that queries a real table and succeeds, and one that queries a non-existent table and fails, triggering retries:

```
"""
DAG: retry_demo
Demonstrates Airflow retry behavior with
a task that fails on the first attempt.
"""
from datetime import datetime, timedelta
from airflow import DAG
from airflow.providers.google.cloud.operators.bigquery import (
    BigQueryInsertJobOperator
)

PROJECT_ID = "your-project-id"
DATASET = "composer_lab"

default_args = {
    "owner": "data-team",
    "retries": 3,
    "retry_delay": timedelta(seconds=30),
}

with DAG(
    dag_id="retry_demo",
    default_args=default_args,
    description="Demonstrates retry and failure handling",
    schedule_interval=None,
    start_date=datetime(2024, 1, 1),
    catchup=False,
    tags=["demo", "reliability"],
) as dag:

    working_query = BigQueryInsertJobOperator(
        task_id="healthy_query",
```

```
            configuration={
                "query": {
                    "query": f"""
                        SELECT COUNT(*) AS total
                        FROM `{PROJECT_ID}.{DATASET}.raw_sales`
                    """,
                    "useLegacySql": False,
                }
            },
            location="US",
        )

        failing_query = BigQueryInsertJobOperator(
            task_id="failing_query",
            configuration={
                "query": {
                    "query": f"""
                        SELECT * FROM `{PROJECT_ID}.{DATASET}.table_
    that_does_not_exist`
                    """,
                    "useLegacySql": False,
                }
            },
            location="US",
        )

        working_query >> failing_query
```

Deploy the preceding DAG to Composer and trigger it from the Airflow UI:

```
sed -i '' "s/your-project-id/${PROJECT_ID}/g" retry_demo.py
gcloud storage cp retry_demo.py ${DAGS_BUCKET}/
```

In the Airflow UI, you will see the **healthy_query** task turns green (indicating success) immediately. The **failing_query** task will turn orange (**up_for_retry**) after each failure, with a 30-second delay between attempts. After 3 retries, it transitions to red (indicating failure), and the overall DAG run is marked as "**failed**." Click on the "**failing_query**" task to see the Task Instance Details panel, which shows the attempt number and the exact error message for each retry.

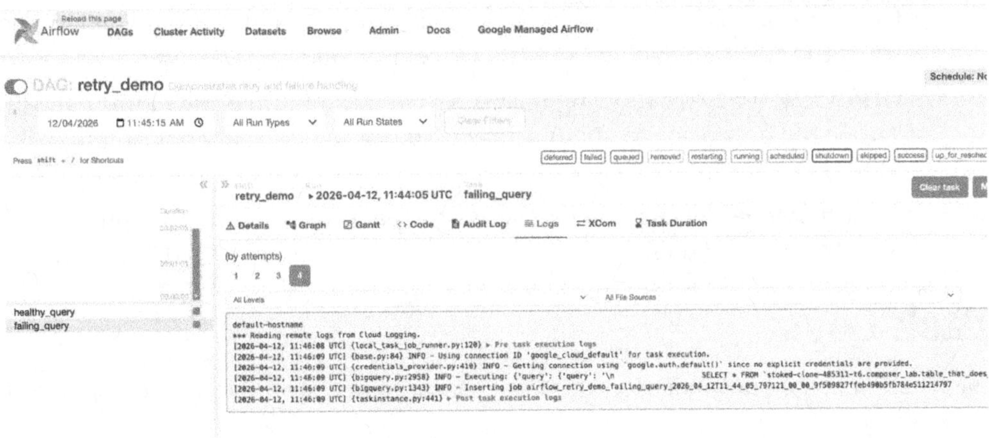

Figure 10.13: *Airflow UI Showing `retry_demo` DAG with `healthy_query` Succeeded and `failing_query` Failed After 3 Retry Attempts*

Idempotency

Beyond retries, idempotency is the most important reliability pattern. As mentioned earlier, every task should produce the same result regardless of how many times it executes. For BigQuery, this means:

- Use **`CREATE OR REPLACE TABLE`** instead of **`INSERT INTO`**.
- Use **`MERGE`** statements for incremental loads.
- Avoid **`INSERT`** without deduplication—if a retry reprocesses the same data, you will get duplicate rows.

Backfills

Airflow's backfill capability allows you to reprocess historical dates. If your pipeline was broken for three days and you fix the bug, you can trigger DAG Runs for the missed dates. As tasks should be idempotent, backfilling is safe—rerunning a historical date produces the same correct result.

Monitoring and Operational Visibility

Once your DAGs are deployed to production, maintaining visibility into their execution health and performance becomes critical.

The Airflow UI

The Airflow web UI is your primary monitoring tool. Key views include:

- **DAGs List**: Shows all registered DAGs, their schedule, last run status, and recent history. A quick glance tells you if anything is broken.

- **Graph View**: Visualizes task dependencies as a flowchart. Color-coded nodes show the status of each task in the current or selected DAG Run.
- **Grid View**: A matrix showing task status across multiple DAG Runs over time. This is the best place to spot patterns—such as a task that consistently fails on Mondays.
- **Task Instance Details**: Click any task to see its execution attempts, logs, and rendered parameters.

Task Logs

Every task instance produces logs that are captured and stored in Cloud Logging. The logs include:

- The exact SQL query that was submitted to BigQuery.
- The BigQuery job ID, which you can use to investigate in the BigQuery console.
- Timing information, such as when the task started, how long it ran, and when it completed.
- Error messages and stack traces for failed attempts.

For production environments, you should also configure Airflow to send email or Slack notifications on task failure using the `on_failure_callback` parameter or the `email_on_failure` default argument.

Cloud Logging Integration

As Cloud Composer runs on GKE, all Airflow logs are automatically exported to Cloud Logging. This means that you can query task logs using standard Cloud Logging filters, set up log-based alerts, and integrate with your existing monitoring stack. For example, to find all failed tasks across all DAGs in the last 24 hours:

```
resource.type="cloud_composer_environment"
severity="ERROR"
textPayload:"Task failed with exception"
```

Cleanup

Cloud Composer environments incur costs even when idle (approximately $0.35/hour). Always delete test environments when you are done in the following way:

```
gcloud composer environments delete composer-bq-lab \
  --location=${REGION} \
  --quiet
```

Optionally, remove the BigQuery dataset and export bucket to avoid residual storage costs in the following manner:

```
bq rm -r -f -d ${PROJECT_ID}:composer_lab
gcloud storage rm --recursive gs://${EXPORT_BUCKET}
```

Conclusion

Orchestration is the connective tissue of production data engineering. Individual tools such as BigQuery, Dataflow, and Spark are powerful; however, without a system to coordinate them—to enforce dependencies, handle failures, and provide visibility—they remain isolated components that require manual intervention to operate.

Cloud Composer—built on Apache Airflow—provides the coordination layer. By defining pipelines as Python DAGs and deploying them to a managed environment, you gain automatic scheduling, dependency resolution, retry logic, parallel execution, backfill capability, and centralized logging. These are not merely nice-to-have features. Rather, they are the baseline requirements for any data system that needs to run reliably on a daily basis, without someone manually babysitting it.

In the next chapter, we will shift our focus from how data moves to how it is protected. *Chapter 11: Security, Governance, and Data Quality* will cover security, governance, and data quality in BigQuery—implementing IAM controls, row-level and column-level security, Data Catalog integration, and quality checks, ensuring that your pipelines produce trustworthy results.

Points to Remember

- **Orchestration bridges the gap** between individual pipeline tools and production-ready data systems. Scheduling, dependency management, retry logic, and monitoring are fundamental requirements—not merely optional extras.
- **DAGs are declarative.** Define what tasks exist and how they depend on each other. Let Airflow handle the scheduling and execution.
- **Cloud Composer eliminates infrastructure management.** Deploy DAGs by copying Python files to a GCS bucket. No servers to maintain.
- **Parallel execution is automatic.** When tasks have no dependency on each other, Airflow runs them simultaneously without any special configuration.
- **BigQueryCheckOperator** enables data quality gates directly inside your pipeline. If the check fails, downstream tasks do not execute.
- **Retries handle transient failures.** Setting `retries=3` with a short delay handles the vast majority of intermittent cloud service errors.

- **Idempotency is non-negotiable.** Use `CREATE OR REPLACE` and `MERGE` to ensure that tasks produce the same result whether run once or ten times.
- **Dataflow integration** through `DataflowStartFlexTemplateOperator` allows Airflow to launch, monitor, and report on Dataflow jobs as part of a broader pipeline.

Multiple Choice Questions

1. What is the primary advantage of using Cloud Composer over manually scheduling cron jobs for data pipeline orchestration?
   a. Cron jobs cannot execute Python scripts.
   b. Cloud Composer provides dependency management, retry logic, backfill capability, and a visual UI for monitoring.
   c. Cron jobs cannot connect to BigQuery.
   d. Cloud Composer is always free of charge.
2. In an Airflow DAG, what does the >> operator define?
   a. The schedule interval between tasks
   b. A task dependency–the downstream task waits for the upstream task to succeed
   c. A data transfer between two BigQuery tables
   d. A retry configuration for the downstream task
3. An Airflow DAG has the following dependency: `task_a >> [task_b, task_c] >> task_d`. Which statement is correct?
   a. Tasks B and C run sequentially after Task A
   b. Task D runs in parallel with Tasks B and C
   c. Tasks B and C run in parallel after Task A, and Task D waits for both to complete
   d. Task A runs after Tasks B and C complete
4. What does the setting "`catchup=False`" in a DAG definition prevent?
   a. The DAG from being triggered manually
   b. Airflow from backfilling DAG Runs for all dates between `start_date` and today

   c. The DAG from retrying failed tasks

   d. The DAG from running on weekends

5. Which Airflow operator is most appropriate for implementing a data quality gate that fails the pipeline if a BigQuery table has zero rows?

   a. `BigQueryInsertJobOperator`

   b. `BigQueryCheckOperator`

   c. `PythonOperator`

   d. `BashOperator`

6. What happens when a task configured with `retries=3` fails for the first time?

   a. The entire DAG Run is immediately marked as failed

   b. The task is marked as `up_for_retry`, and Airflow waits the `retry_delay` before attempting again

   c. Airflow skips the task and proceeds to downstream tasks

   d. The Composer environment restarts

7. Why is using `CREATE OR REPLACE TABLE` preferred over `INSERT INTO` for BigQuery tasks in Airflow?

   a. It runs faster

   b. It ensures idempotency—running the task multiple times produces the same result without duplicate rows

   c. It costs less slot-seconds

   d. It is required by the `BigQueryInsertJobOperator`

8. How does the `DataflowStartFlexTemplateOperator` differ from a fire-and-forget approach to launching Dataflow jobs?

   a. It does not support Flex Templates

   b. It submits the job and immediately marks the task as successful

   c. It polls the Dataflow API, waiting for the job to complete before marking the task as successful or failed

   d. It requires the Dataflow job to be manually approved

Answers

1. b
2. b
3. c
4. b
5. b
6. b
7. b
8. c

Questions

1. Explain the difference between scheduling a pipeline with cron and orchestrating it with Airflow. What specific capabilities does Airflow provide that cron cannot?
2. Describe the purpose of `BigQueryCheckOperator` in data pipeline design. How does it differ from `BigQueryInsertJobOperator`, and when would you use each?
3. A data engineer has a pipeline with five tasks: ingest data, validate schema, build dimension table, build fact table, and run quality checks. The dimension and fact tables can be built independently, but both depend on schema validation. Draw the dependency graph and write the corresponding Airflow dependency code.
4. Explain why idempotency matters in Airflow DAGs. Provide a concrete example of a non-idempotent BigQuery task and explain how to make it idempotent.
5. Your daily pipeline has been failing for the past three days due to a permissions issue that has now been fixed. Describe how you would use Airflow's backfill capability to reprocess the missed data, and explain why idempotent tasks make this safe.

Key Terms

- **Apache Airflow:** An open-source platform for programmatically authoring, scheduling, and monitoring data workflows using Directed Acyclic Graphs (DAGs).
- **Cloud Composer:** Google Cloud's fully managed service for Apache Airflow that provisions and operates the scheduler, web server, workers, metadata database, and logging infrastructure.
- **Directed Acyclic Graph (DAG):** A Python file that defines a collection of tasks and their dependencies. "Directed" means tasks flow one way; "Acyclic" means no circular dependencies.
- **DAG Run:** A specific execution instance of a DAG, tied to a logical execution date and containing individual task instances.
- **Task Instance:** A specific execution of a task within a DAG Run, with its own state (queued, running, success, failed, up_for_retry).
- **Operator:** A pre-built class that defines a single unit of work. Examples include `BigQueryInsertJobOperator`, `BigQueryCheckOperator`, and `DataflowStartFlexTemplateOperator`.
- **BigQueryInsertJobOperator:** An Airflow operator that submits SQL queries (DDL, DML, or SELECT) as BigQuery jobs.
- **BigQueryCheckOperator:** An Airflow operator that runs a SQL query and fails the task if the result evaluates to false or zero, commonly used for data quality gates.
- **DataflowStartFlexTemplateOperator:** An Airflow operator that launches Google Cloud Dataflow jobs using Flex Templates and monitors them until completion.
- **Idempotency:** The property that running a task multiple times produces the same result. Achieved in BigQuery using **`CREATE`** or **`REPLACE TABLE`** or **`MERGE`** statements.
- **Catchup:** An Airflow feature that, when enabled, automatically creates DAG Runs for all dates between **`start_date`** and the current date. Typically disabled (**`catchup=False`**) for non-historical pipelines.
- **Backfill:** The process of reprocessing the historical data by triggering DAG Runs for past dates, relying on idempotent tasks to produce correct results.
- **Default Args:** A dictionary of parameters applied to all tasks in a DAG, commonly used for retry configuration, timeouts, and ownership metadata.

CHAPTER 11
Security, Governance, and Data Quality

Introduction

Over the past several chapters, you have built data pipelines that ingest, transform, and orchestrate data through BigQuery at scale. *Chapter 7, ELT with dbt and BigQuery* introduced the data build tool (dbt) for modular transformations. *Chapter 8, Apache Beam and Dataflow* demonstrated streaming and batch ingestion with Dataflow. *Chapter 9, Spark and BigQuery Integration* brought Spark into the picture for hybrid workloads. *Chapter 10, Orchestration with Cloud Composer* tied everything together with Cloud Composer orchestration. By now, your data platform can move data reliably from source to warehouse to analytics layer.

However, there is a question we have not addressed yet: Who is allowed to see this data?

Consider the "`employees`" table we have been building pipelines around. It contains salary information, email addresses, and department classifications. In a real organization, not everyone should see every column. The finance team needs salary data; the marketing team does not. A regional manager should see records for their own region, not for the entire company. An external auditor might need transaction summaries without any Personally Identifiable Information (PII).

This is a security and governance problem, which is not optional. Regulations such as GDPR, HIPAA, and SOC 2 impose legal requirements on how sensitive data is accessed, by whom, and with what level of auditability. Even without regulatory pressure, data governance is simply good engineering. A data platform without access controls is a data leak waiting to happen.

In this chapter, you will implement the full security and governance stack available in BigQuery. We will build layered access controls—starting with Identity and Access Management (IAM) roles at the dataset level, then narrowing access with authorized views that hide sensitive columns, then applying row-level security that filters data per user, and finally adding column-level security that masks specific fields based on policy tags. Along the way, we will also build data quality assertions, audit table metadata through `INFORMATION_SCHEMA`, and use Data Catalog for discoverability.

By the end of this chapter, you will understand not just how to build pipelines that move data, but also how to build platforms that protect it.

Structure

In this chapter, we will cover the following topics:

- The Security Layer Model
- Identity and Access Management (IAM) Access Controls
- Authorized Views
- Row-Level Security
- Column-Level Security
- Data Quality Assertions
- Metadata Auditing with `INFORMATION_SCHEMA`
- Data Catalog and Discoverability

The Security Layer Model

BigQuery does not have a single security switch. Instead, it provides multiple independent layers that stack on top of each other—with each progressively narrowing what a user can see. Understanding this layered model is essential before diving into the implementation.

Layer	**What It Controls**	**Scope**
IAM Roles	Who can access a dataset or table at all	Project/Dataset/Table
Authorized Views	Which columns a user can see through a view	View definition
Row Access Policies	Which rows a user can see in a table	Per-user/per-group
Column-Level Security	Which columns a user can read, even in direct queries	Per-column via policy tags

Table 11.1: *BigQuery Security Layers and Their Scope*

The layers mentioned in *Table* 11.1 are additive. A user must pass through every layer to see a specific piece of data. If IAM grants them read access to a dataset, but a row access policy restricts them to one region, they will only see rows from that region. If a column-level policy tag masks the `"salary"` column and they lack the Fine-Grained Reader role, they will see an "access denied" error on that column—even though IAM granted them table-level read access.

Think of it as a building. IAM is the front door—it determines whether you can enter at all. Authorized views are the floor directory—they show you only the rooms you are supposed to visit. Row-level security is the keycard system—it limits which rooms on each floor you can actually open. Column-level security is the locked filing cabinet inside the room—even if you can enter the room, certain drawers require additional clearance.

This layered model means that you can implement defense in depth without any single point of failure. Even if one layer is misconfigured, the other layers still protect the data.

Identity and Access Management (IAM) Access Controls

The first and most fundamental security layer in BigQuery is IAM. Every interaction with BigQuery—running a query, creating a table, reading data, modifying a schema—requires the user to have an appropriate IAM role.

Predefined BigQuery Roles

BigQuery provides several predefined roles that cover common access patterns, as demonstrated in *Table 11.2*:

Role	Permissions	Typical Use Case
`` `roles/bigquery.dataViewer` ``	Read tables and views	Analysts who query data
`` `roles/bigquery.dataEditor` ``	Read, create, update, delete tables	Engineers who build pipelines
`` `roles/bigquery.dataOwner` ``	Full control over datasets	Dataset administrators
`` `roles/bigquery.jobUser` ``	Run queries (but no table access)	Users who need compute only
`` `roles/bigquery.admin` ``	Full BigQuery access	Platform administrators

Table 11.2: *Predefined BigQuery IAM Roles*

The principle of least privilege applies here. A data analyst who only needs to run "`SELECT`" queries should receive "`dataViewer`," and not "`dataOwner`." An orchestration service account that creates and updates tables should receive "`dataEditor`," and not "`admin`." Over-granting permissions is the single most common security mistake in data platforms.

Dataset-Level Permissions

Let us build a concrete example. We will create a dataset called "`governance_lab`" with simulated employee and financial data—the kind of data that demands strict access controls.

First, set up the project and enable the required APIs in the following manner:

```
# Set your project
export PROJECT_ID="your-project-id"
gcloud config set project $PROJECT_ID

# Enable APIs
gcloud services enable bigquery.googleapis.com
gcloud services enable datacatalog.googleapis.com
gcloud services enable bigquerydatapolicy.googleapis.com
```

Now, create the dataset and populate it with sample data:

```
-- Create the governance lab dataset
CREATE SCHEMA `your-project-id.governance_lab`
OPTIONS (
  location = 'US',
  description = 'Security, governance, and data quality lab'
);

-- Create an employees table with PII data
CREATE OR REPLACE TABLE `your-project-id.governance_lab.employees` AS
SELECT *
FROM UNNEST([
  STRUCT('EMP001' AS employee_id, 'Alice Johnson' AS full_name,
         'alice@company.com' AS email, 'Engineering' AS department,
         'US-West' AS region, 125000.00 AS salary, DATE '2020-03-15'
AS hire_date),
  STRUCT('EMP002', 'Bob Smith', 'bob@company.com',
         'Engineering', 'US-East', 118000.00, DATE '2021-06-01'),
  STRUCT('EMP003', 'Carol White', 'carol@company.com',
         'Marketing', 'EU-West', 95000.00, DATE '2019-11-20'),
  STRUCT('EMP004', 'David Chen', 'david@company.com',
         'Finance', 'APAC', 140000.00, DATE '2018-01-10'),
  STRUCT('EMP005', 'Eve Martinez', 'eve@company.com',
         'Engineering', 'US-West', 132000.00, DATE '2022-02-28'),
  STRUCT('EMP006', 'Frank Brown', 'frank@company.com',
         'Marketing', 'US-East', 88000.00, DATE '2023-07-15'),
  STRUCT('EMP007', 'Grace Lee', 'grace@company.com',
         'Finance', 'EU-West', 145000.00, DATE '2017-09-01'),
  STRUCT('EMP008', 'Henry Wilson', 'henry@company.com',
         'Engineering', 'APAC', 115000.00, DATE '2021-04-12'),
  STRUCT('EMP009', 'Irene Davis', 'irene@company.com',
         'HR', 'US-West', 98000.00, DATE '2020-08-30'),
  STRUCT('EMP010', 'Jack Taylor', 'jack@company.com',
         'HR', 'US-East', 92000.00, DATE '2022-11-05')
]);
```

This "**employees**" table contains several categories of sensitive data, including salary figures (financial PII), email addresses (personal PII), and department/region classifications (organizational data). In a production environment, different teams would need different levels of access to these columns.

Next, create a transactions table that we will use later for row-level security:

```
-- Create a transactions table with 500 rows across 4 regions
CREATE OR REPLACE TABLE `your-project-id.governance_lab.transactions` AS
SELECT
  CONCAT('TXN', LPAD(CAST(num AS STRING), 5, '0')) AS transaction_id,
  CONCAT('EMP', LPAD(CAST(CAST(FLOOR(RAND() * 10 + 1) AS INT64) AS
STRING), 3, '0')) AS employee_id,
  ROUND(RAND() * 5000, 2) AS amount,
  CASE MOD(num, 4)
    WHEN 0 THEN 'US-West'
    WHEN 1 THEN 'US-East'
    WHEN 2 THEN 'EU-West'
    WHEN 3 THEN 'APAC'
  END AS region,
  DATE_SUB(CURRENT_DATE(), INTERVAL CAST(FLOOR(RAND() * 365) AS
INT64) DAY) AS transaction_date,
  CASE WHEN RAND() > 0.1 THEN 'approved' ELSE 'pending' END AS status
FROM UNNEST(GENERATE_ARRAY(1, 500)) AS num;
```

Verify that both tables were created in the following manner:

```
-- Verify the data
SELECT 'employees' AS table_name, COUNT(*) number_of_rows
FROM `your-project-id.governance_lab.employees`
UNION ALL
SELECT 'transactions', COUNT(*)
FROM `your-project-id.governance_lab.transactions`;
```

You should see 10 employees and 500 transactions, as demonstrated in *Figure 11.1*:

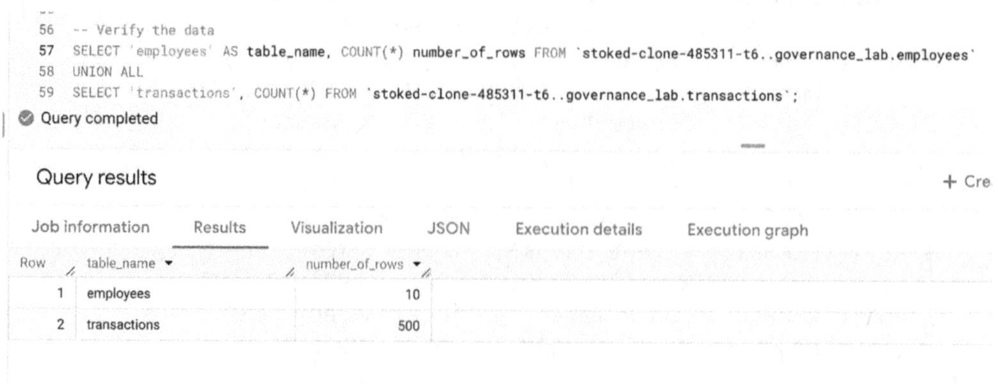

Figure 11.1: *BigQuery Console Showing "governance_lab" Dataset with Table Row Counts*

Now, let us configure dataset-level permissions. Navigate to the BigQuery console, click on the "**`governance_lab`**" dataset, then click the **`+ Share ▼`** dropdown in the toolbar and select **`Permissions`**. This opens the dataset permissions panel.

Here, you can see the IAM roles assigned to the dataset. By default, the project owner has full access, and project viewers can read data. To follow the principle of least privilege, you would grant specific users or service accounts only the roles they need. For example, granting "**`BigQuery Data Viewer`**" to an analyst ensures that they can read the data, but they cannot modify or delete anything.

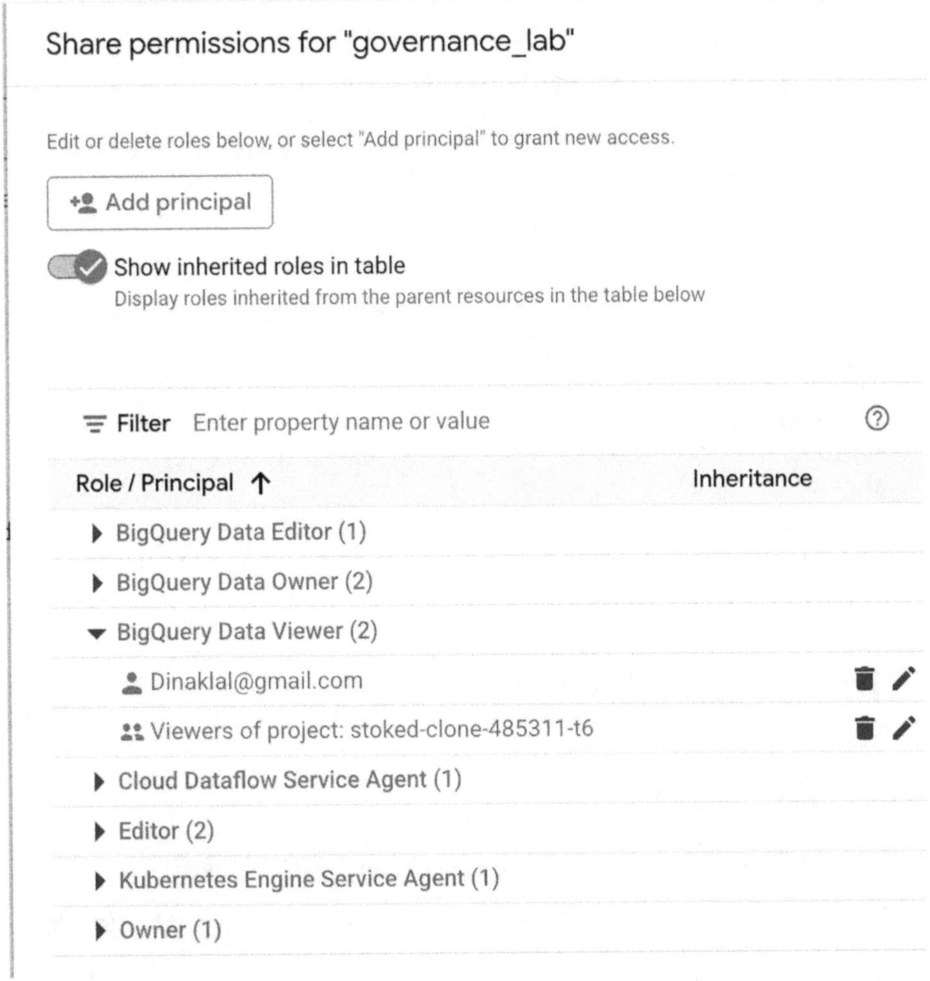

Figure 11.2: *Dataset Permissions Panel Showing IAM Roles Assigned*

Best Practice: Always assign permissions at the dataset level, not at the project level, unless a user genuinely needs access to all datasets. Dataset-level permissions prevent accidental access to unrelated data and make auditing significantly easier.

Authorized Views

IAM controls who can access a dataset, but it does not control which columns they see. If a user has a dataViewer on a dataset, they can query all columns of all tables in that dataset. For sensitive data such as salaries and email addresses, this is often too permissive.

Authorized views solve this by creating a view that exposes only specific columns, and then granting the view permission to read the underlying table—even if the user does not have direct table access.

Creating an Authorized View

Let us create a view that exposes the employee directory without any PII columns in the following way:

```
-- Create a view that excludes salary and email
CREATE OR REPLACE VIEW `your-project-id.governance_lab.employee_
directory` AS
SELECT
  employee_id,
  full_name,
  department,
  region,
  hire_date
FROM `your-project-id.governance_lab.employees`;
```

Notice what this view excludes: "**`salary`**" and "**`email`**." Anyone querying through this view will only see the non-sensitive columns.

Authorizing the View

Creating the view is only half the solution. You also need to authorize it, so that it can access the underlying data on behalf of users who may not have direct table access. The following steps show how:

1. In the BigQuery console, click the **`governance_lab`** dataset.
2. Click the **`+ Share ▼`** dropdown in the toolbar and select **`Authorize Views`**.
3. In the **`Authorized Views`** panel, enter **`your-project-id.governance_lab.employee_directory`** and click **`Add authorization`**.

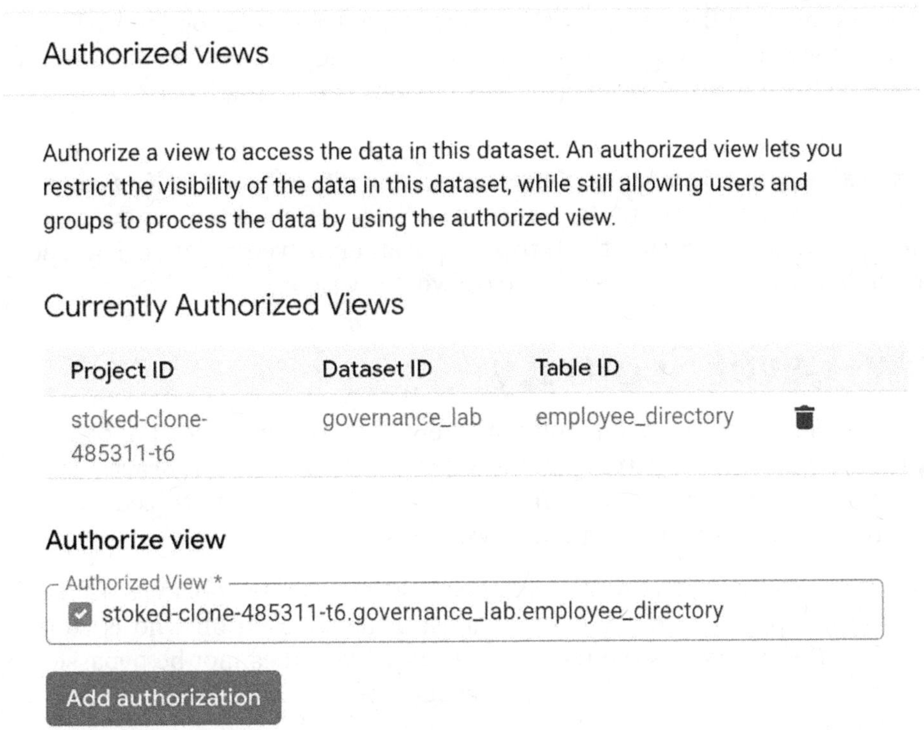

Figure 11.3: *Authorized Views Panel with "employee_directory" View Configured*

Now, query the view to confirm that it works:

```
-- Query the authorized view
SELECT * FROM `your-project-id.governance_lab.employee_directory`;
```

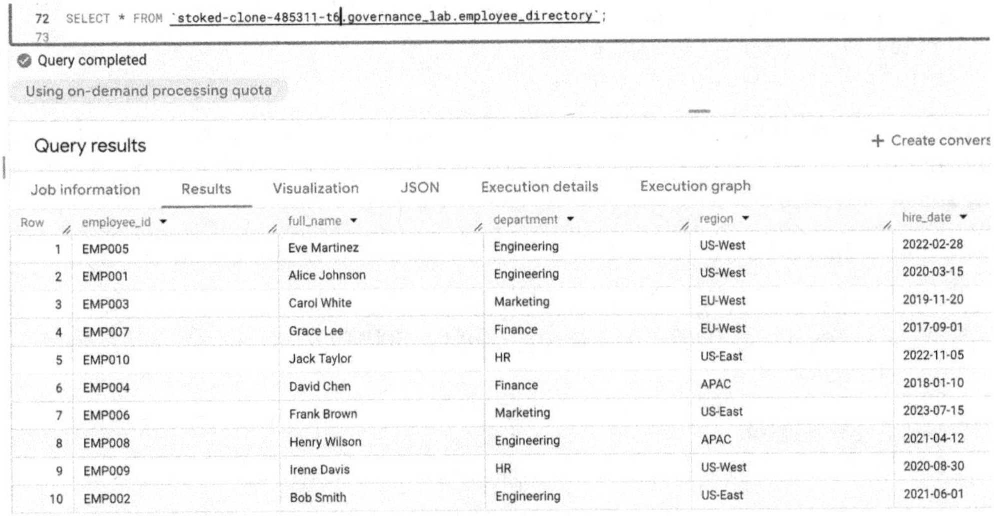

Figure 11.4: *Query Results from "employee_directory" View without PII Columns*

The results show "**employee_id**," "**full_name**," "**department**, **region**," and "**hire_date**"–but no "**salary**" or "**email**." A user with access only to this view would never see the sensitive columns, regardless of other permissions they might have.

This pattern is extremely common in production. You might create a "**public_customers**" view that excludes phone numbers and addresses, a "**finance_summary**" view that shows aggregated totals without individual transaction amounts, or a "**hr_directory**" view as this one that strips PII from employee records. The underlying table retains all the data; the view controls what is visible.

Row-Level Security

Authorized views control which columns are visible. However, what about the rows? Suppose that the US-West regional manager should only see transactions from the US-West region, not transactions from APAC or EU-West. Authorized views cannot help here, as they filter columns, not rows.

BigQuery solves this with row access policies. A row access policy is a filter that is automatically applied to every query against a table, based on who is running the query. The user never sees the filter, as it is invisible and cannot be bypassed, unless the user is a project owner or has the "**bigquery.admin**" role.

Creating a Row Access Policy

Let us create a policy that restricts a specific user to see only US-West transactions:

```
-- Create a row access policy for US-West region only
CREATE OR REPLACE ROW ACCESS POLICY us_west_only
ON `your-project-id.governance_lab.transactions`
GRANT TO ('user:your-email@gmail.com')
FILTER USING (region = 'US-West');
```

Replace `your-email@gmail.com` with your actual email address. This policy tells BigQuery: "When this user queries the transactions table, only return rows where **region = 'US-West'**."

Now, query the table:

```
-- As the policy-granted user, you'll only see US-West rows
SELECT region, COUNT(*) AS row_count, ROUND(SUM(amount), 2)
AS total_amount
FROM `your-project-id.governance_lab.transactions`
GROUP BY region
ORDER BY region;
```

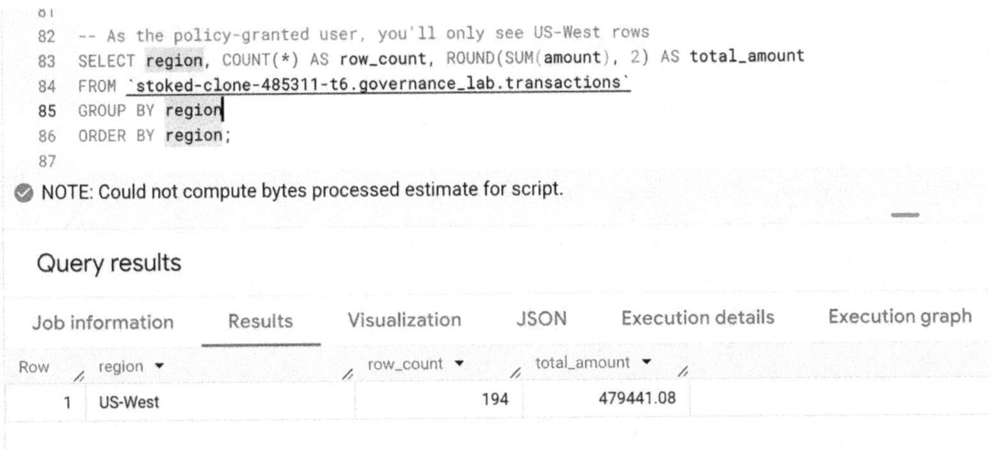

Figure 11.5: *Row-Level Security Filtering Showing Only US-West Transactions*

The results show only one row–US-West–with approximately 194 transactions. The other three regions (APAC, EU-West, and US-East) are completely invisible. The query did not fail; it simply returned a filtered result set, as if the other rows did not exist.

Note: *Row access policies are additive–if a user matches multiple policies, they can see rows from all matching policies combined.*

Restoring Full Access

In a real scenario, administrators need to maintain full visibility. You can grant full access by creating an additional policy with "**FILTER USING (TRUE)**" in the following manner:

```
-- Grant admin full access (sees all rows)
CREATE OR REPLACE ROW ACCESS POLICY admin_full_access
ON `your-project-id.governance_lab.transactions`
GRANT TO ('user:your-email@gmail.com')
FILTER USING (TRUE);
```

Now, run the same query again:

```
-- After adding admin_full_access, all regions are visible
SELECT region, COUNT(*) AS row_count, ROUND(SUM(amount), 2) AS to-
tal_amount
FROM `your-project-id.governance_lab.transactions`
GROUP BY region
ORDER BY region;
```

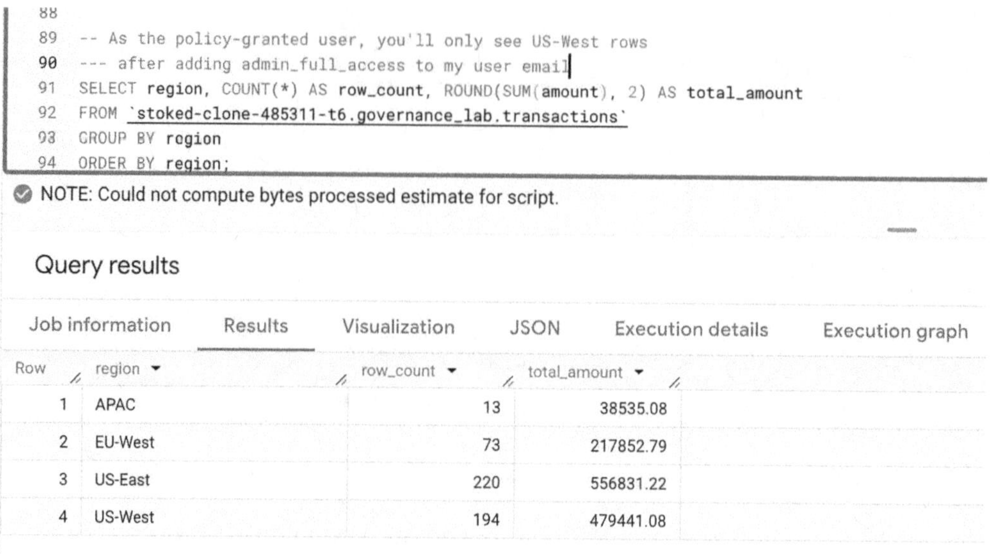

***Figure 11.6:** All Regions Visible after Adding Admin Full Access Policy*

This time, all four regions appear in the results. The "**`FILTER USING (TRUE)`**" policy grants access to every row, and since policies are additive, the user can now see all data. This is the pattern you would use for data platform administrators or compliance teams that need unrestricted access.

Inspecting Row Access Policies

You can inspect all row access policies on a table by using the `bq` CLI in the following manner:

```
bq ls --row_access_policies=true \
  ${PROJECT_ID}:governance_lab.transactions
```

This will display the policy names, grantees, and filter predicates for all row access policies on the table. You should see both "**`us_west_only`**" and "**`admin_full_access`**" policies listed.

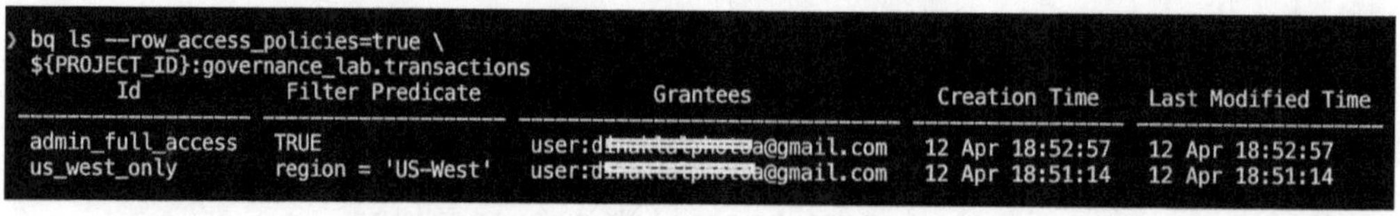

***Figure 11.7:** bq CLI Output Listing Row Access Policies on Transactions Table*

Note: *The "`INFORMATION_SCHEMA.ROW_ACCESS_POLICIES`" view also exposes this data via SQL, but requires the "`bigquery.rowAccessPolicies.list`" IAM permission, which is not included in the default "Owner" role. The `bq` CLI approach works reliably with standard project permissions.*

Column-Level Security

We have now covered three layers of security: IAM (who can access the dataset), authorized views (which columns are visible through a view), and row access policies (which rows are visible per user). Yet, there is still a gap.

Authorized views only protect data when users query through the view. If a user has direct "**dataViewer**" access to the underlying table, they can bypass the view entirely and see all columns. Column-level security closes this gap by protecting individual columns, regardless of how the table is accessed.

BigQuery implements column-level security through "**Data Catalog**" policy tags. You create a taxonomy (a classification hierarchy), define policy tags within it, and then attach those tags to specific table columns. Any user who queries a tagged column must have the "**Fine-Grained Reader**" role on that tag–otherwise, they will receive an "**access denied**" error.

Creating a Taxonomy and Policy Tags

Column-level security uses "**Data Catalog**" policy tags to mask or restrict access to specific columns. First, create a taxonomy with policy enforcement enabled using the Data Catalog REST API:

```
# Create the taxonomy
ACCESS_TOKEN=$(gcloud auth print-access-token)

curl -s -X POST \
  "https://datacatalog.googleapis.com/v1/projects/${PROJECT_ID}/
locations/us/taxonomies" \
  -H "Authorization: Bearer ${ACCESS_TOKEN}" \
  -H "Content-Type: application/json" \
  -d '{
    "displayName": "Data Sensitivity",
    "description": "Classifies data by sensitivity level",
    "activatedPolicyTypes": ["FINE_GRAINED_ACCESS_CONTROL"]
  }'
```

Note the taxonomy ID from the JSON response (the number at the end of the "**name**" field). Then, create two policy tags:

```
# Get the taxonomy ID
export TAXONOMY_ID=$(gcloud data-catalog taxonomies list \
  --location=us --project=${PROJECT_ID} \
  --format="value(name)" | head -1 | awk -F'/' '{print $NF}')
echo "Taxonomy ID: ${TAXONOMY_ID}"
```

```
# Create "Highly Confidential" policy tag
curl -s -X POST \
  "https://datacatalog.googleapis.com/v1/projects/${PROJECT_ID}/
locations/us/taxonomies/${TAXONOMY_ID}/policyTags" \
  -H "Authorization: Bearer $(gcloud auth print-access-token)" \
  -H "Content-Type: application/json" \
  -d '{
    "displayName": "Highly Confidential",
    "description": "PII and financial data requiring strict access
control"
  }'

# Create "Internal" policy tag
curl -s -X POST \
  "https://datacatalog.googleapis.com/v1/projects/${PROJECT_ID}/
locations/us/taxonomies/${TAXONOMY_ID}/policyTags" \
  -H "Authorization: Bearer $(gcloud auth print-access-token)" \
  -H "Content-Type: application/json" \
  -d '{
    "displayName": "Internal",
    "description": "Internal business data with limited exposure"
  }'

# Verify the policy tags
gcloud data-catalog taxonomies policy-tags list \
  --taxonomy=${TAXONOMY_ID} \
  --location=us \
  --project=${PROJECT_ID}
```

Figure 11.8: *Policy Tags Listed via gcloud CLI Showing Highly Confidential and Internal*

Applying Policy Tags to Columns

Navigate to the BigQuery console. Click on the "`employees`" table, then select the "`Schema`" tab and click "`Edit Schema`."

Apply the "`Highly Confidential`" policy tag to these columns, such as:

- `salary`
- `email`

Apply the "**Internal**" tag to:

- `full_name`

Click "**Save**."

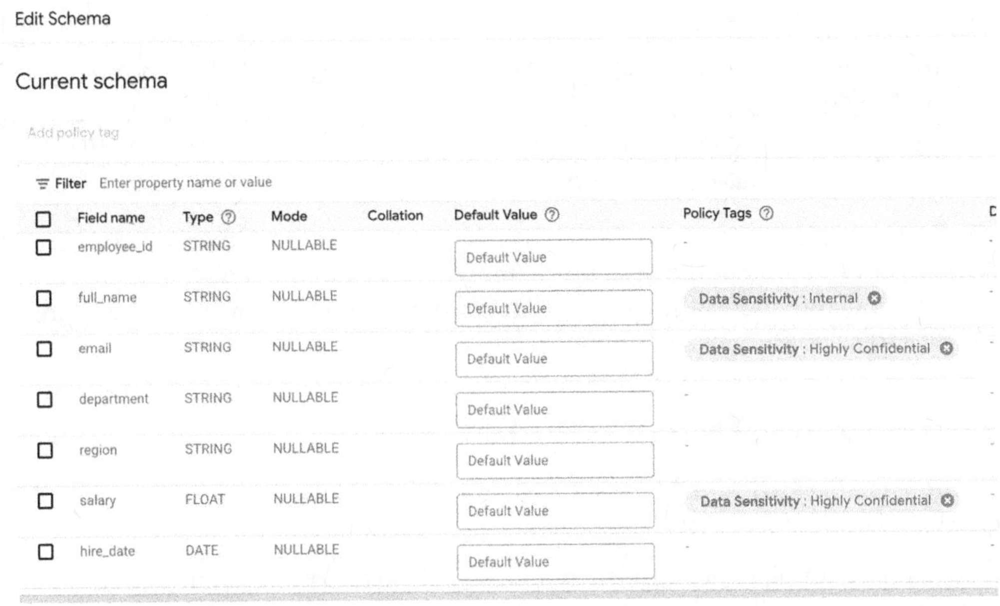

***Figure 11.9**: BigQuery Schema Editor with Policy Tags Applied to Columns*

Now, any user without the "**Fine-Grained Reader**" role on the "**Highly Confidential**" tag will receive an "**access denied**" error when querying "**salary**" or "**email**"—even if they have full "**dataViewer**" access to the dataset:

```
-- Users without Fine-Grained Reader access will get an access
denied error
-- on the tagged columns
SELECT employee_id, full_name, email, salary
FROM `your-project-id.governance_lab.employees`
LIMIT 5;
```

Note: *As the project owner, you will still see all data. To test masking behavior, query from a different account that has the BigQuery "Data Viewer," but NOT the "Fine-Grained Reader" role.*

Security Layers' Functionality

At this point, we have built four independent security layers. Here is how they interact for different user types:

User Type	Dataset Access	Row Filter	Column Masking	What They See
Project Owner	Full	Bypassed	Bypassed	Everything
Data Viewer + RLS (US-West)	Read-only	US-West only	Salary/email masked	US-West rows, no PII
Data Viewer + Fine-Grained Reader	Read-only	US-West only	No masking	US-West rows, with PII
No IAM role	None	N/A	N/A	Access denied

Table 11.3: *Security Layer Interactions by User Type*

This is defense in depth. Even if one layer is misconfigured or overly permissive, the other layers still protect the sensitive data. The combination of all four layers creates a security posture that satisfies most regulatory requirements–without requiring any external tools or third-party solutions.

Data Quality Assertions

Security controls who can see the data. However, there is an equally important question: Is the data trustworthy?

Production data pipelines inevitably encounter dirty data. A source system might send null values where IDs are expected. A currency conversion might produce negative amounts. A timestamp field might contain dates that are set in the future. Without explicit quality checks, these issues flow silently through the pipeline, corrupting downstream tables and producing incorrect dashboards.

In the previous chapter, we used the **`BigQueryCheckOperator`** in Airflow to create quality gates. Here, we will build a standalone quality assertion query that can be used in any context–inside a DAG, as a scheduled query, or as a manual audit.

Writing SQL-Based Quality Assertions

The following is a comprehensive quality check query that validates the "**`transactions`**" table:

```
-- Data quality assertion query
WITH quality_checks AS (
  SELECT
    -- Completeness checks
    COUNTIF(transaction_id IS NULL) AS null_transaction_ids,
    COUNTIF(employee_id IS NULL) AS null_employee_ids,
    COUNTIF(amount IS NULL) AS null_amounts,

    -- Validity checks
```

```
    COUNTIF(amount <= 0) AS negative_amounts,
    COUNTIF(amount > 50000) AS suspicious_large_amounts,
    COUNTIF(transaction_date > CURRENT_DATE()) AS future_dates,
    COUNTIF(status NOT IN ('approved', 'pending')) AS invalid_sta-
tuses,

    -- Referential integrity
    COUNT(DISTINCT t.employee_id) AS unique_employees_in_txn,
    (SELECT COUNT(*) FROM `your-project-id.governance_lab.employ-
ees`) AS total_employees,

    -- Volume check
    COUNT(*) AS total_rows
  FROM `your-project-id.governance_lab.transactions` t
)
SELECT
  total_rows,
  CASE WHEN null_transaction_ids = 0 THEN '✅ PASS' ELSE '❌ FAIL'
END AS pk_not_null,
  CASE WHEN null_amounts = 0 THEN '✅ PASS' ELSE '❌ FAIL' END AS
amount_not_null,
  CASE WHEN negative_amounts = 0 THEN '✅ PASS' ELSE '❌ FAIL' END
AS amount_positive,
  CASE WHEN suspicious_large_amounts = 0 THEN '✅ PASS' ELSE '⚠
WARNING' END AS amount_range,
  CASE WHEN future_dates = 0 THEN '✅ PASS' ELSE '❌ FAIL' END AS
no_future_dates,
  CASE WHEN invalid_statuses = 0 THEN '✅ PASS' ELSE '❌ FAIL' END
AS valid_statuses,
  CONCAT(CAST(unique_employees_in_txn AS STRING), '/', CAST(total_
employees AS STRING)) AS referential_coverage
FROM quality_checks;
```

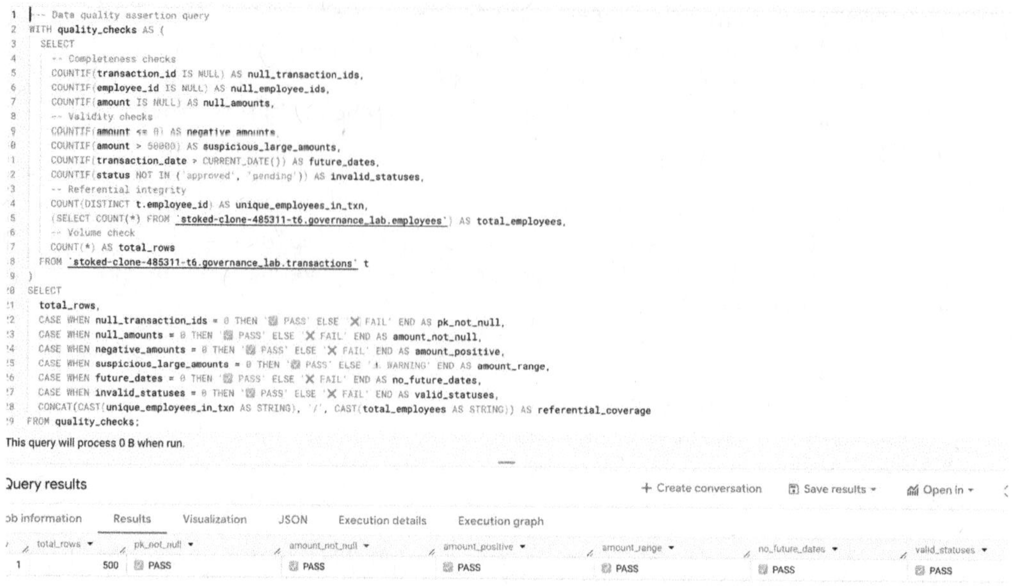

***Figure 11.10**: Data Quality Assertion Results with PASS/FAIL Indicators*

The preceding single query checks six dimensions of data quality in one pass:

- **Completeness**: Are critical fields (such as **`transaction_id`**, **`amount`**) ever null?
- **Validity**: Are amounts positive? Are dates in the past? Are statuses from the allowed set?
- **Referential Integrity**: Do all employee IDs in transactions exist in the employees table?
- **Volume**: Is the total row count within expected bounds?

Each check produces a clear "**`PASS`**," "**`FAIL`**," or "**`WARNING`**" indicator. In a production pipeline, you would embed this pattern as a "**`BigQueryCheckOperator`**" task in your Airflow DAG (as demonstrated in the previous chapter), failing the pipeline if any critical check returns "**`FAIL`**."

Best Practice: Quality checks should be embedded directly in your pipelines rather than run as afterthoughts. A pipeline that loads data without verifying is a pipeline that will eventually corrupt a production dashboard.

Metadata Auditing with `INFORMATION_SCHEMA`

`INFORMATION_SCHEMA` provides a SQL-queryable audit trail of your entire BigQuery estate. Unlike navigating through the console, SQL queries against **`INFORMATION_SCHEMA`** can be automated, scheduled, and incorporated into monitoring pipelines.

Auditing Table Metadata

The "**__TABLES__**" metadata table provides a quick overview of every table in a dataset—including size, row count, and modification timestamps:

```
-- Audit all tables: type, size, row count, and last modified
SELECT
  table_id AS table_name,
  CASE type
    WHEN 1 THEN 'TABLE'
    WHEN 2 THEN 'VIEW'
    ELSE 'OTHER'
  END AS table_type,
  TIMESTAMP_MILLIS(creation_time) AS created_at,
  TIMESTAMP_MILLIS(last_modified_time) AS last_modified,
  ROUND(size_bytes / 1024, 2) AS size_kb,
  row_count
FROM `your-project-id.governance_lab.__TABLES__`
ORDER BY creation_time DESC;
```

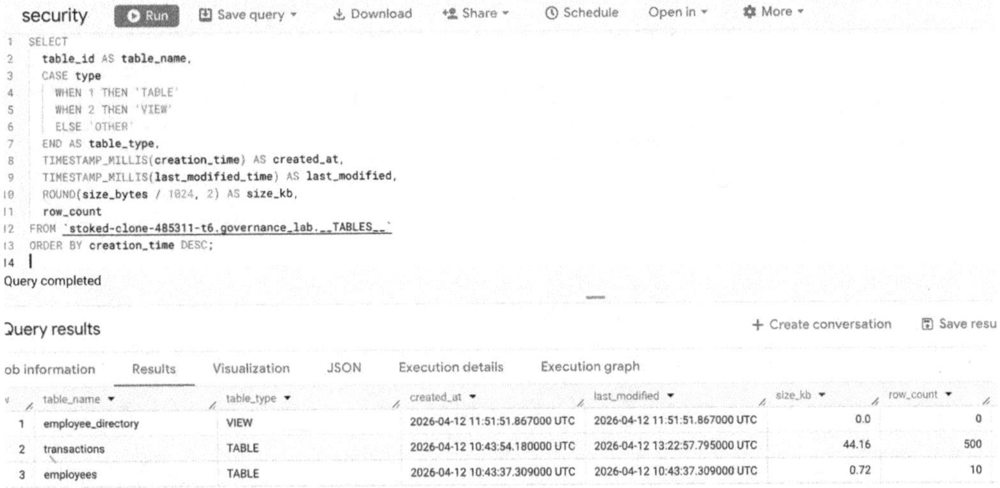

***Figure 11.11:** Table Metadata Audit Using __TABLES__ with Size and Row Counts*

This query reveals the complete inventory of the "**governance_lab**" dataset: two base tables ("**employees**" at 0.72 KB with 10 rows, "**transactions**" at 44.16 KB with 500 rows) and one view ("**employee_directory**" at 0 KB with 0 rows—views have no physical storage).

Auditing Column Schemas

For a deeper audit, query "**INFORMATION_SCHEMA.COLUMNS**" to inspect every column across all tables in the following way:

```
-- Audit all columns and their data types
SELECT
  table_name,
  column_name,
  data_type,
  is_nullable
FROM `your-project-id.governance_lab.INFORMATION_SCHEMA.COLUMNS`
ORDER BY table_name, ordinal_position;
```

Figure 11.12: "`INFORMATION_SCHEMA`" *Column Audit Showing All Table Schemas*

This gives you a complete schema inventory–useful for detecting schema drift, identifying columns that should have "**`NOT NULL`**" constraints, and documenting the data model for new team members.

In a production governance workflow, you would schedule these queries daily and compare results across runs. If a column disappears, a data type changes, or a table's row count drops to zero, an alert should fire. Combined with the quality assertions from the previous section, "**`INFORMATION_SCHEMA`**" queries form the backbone of automated data governance.

Data Catalog and Discoverability

Creating security controls and quality checks is essential. However, there is one more piece of the governance puzzle: discoverability. As data platforms grow, finding the right table becomes increasingly difficult. A data engineer might create dozens of datasets and hundreds of tables. Without documentation, new team members waste hours searching for data that already exists, or worse, creating duplicate tables because they could not find the original.

Google Cloud Data Catalog solves this by indexing every BigQuery table and making it searchable–complete with schema information, policy tags, and user-defined descriptions.

Discovering Tables in Data Catalog

Open Data Catalog in the GCP Console:

1. Navigate to ≡ → **`Dataplex`** → **`Search`** (or search for "**`Data Catalog`**" in the console search bar).
2. In the search bar, type "**`governance_lab`**."
3. Filter by **`Systems`** → **`BigQuery`** on the left panel.
4. Click the "**`governance_lab`**" dataset entry.

You will see all tables and views in the dataset, along with their types and creation timestamps:

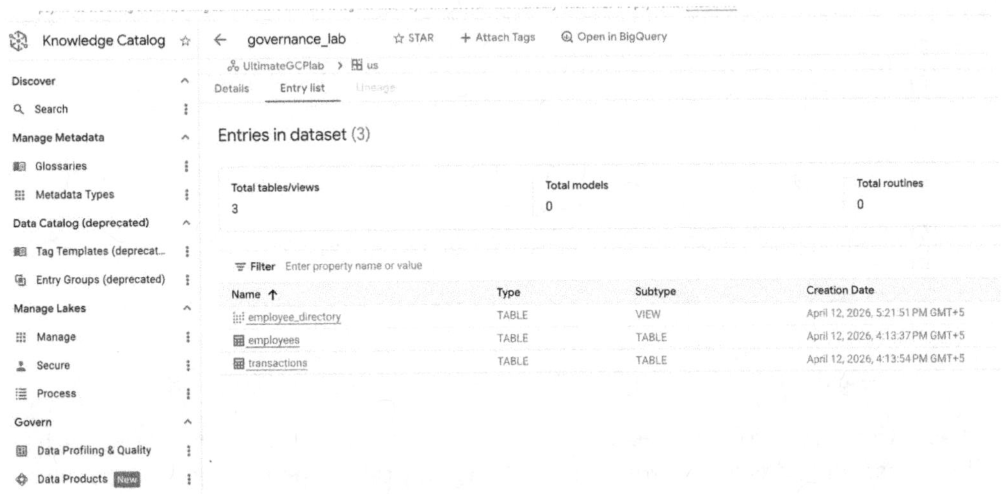

Figure 11.13: Data Catalog Dataset Entry Listing "`governance_lab`" Tables

Adding Table and Column Descriptions

Documentation is only useful if it exists. Add descriptions to make tables discoverable and self-documenting in the following way:

```
ALTER TABLE `your-project-id.governance_lab.employees`
ALTER COLUMN salary SET OPTIONS (description = 'Annual base salary
in USD. Tagged as Highly Confidential.');

ALTER TABLE `your-project-id.governance_lab.employees`
ALTER COLUMN email SET OPTIONS (description = 'Corporate email
address. Tagged as Highly Confidential PII.');

ALTER TABLE `your-project-id.governance_lab.employees`
ALTER COLUMN department SET OPTIONS (description = 'Business
department. Used for row-level security filtering.');
```

These descriptions are immediately visible in both BigQuery and Data Catalog. When a colleague browses the "**employees**" table schema, they will see not only the column name and data type, but also the business context and security classification.

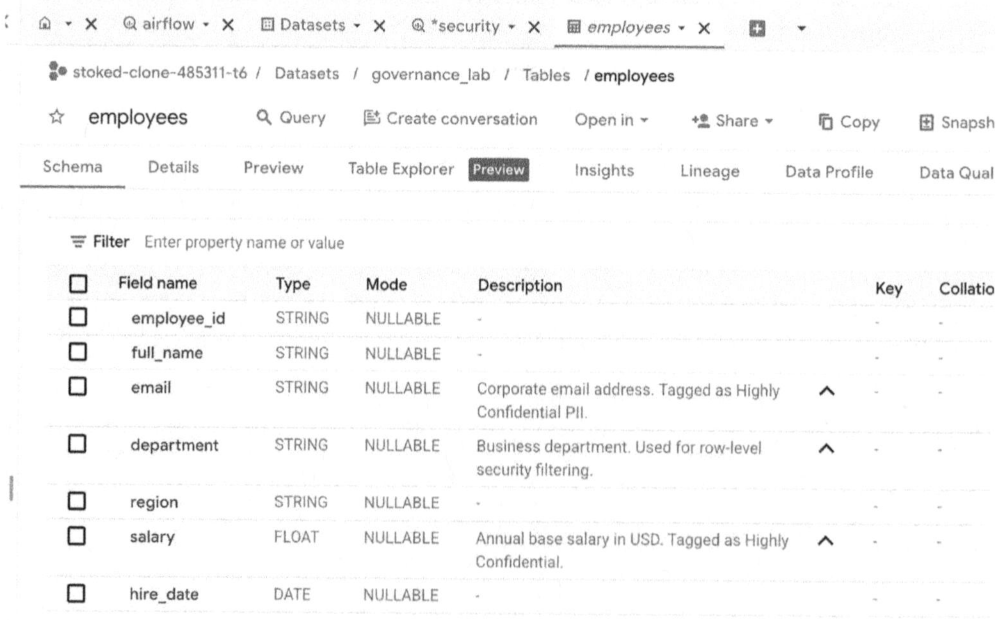

***Figure 11.14**: Employees Table Schema with Column-Level Descriptions*

Best Practice: Treat column descriptions as part of your code review process. When a Pull Request (PR) adds a new column to a BigQuery table, the review should include a meaningful description—just as it would include a code comment for a new function.

Putting It All Together

Let us step back and look at what we have built in this chapter. Starting from a raw dataset with sensitive employee and financial data, we implemented a complete governance framework, including:

- **IAM Access Controls:** Restricted dataset access to only the users and service accounts that need it, following the principle of least privilege.
- **Authorized Views:** Created the "`employee_directory`" view that exposes non-sensitive columns while hiding salary and email. Users who can only access the view never see PII.
- **Row-Level Security:** Applied row access policies that automatically filter transactions by region, per user. The US-West regional manager sees only US-West data. Administrators see everything via the `FILTER USING (TRUE)` policy.
- **Column-Level Security:** Attached "`Data Catalog`" policy tags to "`salary`," "`email`," and "`full_name` **columns**." Users without the "`Fine-Grained Reader`" role cannot query these columns, regardless of their other permissions.
- **Data Quality Assertions:** Built a SQL query that checks completeness, validity, referential integrity, and volume in a single pass, producing `PASS/FAIL` indicators that can be integrated into any pipeline.
- **Metadata Auditing:** Used "`__TABLES__`" and "`INFORMATION_SCHEMA.COLUMNS`" to inventory all tables, columns, sizes, and data types, forming the basis of automated governance monitoring.
- **Data Catalog Discovery:** Made tables searchable and self-documenting with column descriptions that appear in both BigQuery and Data Catalog.

None of these capabilities require external tools. Everything–IAM, row-level security, column-level masking, Data Catalog, `INFORMATION_SCHEMA`–is built into BigQuery at no additional cost. Governance has no billing impact.

Cleanup

If you are working in a lab environment, remove the resources created in this chapter in the following manner:

```
# Remove row access policies
bq query --use_legacy_sql=false \
  "DROP ALL ROW ACCESS POLICIES ON \`${PROJECT_ID}.governance_lab.
transactions\`"

# Delete the taxonomy (if it exists)
```

```
export TAXONOMY_NAME=$(gcloud data-catalog taxonomies list \
  --location=us --project=${PROJECT_ID} \
  --filter="displayName='Data Sensitivity'" \
  --format="value(name)")

if [ -n "$TAXONOMY_NAME" ]; then
  gcloud data-catalog taxonomies delete ${TAXONOMY_NAME} --quiet
  echo "Taxonomy deleted."
else
  echo "No taxonomy found to delete."
fi

# Delete the dataset
bq rm -r -f -d ${PROJECT_ID}:governance_lab
```

Conclusion

This chapter addressed the critical question that separates a data pipeline from a data platform: Who is allowed to see what?

BigQuery provides a layered security model where IAM controls dataset access, authorized views restrict column visibility, row access policies filter rows per user, and column-level policy tags mask sensitive fields. These layers stack independently, creating defense in depth without any single point of failure.

However, security without quality is incomplete. We built SQL-based quality assertions that check completeness, validity, and referential integrity—the same patterns that should run inside every production pipeline via the `BigQueryCheckOperator` tasks we created in the previous chapter.

Furthermore, governance without discoverability is governance that nobody uses. Data Catalog and `INFORMATION_SCHEMA` provide the tools to inventory, document, and monitor your entire data estate from SQL.

In the next chapter, we will explore how Machine Learning (ML) workflows can be built directly inside of BigQuery by using BigQuery ML and Vertex AI—training, evaluating, and deploying models using SQL, without moving data out of the warehouse.

Points to Remember

- **BigQuery security uses four independent layers -** IAM, authorized views, row-level security, and column-level security - each progressively narrowing data access.

- **Always assign IAM permissions at the dataset level following the principle of least privilege** – grant **dataViewer**, not **dataOwner**, unless broader access is genuinely needed.
- **Authorized views restrict column visibility** but only protect data when users query through the view, not when accessing the underlying table directly.
- **Row access policies are additive** – if a user matches multiple policies, they see rows from all matching policies combined.
- Column-level security via Data Catalog policy tags enforces restrictions regardless of how the table is accessed, closing the gap that authorized views leave open.
- **Data quality assertions should be embedded directly in pipelines,** checking completeness, validity, referential integrity, and volume in a single SQL pass.
- **`INFORMATION_SCHEMA`** and **`__TABLES__`** provide SQL-queryable metadata for automated governance monitoring and schema drift detection.
- All governance capabilities – IAM, row-level security, column masking, Data Catalog – are built into BigQuery at no additional cost.

Multiple Choice Questions

1. A data engineer needs to grant a business analyst read-only access to a single BigQuery dataset without allowing them to modify or delete any tables. Which IAM role should they assign?

    a. `roles/bigquery.admin`

    b. `roles/bigquery.dataViewer`

    c. `roles/bigquery.dataEditor`

    d. `roles/bigquery.jobUser`

2. What is the primary purpose of an authorized view in BigQuery?

    a. To improve query performance by caching results

    b. To restrict which columns are visible to users who query through the view

    c. To create a materialized copy of the underlying table

    d. To enable row-level security on the underlying data

3. A row access policy is created with `FILTER USING (region = 'US-West')` and granted to a specific user. What happens when that user runs `SELECT * FROM table`?

   a. The query fails with an access denied error

   b. The query returns all rows but masks the region column

   c. The query returns only rows where `region = 'US-West'`, as if the other rows do not exist

   d. The query returns all rows with a warning about the policy

4. Two row access policies exist on the same table for the same user–one with `FILTER USING (region = 'US-West')` and another with `FILTER USING (region = 'APAC')`. What rows does the user see?

   a. Only US–West rows (the first policy takes precedence)

   b. Only APAC rows (the last policy takes precedence)

   c. Rows from both US–West and APAC (policies are additive)

   d. No rows (conflicting policies cancel each other out)

5. How does column-level security in BigQuery differ from authorized views?

   a. Column-level security only works with views, not base tables

   b. Authorized views enforce restrictions regardless of how the table is accessed; column-level security does not

   c. Column-level security enforces restrictions regardless of how the table is accessed; authorized views only work when users query through the view

   d. There is no difference–they achieve the same result

6. A data engineer attaches a "Highly Confidential" policy tag to the `"salary"` column and does NOT grant Fine-Grained Reader access to User A. What happens when User A queries `SELECT employee_id, salary FROM employees`?

   a. The query returns all rows with salary values masked as NULL

   b. The query returns all rows, but the salary column is hidden

   c. The query fails with an access denied error on the salary column

   d. The query succeeds because IAM Data Viewer overrides policy tags

7. Which approach provides a reliable way to audit all tables, their sizes, and row counts in a BigQuery dataset?
    a. `INFORMATION_SCHEMA.TABLE_STORAGE`
    b. `dataset.__TABLES__`
    c. `INFORMATION_SCHEMA.ROW_ACCESS_POLICIES`
    d. `INFORMATION_SCHEMA.SCHEMATA`
8. In a data quality assertion query, what does a check such as `COUNTIF (transaction_date > CURRENT_DATE()) AS future_dates` validate?
    a. That all transactions occurred in the future
    b. That no transactions have dates beyond today, which would indicate data integrity issues
    c. That the "`transaction_date`" column is not null
    d. That the data was loaded today
9. What is the purpose of a Data Catalog taxonomy in BigQuery column-level security?
    a. To organize tables into logical groups for query optimization
    b. To classify data sensitivity levels and enforce fine-grained access control on columns
    c. To create backup copies of tables across regions
    d. To schedule automatic data quality checks
10. Which of the following is NOT a dimension of data quality that can be validated with SQL assertions?
    a. Completeness: checking for null values in required fields
    b. Validity: checking that values fall within expected ranges
    c. Latency: measuring how fast a query executes
    d. Referential integrity: checking that foreign keys match primary keys

Answers

1. b
2. b

3. c
4. c
5. c
6. c
7. b
8. b
9. b
10. c

Questions

1. Explain the BigQuery security layer model (IAM, authorized views, row-level security, column-level security). How do these layers interact, and why is layered security preferable to a single access control mechanism?
2. A company has an "**`employees`**" table with columns: **`employee_id`**, **`full_name`**, **`email`**, **`salary`**, **`department`**, and **`region`**. The marketing team needs to see employee names and departments but not salaries or emails. The finance team needs full access to salary data. Design a security architecture using the techniques covered in this chapter.
3. Describe the difference between authorized views and column-level security. In what scenarios would you use one over the other, and when would you use both together?
4. A data engineer runs a quality assertion query and discovers that 15% of transaction amounts are negative. Describe how you would integrate this quality check into a Cloud Composer pipeline (refer to the previous chapter), so that the pipeline automatically halts if the check fails.
5. Explain why **`FILTER USING (TRUE)`** is used in row access policies for administrators. What would happen if an administrator's row access policy were accidentally deleted, and how would this affect their ability to query the table?

Key Terms

- **Identity and Access Management (IAM):** Google Cloud's system for controlling who can perform actions on resources. In BigQuery, IAM roles determine whether users can read, write, or administer datasets and tables.
- **Principle of Least Privilege:** A security best practice where users are granted only the minimum permissions necessary to perform their job functions, reducing the risk of accidental or intentional data exposure.
- **Authorized View:** A BigQuery view that has been granted permission to read data from a dataset on behalf of users, even if those users do not have direct access to the underlying tables. Used to restrict which columns are visible.
- **Row Access Policy:** A BigQuery security feature that automatically filters table rows based on who is running the query. Policies are defined with SQL predicates (for example, `region = 'US-West'`) and are invisible to the querying user.
- **Policy Tag:** A Data Catalog label that can be attached to BigQuery table columns to enforce column-level security. Users must have the Fine-Grained Reader role on the tag to query tagged columns.
- **Taxonomy:** A hierarchical classification structure in Data Catalog that organizes policy tags (for example, "`Data Sensitivity`" taxonomy containing "`Highly Confidential`" and "`Internal`" tags).
- **Fine-Grained Reader:** A Data Catalog IAM role that grants permission to read data in columns protected by a specific policy tag. Without this role, queries on tagged columns return an access denied error.
- **Column-Level Security:** A BigQuery feature that restricts access to individual table columns using Data Catalog policy tags, enforced regardless of how the table is accessed (direct query, view, export, or copy).
- **Data Quality Assertion:** A SQL query that validates data against expected conditions (completeness, validity, referential integrity) and produces PASS/FAIL results, used to prevent corrupt data from entering downstream tables.
- **`INFORMATION_SCHEMA`:** A set of BigQuery system views that expose metadata about tables, columns, partitions, and access policies in a SQL-queryable format.
- **Data Catalog:** A Google Cloud service that indexes BigQuery tables and other data assets, making them searchable and discoverable with schema information, policy tags, and user-defined descriptions.
- **Defense in Depth:** A security strategy that uses multiple independent layers of protection so that if one layer fails, the remaining layers still protect the data.

CHAPTER 12

BigQuery ML and Vertex AI

Introduction

So far, we have built a robust data platform. We have established secure ingestion patterns, automated transformations, implemented strict governance rules, and orchestrated everything through Cloud Composer. Now, data flows reliably from source systems into refined analytical tables.

However, data sitting in a table is only providing historical insights–what happened yesterday or last month. The next frontier in data engineering is moving from descriptive analytics (what happened) to predictive analytics (what is going to happen).

Traditionally, adding Machine Learning (ML) to a data platform involved heavy lifting. Data engineers had to build complex Extract, Transform, Load (ETL) pipelines to extract large volumes of data from the data warehouse, load it into an external ML environment (such as Spark MLlib, TensorFlow, or Scikit-Learn instances), manage the infrastructure for training, and then figure out how to serve those models back into the business systems. This process introduced latency, duplicated data, created complex governance nightmares, and required specialized tooling.

Google Cloud changed this paradigm entirely with BigQuery ML. Instead of moving the data to the ML algorithms, BigQuery ML brings the algorithms to the data. It allows data engineers and analysts to train, evaluate, and deploy ML models by using standard SQL directly inside the data warehouse. As for advanced production serving–such as low-latency online predictions–BigQuery ML seamlessly integrates with Vertex AI, that is, Google's enterprise ML platform.

In this chapter, we will bridge the gap between data engineering and ML. We will explore how to build and train models using SQL, efficiently engineer features, tune hyperparameters, and eventually export and deploy models via Vertex AI for production use cases. Along the way, we will discuss architecture patterns, orchestration, and cost optimization, proving that you do not need to be a data scientist to build production-grade AI pipelines.

By the end of this chapter, you will have a solid understanding of how to train, evaluate, and deploy ML models natively by using standard SQL. The broader implication of these insights is a massive architectural shift: you no longer need disjointed, complex infrastructure outside the warehouse to build production-grade AI pipelines.

Structure

In this chapter, we will cover the following topics:

- The Machine Learning (ML) Paradigm Shift
- Building Models in BigQuery ML
- Feature Engineering
- Evaluating and Tuning Models
- Vertex AI Integration
- Productionizing ML Workflows
- Cost and Performance Considerations

The Machine Learning (ML) Paradigm Shift

In a traditional ML architecture, the workflow looks as follows: the data warehouse acts merely as a storage layer. When data scientists need to train a model, they execute large "`SELECT *`" queries or use specialized connectors to pull terabytes of data out of the warehouse and into an external processing cluster (such as a managed notebook or a Dataproc cluster). There, the data is preprocessed, models are trained, and predictions are generated. The predictions are then written back into the data warehouse using another pipeline.

This architecture introduces the following challenges for the data engineering team:

- **Data Movement and Duplication:** Moving terabytes of data over the network is slow, expensive, and leads to multiple out-of-sync copies of the data.
- **Security and Governance Gaps:** The moment data leaves the heavily governed data warehouse (where you spent the previous chapter setting up Row-Level and Column-Level Security), it enters a new environment. Ensuring that those security policies travel with the data is incredibly difficult.
- **Complexity and Tool Sprawl:** It forces the organization to maintain distinct technology stacks–SQL/dbt for data engineering and Python/Scala for ML.
- **Operational Latency:** By the time data is extracted, trained, and predictions are written back, the underlying business reality may have already changed.

Enter BigQuery ML

BigQuery ML flips the architecture on its head. It treats the ML algorithm as just another query function. Under the hood, BigQuery provisions the compute resources–including servers and, if needed, GPUs/TPUs–distributes the training workload across its massive execution engine, and stores the resulting model as an object directly beside your tables.

Consideration	BigQuery ML	Traditional Frameworks (for example, Scikit-learn, PyTorch)
Language	Standard SQL	Python, R, Scala
Data Movement	None–models train where the data lives.	High–data must be extracted and loaded into memory.
Governance	Inherits BigQuery IAM, RLS, and CLS automatically.	Requires rebuilding security rules in the ML environment.
Best For	Structured/tabular data, fast iteration, team democratizing ML.	Computer vision, NLP, massive deep learning grids, highly customized architectures.

Table 12.1: *BigQuery ML versus Traditional ML Frameworks*

Use **`CasesBigQuery`** ML is not a replacement for every ML workflow. It is highly optimized for structured tabular data and time series.

Use BigQuery ML in the following scenarios:

- Your inputs are already housed in BigQuery tables or views.
- The use case involves standard predictive tasks such as classification (churn prediction), regression (lifetime value prediction), k-means clustering (customer segmentation), or time series forecasting (sales projections).
- You want to empower SQL-fluent data engineers and domain experts to build models without learning Python.

Use Vertex AI Custom Training (Traditional Frameworks) in the following scenarios:

- You are processing unstructured data such as raw images, video, or massive corpora of text.
- You require complex and deep neural network architectures that are unsupported by standard algorithms.
- You are importing a highly customized model trained entirely outside of Google Cloud.

In modern data platform design, BigQuery ML acts as the foundational ML layer, handling 80% of business prediction tasks natively, while leaving Vertex AI to handle specialized, heavy-artillery modeling.

Building Models with SQL

Building an ML model in BigQuery is syntactically nearly identical to creating a table or a view. Instead of "CREATE TABLE," you simply use the "CREATE MODEL" statement.

The Problem: Customer Churn Prediction

For our practical example, we will tackle Customer Churn–predicting whether a customer will cancel their subscription. Let us build a concrete dataset to work with. We will create a dedicated dataset called "**bqml_lab**" and populate it with realistic customer activity data that tracks engagement metrics over time:

```
CREATE SCHEMA `bqml_lab`
OPTIONS (location = 'US', description = 'BigQuery ML lab dataset');
```

Next, we will generate 1,000 synthetic customer records. Each record captures a customer's plan type, login frequency, support ticket history, and spending patterns. The target variable–**churned**–is derived from behavioral indicators: customers with low engagement, payment failures, or plan downgrades are more likely to churn.

```
CREATE OR REPLACE TABLE `bqml_lab.customer_activity` AS
WITH customer_base AS (
  SELECT
    CONCAT('CUST', LPAD(CAST(num AS STRING), 4, '0')) AS customer_id,
    DATE_SUB(CURRENT_DATE(), INTERVAL CAST(RAND() * 730 AS INT64)
DAY) AS signup_date,
    CASE
      WHEN RAND() < 0.3 THEN 'Enterprise'
      WHEN RAND() < 0.7 THEN 'Professional'
      ELSE 'Starter'
    END AS plan_type,
    ROUND(RAND() * 500 + 50, 2) AS monthly_charges
  FROM UNNEST(GENERATE_ARRAY(1, 1000)) AS num
),
activity AS (
  SELECT *,
    CAST(RAND() * 30 AS INT64) AS logins_last_month,
    CAST(RAND() * 100 AS INT64) AS feature_usage_count,
    CAST(RAND() * 10 AS INT64) AS support_tickets,
    ROUND(RAND() * 1000, 2) AS total_spend,
    DATE_DIFF(CURRENT_DATE(), signup_date, DAY) AS customer_age_days,
    CASE WHEN RAND() < 0.2 THEN 1 ELSE 0 END AS payment_failed,
    CASE WHEN RAND() < 0.15 THEN 1 ELSE 0 END AS downgraded_plan
  FROM customer_base
```

```
)
SELECT *,
  CASE
    WHEN logins_last_month < 5 AND payment_failed = 1 THEN 1
    WHEN logins_last_month < 3 AND support_tickets > 5 THEN 1
    WHEN downgraded_plan = 1 AND logins_last_month < 10 THEN 1
    WHEN feature_usage_count < 20 AND customer_age_days > 180 THEN 1
    WHEN RAND() < 0.15 THEN 1
    ELSE 0
  END AS churned
FROM activity;
```

We can verify the churn distribution immediately in the following manner:

```
SELECT churned, COUNT(*) AS customer_count,
  ROUND(COUNT(*) * 100.0 / SUM(COUNT(*)) OVER(), 2) AS percentage
FROM `bqml_lab.customer_activity`
GROUP BY churned;
```

This gives us a realistic imbalanced dataset–roughly 30–40% churn versus 60–70% active–which mirrors the real-world subscription data.

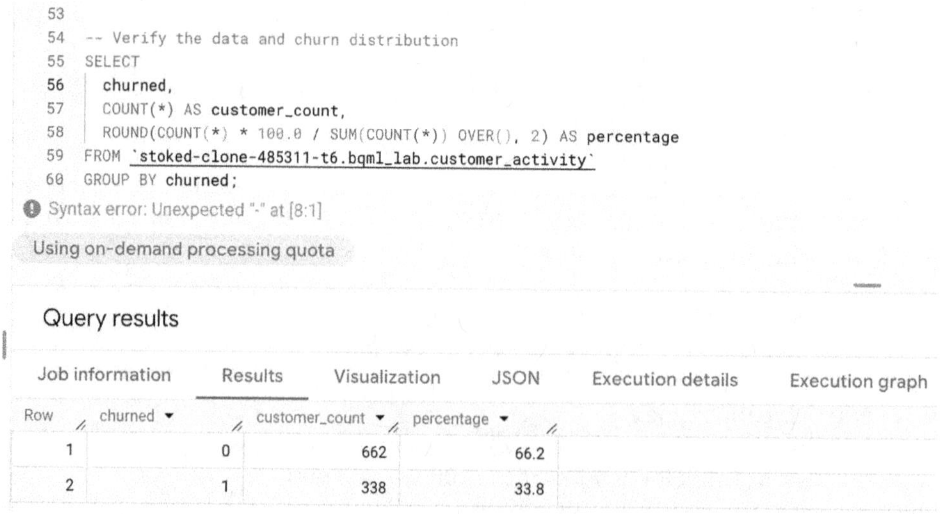

Figure 12.1: *Customer Activity Table with Churn Distribution*

We want to predict whether a customer will cancel their subscription (that is, **`churned = 1`**) or stay active (that is, **`churned = 0`**). As we are predicting a binary categorical outcome, this is a Classification problem. Therefore, we will use a Logistic Regression model.

Feature Engineering Natively

A model is only as good as the data fed into it. Feature engineering is the process of taking raw data and manipulating it into a format that the ML algorithm can understand and learn from more effectively.

In Python environments, data scientists use libraries such as Pandas or Scikit-Learn pipelines to impute null values, bucketize geographic data, or one-hot encode categorical strings. In BigQuery, you do this entirely in SQL.

Standard SQL Feature Engineering

Your first line of defense is standard SQL functions. You can create a view that transforms the raw "**customer_activity**" table into rich ML features before feeding it to "**CREATE MODEL**."

```
CREATE OR REPLACE VIEW `bqml_lab.customer_features` AS
SELECT
  customer_id,
  plan_type,
  customer_age_days,
  monthly_charges,
  logins_last_month,
  feature_usage_count,
  support_tickets,
  total_spend,
  ROUND(total_spend / NULLIF(customer_age_days, 0) * 30, 2) AS avg_
monthly_spend,
  ROUND(feature_usage_count / NULLIF(logins_last_month, 0), 2) AS
features_per_login,
  payment_failed,
  downgraded_plan,
  churned
FROM `bqml_lab.customer_activity`;
```

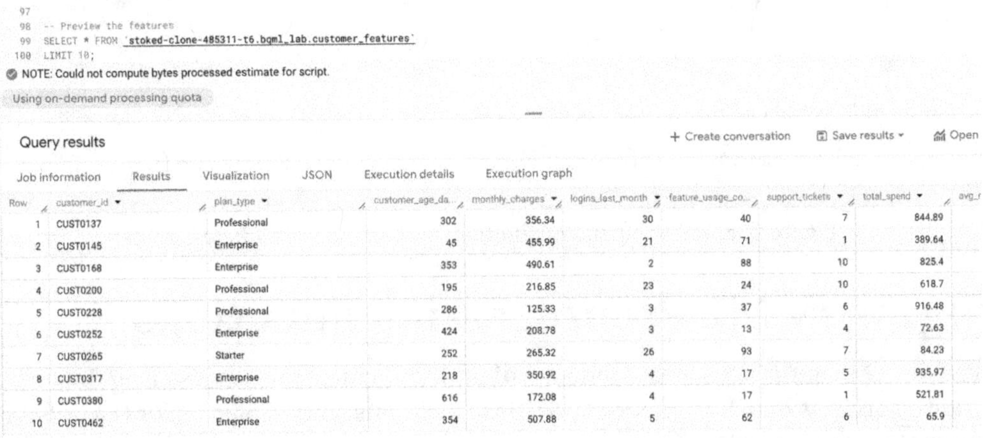

```
97
98  -- Preview the features
99  SELECT * FROM `stoked-clone-485311-t6.bqml_lab.customer_features`
100 LIMIT 10;
```


Row	customer_id	plan_type	customer_age_da...	monthly_charges	logins_last_month	feature_usage_co...	support_tickets	total_spend	avg_r
1	CUST0137	Professional	302	356.34	30	40	7	844.89	
2	CUST0145	Enterprise	45	455.99	21	71	1	389.64	
3	CUST0168	Enterprise	353	490.61	2	88	10	825.4	
4	CUST0200	Professional	195	216.85	23	24	10	618.7	
5	CUST0228	Professional	286	125.33	3	37	6	916.48	
6	CUST0252	Enterprise	424	208.78	3	13	4	72.63	
7	CUST0265	Starter	252	265.32	26	93	7	84.23	
8	CUST0317	Enterprise	218	350.92	4	17	5	935.97	
9	CUST0380	Professional	616	172.08	4	17	1	521.81	
10	CUST0462	Enterprise	354	507.88	5	62	6	65.9	

Figure 12.2: *Feature Engineering View Results Showing Derived Features*

Once the features are engineered, it is standard practice to split the data into training and evaluation sets. We use **FARM_FINGERPRINT** to create a deterministic 80/20 split that remains consistent across reruns.

```
CREATE OR REPLACE TABLE `bqml_lab.training_data` AS
SELECT * FROM `bqml_lab.customer_features`
WHERE MOD(ABS(FARM_FINGERPRINT(customer_id)), 10) < 8;

CREATE OR REPLACE TABLE `bqml_lab.evaluation_data` AS
SELECT * FROM `bqml_lab.customer_features`
WHERE MOD(ABS(FARM_FINGERPRINT(customer_id)), 10) >= 8;
```

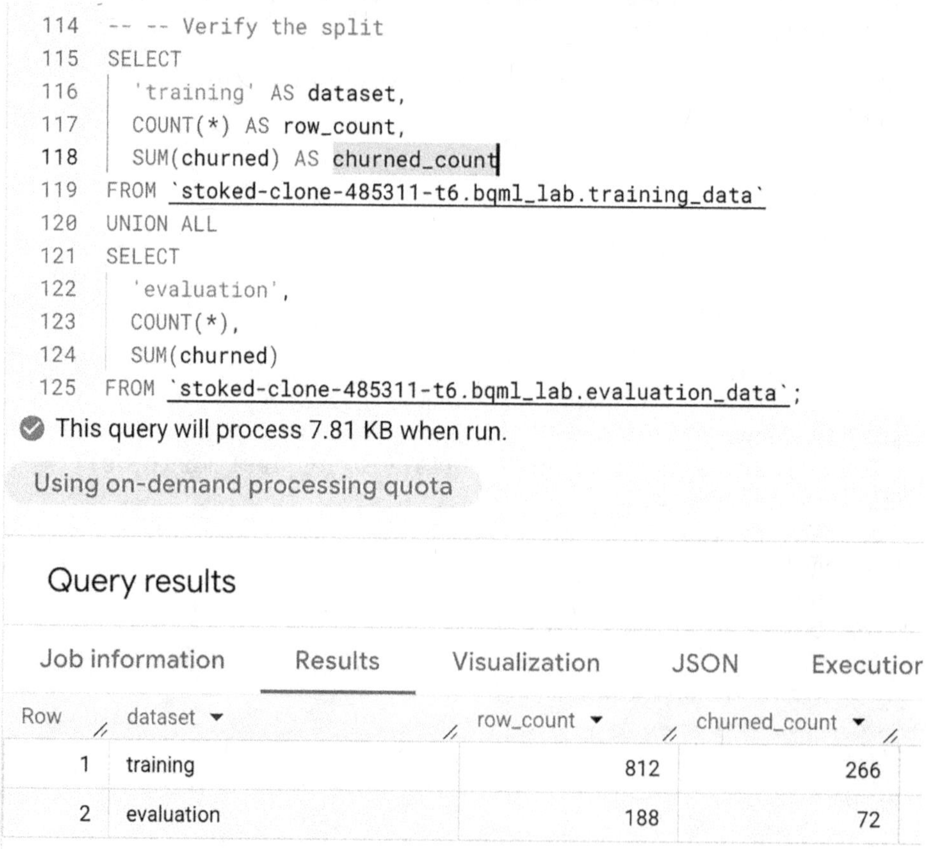

Figure 12.3: *Training and Evaluation Dataset Split with Row Counts*

BigQuery ML Preprocessing Functions

BigQuery ML automates a vast amount of underlying feature engineering. By default, it automatically one-hot encodes "**STRING**" columns and scales "**FLOAT64**" columns during the "**CREATE MODEL**" process.

However, BQML also provides specific preprocessing functions via the "**TRANSFORM**" clause. Using the "**TRANSFORM**" clause inside a "**CREATE MODEL**" statement ensures that whatever feature scaling or bucketizing you apply to the training data is automatically applied to production data when you run a prediction.

```
CREATE OR REPLACE MODEL `bqml_lab.churn_with_transform`
TRANSFORM(
  -- Bucketize continuous age into discrete categories
  ML.BUCKETIZE(customer_age_days, [0, 30, 90, 180, 365])
AS age_buckets,
  -- Combine plan_type with payment_failed to learn how the
  -- plan-vs-churn relationship shifts when a customer has had a
payment issue
  ML.FEATURE_CROSS(STRUCT(plan_type, CAST(payment_failed AS STRING)))
AS plan_payment_cross,
  churned
)
OPTIONS(model_type='LOGISTIC_REG', input_label_cols=['churned'])
AS
SELECT * FROM `bqml_lab.training_data`;
```

Training the Model

Now that we have our customer activity data with churn labels and engineered features, we can train the model. We provide BigQuery with the target column (what we want to predict) and the feature columns (what we are using to make the prediction).

```
CREATE OR REPLACE MODEL `bqml_lab.churn_model_v1`
OPTIONS(
  model_type='LOGISTIC_REG',
  input_label_cols=['churned'],
  auto_class_weights=TRUE,
  max_iterations=20
) AS
SELECT
  plan_type,
  customer_age_days,
  monthly_charges,
  logins_last_month,
  support_tickets,
  churned
FROM `bqml_lab.training_data`;
```

Let us break down the "OPTIONS" clause, which is where the magic happens:

- **model_type='LOGISTIC_REG'**: Tells BigQuery ML the specific algorithm to use. BigQuery supports many types, including linear regression (**LINEAR_**

REG), boosted trees (**BOOSTED_TREE_CLASSIFIER**), neural networks (**DNN_CLASSIFIER**), and more.

- **input_label_cols=['churned']:** This is critical. It identifies the target column that the model is trying to learn to predict. BigQuery assumes all other columns returned by the "**SELECT**" statement are the input features.
- **auto_class_weights=TRUE:** In churn datasets, there are usually far more active users than churned users. This option tells BigQuery to automatically balance the weights so the model is not biased toward predicting the majority class.

When you execute this query, BigQuery spins up the training job in the background. It reads the data, normalizes the inputs, performs gradient descent to find the optimal weights, and saves the trained artifact as a model object in the dataset.

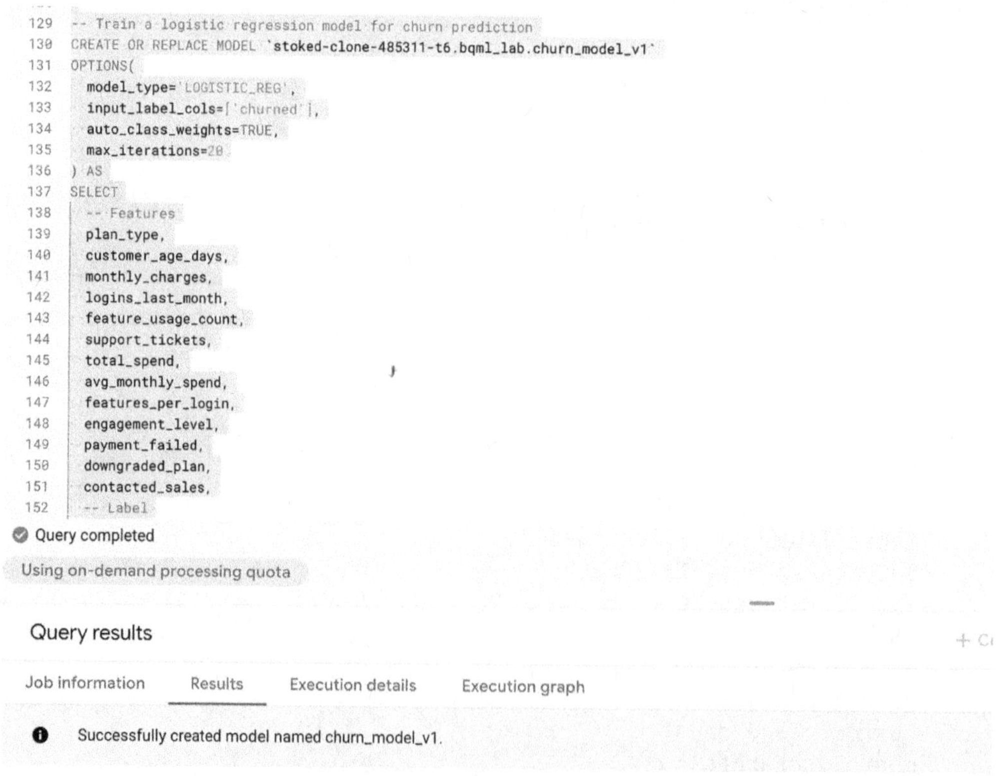

***Figure 12.4:** BigQuery Console Showing `CREATE MODEL` Job with Progress*

Evaluating and Tuning Models

Once a model is trained, how do we know if it is actually good? Assessing model quality involves evaluating its predictions against data it has never seen before–including a holdout or evaluation dataset.

The `ML.EVALUATE` Function

BigQuery provides the built-in **`ML.EVALUATE`** function, which automatically calculates standard data science metrics.

```
SELECT *
FROM ML.EVALUATE(MODEL `bqml_lab.churn_model_v1`,
  (SELECT * FROM `bqml_lab.evaluation_data`)
);
```

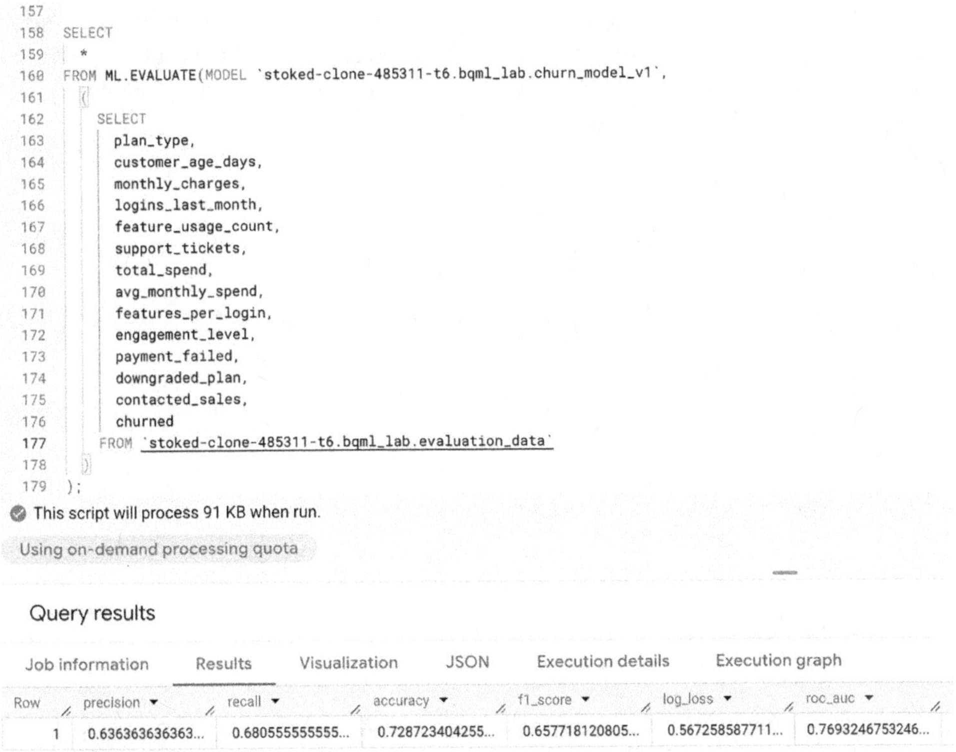

Figure 12.5: *`ML.EVALUATE` Results Showing ROC-AUC, Precision, Recall, and Accuracy*

The output will include:

- **Precision:** When the model predicted a customer would churn, what percentage of the time was it correct? Highly important if intervening is expensive.
- **Recall:** Of all the customers who actually churned, what percentage did the model successfully identify? Highly important if losing a customer is devastating and you want to cast a wide net.
- **Area Under Curve (ROC-AUC):** A single metric telling you how well the model separates the classes. 0.5 is a coin flip; 1.0 is a perfect prediction. Anything above 0.8 is generally solid.

Understanding Feature Importance

If the model is performing well, business stakeholders will inevitably ask: "Why is it predicting that?" BQML allows you to peek inside the black box.

```
SELECT *
FROM ML.WEIGHTS(MODEL `bqml_lab.churn_model_v1`)
ORDER BY ABS(weight) DESC;
```

Executing the preceding query displays the input columns that most strongly influenced the outcome. You might discover that behavioral indicators such as `**logins_last_month**` or `**payment_failed**` have the highest weights, giving the business actionable insights such as: improve engagement or reduce payment friction to prevent churn.

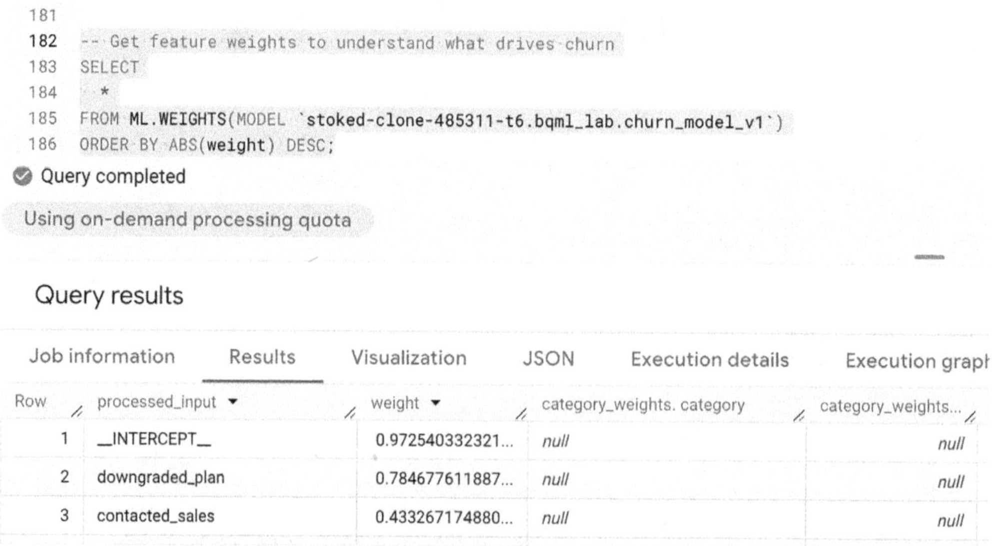

Figure 12.6: *Feature Importance Weights Showing Top Predictors of Churn*

Generating Batch Predictions

By this point, **bqml_lab.churn_model_v1** exists inside BigQuery and predicts accurately on data it has never seen. If your use case is Batch Scoring–for instance, generating a report every night at 2:00 AM of high-risk customers, BigQuery ML handles that beautifully out of the box by using **ML.PREDICT**. We will score the held-out "**evaluation-data**" table we created earlier; in production you would point **ML.PREDICT** at whatever table contains the customers you want to score.

```
-- Generating Batch Predictions
CREATE OR REPLACE TABLE `bqml_lab.daily_churn_scores` AS
SELECT
  customer_id,
```

```
  predicted_churned_probs[OFFSET(1)].prob AS churn_score
FROM ML.PREDICT(MODEL `bqml_lab.churn_model_v1`,
  (SELECT * FROM `bqml_lab.evaluation_data`)
);
```

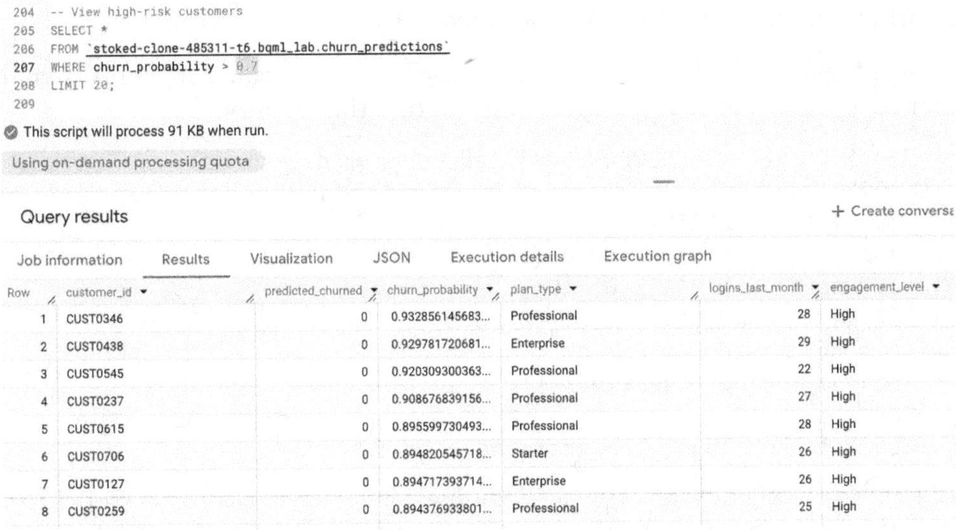

Figure 12.7: *Churn Predictions for High-Risk Customers*

We can also build a confusion matrix to evaluate false positives and false negatives directly in the following manner:

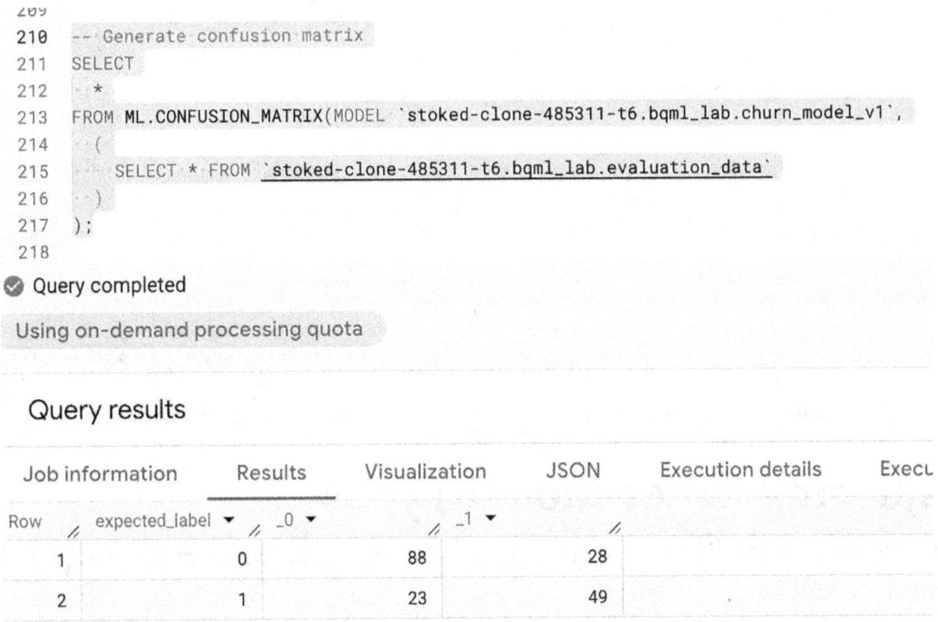

Figure 12.8: *Confusion Matrix Showing True Positives, False Positives, and Errors*

Hyperparameter Tuning

Most ML algorithms have "dials" that you can turn to adjust how they learn. These are called hyperparameters. For example, in a logistic regression, you can adjust the L1 regularization, which penalizes complex models to prevent overfitting.

Instead of guessing the right numbers, BigQuery ML can run automated trial searches. You provide a range, and BQML handles the iteration.

```
CREATE OR REPLACE MODEL `bqml_lab.churn_model_tuned`
OPTIONS(
  model_type='LOGISTIC_REG',
  input_label_cols=['churned'],
  l1_reg=HPARAM_RANGE(0, 10),
  l2_reg=HPARAM_CANDIDATES([0, 0.1, 1, 10]),
  num_trials=10,
  hparam_tuning_objectives=['roc_auc']
) AS
SELECT * FROM `bqml_lab.training_data`;
```

In this query, BigQuery ML trains 10 independent versions of the model (trials), automatically distributing them across its execution engine. By the end, the "**churn_model_tuned**" object will permanently retain the weights from the trial that yielded the highest **roc_auc**.

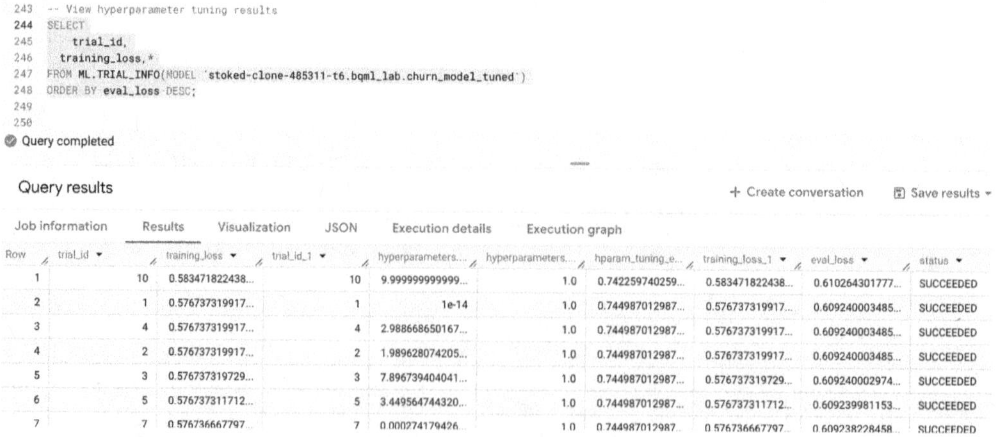

Figure 12.9: *Hyperparameter Tuning Results Showing Trial Performance*

Exploring Other Model Types

While logistic regression is a great baseline, BigQuery supports a wide array of models, including:

1. **Boosted Trees (XGBoost):** If you need higher accuracy and can sacrifice

a bit of interpretability, boosted trees often outperform simple logistic regression on tabular data.

```
OPTIONS(model_type='BOOSTED_TREE_CLASSIFIER', max_iterations=50)
```

2. **Time Series Forecasting (`ARIMA_PLUS`):** For predicting continuous values over time (such as daily revenue or inventory demands), BQML provides a robust automated time series engine. **`ARIMA_PLUS`** automatically handles seasonality, holiday effects, and anomaly detection.

```
OPTIONS(
  model_type='ARIMA_PLUS',
  time_series_timestamp_col='sales_date',
  time_series_data_col='revenue',
  data_frequency='DAILY'
)
```

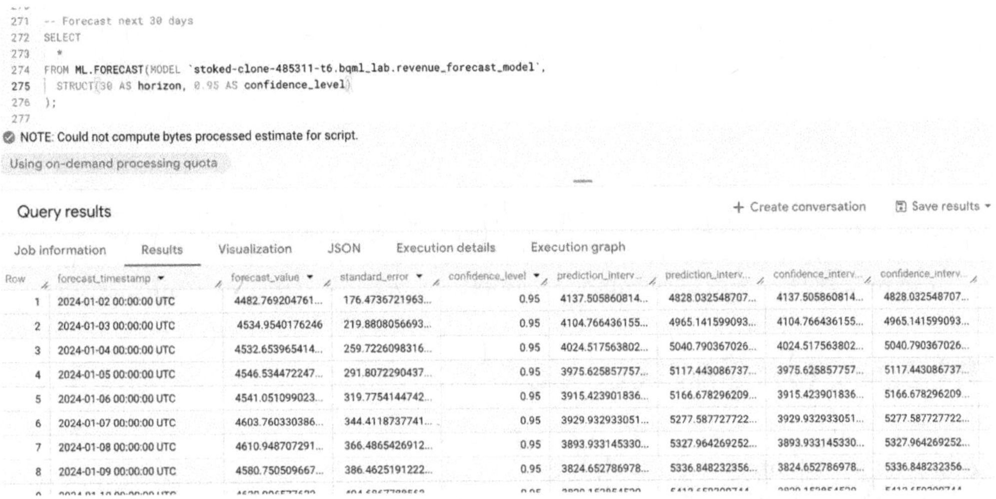

Figure 12.10: *Time Series Forecast Showing Predicted Revenue for Next 30 Days*

3. **Unsupervised Clustering (K-Means):** When you do not have a label to predict (for example, trying to segment customers into groupings based on behavior), you can use an unsupervised model.

```
OPTIONS(model_type='KMEANS', num_clusters=4,
standardize_features=TRUE)
```

```
-- Assign customers to segments
SELECT
  CENTROID_ID AS segment,
  COUNT(*) AS customer_count,
  ROUND(AVG(monthly_charges), 2) AS avg_monthly_charges,
  ROUND(AVG(logins_last_month), 1) AS avg_logins,
  ROUND(AVG(total_spend), 2) AS avg_total_spend
FROM ML.PREDICT(MODEL `stoked-clone-485311-t6.bqml_lab.customer_segments`,
  (SELECT * FROM `stoked-clone-485311-t6.bqml_lab.customer_activity`)
)
GROUP BY segment
ORDER BY segment;
```

This script will process 39.06 KB when run.

Using on-demand processing quota

Query results

Job information | Results | Visualization | JSON | Execution details | Execution gr

Row	segment	customer_count	avg_monthly_cha...	avg_logins	avg_total_spend
1	1	222	403.59	7.7	651.85
2	2	292	325.7	16.2	518.99
3	3	228	185.45	12.6	326.29
4	4	258	260.79	21.0	506.62

Figure 12.11: *Customer Segmentation Results Showing 4 Clusters with Characteristics*

Integrating with Vertex AI

While BigQuery ML excels at batch predictions, many operational applications require seamless integration with a dedicated enterprise ML platform for advanced deployment capabilities.

The Online Serving Problem

However, what if the business application requires "**Online Serving**"? Imagine a customer logging into the SaaS portal. The website needs to immediately query the churn model to decide whether to offer a 20% discount pop-up in real-time.

BigQuery is an analytical data warehouse. Its execution engine is famously optimized for scanning terabytes of data across thousands of node workers, which takes a minimum of one or two seconds to spin up. It is NOT optimized for generating millisecond-latency REST API inferences for single-row requests.

This is where Vertex AI integration enters the picture. BigQuery ML allows you to seamlessly bridge the gap from data warehouse training to Vertex AI production serving.

Step 1: Exporting the Model

We must first extract the mathematical weights and architecture from the BigQuery storage into a format that standard ML serving systems can understand (such as TensorFlow **SavedModel**). We can then export the artifacts to a Cloud Storage bucket:

```
EXPORT MODEL `bqml_lab.churn_model_tuned`
OPTIONS(
  uri='gs://my-project-bqml-models/churn_model_v1/*'
);
```

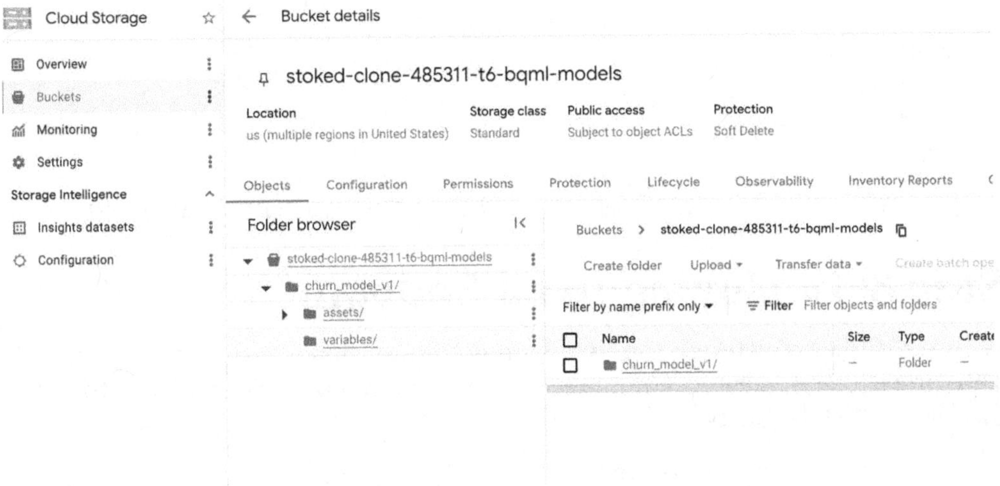

Figure 12.12: *Cloud Storage Showing Exported Model Artifacts*

Step 2: Upload to Vertex AI Model Registry

The Vertex AI Model Registry is a central repository where data science and engineering teams track the lifecycles and versions of their models across the organization.

By using the **gcloud** CLI, we instruct Vertex AI to register the extracted model. We must also specify the pre-built serving container—for instance, a Docker image managed by Google that knows how to turn a TensorFlow graph into a REST API.

```
gcloud ai models upload \
  --region=us-central1 \
  --display-name=churn-prediction-model \
  --container-image-uri=us-docker.pkg.dev/vertex-ai/prediction/
tf2-cpu.2-12:latest \
  --artifact-uri=gs://my-project-bqml-models/churn_model_v1/
```

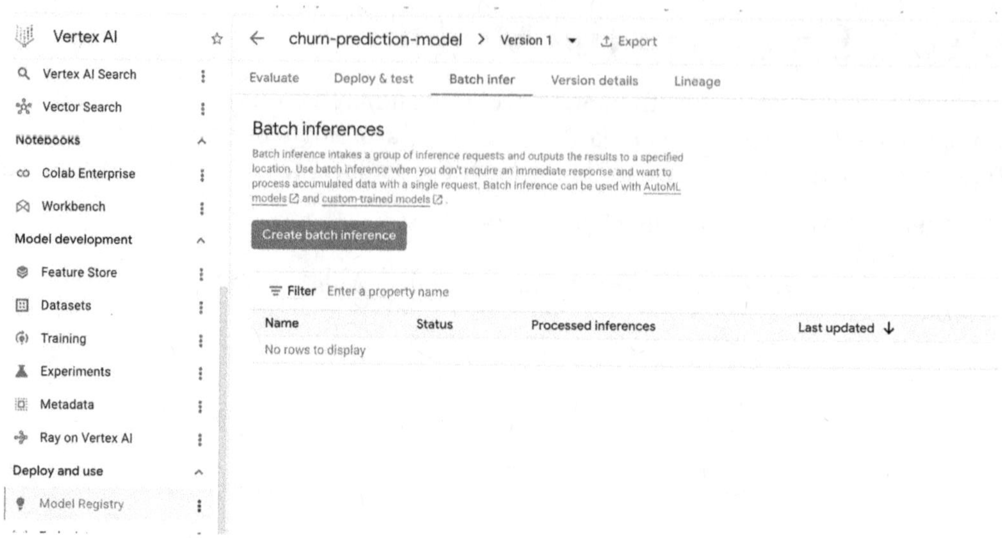

Figure 12.13: *Vertex AI Model Registry Showing Imported BigQuery ML Model*

Step 3: Deploying to an Endpoint

With the model registered, the final step is to provision a live Vertex AI Endpoint. This provisions dedicated compute engines that remain "**`always on`**" to receive incoming HTTP requests.

```
# 1. Create the empty endpoint
gcloud ai endpoints create \
  --region=us-central1 \
  --display-name=churn-prediction-endpoint

# 2. Deploy the Registered Model to the Endpoint
gcloud ai endpoints deploy-model $ENDPOINT_ID \
  --region=us-central1 \
  --model=$MODEL_ID \
  --display-name=churn-model-deployment \
  --machine-type=n1-standard-2 \
  --min-replica-count=1 \
  --max-replica-count=2 \
  --traffic-split=0=100
```

This deploys the model to autoscaling infrastructure. If your website spikes in traffic and thousands of inference calls flood the API, Vertex AI will spin up additional nodes; if traffic drops, it scales down to the **`min-replica-count`**.

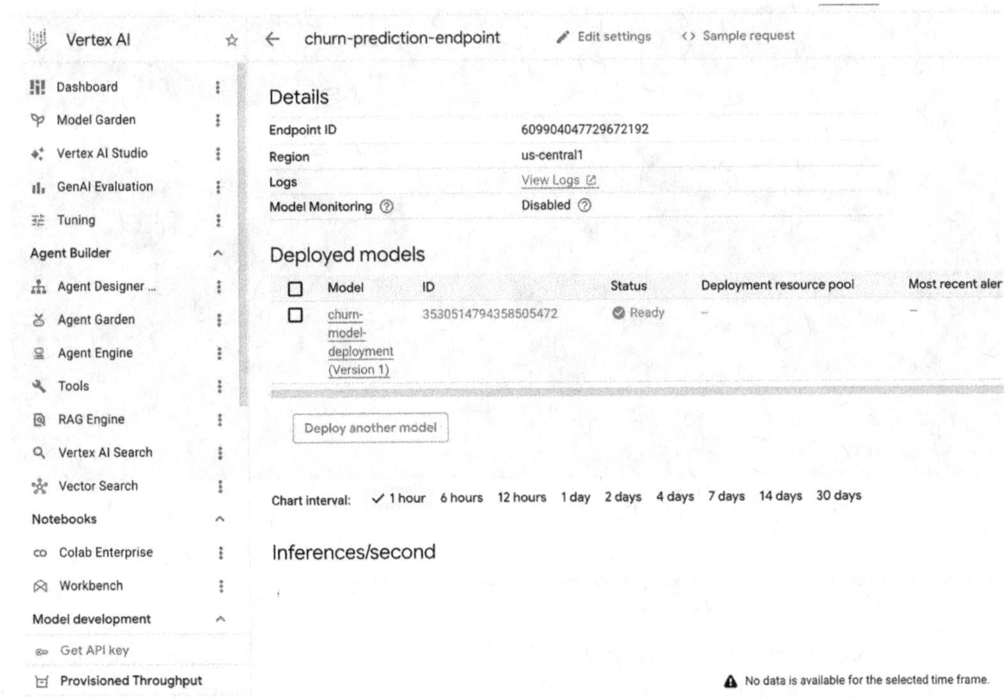

Figure 12.14: *Vertex AI Endpoint Showing Deployed Model with Status*

Making Online Predictions

Once the endpoint is "**ACTIVE**," developers of the frontend application or microservice can issue standard JSON payload POST requests to the Vertex REST API. The model will ingest the JSON and return the prediction in milliseconds.

```
# Issuing a simulated payload test to the API
gcloud ai endpoints predict $ENDPOINT_ID \
  --region=us-central1 \
  --json-request=prediction_request.json
```

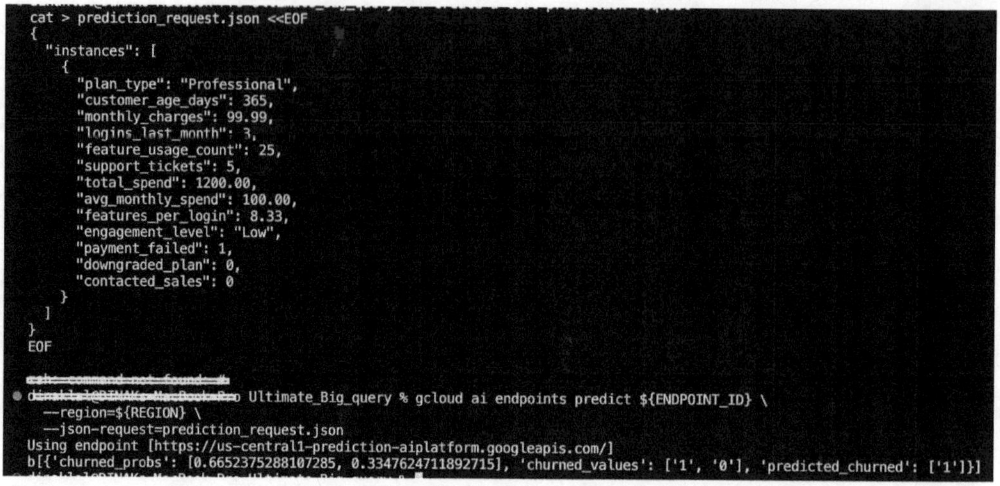

Figure 12.15: *Online Prediction Response from Vertex AI Endpoint*

Productionizing ML Workflows

A model deployed today will silently degrade tomorrow. Data distributions shift; customer behaviors change. Managing the ML lifecycle in production is heavily reliant on orchestration tools, namely Cloud Composer.

Automated Retraining Pipelines

In *Chapter 10, Orchestration with Cloud Composer*, we built Directed Acyclic Graphs (DAGs) using Airflow to sequence dbt and Dataflow jobs. As BigQuery ML uses standard SQL, and integrating ML into your data pipelines leverages the same Airflow operators.

A production ML workflow typically appears as follows:

1. **`BigQueryInsertJobOperator`** rebuilds the **`training_data`** tables based on the past 6 months of data.
2. **`BigQueryInsertJobOperator`** executes **`CREATE OR REPLACE MODEL ...`** to retrain the model on the latest data.
3. **`BigQueryInsertJobOperator`** runs an **`ML.EVALUATE`** statement. You construct a Python callable step to verify that the returned `roc_auc` value is higher than an established baseline threshold (for example, > 0.80).
4. If the check passes, the DAG proceeds to execute an **`EXPORT MODEL`** task.
5. Finally, Vertex AI Airflow operators are utilized to register the new model version and update traffic routed to the Vertex Endpoint.

This creates a fully hands-off Continuous Training (CT) and Continuous Deployment (CD) pipeline.

Detecting Data Drift

When using batch predictions natively inside BigQuery, comparing changes over time becomes a straightforward data engineering exercise. Ensure that your daily inference jobs (your "`daily_churn_scores`" tables) capture not just the user ID and the result, but also the timestamp of the inference.

By persisting your daily inference results natively into standard partitioned tables, you can write downstream data quality assertions (similar to those covered in the previous chapter) that alert you if the average churn probability across the entire user base unexpectedly jumps by 20% overnight–a prime indicator of data drift or upstream data corruption.

Cost and Performance Considerations

While BigQuery ML simplifies the development experience, neglecting operational mechanics can result in unexpectedly high costs.

- **Training Costs (Slot Consumption):** The `CREATE MODEL` query utilizes your BigQuery compute slots. Simple models such as Logistic Regression solve very quickly and incur negligible costs. However, operations such as Deep Neural Networks, Boosted Trees, and particularly Hyperparameter Tuning (which trains multiple models sequentially) are highly compute-intensive. If you run it under the On-Demand pricing model (charging by bytes processed), automated hyperparameter tuning can result in expensive query scans. Ensure that your training datasets are appropriately sampled down to a minimum viable size (for example, 500,000 randomized rows rather than 5 billion) during the prototyping phase.
- **Batch Prediction Costs:** Relying on `ML.PREDICT` works similarly to a "`SELECT`" statement, mapping data against the model artifact. It incurs the standard querying and byte processing costs associated with your BigQuery deployment. For daily batch syncs affecting millions of users, this cost is minimal and highly efficient compared to sending millions of row calls to a REST API.
- **Vertex AI Endpoint Costs:** Unlike BigQuery, which scales down to zero when no queries are actively running, a deployed Vertex AI endpoint provisions dedicated compute machines (for example, `n1-standard-2`). You pay hourly runtime costs for the underlying VMs for as long as the endpoint remains deployed, regardless of whether a prediction is requested. In enterprise environments, ensuring that you have teardown scripts for non-production development endpoints is a crucial cost-optimization measure.

Conclusion

In this chapter, we bridged the gap between the modern data platform and advanced predictive analytics. We discovered that data engineers do not need to rely on fully detached infrastructures or specialized Python architectures to implement the vast majority of enterprise ML workloads.

Using BigQuery ML, you wrote standard SQL to define features, specify modeling algorithms, interpret feature weights, and conduct automated hyperparameter tuning—leveraging the immense parallel execution power of the data warehouse. Finally, for low-latency online application integrations, we mapped a direct path to deploy resilient internal models securely to real-time Vertex AI endpoints.

In the next chapter, we will move from batch ML to the real-time world: building a complete streaming analytics platform on Pub/Sub, Dataflow, BigQuery's storage Write API—visualized through a live Looker Studio dashboard.

Points to Remember

- **BigQuery ML brings algorithms to the data** - models train where the data lives, eliminating data movement, security gaps, and tool sprawl.
- Use `CREATE MODEL` with standard SQL to train classification, regression, clustering, and time series models directly inside BigQuery.
- Use `ML.EVALUATE` against a holdout dataset to assess precision, recall, and **ROC-AUC** – anything above **0.8 ROC-AUC** is generally solid.
- For low-latency online serving, export BigQuery ML models to Vertex AI endpoints – BigQuery is optimized for analytics, not millisecond REST API responses.
- Hyperparameter tuning with `num_trials` runs multiple model variants automatically.
- **Vertex AI endpoints provision always-on compute and bill continuously** - implement teardown scripts for non-production endpoints to avoid surprise costs.

Multiple Choice Questions

1. What is the primary operational advantage of using BigQuery ML over pulling data into a separate Jupyter Notebook infrastructure?

    a. It supports a wider array of unsupported custom Neural Architectures.

    b. It reduces data movement, security gaps, and limits tooling sprawl.

   c. It completely bypasses Google Cloud IAM permissions.

   d. BigQuery SQL processing is strictly faster for processing images.

2. Which SQL keyword is used to instigate the automated training of a model in BigQuery ML?

   a. `TRAIN ALGORITHM`

   b. `CREATE EXPERIMENT`

   c. `CREATE MODEL`

   d. `EXPORT ML`

3. In a BigQuery ML `OPTIONS` clause, what parameter defines the target variable the algorithm is attempting to predict?

   a. `label_prediction`

   b. `target_variable`

   c. `variable_target`

   d. `input_label_cols`

4. If you needed to generate a daily forecast of predicted inventory shipments for the upcoming month, which model type would be most appropriate?

   a. `LOGISTIC_REG`

   b. `KMEANS`

   c. `ARIMA_PLUS`

   d. `BOOSTED_TREE_CLASSIFIER`

5. Which function is used to capture accuracy metrics (such as precision, recall, and ROC AUC) against a hold-out test dataset?

   a. `ML.ACCURACY`

   b. `ML.WEIGHTS`

   c. `ML.PREDICT`

   d. `ML.EVALUATE`

6. What is the primary purpose of the `TRANSFORM` clause in a `CREATE MODEL` script?

   a. It converts BigQuery model types to Vertex model types natively.

   b. It ensures preprocessing steps are intrinsically attached to the model for future predictions.

c. It enforces strict column level security formats.

d. It prevents the model from automatically balancing class weights.

7. Why would an engineering team prioritize deploying a BigQuery ML model to a Vertex AI Endpoint rather than using `ML.PREDICT` natively?

   a. Vertex AI provides heavily reduced billing metrics for batch analytics

   b. BigQuery ML does not support generating actual prediction outputs natively

   c. The business application requires sub-second, low-latency online serving via a REST API

   d. Vertex AI is required to utilize standard Logistic Regression algorithms

8. When utilizing `num_trials` and defining testing objective ranges inside the `OPTIONS` clause, what ML process is being engaged?

   a. Hold-Out Test Evaluation

   b. Automated Hyperparameter Tuning

   c. Neural Feature Processing

   d. K-Means Centroid Splitting

9. You want to understand which specific input column contributed the most significant influence over a Logistic Regression model's predictions. What function should you execute?

   a. `ML.INFLUENCE`

   b. `ML.PREDICT_EXPLAIN`

   c. `ML.WEIGHTS`

   d. `ML.COLUMNS`

10. What cost dynamic remains continuously active and billing the project in the Vertex AI serving architecture, even when predictions are not actively executing?

    a. Exporting the model binary to Cloud Storage

    b. Retaining a deployed Endpoint supported by active Compute instances

    c. Executing `ML.EVALUATE` routines inside BigQuery

    d. Saving a model inside the Vertex AI Model Registry

Answers

1. b
2. c
3. d
4. c
5. d
6. b
7. c
8. b
9. c
10. b

Questions

1. Describe the key architectural differences in data movement and security handling between BigQuery ML and a traditional extract-and-train Python architecture.
2. Under what circumstances would it be more appropriate to use Vertex AI Custom Training instead of BigQuery ML algorithms?
3. What is the purpose of tracking the `ROC-AUC` evaluation metric, and what does a value of 0.5 indicate functionally?
4. Explain how utilizing the `TRANSFORM` model clause mitigates operational risk when creating prediction datasets downstream.
5. Detail the operational steps required to take a model trained purely in BigQuery SQL and expose it successfully to external software applications utilizing Vertex AI.

Key Terms

- **BigQuery ML:** A native BigQuery capability allowing users to build, evaluate, and execute ML models using standard SQL leveraging the data warehouse's compute engines.
- **Classification:** A type of ML problem where the objective is to predict discrete, categorical target outcomes (for example, predicting whether a customer will churn or not).
- **Hyperparameter Tuning:** The automated process of iterating and adjusting high-level model configuration parameters to discover the permutation yielding the highest accuracy constraints.
- **Vertex AI Model Registry:** A central, organized repository within Google Cloud utilized to track model versions, lineages, and readiness states across the entire organization.
- **Vertex AI Endpoint:** A deployed software construct that attaches live compute resources to a mathematical ML model, actively exposing it to receive external traffic via REST APIs for online serving constraints.
- **Batch Scoring:** The process of executing predictions offline on millions of stored database rows efficiently on a predefined schedule (for example, nightly `ML.PREDICT` aggregations).
- **Online Serving:** Exposing prediction engines to handle immediate, real-time inferences individually as they happen, specifically requiring latency measured in milliseconds.
- **Data Drift:** The phenomenon where the underlying statistical distribution of production input data diverges significantly from the historical distributions seen during the model's training, leading to degraded accuracy.

CHAPTER 13
Real-Time Streaming Analytics

Introduction

In the previous chapters, we focused heavily on building a robust, automated batch processing platform. Tools such as the data build tool (dbt) and Cloud Composer excel at taking massive volumes of data that landed yesterday, transforming them overnight, and presenting a pristine dashboard to the business the next morning. For many business functions–such as monthly financial reporting or daily inventory reconciliation–this "T+1" (transaction plus one day) latency is perfectly acceptable.

However, the modern business landscape increasingly operates in the "now." When a user is browsing an e-commerce catalog, knowing what they clicked on yesterday is not enough; the recommendation engine needs to know what they clicked on five seconds ago. When a credit card transaction occurs, the fraud detection system cannot wait for an overnight batch job to flag it.

This is the domain of real-time streaming analytics.

In *Chapter 8, Apache Beam and Dataflow*, we introduced Apache Beam and Google Cloud Dataflow as the unified programming model for both batch and streaming pipelines. We covered the core abstractions–including PCollections, PTransforms, windowing strategies, watermarks, and triggers–and built introductory batch and streaming pipelines. We also explored Dead-Letter Queue (DLQ) patterns, late data handling, and the mechanics of Dataflow autoscaling.

This chapter is where those concepts graduate from theory into a production-representative project. Instead of processing simple test messages, we will build a complete, end-to-end real-time streaming analytics platform: a simulated e-commerce clickstream flowing through Pub/Sub, processed by a branched Beam pipeline on Dataflow, landing in BigQuery via the high-performance Storage Write API, and visualized through a live Looker Studio dashboard. Along the way, we will confront challenges that only emerge in real streaming systems, such as choosing the right table structure, handling late-arriving data, managing costs for always-on infrastructure, and building operational guardrails that keep the pipeline healthy.

By the end of this chapter, you will have a solid understanding of how to design, deploy, and monitor a production-grade real-time streaming pipeline on Google Cloud. These skills represent a critical shift from batch-oriented thinking to event-driven architecture, enabling you to build systems that deliver insights in seconds rather than hours.

Structure

In this chapter, we will cover the following topics:

- Understanding the Streaming Architecture
- Core Streaming Concepts
- Building the Foundation
- Simulating the Stream
- Writing the Apache Beam Pipeline
- Deploying to Dataflow
- Serving Real-Time Insights
- Handling the Inevitable: Late Data
- Operational Best Practices

Understanding the Streaming Architecture

Before we write any code, let us look at the blueprint of the system we are going to build across this chapter. Unlike the basic streaming pipeline that we prototyped in *Chapter 8, Apache Beam and Dataflow* (which read test messages and wrote to a single BigQuery table), this project implements a production-grade architecture with multiple output paths, pre-computed aggregations, and a live visualization layer.

The architecture of a modern streaming pipeline typically consists of four distinct layers: Generation, Ingestion, Processing, and Storage/Serving. *Figure* 13.1 illustrates how these layers connect in our e-commerce analytics system:

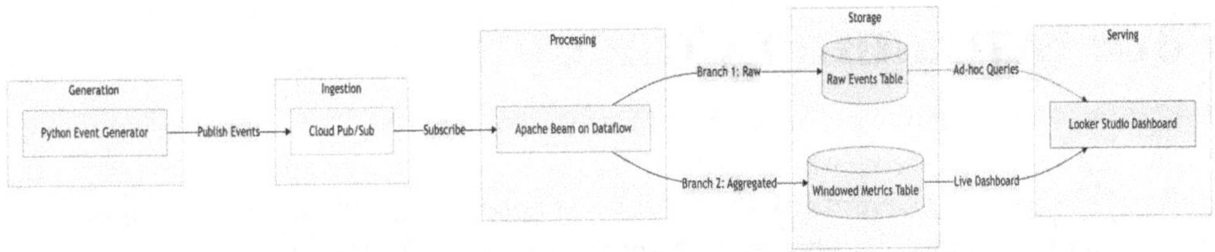

Figure 13.1: *End-to-End Streaming Architecture Showing the Four Layers: A Python Event Generator Publishes to Pub/Sub, Which Feeds Apache Beam on Dataflow*

Note: *Dataflow branches into two BigQuery tables (raw events and windowed metrics), both feeding a Looker Studio dashboard.*

Reading the diagram from left to right showcases events flowing through each layer with increasing refinement. The key architectural decision is the branch in the Processing layer—our Dataflow pipeline will split into two separate write paths, one for raw audit data and one for pre-aggregated dashboard metrics. This "branched pipeline" pattern is common in production streaming systems, as it serves two fundamentally different consumer needs without requiring two separate pipelines.

Let us walk through each layer, including:

1. **Generation (The Source):** In the real world, this would be your mobile app, website backend, or IoT devices emitting telemetry data. For our project, we will use a Python script to simulate hundreds of users clicking around an e-commerce site.
2. **Ingestion (The Buffer):** Data streams are highly unpredictable. Traffic spikes can easily overwhelm downstream databases. Google Cloud Pub/Sub acts as our shock absorber. It is a globally distributed message bus that ingests events instantly and holds them until our processing layer is ready. Pub/Sub guarantees at-least-once delivery and retains unacknowledged messages for up to 7 days by default, meaning that even if your Dataflow pipeline goes down temporarily, no data is lost.
3. **Processing (The Engine):** We will use Apache Beam, that is, a unified programming model for batch and streaming data, and execute it on Google Cloud Dataflow. Dataflow will pull messages from Pub/Sub, assign them to time windows, aggregate the metrics, and handle the complexities of scaling up workers during traffic spikes.
4. **Storage and Serving (The Destination):** Dataflow will write the refined streams directly into BigQuery using the Storage Write API, where it is instantly queryable. Looker Studio will connect to BigQuery to visualize the live data.

Core Streaming Concepts

This project builds on the windowing, watermark, and trigger concepts we covered in *Chapter 8, Apache Beam and Dataflow*. We will use Fixed Windows of 60 seconds to aggregate clickstream events, with an Allowed Lateness of 120 seconds to handle late-arriving data from mobile devices with intermittent connectivity.

The key challenge in our e-commerce pipeline is handling the gap between Event Time (when a user clicks) and Processing Time (when Dataflow receives the event). A user might add an item to their cart while on a train, lose cellular connection, and regain it after two minutes. Our pipeline must handle this gracefully without losing data or producing incorrect aggregations.

If you need a refresher on streaming fundamentals, revisit *Chapter 8, Apache Beam and Dataflow* before proceeding.

Building the Foundation

Let us begin by preparing our Google Cloud infrastructure. We need a Pub/Sub topic to receive the stream, and BigQuery tables to store the results.

First, create the Pub/Sub topic and a corresponding pull subscription so that Dataflow can read the events safely:

```
# Create the topic
gcloud pubsub topics create clickstream-events

# Create the subscription
gcloud pubsub subscriptions create clickstream-sub \
  --topic=clickstream-events \
  --ack-deadline=60

Next, create a Cloud Storage bucket for Dataflow's staging and
temporary files:
export BUCKET_NAME="${PROJECT_ID}-streaming-lab"
gcloud storage buckets create gs://${BUCKET_NAME} --location=US
```

Next, let us set up BigQuery. For this project, we are employing a branched pipeline pattern. We will write every raw event to one table (for auditing and replayability purposes), and write the 60-second windowed aggregations to a second table, which is optimized for dashboards.

```
-- Create the dataset
CREATE SCHEMA `your-project-id.streaming_analytics`
OPTIONS (
  location = 'US',
  description = 'Real-time streaming analytics project'
```

```
);

-- Create the Raw Table (Partitioned by event time for efficient
querying)
CREATE OR REPLACE TABLE `your-project-id.streaming_analytics.raw_
clickstream` (
  event_id STRING NOT NULL,
  user_id STRING,
  session_id STRING,
  event_type STRING,
  page_url STRING,
  product_id STRING,
  product_category STRING,
  price FLOAT64,
  device_type STRING,
  country STRING,
  event_timestamp TIMESTAMP,
  processing_timestamp TIMESTAMP
)
PARTITION BY DATE(event_timestamp)
CLUSTER BY event_type, country;

-- Create the Aggregated Table (Clustered for fast dashboard lookups)
CREATE OR REPLACE TABLE `your-project-id.streaming_analytics.
windowed_metrics` (
  window_start TIMESTAMP,
  window_end TIMESTAMP,
  event_type STRING,
  country STRING,
  event_count INT64,
  unique_users INT64,
  total_revenue FLOAT64,
  avg_price FLOAT64,
  processing_timestamp TIMESTAMP
)
PARTITION BY DATE(window_start)
CLUSTER BY event_type;
```

Choosing the Right Table Structure for Streaming

Designing BigQuery tables for streaming workloads requires fundamentally different thinking than batch-loaded tables. There are the following three key principles to keep in mind:

1. **Partition by Event Time, Not Load Time.** When data arrives via streaming,

BigQuery can automatically partition it by ingestion time (**_PARTITIONTIME**). However, this creates a subtle problem for analytics: if 50 late events from yesterday arrive today, they land in today's partition, despite belonging to yesterday's business window. By explicitly partitioning on **event_timestamp**, we ensure that analytical queries such as "Show me all revenue from April 17th" always return complete and accurate results regardless of when the data physically arrived.

2. **Cluster for Dashboard Access Patterns.** Our Looker Studio dashboard will repeatedly filter by **event_type** (to show purchases separately from page views) and country (for geographic breakdowns). By clustering on these two columns, BigQuery physically co-locates related rows on disk. This means dashboard queries that filter on these fields scan dramatically less data, reducing both latency and cost.

3. **Append-Only Architecture.** Streaming tables in BigQuery are inherently append-only. Unlike batch tables, where you can run MERGE or UPDATE statements to deduplicate records, streaming inserts add new rows without modifying existing ones. This means that if Dataflow emits an updated aggregation for a historical window (due to late data), both the original and the updated row will exist in the table. Your downstream queries should account for this by using **MAX(processing_timestamp)** or row-number deduplication patterns in the following manner:

```
-- Deduplicate windowed metrics by keeping the latest aggregation
per window
SELECT * EXCEPT(row_num) FROM (
  SELECT *,
    ROW_NUMBER() OVER (
      PARTITION BY window_start, event_type, country
      ORDER BY processing_timestamp DESC
    ) AS row_num
  FROM `your-project-id.streaming_analytics.windowed_metrics`
)
WHERE row_num = 1
```

Simulating the Stream

In a production environment, these events would originate from your application's backend, mobile apps, or IoT devices. For our learning environment, we need to generate synthetic clickstream data that mimics real user behavior. We will build a Python event generator that simulates hundreds of users browsing an e-commerce site–viewing pages, clicking products, adding items to carts, and completing purchases.

The event generator uses weighted random selection to create realistic traffic patterns: page views are the most common (50%), followed by product clicks (25%), add-to-cart actions (15%), and purchases (10%). Each event includes a unique ID, user session information, timestamps, and transaction details.

```
import json, time, random, uuid
from datetime import datetime
from google.cloud import pubsub_v1

PROJECT_ID = "your-project-id"
TOPIC_ID = "clickstream-events"

publisher = pubsub_v1.PublisherClient()
topic_path = publisher.topic_path(PROJECT_ID, TOPIC_ID)

EVENT_TYPES = ["page_view", "product_click", "add_to_cart", "purchase"]

def generate_event():
    event_type = random.choices(EVENT_TYPES, weights=[50, 25, 15,
10], k=1)[0]
    price = round(random.uniform(5.99, 299.99), 2) if event_type in
["add_to_cart", "purchase"] else 0.0

    return {
        "event_id": str(uuid.uuid4()),
        "user_id": f"USER-{random.randint(1, 500):04d}",
        "session_id": f"SESS-{random.randint(1, 2000):06d}",
        "event_type": event_type,
        "price": price,
        "country": random.choice(["US", "UK", "DE", "IN"]),
        "event_timestamp": datetime.utcnow().isoformat() + "Z"
    }

def publish_events(events_per_second=10, duration_seconds=300):
    """Publish events at a steady rate."""
    total_published = 0
    start_time = time.time()

    print(f"Publishing {events_per_second} events/sec for
{duration_seconds}s...")

    while time.time() - start_time < duration_seconds:
        for _ in range(events_per_second):
            event = generate_event()
            data = json.dumps(event).encode("utf-8")
            publisher.publish(topic_path, data)
            total_published += 1

        # Status update every 10 seconds
```

```
        elapsed = int(time.time() - start_time)
        if elapsed % 10 == 0 and elapsed > 0:
            print(f"  [{elapsed}s] Published {total_published}
events...")

        time.sleep(1)

    print(f"\nDone. Total events published: {total_published}")

if __name__ == "__main__":
    publish_events()
```

When you run this script, it publishes 10 events per second for 5 minutes (3,000 total events), printing progress updates every 10 seconds as the data flows into Pub/Sub.

Writing the Apache Beam Pipeline

Now, as for the heart of the architecture: the stream processor. In *Chapter 8, Apache Beam and Dataflow*, we built introductory Beam pipelines that read from a single source and wrote to a single sink. This project takes it further—we construct a more sophisticated branched pipeline that reads from Pub/Sub and fans out into two independent BigQuery write paths.

Defining the DoFn Transforms

In *Chapter 8, Apache Beam and Dataflow*, we introduced `ParDo` as Beam's most flexible transform—a user-defined function that processes elements one at a time. We now need to define three concrete `DoFn` classes that form the processing logic of our pipeline.

The first DoFn parses the raw bytes from Pub/Sub into Python dictionaries. Notice the `try-except` block, which is critical in streaming. A single malformed JSON message must not crash the entire pipeline. We log the error and silently skip it in a production system; you would route this to a dead-letter table:

```
class ParseClickEvent(beam.DoFn):
    def process(self, element):
        try:
            record = json.loads(element.decode("utf-8"))
            record["processing_timestamp"] = datetime.utcnow()
.isoformat()
            yield record
        except Exception as e:
            logging.error(f"Failed to parse: {e}")
```

The second DoFn extracts the event timestamp from the JSON payload and assigns it as the Beam element's timestamp. This is what allows Beam to perform event-time windowing rather than processing-time windowing–without this step, all events would be windowed by "when Dataflow received them" rather than "when they actually occurred" in the following way:

```
class AddEventTimestamp(beam.DoFn):
    def process(self, element):
        import apache_beam as beam
        from datetime import datetime
        ts = element.get("event_timestamp", "")
        try:
            dt = datetime.fromisoformat(ts.replace("Z", "+00:00"))
            yield beam.window.TimestampedValue(element, dt.timestamp())
        except Exception:
            yield element
```

The third DoFn receives groups of events that share the same key (event type + country) within the same time window, and computes aggregated metrics. The **`window`** parameter is injected by Beam automatically and provides the window boundaries:

```
class AggregateWindowMetrics(beam.DoFn):
    def process(self, element, window=beam.DoFn.WindowParam):
        key, events = element
        event_type, country = key
        event_list = list(events)

        unique_users = len(set(e.get("user_id", "") for e in event_
list))
        total_revenue = sum(e.get("price", 0) for e in event_list)
        avg_price = total_revenue / len(event_list) if event_list
else 0

        yield {
            "window_start": window.start.to_utc_datetime().isoformat(),
            "window_end": window.end.to_utc_datetime().isoformat(),
            "event_type": event_type,
            "country": country,
            "event_count": len(event_list),
            "unique_users": unique_users,
            "total_revenue": round(total_revenue, 2),
            "avg_price": round(avg_price, 2),
            "processing_timestamp": datetime.utcnow().isoformat(),
        }
```

Assembling the Pipeline

With the three DoFn classes defined, we can now assemble the complete pipeline graph. This is where the branched pipeline pattern comes to life—a single input stream from Pub/Sub fans out into two independent BigQuery write paths in the following manner:

```
with beam.Pipeline(options=pipeline_options) as p:
    # ── Read from Pub/Sub ──
    raw_messages = (
        p
        | "ReadPubSub" >> beam.io.ReadFromPubSub(
            subscription=known_args.input_subscription
        )
        | "ParseJSON" >> beam.ParDo(ParseClickEvent())
        | "AddTimestamp" >> beam.ParDo(AddEventTimestamp())
    )

    # ── Branch 1: Write raw events directly to BigQuery ──
    (
        raw_messages
        | "WriteRawToBQ" >> beam.io.WriteToBigQuery(
            table=known_args.output_raw_table,
            schema=raw_schema,
            write_disposition=beam.io.BigQueryDisposition.WRITE_APPEND,
            create_disposition=beam.io.BigQueryDisposition.CREATE_NEVER,
            method=beam.io.WriteToBigQuery.Method.STORAGE_WRITE_API,
        )
    )

    # ── Branch 2: Window + Aggregate + Write summaries ──
    (
        raw_messages
        | "Window60s" >> beam.WindowInto(
            FixedWindows(60),  # 1-minute fixed windows
            trigger=AfterWatermark(
                early=AfterProcessingTime(30), #Emit partial results
every 30s
              late=AfterProcessingTime(0) #Remit
            ),
            accumulation_mode=AccumulationMode.ACCUMULATING,
            allowed_lateness=120  # Accept late data up to 2 minutes
        )
        | "KeyByTypeCountry" >> beam.Map(
            lambda e: ((e["event_type"], e["country"]), e)
        )
```

```
        | "GroupByKey" >> beam.GroupByKey()
        | "Aggregate" >> beam.ParDo(AggregateWindowMetrics())
        | "WriteAggToBQ" >> beam.io.WriteToBigQuery(
            table=known_args.output_agg_table,
            schema=agg_schema,
            write_disposition=beam.io.BigQueryDisposition.WRITE_APPEND,
            create_disposition=beam.io.BigQueryDisposition.CREATE_NEVER,
            method=beam.io.WriteToBigQuery.Method.STORAGE_WRITE_API,
        )
    )
```

Notice the sophisticated streaming controls in Branch 2, such as:

- **`FixedWindows(60)`**: Slices the infinite stream into 60-second chunks.
- **`AfterProcessingTime(30)`**: Tells Beam to emit early partial results to BigQuery every 30 seconds so that our dashboard updates quickly, rather than waiting a full minute.
- **`allowed_lateness=120`**: Dictates that if an event arrives up to 2 minutes late, Beam should gracefully accept it and update the exact historical window it belonged to.
- **`AccumulationMode.ACCUMULATING`**: Each pane (such as early, on-time, and late) emits the full running total of that window, not just new events.

The Complete Executable Pipeline

For the pipeline to run successfully, we must explicitly declare the **raw_schema** and **agg_schema**, supply the required imports, and scaffold the **PipelineOptions** so that Dataflow understands our custom arguments.

Save the complete, runnable code to a file named **streaming_pipeline.py** in the following way:

```
import argparse
import json
import logging
import apache_beam as beam
from apache_beam.options.pipeline_options import PipelineOptions,
StandardOptions
from apache_beam.transforms.window import FixedWindows
from apache_beam.transforms.trigger import AfterWatermark,
AfterProcessingTime, AccumulationMode
from datetime import datetime

# —— 1. DoFn Classes ——
class ParseClickEvent(beam.DoFn):
    def process(self, element):
```

```
        try:
            record = json.loads(element.decode("utf-8"))
            record["processing_timestamp"] = datetime.utcnow()
.isoformat()
            yield record
        except Exception as e:
            logging.error(f"Failed to parse: {e}")

class AddEventTimestamp(beam.DoFn):
    def process(self, element):
        import apache_beam as beam
        from datetime import datetime
        ts = element.get("event_timestamp", "")
        try:
            dt = datetime.fromisoformat(ts.replace("Z", "+00:00"))
            yield beam.window.TimestampedValue(element, dt.timestamp())
        except Exception:
            yield element

class AggregateWindowMetrics(beam.DoFn):
    def process(self, element, window=beam.DoFn.WindowParam):
        key, events = element
        event_type, country = key
        event_list = list(events)
        unique_users = len(set(e.get("user_id", "") for e in
event_list))
        total_revenue = sum(e.get("price", 0) for e in event_list)
        avg_price = total_revenue / len(event_list) if event_list else 0

        yield {
            "window_start": window.start.to_utc_datetime().isoformat(),
            "window_end": window.end.to_utc_datetime().isoformat(),
            "event_type": event_type,
            "country": country,
            "event_count": len(event_list),
            "unique_users": unique_users,
            "total_revenue": round(total_revenue, 2),
            "avg_price": round(avg_price, 2),
            "processing_timestamp": datetime.utcnow().isoformat(),
        }

# ——— 2. Pipeline Execution ———
def run(argv=None):
    parser = argparse.ArgumentParser()
    parser.add_argument("--input_subscription", required=True)
    parser.add_argument("--output_raw_table", required=True)
    parser.add_argument("--output_agg_table", required=True)
```

```
    known_args, pipeline_args = parser.parse_known_args(argv)

    pipeline_options = PipelineOptions(pipeline_args)
    pipeline_options.view_as(StandardOptions).streaming = True

    # Storage Write API Schemas
    raw_schema = {
        "fields": [
            {"name": "event_id", "type": "STRING", "mode": "REQUIRED"},
            {"name": "user_id", "type": "STRING", "mode": "NULLABLE"},
            {"name": "session_id", "type": "STRING", "mode":
"NULLABLE"},
            {"name": "event_type", "type": "STRING", "mode":
"NULLABLE"},
            {"name": "page_url", "type": "STRING", "mode":
"NULLABLE"},
            {"name": "product_id", "type": "STRING", "mode":
"NULLABLE"},
            {"name": "product_category", "type": "STRING", "mode":
"NULLABLE"},
            {"name": "price", "type": "FLOAT64", "mode": "NULLABLE"},
            {"name": "device_type", "type": "STRING", "mode":
"NULLABLE"},
            {"name": "country", "type": "STRING", "mode":
"NULLABLE"},
            {"name": "event_timestamp", "type": "TIMESTAMP", "mode":
"NULLABLE"},
            {"name": "processing_timestamp", "type": "TIMESTAMP",
"mode": "NULLABLE"},
        ]
    }

    agg_schema = {
        "fields": [
            {"name": "window_start", "type": "TIMESTAMP", "mode":
"NULLABLE"},
            {"name": "window_end", "type": "TIMESTAMP", "mode":
"NULLABLE"},
            {"name": "event_type", "type": "STRING", "mode":
"NULLABLE"},
            {"name": "country", "type": "STRING", "mode":
"NULLABLE"},
            {"name": "event_count", "type": "INT64", "mode":
"NULLABLE"},
            {"name": "unique_users", "type": "INT64", "mode":
"NULLABLE"},
```

```
            {"name": "total_revenue", "type": "FLOAT64", "mode":
"NULLABLE"},
            {"name": "avg_price", "type": "FLOAT64", "mode":
"NULLABLE"},
            {"name": "processing_timestamp", "type": "TIMESTAMP",
"mode": "NULLABLE"},
        ]
    }

    with beam.Pipeline(options=pipeline_options) as p:
        raw_messages = (
            p
            | "ReadPubSub" >> beam.io.ReadFromPubSub(subscription=-
known_args.input_subscription)
            | "ParseJSON" >> beam.ParDo(ParseClickEvent())
            | "AddTimestamp" >> beam.ParDo(AddEventTimestamp())
        )

        (raw_messages
         | "WriteRawToBQ" >> beam.io.WriteToBigQuery(
             table=known_args.output_raw_table, schema=raw_schema,
             write_disposition=beam.io.BigQueryDisposition.WRITE_
APPEND,
             create_disposition=beam.io.BigQueryDisposition.CREATE_
NEVER,
             method=beam.io.WriteToBigQuery.Method.STORAGE_WRITE_
API))

        (raw_messages
         | "Window60s" >> beam.WindowInto(
             FixedWindows(60),
             trigger=AfterWatermark(early=AfterProcessingTime(30),
late=AfterProcessingTime(0)),
             accumulation_mode=AccumulationMode.ACCUMULATING,
             allowed_lateness=120)
         | "KeyByTypeCountry" >> beam.Map(lambda e: ((e["event_
type"], e["country"]), e))
         | "GroupByKey" >> beam.GroupByKey()
         | "Aggregate" >> beam.ParDo(AggregateWindowMetrics())
         | "WriteAggToBQ" >> beam.io.WriteToBigQuery(
             table=known_args.output_agg_table, schema=agg_schema,
             write_disposition=beam.io.BigQueryDisposition.WRITE_
APPEND,
             create_disposition=beam.io.BigQueryDisposition.CREATE_
NEVER,
             method=beam.io.WriteToBigQuery.Method.STORAGE_WRITE_API))
```

```
if __name__ == "__main__":
    logging.getLogger().setLevel(logging.INFO)
    run()
```

Notice the sophisticated streaming controls in Branch 2, including:

- **`FixedWindows(60)`**: Slices the infinite stream into 60-second chunks.
- **`AfterProcessingTime(30)`**: Tells Beam to emit early partial results to BigQuery every 30 seconds, so that our dashboard updates quickly, rather than waiting a full minute.
- **`allowed_lateness=120`**: Dictates that if an event arrives up to 2 minutes late, Beam should gracefully accept it and update the exact historical window it belonged to.
- **`AccumulationMode.ACCUMULATING`**: Each pane (such as early, on-time, and late) emits the full running total of that window, not just new events.

The Storage Write API

You may recall from *Chapter 3, Getting Data into BigQuery* that BigQuery natively offers a streaming insert mechanism (**`tabledata.insertAll`**). However, that is the legacy method. Modern architectures use the BigQuery Storage Write API via gRPC.

Feature	**Legacy `insertAll`**	**Storage Write API**
Delivery Semantics	Best-effort (at-least-once)	Exactly once guaranteed
Throughput	~100,000 rows/sec per project	Millions of rows/sec per project
Protocol	REST/JSON	gRPC/Protocol Buffers
Schema Requirement	Optional (BigQuery infers)	Explicit schema declaration required
Cost	Free tier available, then per-row pricing	Included in BigQuery storage pricing
Beam Integration	`method=STREAMING_INSERTS`	`method=STORAGE_WRITE_API`

Table 13.1: *Storage Write API versus Legacy Streaming Inserts*

To use the Storage Write API with Apache Beam, you must explicitly declare the BigQuery schema as a Python dictionary and pass **`method=beam.io.WriteToBigQuery.Method.STORAGE_WRITE_API`** to your write transform. This is why we defined `raw_schema` and `agg_schema` objects in the pipeline code; the Storage Write API will reject writes that do not match the declared schema exactly.

Note: *The Storage Write API's cross-language transform requires a local Java Runtime Environment (JRE) when running pipelines locally. When deployed to Dataflow, the Java Software Development Kit (SDK) is already available on the worker VMs.*

Deploying to Dataflow

As demonstrated in *Chapter 8, Apache Beam and Dataflow*, Apache Beam is an abstraction layer–a pipeline definition, not an execution engine. Switching from local testing (**DirectRunner**) to cloud execution (**DataflowRunner**) requires only a configuration change. We can now submit our pipeline to Google Cloud Dataflow for distributed, autoscaled processing.

To launch the pipeline, run the following deployment command; note that we define the "REGION" variable explicitly before deploying:

```
export REGION="us-central1"

python3 streaming_pipeline.py \
  --project="${PROJECT_ID}" \
  --input_subscription="projects/${PROJECT_ID}/subscriptions/click-
stream-sub" \
  --output_raw_table="${PROJECT_ID}:streaming_analytics.raw_click-
stream" \
  --output_agg_table="${PROJECT_ID}:streaming_analytics.windowed_
metrics" \
  --runner=DataflowRunner \
  --region="${REGION}" \
  --temp_location="gs://${BUCKET_NAME}/temp" \
  --staging_location="gs://${BUCKET_NAME}/staging" \
  --streaming \
  --num_workers=2 \
  --max_num_workers=5 \
  --autoscaling_algorithm=THROUGHPUT_BASED
```

Monitoring the Live Pipeline

In the Google Cloud Console, navigating to **Dataflow** > **Jobs** reveals what we just built in action. The **Job Graph** tab shows the Directed Acyclic Graph (DAG) of our pipeline with real-time throughput numbers on each edge.

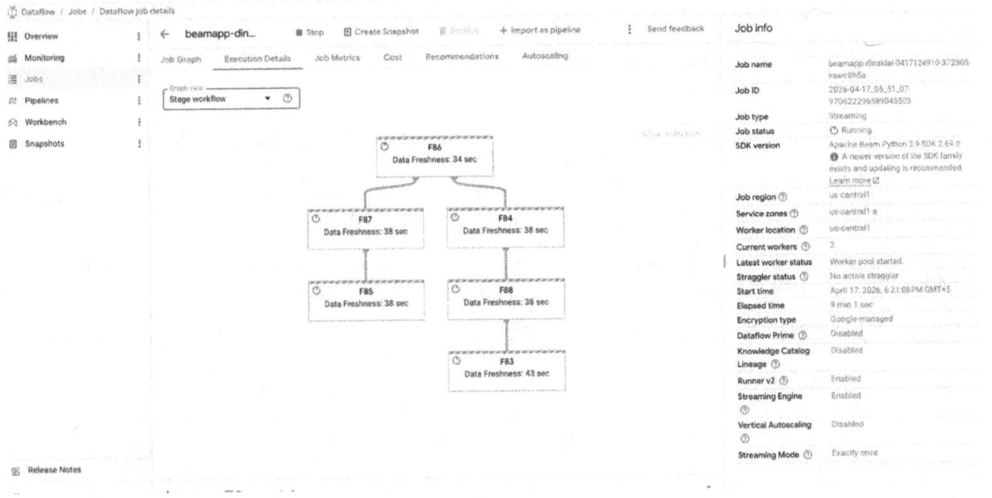

Figure 13.2: *Dataflow Console Showing the Streaming Job's Execution Graph*

Note: *Each transform (such as* ***`ReadPubSub`***, ***`ParseJSON`***, ***`AddTimestamp`***, ***`WriteRawToBQ`***, ***`Window60s`***, *and so on) is displayed as a node, with per-second element counts on the connecting edges.*

As the system processes events, the Dataflow graph comes alive with real-time throughput numbers tracking elements as they pass from Pub/Sub to BigQuery.

If traffic suddenly spikes to 10,000 events per second, Dataflow utilizes its Streaming Autoscaler. By setting **`--max_num_workers=5`** and **`THROUGHPUT_BASED`**, Dataflow constantly monitors CPU utilization and backlogs. It will spin up additional Compute Engine VMs automatically to burn down the queue and scale them neatly back down to **`--num_workers=2`** when traffic subsides.

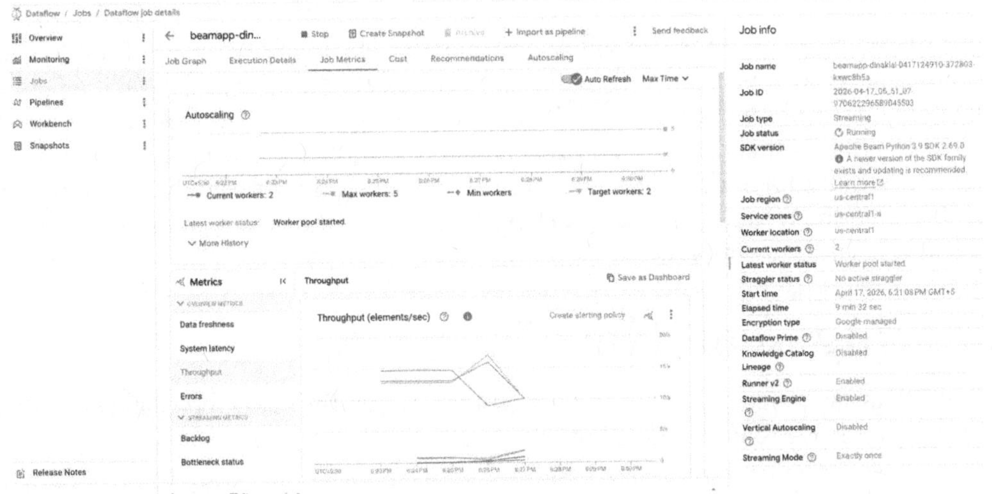

Figure 13.3: *Dataflow Job Metrics Tab Showing System Lag, Data Freshness, and Autoscaling Charts*

Note: *System Lag indicates how far behind the pipeline is in real-time; Data Freshness shows the age of the most recently processed element.*

Understanding Key Streaming Metrics

The "Job Metrics" tab in Dataflow exposes several critical health indicators. Understanding them is essential for operating streaming pipelines in production:

Metric	What It Tells You	Healthy Value	Warning Sign
System Lag	How far behind real-time the pipeline is processing	< 10 seconds	Consistently > 60 seconds means workers are overwhelmed
Data Freshness	Age of the most recently processed element	< 30 seconds	Rising trend indicates a growing backlog
Throughput	Elements processed per second across all workers	Matches your publish rate	Significantly below the publish rate means a bottleneck
Autoscaling	Current worker count versus configured min/max	Stable near `num_workers`	Persistently at `max_num_workers` means your max is too low
Backlog (Bytes)	Unprocessed data waiting in Pub/Sub	Near zero	A growing backlog means processing cannot keep up

Table 13.2: *Key Dataflow Streaming Metrics*

When the System Lag stays elevated, it usually means one of three things: your workers are undersized (try increasing `--num_workers`), your aggregation logic is too expensive (profile the `GroupByKey` step), or your BigQuery writes are throttled (check Storage Write API quotas).

Similarly, a rising Data Freshness metric means that the newest element Dataflow has processed is getting progressively older—a clear sign that the pipeline is falling behind. This often coincides with a growing Pub/Sub Backlog. When the backlog is growing, but System Lag is stable, it typically indicates that Dataflow workers are processing at full capacity, but the incoming event rate has exceeded their throughput ceiling. The fix is to either increase `--max_num_workers` or optimize the most expensive transform step in your pipeline graph.

Serving Real-Time Insights

While Dataflow hums along in the background, check the BigQuery dataset. Data is landing identically to batch data, but with second-level latency.

```
SELECT
  window_start,
  window_end,
  event_type,
  country,
  event_count,
  total_revenue
FROM `your-project-id.streaming_analytics.windowed_metrics`
ORDER BY window_start DESC
LIMIT 5;
```

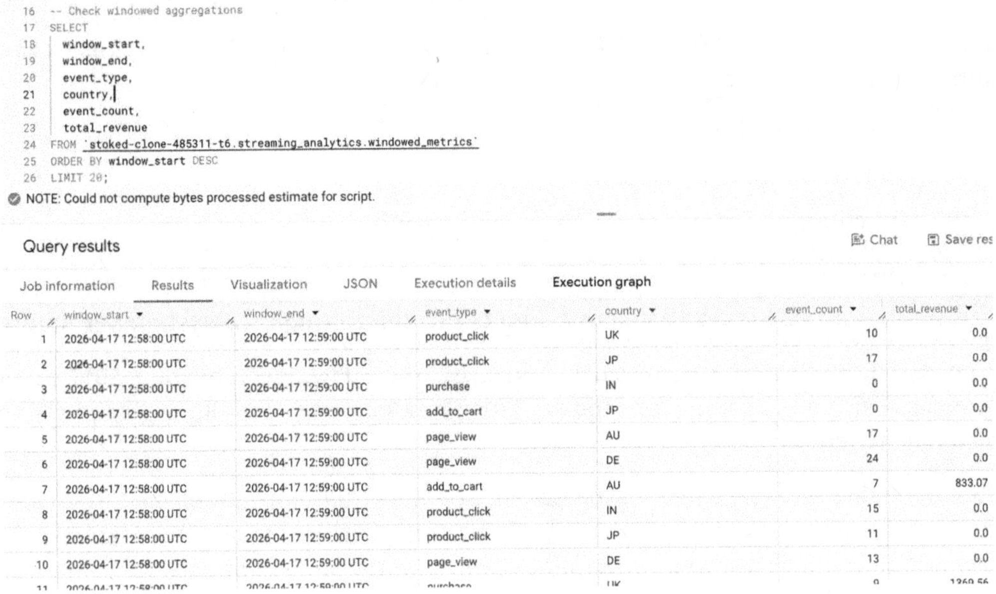

Row	window_start	window_end	event_type	country	event_count	total_revenue
1	2026-04-17 12:58:00 UTC	2026-04-17 12:59:00 UTC	product_click	UK	10	0.0
2	2026-04-17 12:58:00 UTC	2026-04-17 12:59:00 UTC	product_click	JP	17	0.0
3	2026-04-17 12:58:00 UTC	2026-04-17 12:59:00 UTC	purchase	IN	0	0.0
4	2026-04-17 12:58:00 UTC	2026-04-17 12:59:00 UTC	add_to_cart	JP	0	0.0
5	2026-04-17 12:58:00 UTC	2026-04-17 12:59:00 UTC	page_view	AU	17	0.0
6	2026-04-17 12:58:00 UTC	2026-04-17 12:59:00 UTC	page_view	DE	24	0.0
7	2026-04-17 12:58:00 UTC	2026-04-17 12:59:00 UTC	add_to_cart	AU	7	833.07
8	2026-04-17 12:58:00 UTC	2026-04-17 12:59:00 UTC	product_click	IN	15	0.0
9	2026-04-17 12:58:00 UTC	2026-04-17 12:59:00 UTC	product_click	JP	11	0.0
10	2026-04-17 12:58:00 UTC	2026-04-17 12:59:00 UTC	page_view	DE	13	0.0

Figure 13.4: *BigQuery Query Results Showing Windowed Aggregation Data*

Note: *Each row represents a 60-second window with event type, country, event count, and total revenue—confirming that Dataflow is successfully computing and writing real-time metrics.*

Building a Live Dashboard in Looker Studio

Data in a table is not easily digested by the C-Suite. We connect the windowed metrics table directly to Looker Studio to create a live-updating executive dashboard. As we had the pipeline pre-aggregate the data into dense 60-second windows with `SUM` and `COUNT` logic already computed, querying this table is intensely fast and cheap, making it an optimal source for a live-refreshing dashboard.

Follow these steps to build the dashboard:

Step 1: Create a Data Source. Navigate to [Looker Studio](https://lookerstudio.google.com) and click **`Create`** > **`Data Source`**. Select BigQuery as the connector. Browse to your project, select the `streaming_analytics` dataset, and choose the **`windowed_metrics`** table. Click **`Connect`**.

Step 2: Configure Field Types. Looker Studio will auto-detect most field types, but verify that **`window_start`** and **`window_end`** are recognized as **`Date and Time`** fields, not plain strings. If they appear as text, manually change their type in the data source configuration. This is critical for time-series charts to render correctly.

Step 3: Create a Time-Series Chart. Click **`Add a chart`** > **`Time series chart`**. Configure the following:

- **Dimension:** `window_start`
- **Metric:** `SUM(event_count)`
- **Date Range:** Today
- **Sort:** `window_start` ascending

This produces a line chart that shows events flowing through the system per minute.

Step 4: Add a Revenue Scorecard. Add a Scorecard widget showing **`SUM(total_revenue)`** with a date filter for "**`Today`**." This gives executives an at-a-glance view of real-time revenue.

Step 5: Enable Auto-Refresh. In the dashboard view (not edit mode), click the three-dot menu and select Refresh data configuration. Set an auto-refresh interval. As new windowed aggregations land in BigQuery, the dashboard updates automatically without manual intervention.

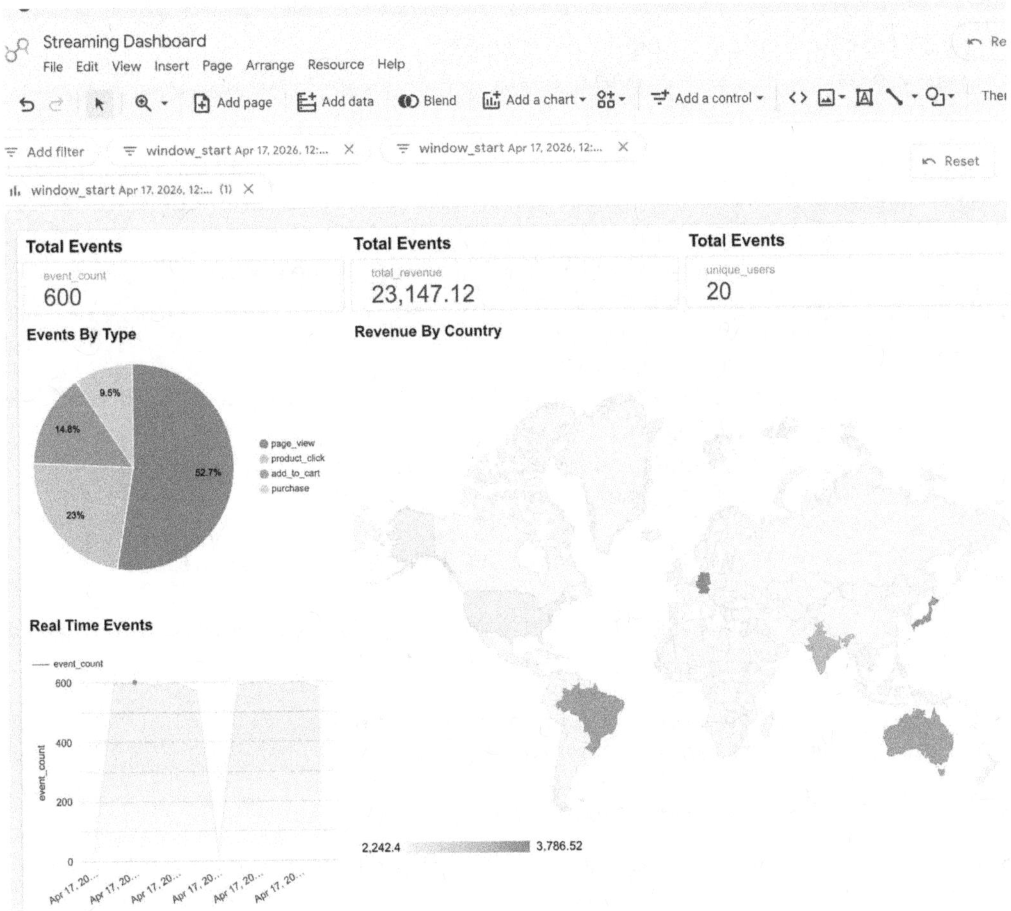

Figure 13.5: *Looker Studio Dashboard Displaying Live Streaming Metrics*

Note: *A time-series chart shows events per minute over time, with scorecard widgets displaying total revenue and event counts—all auto-refreshing from BigQuery.*

Handling the Inevitable: Late Data

One of the true tests of a streaming pipeline is how it behaves when the idyllic network conditions fail. Let us force our system to handle the late-arriving data.

We write a dedicated script (**`late_events.py`**) that actively injects `purchase` events into Pub/Sub, but deliberately overrides the event timestamp to be 90 seconds in the past:

```
# late_events.py — Publish events with timestamps 90 seconds in the past
import json, uuid, random
from datetime import datetime, timedelta
from google.cloud import pubsub_v1
```

```
publisher = pubsub_v1.PublisherClient()
topic_path = publisher.topic_path("your-project-id",
"clickstream-events")

for i in range(50):
    event = {
        "event_id": str(uuid.uuid4()),
        "user_id": f"USER-{random.randint(1, 500):04d}",
        "session_id": f"SESS-LATE-{i:04d}",
        "event_type": "purchase",
        "page_url": "/checkout",
        "product_id": f"PROD-{random.randint(1, 50):04d}",
        "product_category": "Electronics",
        "price": round(random.uniform(50, 500), 2),
        "device_type": "mobile",
        "country": "US",
        # Timestamp is 90 seconds in the past (within allowed_
lateness=120s)
        "event_timestamp": (datetime.utcnow() - timedelta(sec-
onds=90)).isoformat() + "Z"
    }
    data = json.dumps(event).encode("utf-8")
    publisher.publish(topic_path, data)

print("Published 50 late events (90 seconds late)")
```

Since our Beam pipeline was configured with **allowed_lateness=120**, 90 seconds is safely within the grace period. Instead of failing or appending the events to the current minute's aggregations, Dataflow identifies the actual event time, reconstructs the past aggregation state, updates the numbers, and issues an updated row into BigQuery for that specific historical window.

To verify this, query the windowed metrics table and look for multiple rows sharing the same **window_start** but with different **processing_timestamp** values:

```
-- Check for late event processing
SELECT
  window_start,
  window_end,
  event_type,
  event_count,
  processing_timestamp
FROM `your-project-id.streaming_analytics.windowed_metrics`
WHERE event_type = 'purchase'
  AND country = 'US'
ORDER BY window_start DESC
LIMIT 10;
```

This handles edge case consistency automatically, ensuring that your real-time analytics dashboards remain mathematically pure even when mobile networks lag.

Operational Best Practices

Chapter 8, Apache Beam and Dataflow covered the fundamentals of Dataflow job management–drain versus cancel, autoscaling behavior, and DLQ patterns. In this section, we will go deeper with production-hardened practices specific to long-running streaming workloads, such as:

Practice 1: Monitor Dead-Letter Patterns

In *Chapter 8, Apache Beam and Dataflow*, we introduced the DLQ pattern using **`beam.pvalue.TaggedOutput`** to route failed records to a separate output. In our `ParseClickEvent` DoFn, we implemented a simplified version by using `try-except` with logging. In a production system, you would extend this to write failed messages to a dedicated BigQuery table or Cloud Storage bucket for later analysis and reprocessing, without disrupting the flow of healthy data.

You can trace worker exceptions by analyzing Dataflow logs. When you build robust pipelines with proper error handling, this log query should return zero results:

```
gcloud logging read \
  "resource.type=dataflow_step AND severity>=ERROR" \
  --project=$PROJECT_ID \
  --limit=10 \
  --format="table(timestamp, textPayload)"
```

Practice 2: Cleanup and Draining

As highlighted in *Chapter 8, Apache Beam and Dataflow, Section: Key Takeaways*, always drain a streaming job rather than canceling it. Unlike a batch job that terminates after processing its input, a streaming pipeline runs eternally, waiting for more data.

If you forget to shut down a Dataflow streaming job, you will continue to incur hourly compute costs.

Always gracefully terminate your pipeline using the "`drain`" command. Draining tells Dataflow to stop accepting new Pub/Sub messages, but finish processing and writing any data already buffered in memory before deleting the worker VMs.

```
# 1. Drain the Dataflow job (completes in-flight work, then stops)
gcloud dataflow jobs drain $(gcloud dataflow jobs list \
  --region=$REGION \
  --filter="name:beamapp" \
```

```
    --status=active \
    --format="value(id)") \
    --region=$REGION

# 2. Delete Pub/Sub resources
gcloud pubsub subscriptions delete clickstream-sub --quiet
gcloud pubsub topics delete clickstream-events --quiet

# 3. Delete BigQuery dataset
bq rm -r -f -d ${PROJECT_ID}:streaming_analytics

# 4. Delete GCS bucket
gcloud storage rm --recursive gs://${BUCKET_NAME}
```

Figure 13.6: *Dataflow Console Showing the Job in the "Drained" State*

Note: *The Job Info panel confirms 0 current workers, "Worker pool stopped" status, and "Exactly once" streaming mode–indicating that the pipeline was gracefully terminated without data loss.*

Practice 3: Cost Awareness

Streaming architectures are the most expensive workloads in this entire book. Unlike batch jobs that start, process, and terminate, streaming pipelines run continuously. Understanding the cost components is critical:

Component	Billing Model	Typical Cost (Lab)	Production Estimate
Dataflow Workers	Per vCPU-hour + per GB-hour of memory	~$0.50/hr for 2 workers	$360–$720/month for 2 workers running 24/7
Pub/Sub	Per message delivered (first 10GB free)	< $0.01 for lab	$40–$100/month at ~10M messages/day
BigQuery Streaming	Storage Write API included in storage costs	< $0.01 for lab	Varies by volume
BigQuery Storage	Per GB stored, per month	< $0.01 for lab	$0.02/GB/month (active storage)

Table 13.3: *Streaming Pipeline Cost Components*

The single most common cost mistake in streaming is forgetting to drain a development pipeline. A 2-worker Dataflow streaming job running for a forgotten weekend costs approximately $24 in compute alone. Always set budget alerts in the Google Cloud Console.

Practice 4: Production Tips

Teams that have operated streaming pipelines in production consistently report the same lessons learned, such as:

- **Schema Evolution is painful.** Unlike batch tables, in which you can reload historical data with a new schema, streaming pipelines are always running. If you add a new field to your event JSON, the running pipeline's DoFn will ignore it at best or crash at worst. Plan schema changes with a versioning strategy: add new fields as nullable first, deploy the updated pipeline, then backfill historical data if needed.
- **Idempotency is non-negotiable.** Pub/Sub guarantees at-least-once delivery, meaning that a message can be delivered more than once during retries. Your pipeline should handle duplicate messages gracefully. The **`event_id`** field we included serves exactly this purpose: downstream consumers can deduplicate using it.
- **Monitor Pub/Sub subscription age.** In the Pub/Sub console, the metric "Oldest unacknowledged message age" tells you how far behind your consumer (Dataflow) is from the publisher. If this metric climbs steadily, your pipeline cannot keep pace with the event rate.
- **Use `` `drain` ``, never `` `cancel` ``.** The "**`gcloud dataflow jobs cancel`**" command immediately kills all workers, potentially losing any data buffered in memory. The "**`drain`**" command stops accepting new messages but allows workers to flush their in-memory state to BigQuery before shutting down. Always use `drain` unless you are comfortable losing in-flight data.

- **Test Allowed Lateness aggressively.** We tested with 90-second late events, but production systems can experience minutes or even hours of delay (for example, mobile devices syncing after airplane mode). Decide on an "`allowed_lateness`" value that matches your business tolerance, and test it explicitly–do not assume that it works.

Conclusion

In this chapter, we crossed the bridge from historical batch processing into the world of live, real-time streaming analytics. We started by understanding the fundamental paradigm shift from bounded to unbounded data, and explored the core concepts that make streaming possible: windowing, watermarks, and late data handling.

We built a complete, production-representative pipeline using Google Cloud's streaming stack. Pub/Sub served as our decoupled ingestion layer, absorbing unpredictable event traffic without overwhelming downstream systems. Apache Beam on Dataflow processed the continuous stream, applying 60-second fixed windows with early triggers and Allowed Lateness to balance freshness with completeness. The BigQuery Storage Write API provided high-throughput, exactly-once delivery into our warehouse. Looker Studio transformed the dense, pre-aggregated windowed metrics into a live executive dashboard.

We also confronted the messy realities of production streaming: late data that must be assigned to the correct historical windows, malformed messages that require dead-letter routing, cost management for always-on infrastructure, and the critical importance of draining (never canceling) a streaming pipeline.

In the next chapter, we will bring together many of the batch concepts we have explored throughout this book into a comprehensive real-world scenario, building an Enterprise Warehouse and Extract, Load, Transform (ELT) Pipeline using dbt and BigQuery.

Points to Remember

- **Pub/Sub acts as a buffer between event sources and Dataflow -** it absorbs traffic spikes and retains messages for up to 7 days if the pipeline goes down.
- Use the branched pipeline pattern to write raw events and pre-aggregated metrics to separate BigQuery tables from a single Dataflow job.
- Partition streaming tables by event time, not load time - this ensures late-arriving data lands in the correct business date partition.

- The Storage Write API replaces legacy streaming inserts with higher throughput, exactly-once delivery, and lower cost.
- **Always drain a streaming job, never cancel it** – canceling loses in-flight data while draining flushes buffered records to BigQuery before stopping.
- Streaming pipelines run continuously and bill continuously.

Multiple Choice Questions

1. What is the primary operational difference between bounded and unbounded data in streaming architecture?

    a. Bounded data is always strictly numerical, while unbounded data is textual.

    b. Bounded data requires Pub/Sub, while unbounded data requires Dataflow.

    c. Bounded data has a defined end and can be processed fully, while unbounded events arrive continuously forever.

    d. Unbounded data is natively supported by legacy tabledata.insertAll but not the Storage Write API.

2. Which Apache Beam concept is responsible for grouping continuous data streams into finite, discrete time blocks for aggregations?

    a. Watermarks

    b. Triggers

    c. Pub/Sub Topics

    d. Windowing

3. If an upstream system loses network connection and a JSON event is delayed by 90 seconds, what Dataflow parameter allows the system to recalculate historical aggregations rather than safely dropping the event?

    a. `allowed_lateness`

    b. `accumulation_mode`

    c. `early_trigger`

    d. `fixed_windows`

4. When designing a branched streaming architecture, what is standard practice if a malformed JSON message cannot be parsed by your pipeline?

    a. Allow the pipeline to crash and alert administrators

    b. Route the offending message to a Dead-Letter Queue (DLQ) BigQuery table for later inspection

    c. Silently drop the message without logging

    d. Resend the message to Pub/Sub continuously until parsed

5. Why is `--autoscaling_algorithm=THROUGHPUT_BASED` crucial for modern Dataflow pipelines?

    a. Because it reduces the dependency on BigQuery for aggregations

    b. It ensures the streaming job stops automatically when no traffic is detected

    c. It dynamically provisions and terminates Compute Engine VMs based on incoming event volume, preventing backlog and optimizing cost

    d. Because Pub/Sub topics require throughput metrics to acknowledge messages properly

6. What is the highest-performance mechanism recommended to ingest real-time data from an Apache Beam pipeline into BigQuery?

    a. tabledata.insertAll

    b. The BigQuery API Client Libraries

    c. BigQuery Data Transfer Service

    d. BigQuery Storage Write API

7. What metric tracks how far behind real-time the processing engine is operating when reading from Pub/Sub?

    a. System Lag

    b. Worker Utilization

    c. Maximum Throughput

    d. Pipeline CPU utilization

8. Why is it dangerous to leave an active streaming Dataflow pipeline running after a lab or testing session is completed?

   a. It will fill the BigQuery table and crash the GCP project.

   b. Streaming jobs run endlessly and continue accumulating hourly Compute Engine costs regardless of data volumes.

   c. Pub/Sub requires daily renewals of active streaming pulls.

   d. BigQuery disables continuous streaming after 24 hours of no activity.

9. What command safely stops a Dataflow streaming job, allowing it to finish processing currently buffered messages before terminating?

   a. `gcloud dataflow jobs cancel`

   b. `gcloud pubsub pull --stop`

   c. `gcloud dataflow jobs drain`

   d. `python3 streaming_pipeline.py --stop`

10. Looker Studio connects to BigQuery for real-time visualization. Why did we visualize `windowed_metrics` instead of the raw event table?

    a. Looker Studio does not support raw JSON inputs.

    b. Looker Studio only auto-refreshes data that has been processed by Apache Beam.

    c. Querying dense, pre-aggregated windowed tables is incredibly fast and cheap, making it an optimal source for live-refreshing dashboards.

    d. Raw events cannot be assigned timestamps in BigQuery.

Answers

1. c
2. d
3. a
4. b
5. c
6. d
7. a

8. b
9. c
10. c

Questions

1. Explain the "Branched Pipeline" architectural pattern utilized in our Dataflow graph, and why writing to both a raw events table and an aggregated metrics table is important in production.
2. What are the key differences between Fixed Windows, Sliding Windows, and Session Windows when building a streaming analytics process? When would you choose each?
3. Describe the problem caused by "Late Data" in real-time analytics and how Apache Beam's Watermarks and Allowed Lateness settings solve it. What happens to an event that arrives after the allowed lateness period has expired?
4. Why did we utilize the BigQuery Storage Write API instead of legacy streaming inserts, and what architectural requirement does it mandate from the data engineering team?
5. How does decoupled streaming ingestion via Google Cloud Pub/Sub act as a "shock absorber" during rapid, unpredictable traffic spikes on an upstream application frontend?

Key Terms

- **Unbounded Data:** Datasets that have no defined end; events that are generated continuously, constantly flowing into the processing system.
- **Pub/Sub:** Google Cloud's fully-managed real-time messaging service that allows you to send and receive messages between independent applications, decoupling producers and consumers.
- **Apache Beam:** An open-source, unified programming model to define and execute data processing pipelines, encompassing both batch and streaming paradigms.
- **Google Cloud Dataflow:** A managed service for executing Apache Beam data processing pipelines, featuring horizontal autoscaling and serverless operations.
- **DoFn:** A Beam "`Do Function`" – a user-defined processing step that receives individual elements, applies logic, and emits output elements. The fundamental unit of computation in a Beam pipeline.

- **Windowing:** The process of logically dividing continuous unbounded data streams into finite chunks based on time boundaries for mathematical aggregations.
- **Watermark:** A heuristic metric indicating how far along the processing engine believes it is relative to Event Time, used to determine when a window should be calculated and emitted.
- **Allowed Lateness:** An Apache Beam configuration that specifies how long after a window closes the system will continue to accept and re-aggregate late-arriving events.
- **Storage Write API:** High-throughput, gRPC-based data ingestion API for BigQuery that provides high concurrency and exactly-once streaming semantics, replacing the legacy `tabledata.insertAll` endpoint.
- **System Lag:** A critical Dataflow streaming metric representing the delay between when a message was published to Pub/Sub and when it was successfully processed.
- **Dead-Letter Queue (DLQ):** An architectural pattern where messages that cannot be processed successfully (due to schema mismatch or malformed data) are routed to a separate storage table rather than crashing the primary stream.
- **Draining:** The process of gracefully shutting down a streaming Dataflow pipeline by stopping new message ingestion while allowing currently buffered data to be fully processed and written to sinks before workers terminate.

CHAPTER 14
Enterprise Warehouse and ELT Project

Introduction

Most data teams start small. A few CSV files uploaded to BigQuery. Some ad-hoc SQL queries saved in a shared folder. A handful of dashboards built directly on raw tables. This works fine for the first few months. However, as the business grows, cracks begin to appear. Analysts waste hours debugging why revenue numbers do not match between reports. Engineers spend entire sprints untangling spaghetti SQL that nobody documented. New team members struggle to understand which tables are safe to query and which are deprecated experiments.

The solution is not more tools or bigger infrastructure, but rather, it is the structure. A well-architected data warehouse with clear transformation layers, automated quality checks, and proper deployment workflows transforms chaos into reliability.

In *Chapter 7, ELT with dbt and BigQuery*, we introduced the data build tool (dbt) as a framework for managing SQL transformations. We covered models, tests, and documentation through focused examples. Now, we are going to build something complete: a production-grade e-commerce analytics warehouse with staging models that clean raw data, intermediate models that encode business logic, and mart models that are optimized for analyst consumption. We will implement incremental loading for large fact tables, enforce data quality with comprehensive testing, generate documentation that persists into BigQuery metadata, and deploy everything through automated Continuous Integration/Continuous Deployment (CI/CD) workflows.

This chapter will tackle the challenges that only surface in real warehouse projects, such as choosing between table and view materializations, handling slowly changing dimensions, optimizing partitioning and clustering strategies, managing schema evolution, and building operational guardrails that keep pipelines healthy as data volumes grow.

Quick Refresher: In *Chapter 7, ELT with dbt and BigQuery*, we introduced dbt's core concepts, including models (SQL files that define transformations), tests (data quality assertions), and the `ref()` function (which creates dependencies between models). If you need a deeper review of dbt fundamentals, revisit this chapter before proceeding.

Structure

In this chapter, we will cover the following topics:

- Understanding the Extract, Load, Transform (ELT) Architecture
- Setting up the Foundation
- Building the Staging Layer
- Constructing the Intermediate Layer
- Creating the Mart Layer
- Implementing Incremental Models
- Enforcing Data Quality
- Generating Documentation
- Deploying with CI/CD
- Operational Best Practices

Understanding the Extract, Load, Transform (ELT) Architecture

A production data warehouse is not a collection of random SQL scripts. It is a layered system where each transformation has a specific purpose and place. The architecture we are building follows a three-layer pattern that has become the standard across modern analytics teams: Staging, Intermediate, and Marts.

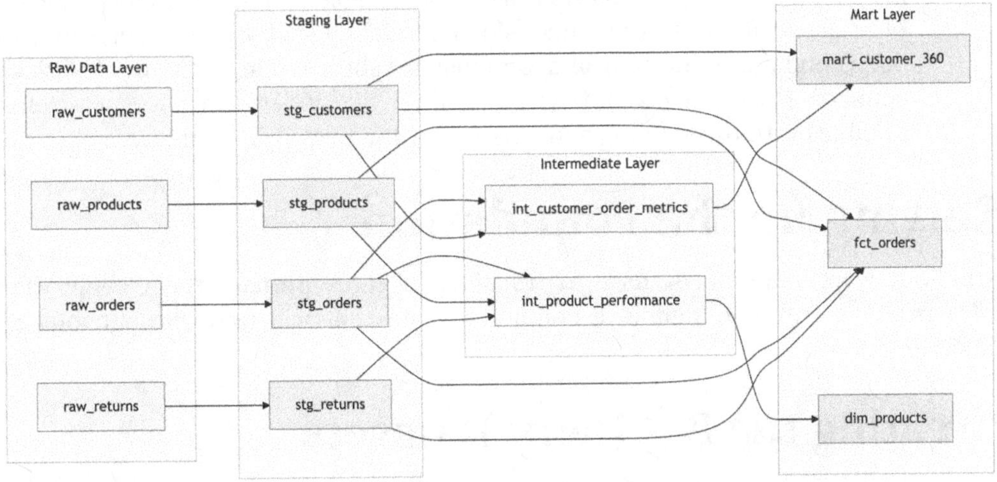

Figure 14.1: *End-to-End ELT Architecture Showing the 3 Transformation Layers*

Note: *Raw data flows into staging models, then intermediate models, and finally mart models.*

Data flows left to right through each layer with increasing refinement. The core principle is Separation of Concerns (SoC): each layer has a specific job, and models never skip layers. A mart model reads from intermediate or staging models, never directly from raw tables. This layered approach creates maintainable, testable, and reusable transformations.

Here is what each layer does:

1. **Raw Data (The Source):** In the real world, this would be data loaded by Fivetran, Airbyte, or BigQuery Data Transfer Service. For our project, we will simulate this with four raw tables: customers, products, orders, and returns.
2. **Staging Layer (The Cleaning Room):** Staging models have a 1:1 relationship with raw tables. They do not perform joins, aggregations, or complex business logic. Their sole purpose is to clean and standardize: rename columns to consistent conventions, cast data types, trim whitespace, filter out invalid records, and extract nested JSON fields. Every downstream model reads from staging, never from raw tables.
3. **Intermediate Layer (The Business Logic Engine):** Intermediate models encode the complex transformations that define your business. This is where you join customers with orders to calculate lifetime value, aggregate product sales to compute return rates, and apply business rules such as customer segmentation. These models are designed to be reusable—a single intermediate model might feed multiple downstream marts.
4. **Mart Layer (The Analytics Interface):** Mart models are the final, polished tables exposed to BI tools such as Looker, Tableau, and Metabase. They are typically structured using dimensional modeling such as: fact tables (narrow, deep, immutable events) and dimension tables (wide, shallow, descriptive context). Marts are often denormalized for query performance, materialized as tables with partitioning and clustering, and heavily documented.

Setting up the Foundation

Now, our warehouse needs data to transform. Let us prepare the Google Cloud infrastructure and load sample e-commerce data that will flow through our ELT pipeline.

Creating the BigQuery Datasets

We need three datasets to simulate proper environment separation. During production, development and production environments are isolated to prevent accidental changes from affecting live dashboards.

```
# Set your project
export PROJECT_ID="your-project-id"
gcloud config set project $PROJECT_ID

# Enable BigQuery API
gcloud services enable bigquery.googleapis.com

# Raw data dataset (simulates data loaded by Fivetran/ETL tools)
bq mk --dataset --location=US ${PROJECT_ID}:ecommerce_raw

# Development dataset (where you'll build models locally)
bq mk --dataset --location=US ${PROJECT_ID}:analytics_dev

# Production dataset (where CI/CD will deploy)
bq mk --dataset --location=US ${PROJECT_ID}:analytics_prod
```

Loading Sample E-Commerce Data

We need realistic sample data representing an e-commerce platform. The following SQL generates four interconnected tables: customers, products, orders, and returns.

```
-- Create raw_customers table (1,000 customers)
CREATE OR REPLACE TABLE `your-project-id.ecommerce_raw.raw_customers` AS
SELECT
  GENERATE_UUID() AS customer_id,
  CONCAT('Customer ', CAST(num AS STRING)) AS customer_name,
  CONCAT('customer', CAST(num AS STRING), '@example.com') AS email,
  CASE MOD(num, 5)
    WHEN 0 THEN 'US'
    WHEN 1 THEN 'UK'
    WHEN 2 THEN 'DE'
    WHEN 3 THEN 'FR'
    ELSE 'CA'
  END AS country,
  DATE_SUB(CURRENT_DATE(), INTERVAL MOD(num, 365) DAY) AS signup_date
FROM UNNEST(GENERATE_ARRAY(1, 1000)) AS num;

-- Create raw_products table (200 products)
CREATE OR REPLACE TABLE `your-project-id.ecommerce_raw.raw_products` AS
SELECT
  CONCAT('PROD-', LPAD(CAST(num AS STRING), 4, '0')) AS product_id,
  CONCAT('Product ', CAST(num AS STRING)) AS product_name,
  CASE MOD(num, 5)
```

```
    WHEN 0 THEN 'Electronics'
    WHEN 1 THEN 'Clothing'
    WHEN 2 THEN 'Home'
    WHEN 3 THEN 'Sports'
    ELSE 'Books'
  END AS category,
  ROUND(10 + (num * 2.5), 2) AS price,
  MOD(num, 2) = 0 AS is_active
FROM UNNEST(GENERATE_ARRAY(1, 200)) AS num;

-- Create raw_orders table (5,000 orders)
CREATE OR REPLACE TABLE `your-project-id.ecommerce_raw.raw_orders` AS
WITH numbered_customers AS (
  SELECT customer_id, ROW_NUMBER() OVER ( ORDER BY customer_id) as rn
FROM `your-project-id.ecommerce_raw.raw_customers`
),
numbered_products AS (
  SELECT product_id, price, ROW_NUMBER() OVER ( ORDER BY product_id)
as rn
 FROM `your-project-id.ecommerce_raw.raw_products` ),
order_data AS (
  SELECT
    CONCAT('ORD-', LPAD(CAST(num AS STRING), 6, '0')) AS order_id,
    c.customer_id,
    p.product_id,
    DATE_SUB(CURRENT_DATE(), INTERVAL MOD(num, 180) DAY) AS order_date,
    CASE MOD(num, 10)
      WHEN 0 THEN 'cancelled'
      WHEN 1 THEN 'pending'
      ELSE 'completed'
    END AS status,
    ROUND(20 + (RAND() * 200), 2) AS amount
  FROM UNNEST(GENERATE_ARRAY(1, 5000)) AS num
  JOIN numbered_customers c on c.rn = MOD(num * 7919, 1000) + 1
  JOIN numbered_products p on p.rn = MOD(num * 31, 200) + 1
--- Prime * num mod count gives an even, shuffled mapping
--- with no accidental correlation to MOD(num, 180 ) used for order_
date
)
SELECT * FROM order_data;

-- Create raw_returns table (400 returns, ~8% return rate)
CREATE OR REPLACE TABLE `your-project-id.ecommerce_raw.raw_returns`
AS
WITH completed_orders AS (
  SELECT order_id, order_date
  FROM `your-project-id.ecommerce_raw.raw_orders`
```

```
    WHERE status = 'completed'
  )
  SELECT
    CONCAT('RET-', LPAD(CAST(num AS STRING), 6, '0')) AS return_id,
    order_id,
    DATE_ADD(order_date, INTERVAL MOD(num, 14) + 1 DAY) AS return_date,
    CASE MOD(num, 3)
      WHEN 0 THEN 'defective'
      WHEN 1 THEN 'wrong_item'
      ELSE 'not_satisfied'
    END AS return_reason
  FROM completed_orders
  CROSS JOIN UNNEST(GENERATE_ARRAY(1, 1)) AS num
  WHERE RAND() < 0.08
  LIMIT 400;
```

Verify that the data is loaded correctly:

```
SELECT 'customers' AS table_name, COUNT(*) AS row_count
FROM `your-project-id.ecommerce_raw.raw_customers`
UNION ALL
SELECT 'products', COUNT(*)
FROM `your-project-id.ecommerce_raw.raw_products`
UNION ALL
SELECT 'orders', COUNT(*)
FROM `your-project-id.ecommerce_raw.raw_orders`
UNION ALL
SELECT 'returns', COUNT(*)
FROM `your-project-id.ecommerce_raw.raw_returns`;
```

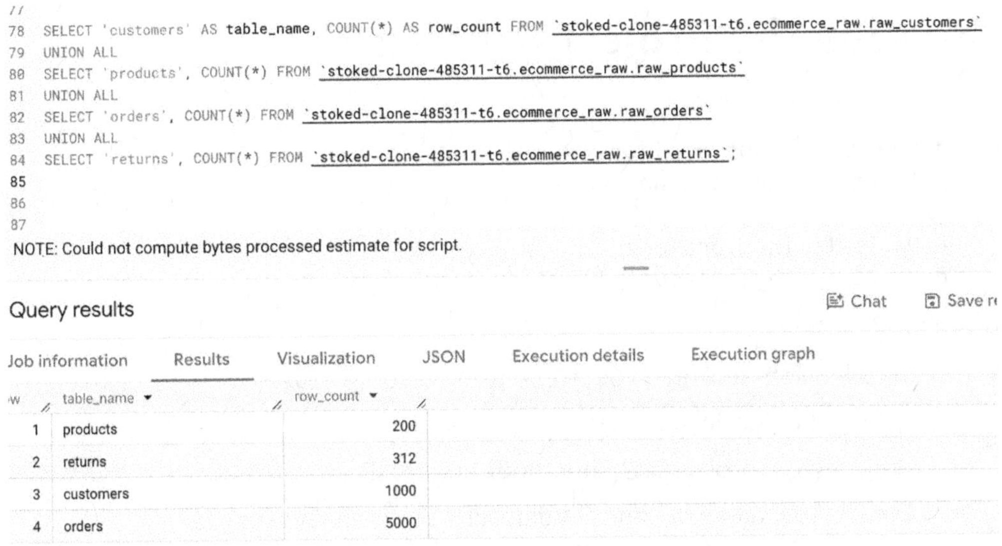

Figure 14.2: *BigQuery Query Results Showing Row Counts*

Initializing the dbt Project

With the raw data loaded, we can now set up the dbt project that will transform it into analytics-ready tables.

Installing dbt-bigquery

dbt requires Python 3.11 or 3.12. Create a virtual environment to isolate dependencies:

```
# Create virtual environment
python3.11 -m venv dbt-venv
source dbt-venv/bin/activate  # On Windows: dbt-venv\Scripts\activate

# Install dbt-bigquery
pip install --upgrade pip
pip install dbt-bigquery

# Verify installation
dbt --version
```

Expected output:

```
Core:
  - installed: 1.8.x
  - latest:    1.8.x

Plugins:
  - bigquery: 1.8.x
```

Creating the Project Structure

Initialize a new dbt project:

```
# Create new dbt project
dbt init enterprise_warehouse

# Navigate into project
cd enterprise_warehouse
```

When prompted:

- Which database would you like to use? Select `bigquery`
- Desired authentication method? Select `oauth`
- Project (GCP project id)? Enter your project ID
- Dataset (the name of your dbt dataset)? Enter `analytics_dev`
- Threads? Enter `4`

- Location? Enter US

Configuring Profiles

dbt uses **profiles.yml** to manage database connections. Edit **~/.dbt/profiles.yml** to add both development and production targets in the following manner:

```
enterprise_warehouse:
  target: dev
  outputs:
    dev:
      type: bigquery
      method: oauth
      project: your-project-id
      dataset: analytics_dev
      threads: 4
      location: US
      priority: interactive

    prod:
      type: bigquery
      method: service-account
      project: your-project-id
      dataset: analytics_prod
      threads: 8
      location: US
      keyfile: ./service-account.json
```

Authenticate with Google Cloud and test the connection:

```
# Authenticate
gcloud auth application-default login

# Test connection
dbt debug
```

You should see all green checkmarks confirming that dbt can connect to BigQuery.

Figure 14.3: *Terminal Showing Successful `dbt Debug` Output with All Checks Passing*

Building the Staging Layer

The staging layer serves as the front door to your dbt project. These models read directly from raw tables and perform the essential yet unglamorous work of data cleaning and standardization.

Defining Sources

Before building staging models, we need to declare our raw tables as "**`sources`**" in **`dbt`**. This creates a centralized registry of external data and enables source freshness monitoring.

Create **`models/sources.yml`**:

```
version: 2

sources:
  - name: ecommerce_raw
    database: your-project-id
    schema: ecommerce_raw
    description: Raw e-commerce data loaded from operational systems

    tables:
      - name: raw_customers
        description: Raw customer information
```

```
      columns:
        - name: customer_id
          description: Unique customer identifier

    - name: raw_products
      description: Raw product catalog
      columns:
        - name: product_id
          description: Unique product identifier

    - name: raw_orders
      description: Raw order transactions
      columns:
        - name: order_id
          description: Unique order identifier

    - name: raw_returns
      description: Raw return records
      columns:
        - name: return_id
          description: Unique return identifier
```

Building Staging Models

Staging models follow strict conventions: they have a 1:1 relationship with source tables, perform no joins or aggregations, and focus solely on cleaning and standardization.

Create **models/staging/stg_customers.sql**:

```
WITH source AS (
    SELECT * FROM {{ source('ecommerce_raw', 'raw_customers') }}
),

cleaned AS (
    SELECT
        customer_id,
        TRIM(customer_name) AS customer_name,
        LOWER(TRIM(email)) AS email,
        UPPER(TRIM(country)) AS country,
        signup_date,
        CURRENT_TIMESTAMP() AS loaded_at
    FROM source
    WHERE email IS NOT NULL
      AND signup_date IS NOT NULL
)

SELECT * FROM cleaned
```

Notice what this model does, such as:

- Uses **`{{ source() }}`** to reference the raw table (not a hardcoded table name).
- Standardizes string casing (lowercase emails, uppercase country codes).
- Trims whitespace.
- Filters out invalid records (missing email or **`signup_date`**).
- Adds a **`loaded_at`** timestamp for audit purposes.
- No joins, no aggregations, no complex business logic.

Create `models/staging/stg_products.sql`:

```
WITH source AS (
    SELECT * FROM {{ source('ecommerce_raw', 'raw_products') }}
),

cleaned AS (
    SELECT
        product_id,
        TRIM(product_name) AS product_name,
        TRIM(category) AS category,
        price,
        is_active,
        CURRENT_TIMESTAMP() AS loaded_at
    FROM source
    WHERE product_id IS NOT NULL
      AND price > 0
)

SELECT * FROM cleaned
```

Create `models/staging/stg_orders.sql`:

```
WITH source AS (
    SELECT * FROM {{ source('ecommerce_raw', 'raw_orders') }}
),

cleaned AS (
    SELECT
        order_id,
        customer_id,
        product_id,
        order_date,
        LOWER(TRIM(status)) AS status,
        amount,
        CURRENT_TIMESTAMP() AS loaded_at
    FROM source
```

```
    WHERE order_id IS NOT NULL
      AND order_date IS NOT NULL
      AND amount >= 0
)

SELECT * FROM cleaned
```

Create `models/staging/stg_returns.sql`:

```
WITH source AS (
    SELECT * FROM {{ source('ecommerce_raw', 'raw_returns') }}
),

cleaned AS (
    SELECT
        return_id,
        order_id,
        return_date,
        LOWER(TRIM(return_reason)) AS return_reason,
        CURRENT_TIMESTAMP() AS loaded_at
    FROM source
    WHERE return_id IS NOT NULL
      AND order_id IS NOT NULL
      AND return_date IS NOT NULL
)

SELECT * FROM cleaned
```

Adding Staging Tests

Tests in dbt are assertions about the state of your data. Define them alongside your model declarations in **`models/staging/schema.yml`**:

```
version: 2

models:
  - name: stg_customers
    description: Cleaned and standardized customer data
    columns:
      - name: customer_id
        description: Unique customer identifier
        tests:
          - unique
          - not_null
      - name: email
        description: Customer email address
        tests:
          - unique
```

```
          - not_null
      - name: country
        tests:
          - accepted_values:
              values: ['US', 'UK', 'DE', 'FR', 'CA']

  - name: stg_products
    description: Cleaned product catalog
    columns:
      - name: product_id
        tests:
          - unique
          - not_null
      - name: price
        tests:
          - not_null
      - name: category
        tests:
          - accepted_values:
              values: ['Electronics', 'Clothing', 'Home', 'Sports',
'Books']

  - name: stg_orders
    description: Cleaned order transactions
    columns:
      - name: order_id
        tests:
          - unique
          - not_null
      - name: customer_id
        tests:
          - not_null
          - relationships:
              to: ref('stg_customers')
              field: customer_id
      - name: product_id
        tests:
          - not_null
          - relationships:
              to: ref('stg_products')
              field: product_id
      - name: status
        tests:
          - accepted_values:
              values: ['completed', 'pending', 'cancelled']

  - name: stg_returns
```

```
    description: Cleaned return records
    columns:
      - name: return_id
        tests:
          - unique
          - not_null
      - name: order_id
        tests:
          - not_null
          - relationships:
              to: ref('stg_orders')
              field: order_id
```

The "**relationships**" test is particularly powerful, as it enforces referential integrity by verifying that every **customer_id** in **stg_orders** exists in **stg_customers**. BigQuery does not enforce foreign keys natively, so that dbt tests serve as your data quality firewall.

Running Staging Models

Build the staging layer in the following manner:

```
# Build staging models
dbt run --select staging
```

When you run `dbt  run`, dbt automatically determines the correct execution order based on dependencies. Since staging models have no dependencies on each other, they run in parallel (up to the "**threads**" limit in your profile).

Now, run the tests:

```
# Run staging tests
dbt test --select staging
```

Most tests pass; however, one fails:

```
12 of 12 FAIL 1 unique_stg_returns_return_id ........ [FAIL 1 in 2.32s]

Completed with 1 error, 0 partial successes, and 0 warnings:

Failure in test unique_stg_returns_return_id (models/staging/schema.yml)
  Got 1 result, configured to fail if != 0
```

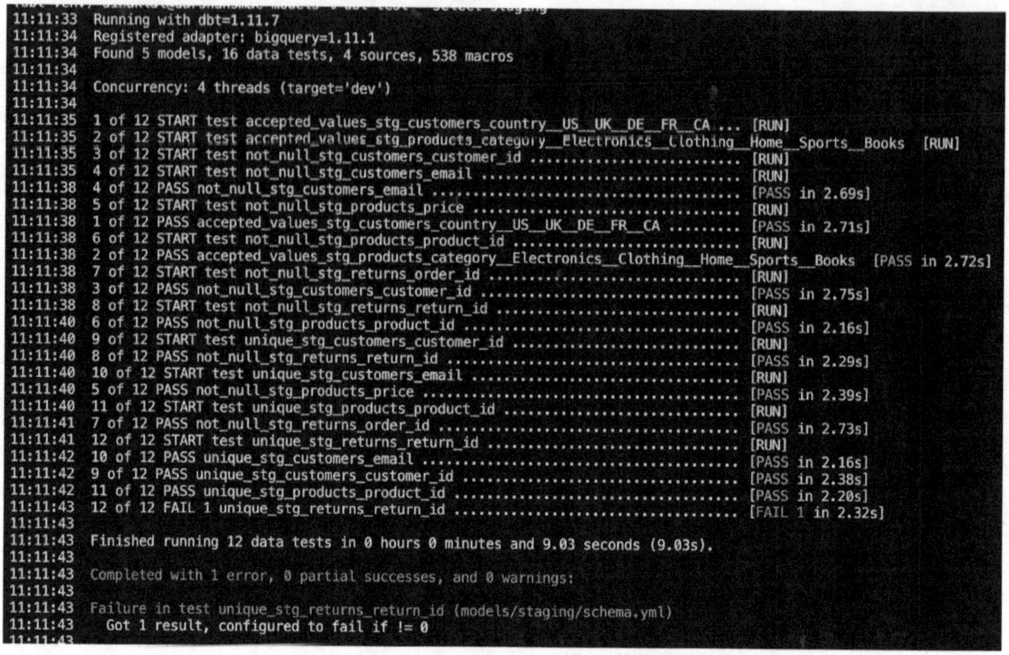

Figure 14.4: *Terminal Showing `dbt test` Output with 11 Tests Passing and 1 Failing: `unique_stg_returns_return_id`.*

This is dbt's testing framework earning its keep. Our "**unique**" test on **return_id** caught duplicate values in the raw data before they could propagate through the pipeline and corrupt downstream analytics.

Debugging the Test Failure

If we look back at our **raw_returns** generation SQL, we used **CROSS JOIN UNNEST(GENERATE_ARRAY(1, 1))**—a single-element array. This means every return record was generated with the same **return_id** of **RET-000001**. In production, this kind of upstream data quality issue is surprisingly common: a source system change, a broken ETL job, or a schema migration gone wrong.

The "**unique**" test caught this before it could infect downstream dashboards. Without dbt, this bug would have silently passed through every transformation and surfaced as duplicated revenue in your Customer 360 mart—the kind of error that erodes trust in the entire analytics platform.

Fixing the Source Data

Re-generate the "**raw_returns**" table with properly unique sequential IDs using **ROW_NUMBER()**:

```
CREATE OR REPLACE TABLE `your-project-id.ecommerce_raw.raw_returns` AS
WITH completed_orders AS (
  SELECT order_id, order_date
  FROM `your-project-id.ecommerce_raw.raw_orders`
  WHERE status = 'completed'
),
sampled_returns AS (
  SELECT
    order_id,
    order_date,
    DATE_ADD(order_date, INTERVAL CAST(FLOOR(1 + RAND() * 14) AS
INT64) DAY) AS return_date,
    CASE CAST(FLOOR(RAND() * 3) AS INT64)
      WHEN 0 THEN 'defective'
      WHEN 1 THEN 'wrong_item'
      ELSE 'not_satisfied'
    END AS return_reason
  FROM completed_orders
  WHERE RAND() < 0.08
  LIMIT 400
)
SELECT
  CONCAT('RET-', LPAD(CAST(ROW_NUMBER() OVER() AS STRING), 6, '0'))
AS return_id,
  order_id,
  return_date,
  return_reason
FROM sampled_returns;
```

Now, re-run the tests:

```
dbt test --select staging
```

All 12 tests pass. The pipeline is clean.

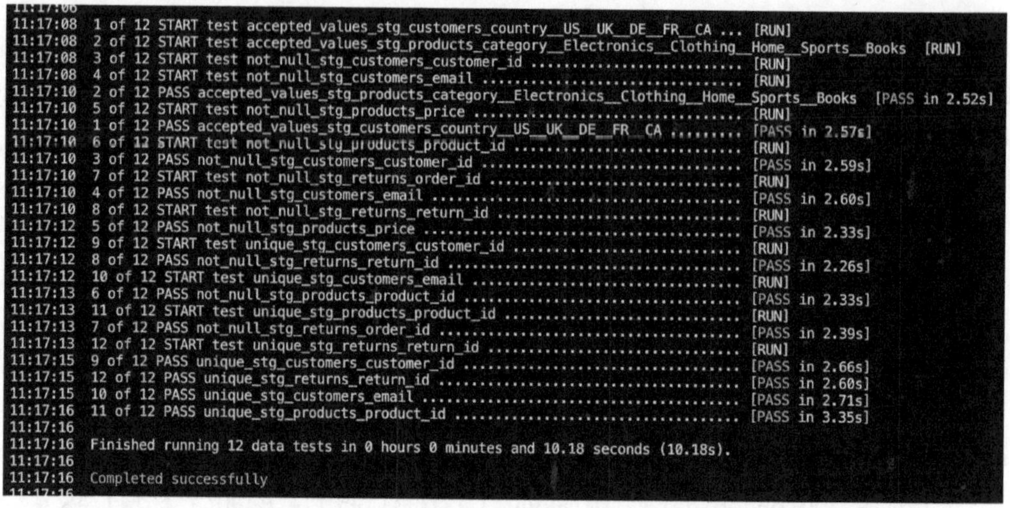

Figure 14.5: *Terminal Showing All 12 Staging Tests Passing after the Raw Data Fix*

Constructing the Intermediate Layer

The intermediate layer handles complex business logic. Customer lifetime value calculations, product return rate aggregations, and business rule applications all happen here.

Building Customer Order Metrics

Create `models/intermediate/int_customer_order_metrics.sql`:

```
{{ config(
    materialized='view'
) }}

WITH orders AS (
    SELECT * FROM {{ ref('stg_orders') }}
),

customer_metrics AS (
    SELECT
        customer_id,
        COUNT(*) AS total_orders,
        COUNT(CASE WHEN status = 'completed' THEN 1 END) AS completed
_orders,
        COUNT(CASE WHEN status = 'cancelled' THEN 1 END)
AS cancelled_orders,
```

```
        COUNT(CASE WHEN status = 'pending' THEN 1 END) AS pending_
orders,
        SUM(CASE WHEN status = 'completed' THEN amount ELSE 0 END) AS
total_revenue,
        AVG(CASE WHEN status = 'completed' THEN amount END) AS avg_
order_value,
        MIN(order_date) AS first_order_date,
        MAX(order_date) AS last_order_date,
        DATE_DIFF(MAX(order_date), MIN(order_date), DAY) AS customer
_lifetime_days,
        DATE_DIFF(CURRENT_DATE(), MAX(order_date), DAY) AS days_
since_last_order
    FROM orders
    GROUP BY customer_id
)

SELECT * FROM customer_metrics
```

The preceding model performs the following tasks:

- Reads from the staging layer (**stg_orders**).
- Performs aggregations to calculate metrics per customer.
- Handles conditional logic (such as completed versus cancelled orders).
- Calculates derived metrics (such as customer lifetime days, days since last order).
- Produces a reusable dataset for downstream marts.

Building Product Performance Metrics

Create `models/intermediate/int_product_performance.sql`:

```
{{ config(
    materialized='view'
) }}

WITH orders AS (
    SELECT * FROM {{ ref('stg_orders') }}
),

products AS (
    SELECT * FROM {{ ref('stg_products') }}
),

returns AS (
    SELECT * FROM {{ ref('stg_returns') }}
),
```

```
product_orders AS (
    SELECT
        o.product_id,
        COUNT(*) AS total_orders,
        COUNT(CASE WHEN o.status = 'completed' THEN 1 END) AS
completed_orders,
        SUM(CASE WHEN o.status = 'completed' THEN o.amount ELSE 0
END) AS total_revenue,
        AVG(CASE WHEN o.status = 'completed' THEN o.amount END) AS
avg_order_value,
        COUNT(DISTINCT o.customer_id) AS unique_customers
    FROM orders o
    GROUP BY o.product_id
),

product_returns AS (
    SELECT
        o.product_id,
        COUNT(*) AS total_returns
    FROM returns r
    INNER JOIN orders o ON r.order_id = o.order_id
    GROUP BY o.product_id
),

final AS (
    SELECT
        p.product_id,
        p.product_name,
        p.category,
        p.price,
        p.is_active,
        COALESCE(po.total_orders, 0) AS total_orders,
        COALESCE(po.completed_orders, 0) AS completed_orders,
        COALESCE(po.total_revenue, 0) AS total_revenue,
        COALESCE(po.avg_order_value, 0) AS avg_order_value,
        COALESCE(po.unique_customers, 0) AS unique_customers,
        COALESCE(pr.total_returns, 0) AS total_returns,
        CASE
            WHEN po.completed_orders > 0
            THEN ROUND(COALESCE(pr.total_returns, 0) / po.completed
_orders * 100, 2)
            ELSE 0
        END AS return_rate_pct
    FROM products p
```

```
    LEFT JOIN product_orders po ON p.product_id = po.product_id
    LEFT JOIN product_returns pr ON p.product_id = pr.product_id
)

SELECT * FROM final
```

The preceding model demonstrates the power of the intermediate layer to:

- Join three staging models (namely, orders, products, returns),
- Calculate complex metrics (such as return rate percentage),
- Use **`COALESCE`** to handle products with no orders, and
- Produce a comprehensive product performance dataset.

Creating Reusable Macros

Macros are reusable functions written in Jinja, that is, a templating language that dbt uses to add dynamic logic (for instance, if statements, loops, and variables) to otherwise static SQL files. They enable code reuse across models.

Create `macros/customer_segmentation.sql`:

```
{% macro customer_segment(days_since_last_order) %}
    CASE
        WHEN {{ days_since_last_order }} IS NULL THEN 'Never Ordered'
        WHEN {{ days_since_last_order }} <= 30 THEN 'Active'
        WHEN {{ days_since_last_order }} <= 90 THEN 'At Risk'
        ELSE 'Churned'
    END
{% endmacro %}
```

The preceding macro encapsulates customer segmentation logic. Any model can now call **`{{ customer_segment('days_since_last_order') }}`** instead of duplicating the "**`CASE`**" statement.

Running Intermediate Models

Build the intermediate layer in the following way:

```
# Build intermediate models
dbt run --select intermediate
```

dbt automatically builds **`int_customer_order_metrics`** and **`int_product_performance`** after the staging models complete, as it parses the **`{{ ref() }}`** functions to understand dependencies.

Creating the Mart Layer

Mart models are the final destination of your data transformation pipeline. These tables serve analysts, BI tools, and Machine Learning (ML) models. They prioritize query performance, comprehensive documentation, and intuitive structure.

Building the Customer 360 Mart

The Customer 360 mart combines customer profile data with behavioral metrics and lifecycle segmentation. This denormalized table makes it easy for analysts to answer questions such as "Show me all high-value customers in the UK who have not ordered in 60 days."

Create `models/marts/mart_customer_360.sql`:

```
{{ config(
    materialized='table',
    cluster_by=['country', 'customer_segment']
) }}

WITH customers AS (
    SELECT * FROM {{ ref('stg_customers') }}
),

metrics AS (
    SELECT * FROM {{ ref('int_customer_order_metrics') }}
),

final AS (
    SELECT
        c.customer_id,
        c.customer_name,
        c.email,
        c.country,
        c.signup_date,
        COALESCE(m.total_orders, 0) AS total_orders,
        COALESCE(m.completed_orders, 0) AS completed_orders,
        COALESCE(m.cancelled_orders, 0) AS cancelled_orders,
        COALESCE(m.pending_orders, 0) AS pending_orders,
        COALESCE(m.total_revenue, 0) AS lifetime_value,
        COALESCE(m.avg_order_value, 0) AS avg_order_value,
        m.first_order_date,
        m.last_order_date,
        COALESCE(m.customer_lifetime_days, 0) AS customer_lifetime_days,
        m.days_since_last_order,
```

```
        {{ customer_segment('m.days_since_last_order') }} AS customer
_segment,
        DATE_DIFF(CURRENT_DATE(), c.signup_date, DAY) AS days_since_
signup,
        CURRENT_TIMESTAMP() AS updated_at
    FROM customers c
    LEFT JOIN metrics m ON c.customer_id = m.customer_id
)

SELECT * FROM final
```

Key design decisions in this mart include:

- **Materialized as Table**: Marts are queried frequently, so we pay the storage cost for faster query performance.
- **Clustered by Country and Segment**: Analysts typically filter by these dimensions, so clustering co-locates related rows on disk.
- **Uses the Macro**: The **`{{ customer_segment() }}`** macro ensures consistent segmentation logic across all models.
- **Handles Nulls Gracefully**: `COALESCE` ensures that customers with no orders still appear with zero values.
- **Includes Audit Timestamp**: The **`updated_at`** field tracks when the mart was last refreshed.

Building the Orders Fact Table

Fact tables record business events. They are typically narrow (for instance, many rows but few columns) and immutable, as events do not change once recorded. Our orders fact table will use incremental materialization to efficiently handle growing data volumes.

Create **`models/marts/fct_orders.sql`**:

```
{{ config(
    materialized='incremental',
    unique_key='order_id',
    partition_by={
        "field": "order_date",
        "data_type": "date",
        "granularity": "day"
    },
    cluster_by=['status', 'customer_id']
) }}

WITH orders AS (
    SELECT * FROM {{ ref('stg_orders') }}
```

```
),

customers AS (
    SELECT
        customer_id,
        country,
        signup_date
    FROM {{ ref('stg_customers') }}
),

products AS (
    SELECT
        product_id,
        product_name,
        category,
        price AS product_price
    FROM {{ ref('stg_products') }}
),

returns AS (
    SELECT
        return_id,
        order_id,
        return_date,
        return_reason
    FROM {{ ref('stg_returns') }}
),

final AS (
    SELECT
        o.order_id,
        o.customer_id,
        c.country AS customer_country,
        o.product_id,
        p.product_name,
        p.category AS product_category,
        o.order_date,
        o.status,
        o.amount,
        p.product_price,
        r.return_date,
        r.return_reason,
        CASE WHEN r.return_id IS NOT NULL THEN TRUE ELSE FALSE END AS
is_returned,
        DATE_DIFF(o.order_date, c.signup_date, DAY) AS days_since_
signup_at_order,
        o.loaded_at
```

```
    FROM orders o
    INNER JOIN customers c ON o.customer_id = c.customer_id
    INNER JOIN products p ON o.product_id = p.product_id
    LEFT JOIN returns r ON o.order_id = r.order_id

    {% if is_incremental() %}
        -- Only process new or updated orders
        WHERE o.loaded_at > (SELECT MAX(loaded_at) FROM {{ this }})
    {% endif %}
)

SELECT * FROM final
```

The incremental configuration is the most important aspect of this model, including:

- **`materialized='incremental'`**: On the first run, dbt builds the full table. On subsequent runs, it only processes new records.
- **`unique_key='order_id'`**: If an order is updated (for example, status changes from pending to completed), dbt replaces the old row.
- **`partition_by order_date`**: BigQuery physically separates data by date, dramatically reducing bytes scanned for date-filtered queries.
- **`cluster_by status and customer_id`**: Further optimizes queries that filter on these columns.
- **`{% if is_incremental() %}`**: This Jinja block only executes on incremental runs, filtering to new records based on **`loaded_at`**.

Building the Products Dimension Table

Dimension tables provide descriptive context about the business entities. They are typically wide with few rows and many columns, and slowly changing as attributes update over time.

Create **`models/marts/dim_products.sql`**:

```
{{ config(
    materialized='table',
    cluster_by=['category', 'is_active']
) }}

SELECT
    product_id,
    product_name,
    category,
    price,
    is_active,
```

```
        total_orders,
        completed_orders,
        total_revenue,
        avg_order_value,
        unique_customers,
        total_returns,
        return_rate_pct,
        CASE
            WHEN total_revenue >= 10000 THEN 'High Performer'
            WHEN total_revenue >= 5000 THEN 'Medium Performer'
            WHEN total_revenue > 0 THEN 'Low Performer'
            ELSE 'No Sales'
        END AS performance_tier,
        CURRENT_TIMESTAMP() AS updated_at
    FROM {{ ref('int_product_performance') }}
```

The preceding dimension table enriches the product catalog data with performance metrics, making it straightforward for analysts to identify top-performing products or categories with high return rates.

Running the Complete Pipeline

With all three layers built now, run the entire pipeline:

```
# Run all models in dependency order
dbt run

# Run all tests
dbt test
```

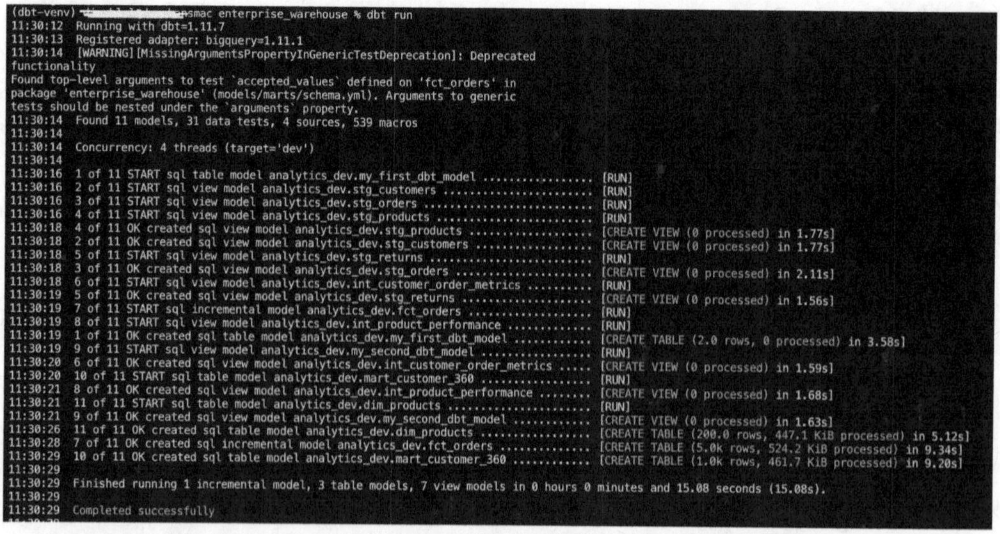

Figure 14.6: *Terminal Showing Successful `dbt run` with All 9 Models Built: 4 Staging Views, 2 Intermediate Views, 2 Mart Tables, and 1 Incremental Fact Table*

Once the entire warehouse is successfully built, running the full test suite acts as our final quality gate. It verifies that all intermediate transformations maintain referential integrity and that our custom testing logic did not spot any anomalies.

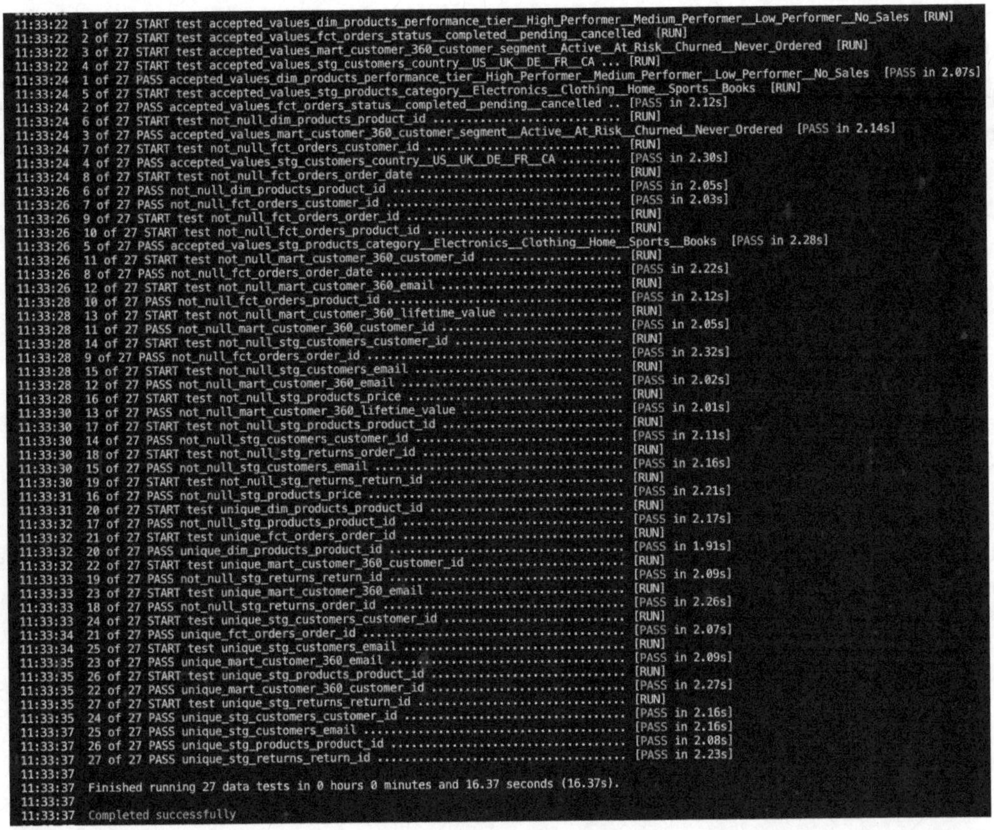

```
11:33:22  1 of 27 START test accepted_values_dim_products_performance_tier__High_Performer__Medium_Performer__Low_Performer__No_Sales  [RUN]
11:33:22  2 of 27 START test accepted_values_fct_orders_status__completed__pending__cancelled  [RUN]
11:33:22  3 of 27 START test accepted_values_mart_customer_360_customer_segment__Active__At_Risk__Churned__Never_Ordered  [RUN]
11:33:22  4 of 27 START test accepted_values_stg_customers_country__US__UK__DE__FR__CA ... [RUN]
11:33:24  1 of 27 PASS accepted_values_dim_products_performance_tier__High_Performer__Medium_Performer__Low_Performer__No_Sales  [PASS in 2.07s]
11:33:24  5 of 27 START test accepted_values_stg_products_category__Electronics__Clothing__Home__Sports__Books  [RUN]
11:33:24  2 of 27 PASS accepted_values_fct_orders_status__completed__pending__cancelled .. [PASS in 2.12s]
11:33:24  6 of 27 START test not_null_dim_products_product_id ........................... [RUN]
11:33:24  3 of 27 PASS accepted_values_mart_customer_360_customer_segment__Active__At_Risk__Churned__Never_Ordered  [PASS in 2.14s]
11:33:24  7 of 27 START test not_null_fct_orders_customer_id ............................ [RUN]
11:33:24  4 of 27 PASS accepted_values_stg_customers_country__US__UK__DE__FR__CA ......... [PASS in 2.30s]
11:33:24  8 of 27 START test not_null_fct_orders_order_date ............................. [RUN]
11:33:26  6 of 27 PASS not_null_dim_products_product_id ................................. [PASS in 2.05s]
11:33:26  7 of 27 PASS not_null_fct_orders_customer_id .................................. [PASS in 2.03s]
11:33:26  9 of 27 START test not_null_fct_orders_order_id ............................... [RUN]
11:33:26  10 of 27 START test not_null_fct_orders_product_id ............................ [RUN]
11:33:26  5 of 27 PASS accepted_values_stg_products_category__Electronics__Clothing__Home__Sports__Books  [PASS in 2.28s]
11:33:26  11 of 27 START test not_null_mart_customer_360_customer_id .................... [RUN]
11:33:26  8 of 27 PASS not_null_fct_orders_order_date ................................... [PASS in 2.22s]
11:33:26  12 of 27 START test not_null_mart_customer_360_email .......................... [RUN]
11:33:28  10 of 27 PASS not_null_fct_orders_product_id .................................. [PASS in 2.12s]
11:33:28  13 of 27 START test not_null_mart_customer_360_lifetime_value ................. [RUN]
11:33:28  11 of 27 PASS not_null_mart_customer_360_customer_id .......................... [PASS in 2.05s]
11:33:28  14 of 27 START test not_null_stg_customers_customer_id ........................ [RUN]
11:33:28  9 of 27 PASS not_null_fct_orders_order_id ..................................... [PASS in 2.32s]
11:33:28  15 of 27 START test not_null_stg_customers_email .............................. [RUN]
11:33:28  12 of 27 PASS not_null_mart_customer_360_email ................................ [PASS in 2.02s]
11:33:28  16 of 27 START test not_null_stg_products_price ............................... [RUN]
11:33:30  13 of 27 PASS not_null_mart_customer_360_lifetime_value ....................... [PASS in 2.01s]
11:33:30  17 of 27 START test not_null_stg_products_product_id .......................... [RUN]
11:33:30  14 of 27 PASS not_null_stg_customers_customer_id .............................. [PASS in 2.11s]
11:33:30  18 of 27 START test not_null_stg_returns_order_id ............................. [RUN]
11:33:30  15 of 27 PASS not_null_stg_customers_email .................................... [PASS in 2.16s]
11:33:30  19 of 27 START test not_null_stg_returns_return_id ............................ [RUN]
11:33:31  16 of 27 PASS not_null_stg_products_price ..................................... [PASS in 2.21s]
11:33:31  20 of 27 START test unique_dim_products_product_id ............................ [RUN]
11:33:32  17 of 27 PASS not_null_stg_products_product_id ................................ [PASS in 2.17s]
11:33:32  21 of 27 START test unique_fct_orders_order_id ................................ [RUN]
11:33:32  20 of 27 PASS unique_dim_products_product_id .................................. [PASS in 1.91s]
11:33:32  22 of 27 START test unique_mart_customer_360_customer_id ...................... [RUN]
11:33:33  19 of 27 PASS not_null_stg_returns_return_id .................................. [PASS in 2.09s]
11:33:33  23 of 27 START test unique_mart_customer_360_email ............................ [RUN]
11:33:33  18 of 27 PASS not_null_stg_returns_order_id ................................... [PASS in 2.26s]
11:33:33  24 of 27 START test unique_stg_customers_customer_id .......................... [RUN]
11:33:34  21 of 27 PASS unique_fct_orders_order_id ...................................... [PASS in 2.07s]
11:33:34  25 of 27 START test unique_stg_customers_email ................................ [RUN]
11:33:35  23 of 27 PASS unique_mart_customer_360_email .................................. [PASS in 2.09s]
11:33:35  26 of 27 START test unique_stg_products_product_id ............................ [RUN]
11:33:35  22 of 27 PASS unique_mart_customer_360_customer_id ............................ [PASS in 2.27s]
11:33:35  27 of 27 START test unique_stg_returns_return_id .............................. [RUN]
11:33:35  24 of 27 PASS unique_stg_customers_customer_id ................................ [PASS in 2.16s]
11:33:37  25 of 27 PASS unique_stg_customers_email ...................................... [PASS in 2.16s]
11:33:37  26 of 27 PASS unique_stg_products_product_id .................................. [PASS in 2.08s]
11:33:37  27 of 27 PASS unique_stg_returns_return_id .................................... [PASS in 2.23s]
11:33:37
11:33:37  Finished running 27 data tests in 0 hours 0 minutes and 16.37 seconds (16.37s).
11:33:37
11:33:37  Completed successfully
```

Figure 14.7: *Terminal Showing All Tests Passing across Staging, Intermediate, and Mart Layers*

When you run `dbt run`, dbt constructs a Directed Acyclic Graph (DAG) of dependencies and executes models in the following topological order:

1. Staging models (no dependencies)
2. Intermediate models (depend on staging)
3. Mart models (depend on staging and intermediate)

Enforcing Data Quality

Testing is essential in production data warehouses. Without automated tests, bad data silently propagates through pipelines, inflating revenue dashboards, breaking ML models, and eroding trust in analytics.

Generic Tests

Generic tests are reusable assertions that dbt provides out of the box. We have already seen examples in our staging layer **`schema.yml`**: **`unique`**, **`not_null`**, **`accepted_values`**, and **`relationships`**.

However, dbt also supports custom generic tests. Create **`macros/test_revenue_positive.sql`**:

```
{% test revenue_positive(model, column_name) %}

SELECT
    {{ column_name }},
    COUNT(*) AS invalid_count
FROM {{ model }}
WHERE {{ column_name }} < 0
GROUP BY {{ column_name }}
HAVING COUNT(*) > 0

{% endtest %}
```

The preceding custom test fails if any revenue value is negative. Apply it in `models/marts/schema.yml`:

```
models:
  - name: mart_customer_360
    columns:
      - name: lifetime_value
        tests:
          - revenue_positive
```

Singular Tests

Singular tests are one-off SQL queries that return failing records. If the query returns any rows, the test fails. Create **`tests/assert_return_date_after_order.sql`**:

```
-- Returns should always occur after the order date
SELECT
    f.order_id,
    f.order_date,
    f.return_date
FROM {{ ref('fct_orders') }} f
WHERE f.is_returned = TRUE
  AND f.return_date < f.order_date
```

The preceding test catches a critical business rule violation: a return that cannot be dated before the original order.

Comprehensive Mart Documentation

Add detailed descriptions to **models/marts/schema.yml**:

```
version: 2

models:
  - name: mart_customer_360
    description: |
      Complete customer analytics mart combining profile data,
      order metrics, and lifecycle segmentation. Primary table
      for customer analysis and segmentation workflows.

      Refresh: Daily at 6 AM UTC
      Materialization: Table with clustering on country and segment

    columns:
      - name: customer_id
        description: Unique customer identifier (UUID)
        tests:
          - unique
          - not_null

      - name: customer_segment
        description: |
          Customer lifecycle segment based on recency:
          - Active: Ordered in last 30 days
          - At Risk: Last order 30-90 days ago
          - Churned: No orders in 90+ days
          - Never Ordered: Signed up but never purchased
        tests:
          - accepted_values:
              values: ['Active', 'At Risk', 'Churned', 'Never Ordered']

      - name: lifetime_value
        description: Total revenue from all completed orders
(excludes cancelled/pending)
        tests:
          - not_null
          - revenue_positive

  - name: fct_orders
    description: |
      Incremental fact table of all orders with enriched customer
      and product context. Partitioned by order_date for optimal
      query performance on date-filtered analytics.
```

```
        Refresh: Incremental (processes only new orders)
        Materialization: Incremental table, partitioned daily

      columns:
        - name: order_id
          description: Unique order identifier
          tests:
            - unique
            - not_null
        - name: status
          tests:
            - accepted_values:
                values: ['completed', 'pending', 'cancelled']

  - name: dim_products
    description: |
      Product dimension table with performance metrics and
      categorization. Combines catalog data with aggregated
      sales performance for product analysis.

    columns:
      - name: product_id
        tests:
          - unique
          - not_null
      - name: performance_tier
        tests:
          - accepted_values:
              values: ['High Performer', 'Medium Performer', 'Low
Performer', 'No Sales']
```

Run the complete test suite in the following way:

```
# Run all tests
dbt test

# Run only singular tests
dbt test --select test_type:singular

# Run only schema tests
dbt test --select test_type:schema
```

All tests should pass, giving you the confidence that your data quality is intact.

Generating Documentation

Documentation in traditional data warehouses quickly becomes outdated. A wiki page, written six months ago, describing a table's schema rarely gets updated when columns change. dbt solves this by keeping documentation as code, right alongside SQL models.

Configuring Documentation Persistence

By default, dbt documentation lives only on the **dbt** Docs website. However, with **persist_docs**, **dbt** pushes your descriptions directly into BigQuery's metadata, making them visible to anyone querying the tables.

Update **dbt_project.yml**:

```
name: 'enterprise_warehouse'
version: '1.0.0'
config-version: 2

profile: 'enterprise_warehouse'

model-paths: ["models"]
analysis-paths: ["analyses"]
test-paths: ["tests"]
seed-paths: ["seeds"]
macro-paths: ["macros"]
snapshot-paths: ["snapshots"]

target-path: "target"
clean-targets:
  - "target"
  - "dbt_packages"

models:
  enterprise_warehouse:
    +persist_docs:
      relation: true    # Table-level descriptions
      columns: true     # Column-level descriptions

    staging:
      +materialized: view
      +schema: staging

    intermediate:
      +materialized: view
      +schema: intermediate

    marts:
      +materialized: table
      +schema: marts
```

After running **dbt run**, your descriptions from **schema.yml** will appear in BigQuery Console. When an analyst opens **mart_customer_360** and clicks the **Schema** tab, they will see your column descriptions without needing to check **dbt** Docs.

Generating the Documentation Site

Execute the following commands to generate and serve the documentation:

```
# Generate documentation
dbt docs generate

# Serve documentation locally
dbt docs serve
```

This opens **http://localhost:8080** with an interactive documentation site featuring:

- Searchable data dictionary of every model, column, test, and macro,
- Column-level descriptions with data types,
- Test coverage indicators,
- Source freshness checks, and
- Macro documentation.

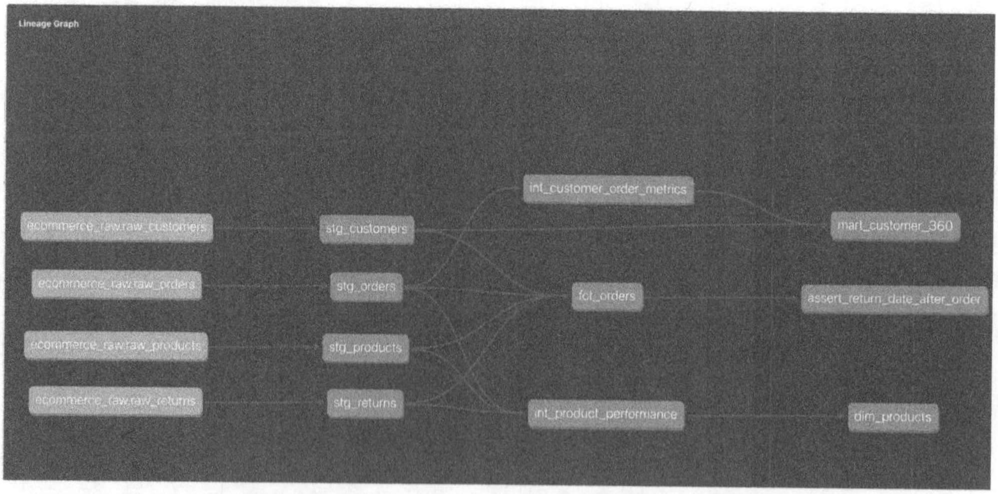

Figure 14.8: *dbt Docs Interface Showing the Lineage DAG with All Models Connected from Sources through Staging, Intermediate, and Marts*

Exploring the Lineage Graph

The most powerful feature of dbt Docs is the interactive lineage graph. Click the blue

`View Lineage Graph` button in the bottom right corner. The graph will show the following:

- All source tables (green nodes)
- All staging models (blue nodes)
- All intermediate models (purple nodes)
- All mart models (orange nodes)
- Dependencies flowing left to right

Click on any node to see:

- The compiled SQL that BigQuery actually executes,
- Column descriptions and data types,
- Tests applied to the model,
- Upstream dependencies (what this model reads from), and
- Downstream dependencies (what reads from this model).

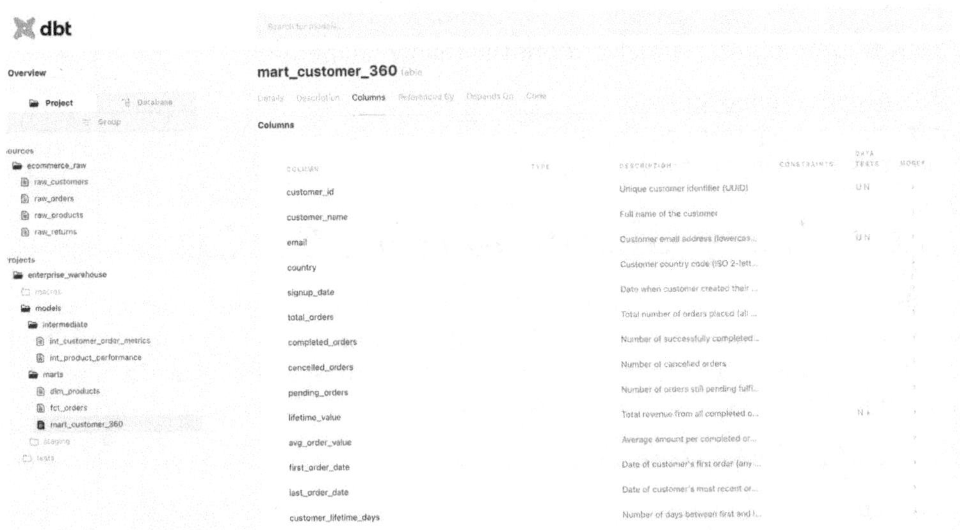

Figure 14.9: *dbt Docs Showing mart_customer_360 with Comprehensive Column Descriptions, Test Coverage, and Dependency Information*

For our e-commerce pipeline, the DAG shows 4 raw sources → 4 staging models → 2 intermediate models → 3 mart models.

This visual representation makes it easy to trace the lineage of any metric. If an analyst asks "Where does the "**`lifetime_value`**" field in `mart_customer_360` come from?", you can click through the graph to see that it originates from the "**`amount`**" field in **`raw_orders`**, flows through **`stg_orders`**, gets aggregated in **`int_customer_order_metrics`**, and finally lands in the mart.

Deploying with CI/CD

Transforming data on your laptop is just the beginning. Production data warehouses require automated deployment, environment separation, and continuous integration to prevent broken code from reaching analysts.

Setting up Environment Separation

In a proper dbt workflow, development and production environments are strictly separated. Analysts work in isolated sandbox datasets where they can experiment freely, without affecting live dashboards.

Your `profiles.yml` already defines the following two targets:

- **`dev`**: Uses OAuth authentication, writes to **`analytics_dev`**, and runs on your laptop.
- **`prod`**: Uses service account authentication, writes to **`analytics_prod`**, and runs in CI/CD.

To deploy to production manually, adopt the following method:

```
# Deploy to production
dbt run --target prod
dbt test --target prod
```

Implementing GitHub Actions CI/CD

Automated deployment ensures that every code change is tested before reaching production. When an analyst opens a Pull Request (PR), a CI bot automatically builds the proposed changes in an isolated environment and runs all the tests. If any test fails, the PR cannot be merged.

Create **`.github/workflows/dbt_ci.yml`**:

```
name: dbt CI/CD

on:
  pull_request:
    branches: [main]
  push:
    branches: [main]

env:
  DBT_PROFILES_DIR: ./

jobs:
```

```
  dbt-ci:
    name: dbt Build and Test
    runs-on: ubuntu-latest

    steps:
      - name: Checkout code
        uses: actions/checkout@v3

      - name: Set up Python
        uses: actions/setup-python@v4
        with:
          python-version: '3.11'

      - name: Install dbt
        run: |
          pip install --upgrade pip
          pip install dbt-bigquery

      - name: Create profiles.yml
        run: |
          mkdir -p ~/.dbt
          echo "${{ secrets.DBT_PROFILES_YML }}" > ~/.dbt/profiles.yml

      - name: Create service account key
        run: |
          echo "${{ secrets.GCP_SERVICE_ACCOUNT_KEY }}" > ./service-
account.json

      - name: dbt Debug
        run: dbt debug --target prod

      - name: dbt Deps
        run: dbt deps

      - name: dbt Build (Run + Test)
        run: dbt build --target prod

      - name: dbt Docs Generate
        if: github.event_name == 'push' && github.ref == 'refs/heads/
main'
        run: dbt docs generate --target prod
```

The preceding workflow goes through the following steps:

1. Triggers on every PR and push to main.
2. Installs **`dbt-BigQuery`** in a fresh Ubuntu environment.

3. Authenticates using a service account stored in GitHub Secrets.
4. Runs **dbt build**, executing both **dbt run** and **dbt test**.
5. Generates documentation on successful main branch deployments.

Configuring GitHub Secrets

In your GitHub repository, navigate to **Settings → Secrets and variables → Actions** and add:

GCP_SERVICE_ACCOUNT_KEY: The JSON key for a service account with BigQuery permissions:

```
# Create service account
gcloud iam service-accounts create dbt-ci-cd \
  --display-name="dbt CI/CD Service Account"

# Grant BigQuery permissions
gcloud projects add-iam-policy-binding $PROJECT_ID \
  --member="serviceAccount:dbt-ci-cd@${PROJECT_ID}.iam.gservice
account.com" \
  --role="roles/bigquery.dataEditor"

gcloud projects add-iam-policy-binding $PROJECT_ID \
  --member="serviceAccount:dbt-ci-cd@${PROJECT_ID}.iam.gservice
account.com" \
  --role="roles/bigquery.jobUser"

# Create and download key
gcloud iam service-accounts keys create service-account-key.json \
  --iam-account=dbt-ci-cd@${PROJECT_ID}.iam.gserviceaccount.com
```

DBT_PROFILES_YML: The production profile configuration:

```
enterprise_warehouse:
  target: prod
  outputs:
    prod:
      type: bigquery
      method: service-account
      project: your-project-id
      dataset: analytics_prod
      threads: 8
      location: US
      keyfile: ./service-account.json
```

Testing the CI/CD Pipeline

Create a new branch, make a change, and push:

```
# Create feature branch
git checkout -b feature/add-customer-cohorts

# Make changes to models or tests
# ... edit files ...

# Commit and push
git add .
git commit -m "Add customer cohort analysis"
git push origin feature/add-customer-cohorts
```

Open a PR on GitHub. The CI/CD pipeline runs automatically, building your models in an isolated environment and running all tests. If any test fails, the PR is blocked from merging. If all tests pass, the PR can be safely merged, triggering an automatic deployment to production.

Once merged, your final tables are securely built inside your production dataset, entirely untouched by manual human queries or local development experiments.

This workflow prevents the broken code from reaching production and gives teams the confidence to iterate quickly.

Operational Best Practices

Running a production data warehouse requires more than just writing SQL. Here are the practical lessons from teams operating dbt pipelines at scale.

Schema Evolution is Inevitable

Unlike application databases where schema changes are carefully planned migrations, data warehouses constantly evolve. New columns appear in source systems, business definitions change, and analysts request new metrics.

When adding a new column to a staging model:

1. Add the column as `NULLABLE` first,
2. Deploy to production,
3. Backfill historical data if needed, and
4. Only then make it `NOT NULL` if required.

Never remove columns without checking downstream dependencies. Use **`dbt ls --select +model_name`** to see all models that depend on a given model.

Incremental Models Require Care

Incremental models are powerful, but they introduce complexity. Common pitfalls include:

Forgetting to Handle Late-Arriving Data: If your source system can update historical records, your incremental logic must account for this. Consider using a lookback window in the following way:

```
{% if is_incremental() %}
    WHERE o.loaded_at > (SELECT MAX(loaded_at) - INTERVAL 3 DAY FROM
{{ this }})
{% endif %}
```

Not Testing Incremental Logic: Always test your incremental model by running it twice:

```
# First run (full refresh)
dbt run --select fct_orders --full-refresh

# Second run (incremental)
dbt run --select fct_orders

# Verify row counts match expectations
```

Monitor dbt Run Times

As your warehouse grows, model run times increase. Use **`dbt run --profile`** to identify slow models. Some common optimizations are as follows:

- Materialize frequently-queried intermediate models as tables instead of views.
- Add partitioning and clustering to large tables.
- Use incremental models for fact tables over 10 million rows.
- Break complex models into smaller, reusable pieces.

To quantify the impact: a **`fct_orders`** table with 50 million rows and daily partitioning might scan 2 TB on a full refresh, costing approximately $12.50 per run in on-demand pricing. With incremental loading processing only today's 100,000 new rows, the same model scans roughly 40 GB—reducing cost to under $0.25 per run. Over a month of daily runs, that is the difference between $375 and $7.50.

Document Everything

Future you (and your teammates) will appreciate comprehensive documentation. Every model should have:

- A description explaining what it contains and why it exists,
- Column descriptions for non-obvious fields,
- Notes about refresh schedule and materialization strategy, and
- Links to relevant business logic documentation.

Version Control Best Practices

Keep your dbt project organized in the following ways:

1. Use feature branches for all changes; never commit directly to main.
2. Write descriptive commit messages that explain WHY, and not just WHAT.
3. Tag releases with semantic versioning (such as v1.0.0, v1.1.0, and v1.2.0).
4. Keep your **`.gitignore`** updated to exclude **`target/`**, **`dbt_packages/`**, and service account keys.
5. Review the diff before committing to catch accidental changes.
6. Use PR templates to standardize code reviews.

Example `.gitignore` for dbt projects:

```
target/
dbt_packages/
logs/
*.json
*.log
.env
.DS_Store
```

Cleanup

Important: *BigQuery datasets incur storage costs even when idle. Clean up lab resources when finished to avoid the ongoing charges.*

```
# Delete the development dataset
bq rm -r -f -d ${PROJECT_ID}:analytics_dev

# Delete the production dataset
bq rm -r -f -d ${PROJECT_ID}:analytics_prod
```

```
# Delete the raw data dataset
bq rm -r -f -d ${PROJECT_ID}:ecommerce_raw

# Deactivate the Python virtual environment
Deactivate
```

Conclusion

You have just built a production-grade data warehouse. Over the course of this chapter, you have created 4 staging models cleaning 1,000 customers, 200 products, 5,000 orders, and 400 returns; 2 intermediate models calculating customer lifetime value and product performance metrics; and 3 mart models including a Customer 360 table, an incremental fact table with partitioning, and a product dimension. You implemented 24+ data quality tests to catch issues before they reach dashboards, set up a complete CI/CD pipeline deploying changes automatically through GitHub Actions, generated interactive documentation with full lineage graphs persisted to BigQuery metadata, and established production-ready infrastructure with dev/prod environment separation.

This chapter also built a complete enterprise data warehouse from raw data to analytics-ready tables. We started with the three-layer architecture that separates concerns: staging for cleaning, intermediate for business logic, and marts for analytics. We loaded sample e-commerce data into BigQuery and initialized a dbt project with proper environment separation.

We built 4 staging models that cleaned and standardized raw data, enforcing data quality with generic tests for uniqueness, nullability, and referential integrity. We constructed 2 intermediate models that encoded complex business logic such as: customer order metrics and product performance analytics. We created 3 mart models optimized for end-user consumption: A Customer 360 table with lifecycle segmentation, an incremental orders fact table partitioned by date, and a products dimension table enriched with performance metrics.

We enforced data quality with custom test macros and singular tests that catch business rule violations. We generated comprehensive documentation with lineage graphs and persisted descriptions into BigQuery metadata. We deployed the entire pipeline through automated CI/CD workflows that test every change before it even reaches production.

The patterns explored here–layered transformations, incremental loading, automated testing, and continuous deployment–come from teams running data warehouses at scale. These are not theoretical best practices; rather, they are practical solutions to real problems that emerge when data volumes grow, teams expand, and stakeholders depend on accurate analytics.

In the next chapter, we will look at where BigQuery and the broader data ecosystem are heading, exploring emerging trends such as real-time analytics, AI-driven systems, Data Mesh architectures, and the skills that will matter as the field continues to evolve.

Points to Remember

- Organize your warehouse into three distinct layers: staging for cleaning, intermediate for business logic, and marts for BI tools. Models should never skip layers.
- **BigQuery does not enforce primary or foreign keys** - use tests (unique, not_null, relationships) to catch bad data before it corrupts your dashboards.
- Use **`is_incremental()`** configurations to only process new or updated records on subsequent runs. This significantly reduces BigQuery compute costs for large tables.
- Partition and cluster your mart tables based on how analysts query them. Partitioning splits data by date, while clustering co-locates related rows on disk.
- Separate local development (**`analytics_dev`**) from production (**`analytics_prod`**) and use CI/CD pipelines (like GitHub Actions) to test all changes before they are deployed.
- Turn on **`persist_docs`** in your configuration to automatically push your model and column descriptions from your dbt code into BigQuery Console metadata.

Multiple Choice Questions

1. What is the primary purpose of the staging layer in a dbt project?
    a. To perform complex joins and aggregations
    b. To clean and standardize raw data with 1:1 source mappings
    c. To create denormalized tables for BI tools
    d. To enforce business rules and calculate KPIs
2. Which dbt function should you use to reference another model in your SQL?
    a. `{{ source() }}`
    b. `{{ ref() }}`

   c. `{{ model() }}`
   d. `{{ include() }}`

3. What happens when you run `dbt test` on a model with a "`unique`" test that fails?
   a. dbt automatically fixes the duplicate records
   b. dbt skips the model and continues with other models
   c. dbt returns the duplicate values and fails the test
   d. dbt deletes the duplicate records from BigQuery
4. In an incremental dbt model, what does the `unique_key` configuration do?
   a. Creates a primary key constraint in BigQuery
   b. Tells dbt which column to use for deduplication when merging new data
   c. Automatically generates unique IDs for new records
   d. Prevents duplicate records from being inserted
5. Why should intermediate models typically be materialized as views rather than tables?
   a. Views use less storage and are only materialized when queried
   b. Views are faster to query than tables
   c. Views automatically update when source data changes
   d. Views support partitioning and clustering
6. What is the purpose of the **`{{ config(persist_docs=true) }}`** setting in **`dbt_project.yml`**?
   a. To generate the dbt docs website
   b. To push table and column descriptions into BigQuery metadata
   c. To create PDF documentation
   d. To back up documentation to Cloud Storage
7. In a production dbt deployment, what is the recommended way to stop a broken model from reaching analysts?
   a. Delete the model file immediately
   b. Manually review every SQL query before deployment

c. Disable automated deployments entirely

d. Use CI/CD to test all changes before merging to main

8. What does the "`relationships`" test verify in dbt?

a. That two tables have the same number of rows

b. That a foreign key value exists in the referenced parent table

c. That two columns have the same data type

d. That a table has a primary key defined

9. When should you use an incremental materialization instead of a table materialization?

a. For small dimension tables with frequent updates

b. For staging models that clean raw data

c. For large fact tables where you only need to process new records

d. For intermediate models with complex joins

10. What is the primary benefit of partitioning a BigQuery table by date in a dbt model?

a. It reduces bytes scanned and cost for date-filtered queries.

b. It automatically deletes old data.

c. It improves write performance for inserts.

d. It enables real-time streaming inserts.

Answers

1. b
2. b
3. c
4. b
5. a
6. b
7. d
8. b
9. c
10. a

Questions

1. Explain the difference between the staging, intermediate, and mart layers in a dbt project. Why is this Separation of Concerns (SoC) important for maintainability?
2. Describe how incremental models work in dbt. What are the key configuration parameters, and what happens on the first run versus subsequent runs?
3. Why does BigQuery not enforce primary keys or foreign keys natively, and how does dbt's testing framework compensate for this limitation?
4. Explain the purpose of the `{{ ref() }}` function in dbt. How does it enable environment-aware deployments and automatic dependency resolution?
5. Describe the CI/CD workflow for a dbt project. What happens when an analyst opens a pull request, and how does this prevent broken code from reaching production?

Key Terms

- **Extract, Load, Transform (ELT):** A data integration pattern where raw data is loaded directly into the warehouse, and transformations are executed using the warehouse's compute power.
- **Staging Layer:** The first transformation layer in a dbt project that performs 1:1 cleaning and standardization of raw source tables.
- **Intermediate Layer:** The middle transformation layer that encodes complex business logic, joins, and reusable transformations.
- **Mart Layer:** The final transformation layer that produces analytics-ready tables optimized for end-user consumption and BI tools.
- **Incremental Materialization:** A dbt materialization strategy that only processes new or updated records on subsequent runs, optimizing performance for large tables.
- **Generic Test:** A reusable dbt test (unique, not_null, accepted_values, relationships) that can be applied to any model or column.
- **Singular Test:** A one-off SQL query in the `tests/` directory that returns failing records if the test fails.
- **Lineage Graph:** A visual representation of data dependencies showing how models connect from sources through transformations to final marts.
- **Persist Docs:** A dbt configuration that pushes table and column descriptions from schema.yml into BigQuery metadata.

- **Continuous Integration/Continuous Deployment (CI/CD):** An automated workflow that tests and deploys code changes, preventing broken models from reaching production.
- **Partitioning:** A BigQuery optimization that physically separates table data by a column (typically date), reducing bytes scanned for filtered queries.
- **Clustering:** A BigQuery optimization that co-locates rows with similar values in the same storage blocks, improving query performance for filtered columns.

CHAPTER 15

The Future of BigQuery and Emerging Trends

Introduction

Throughout this book, we have built a comprehensive foundation in BigQuery and modern data engineering. We started with the fundamentals of data warehousing, explored BigQuery's architecture and storage engine, mastered ingestion patterns and transformation workflows, orchestrated complex pipelines, implemented real-time streaming, and deployed production-grade Extract, Load, Transform (ELT) systems. Each chapter equipped you with the practical skills that work today.

However, data engineering does not stand still. The field evolves rapidly, driven by changing business needs, technological breakthroughs, and shifting architectural patterns. What worked five years ago—nightly batch jobs, manual schema management, siloed data teams—no longer scales for organizations that need real-time insights, AI-driven automation, and decentralized data ownership.

This final chapter looks ahead. We will explore where BigQuery and the broader Google Cloud data ecosystem are heading, examine emerging patterns reshaping how data platforms are built, and identify the skills that will matter most in the coming years. The goal is not to predict the future with certainty, but rather to help you recognize the trends gaining momentum, so that you can invest your learning time wisely.

This chapter explores four key areas to reshape the data engineering landscape: real-time data platforms, intelligent and decentralized architectures, automation-first workflows, and the evolving role of data engineers. BigQuery is evolving to meet these demands with enhanced streaming capabilities, deeper Artificial Intelligence (AI) integration, and serverless frameworks that eliminate infrastructure management. Understanding these trends will help you build systems that remain relevant as the field continues to evolve.

Structure

This chapter will explore the following four key areas reshaping the data engineering landscape:

- The Shift to Real-Time Data Platforms
- Intelligent and Decentralized Architectures
- Automation-First Workflows
- The Future Data Engineer

The Shift to Real-Time Data Platforms

The most fundamental change in data engineering today is the transition from batch-first to streaming-first architectures.

Real-Time Analytics as the New Default

For decades, data warehousing operated on a simple assumption: yesterday's data is good enough for today's decisions. Batch jobs ran overnight, dashboards refreshed at 6 AM, and analysts queried data that was hours or days old. This worked fine for monthly reports, quarterly planning, and historical analysis.

That assumption is breaking down now. Modern businesses operate in real-time. E-commerce platforms adjust pricing based on current inventory and competitor actions. Fraud detection systems block suspicious transactions within milliseconds. Supply chain operations reroute shipments based on live traffic data. Marketing teams personalize content based on what users clicked seconds ago.

The shift from batch to streaming is not just about speed, but it is also about fundamentally different business capabilities. When data arrives in real-time, you can:

- Detect and respond to anomalies immediately rather than discovering problems in tomorrow's report.
- Personalize experiences based on current behavior instead of yesterday's profile.
- Optimize operations dynamically as conditions change, not after the fact.
- Enable interactive analytics where users explore live data, not stale snapshots.

BigQuery is adapting to this reality. The Storage Write API—as introduced in *Chapter 13, Real-Time Streaming Analytics*—now supports sub-second latency with exactly-once semantics, making real-time analytics practical at scale. Streaming inserts—

that once took 30–90 seconds to become queryable—now appear in under a second. The line between "batch" and "streaming" is blurring; soon, all data will be treated as continuous streams, with batch processing becoming a special case of windowed streaming.

Building for Real-Time

Designing a real-time platform requires rethinking every layer of the traditional data stack—from ingestion through to consumption.

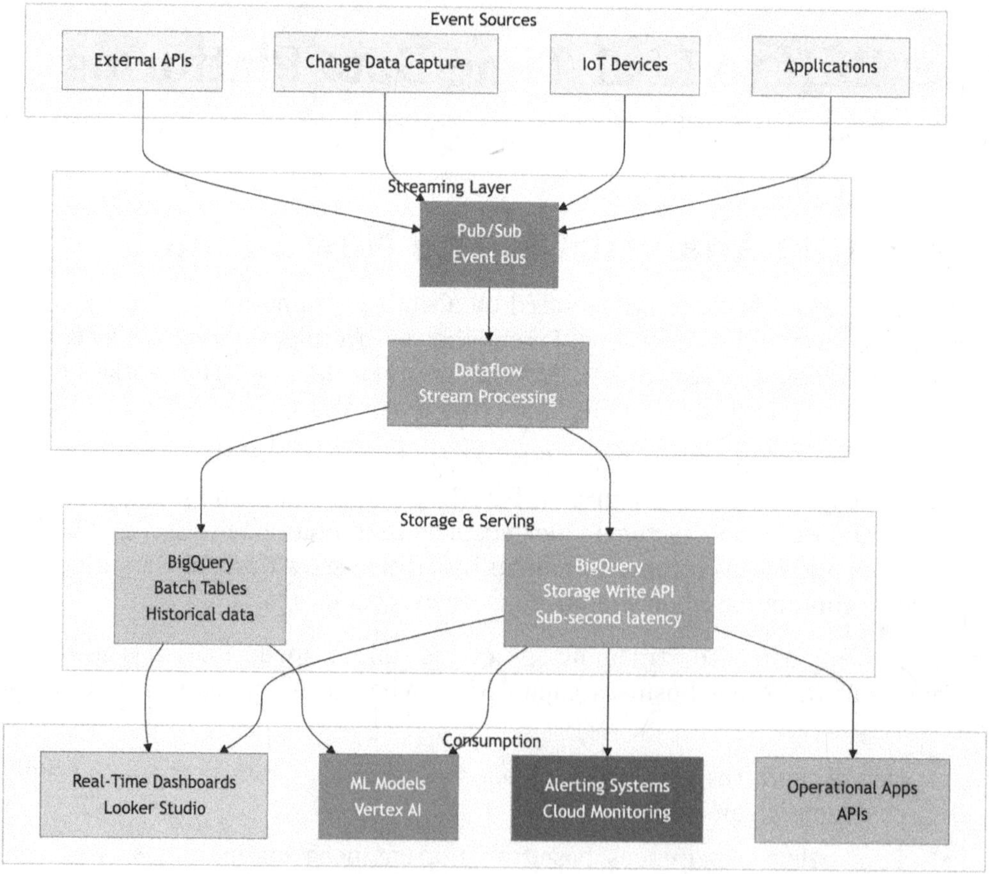

Figure 15.1: *Modern Real-Time Analytics Architecture*

This architecture represents a fundamental shift from the traditional batch-oriented warehouse. Notice that streaming is not a separate path—it is the primary path. Batch processing still exists for historical data and complex transformations, but the default assumption is that data flows continuously.

The Implications for You If you are building new data platforms today, design for streaming first in the following ways:

- **Choose Ingestion Methods That Support Streaming:** Storage Write API over batch loads.
- **Design Schemas for Append-Only Patterns:** Immutable events, not mutable dimensions.
- **Build Transformations That Handle Late Data:** Watermarks and allowed lateness are not optional.
- **Test with Realistic Event Volumes:** Streaming systems fail differently than batch systems.
- **Monitor Lag Metrics:** System lag and data freshness become critical SLOs.

The batch-first mindset that dominated data warehousing for decades is giving way to streaming-first thinking. This does not mean batch processing disappears; rather, it means that streaming becomes the default and batch becomes a special case.

Continuous Queries: BigQuery as an Active Engine

One of the most significant recent additions to BigQuery is Continuous Queries, which fundamentally transforms BigQuery from a passive data warehouse into an active operational engine. Traditionally, BigQuery waited for you to query it—you ran a "`SELECT`" statement, received results, and that was the end of the interaction. Continuous Queries flip this model: you define a query once using `CREATE CONTINUOUS QUERY`, and BigQuery runs it continuously in the background, processing new data as it arrives and pushing results in real-time to downstream systems.

This enables entirely new use cases. Instead of building a separate streaming infrastructure with Dataflow or Flink to compute real-time aggregations, you can now do it directly in BigQuery. For example, you can create a continuous query that monitors incoming transaction events, detects fraud patterns in real-time, and immediately writes alerts to Pub/Sub or Bigtable. The query never stops—it processes each new row as it arrives, maintains stateful aggregations (such as running totals or session windows), and delivers results with sub-second latency. This turns BigQuery into an event-driven platform that can trigger downstream workflows, update operational databases, or feed real-time dashboards without any external orchestration. For data engineers, this means fewer moving parts: instead of managing Dataflow jobs, Pub/Sub subscriptions, and BigQuery separately, you can consolidate real-time processing logic directly in SQL where your data already lives.

Intelligent and Decentralized Architectures

As data platforms grow in scale, two architectural shifts are converging: decentralizing ownership through Data Mesh and embedding AI directly into the engineering workflow.

Data Mesh: Decentralizing Data Ownership

For the past two decades, data warehousing followed a centralized model: a single team (the data engineering team) owned all data pipelines, transformations, and quality. Business teams submitted requests, and the data team built and maintained everything. This worked when data volumes were manageable, and use cases were limited.

However, as organizations scale, the centralized model breaks down in the following ways:

- **The Data Team Becomes a Bottleneck:** Every new dashboard, report, or Machine Learning (ML) model requires the data team's involvement.
- **Domain Knowledge is Lost:** The data team does not understand the nuances of every business domain.
- **Quality Suffers:** The data team cannot validate the correctness of data that they do not own.
- **Innovation Slows:** Business teams wait weeks or months for new data products.

Data Mesh is an emerging architectural pattern that decentralizes data ownership. Instead of a central warehouse owned by one team, each business domain owns its data as a product.

The Data Mesh Principles

Data Mesh is built on the following four principles:

1. **Domain-Oriented Ownership**: The marketing team owns marketing data, the supply chain team owns logistics data, and so on.
2. **Data as a Product**: Each domain treats its data as a product with Service Level Agreements (SLAs), documentation, and quality guarantees.
3. **Self-Serve Data Platform**: A centralized platform team provides tools (such as BigQuery, dbt, Dataflow, and more) that domain teams use independently.

4. **Federated Computational Governance**: Policies (such as security, privacy, quality, and so on) are enforced automatically by the platform, and not manually by a central team.

Data Mesh on BigQuery

BigQuery's multi-project architecture and fine-grained Identity and Access Management (IAM) controls make it a natural fit for implementing Data Mesh at scale.

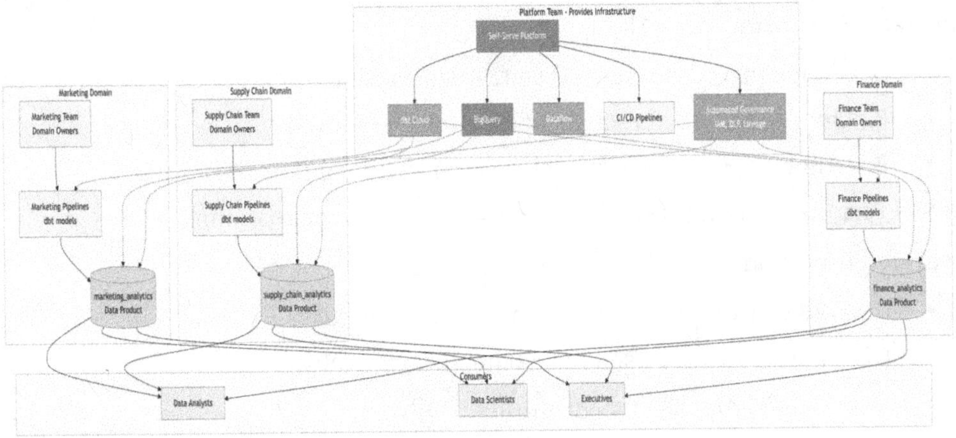

***Figure 15.2**: Data Mesh Architecture on BigQuery*

In this model:

- **Platform team** provides BigQuery, dbt Cloud, Dataflow, Continuous Integration/Continuous Deployment (CI/CD) templates, and automated governance.
- **Domain teams** (such as Marketing, Supply Chain, Finance, and more) own their data products and pipelines.
- **Consumers** (such as analysts, data scientists, executives, and more) access data products from any domain.
- **Governance** is automated through IAM policies, Data Loss Prevention (DLP), and lineage tracking.

Implementing Data Mesh with BigQuery

BigQuery's features align well with Data Mesh principles in the following ways:

Domain Ownership:

- Each domain gets its own BigQuery dataset (for example, **`marketing_analytics`**, **`supply_chain_analytics`**, and so on).

- IAM policies grant domain teams full control over their datasets.
- Authorized views allow controlled sharing without copying data.

Data as a Product:

- dbt documentation serves as the product catalog.
- Column descriptions and lineage graphs document the product.
- dbt tests enforce quality SLAs.
- Materialized views provide performance guarantees.

Self-Serve Platform:

- dbt Cloud provides a self-serve transformation framework.
- BigQuery Studio offers a no-code interface for analysts.
- Dataflow templates enable self-serve streaming pipelines.
- Terraform modules standardize infrastructure provisioning.

Federated Governance:

- IAM policies enforce access control automatically.
- DLP policies scan for sensitive data automatically.
- Data Catalog tracks lineage automatically.
- Policy tags enforce column-level security automatically.
- Data Clean Rooms allow secure, privacy-preserving data sharing across organizations (for example, marketing attribution) without exposing the underlying Personally Identifiable Information (PII).

Instances to Adopt Data Mesh

Data Mesh is not for everyone. Consider it only in the following instances:

- Your organization has a large data engineering presence (for example, 50+ engineers) across multiple teams.
- Business domains have distinct data needs and expertise.
- The central data team is a bottleneck.
- You need to scale data product development.

Do not adopt Data Mesh if:

- You have a small team (< 10 people).
- Your data use cases are simple and centralized.
- You lack organizational buy-in for decentralization.

The Lakehouse: BigLake and Open Table Formats

For years, the industry debated between "Data Lakes" (cheap, flexible object storage) and "Data Warehouses" (fast, structured, but proprietary storage). The modern solution is the Lakehouse Architecture, which converges the best of both workflows by decoupling compute from storage.

Instead of forcing you to load all your data into native BigQuery storage, Google introduced BigLake, which is a unified query engine. BigLake allows BigQuery to execute high-performance queries directly against data files sitting in Google Cloud Storage, AWS S3, or Azure Blob Storage. Most importantly, it natively supports Open Table Formats such as Apache Iceberg, Delta Lake, and Apache Hudi.

This is a monumental shift. By storing data in an open format such as Iceberg rather than a proprietary warehouse format, you eliminate vendor lock-in. Your data becomes perfectly interoperable, as you can have BigQuery, Spark clusters, and third-party tools all securely querying the same bucket simultaneously without duplicating data or paying redundant storage costs.

AI-Driven Data Engineering

AI is not just a consumer of data, but it is also becoming a builder of data systems. The integration of BigQuery with Vertex AI and Generative AI (GenAI) is creating a new category of AI-native data platforms where ML models design schemas, write transformations, optimize queries, and detect anomalies.

BigQuery and Vertex AI Integration

We covered BigQuery ML in *Chapter 12, BigQuery ML and Vertex AI*, yet the integration is deepening:

Remote Models in BigQuery

You can now call Vertex AI models directly from SQL. As **`ML.PREDICT`** is a table-valued function, the input table is passed as the second argument, and the prediction columns are returned alongside the input columns:

```
SELECT
  customer_id,
  predicted_churn,
  predicted_churn_probs
FROM ML.PREDICT(MODEL `your-project-id.bqml_lab.vertex_churn_model`,
```

```
    (SELECT
      customer_id,monthly_charges,
      tenure_months,support_tickets
     FROM `your-project-id.bqml_lab.customer_features`))
```

This brings custom TensorFlow, PyTorch, and scikit-learn models into BigQuery without exporting data.

Feature Store Integration:

Vertex AI Feature Store now syncs with BigQuery tables, enabling:

- Real-time feature serving for online predictions,
- Historical feature lookups for training, and
- Automatic feature freshness monitoring.

AutoML Integration: BigQuery can trigger Vertex AI AutoML training jobs automatically when new data arrives, creating a continuous learning loop.

GenAI for Data Engineering

Large Language Models (LLMs) are beginning to assist with data engineering tasks, such as:

SQL Generation:

Tools such as Gemini in BigQuery can:

- Generate SQL queries from natural language descriptions.
- Explain the existing queries in plain English.
- Suggest optimizations for slow queries.
- Auto-complete complex joins and window functions.

Schema Design:

LLMs can analyze sample data and suggest:

- Appropriate data types and constraints,
- Partitioning and clustering strategies, and
- Normalization versus denormalization trade-offs.

Data Quality Rules:

Given a table schema and business context, LLMs can generate:

- dbt test definitions,
- Anomaly detection rules, and
- Data validation logic.

Pipeline Code Generation:

By describing a pipeline in natural language, LLMs can generate:

- Dataflow pipeline code,
- dbt model definitions, and
- Airflow DAG configurations.

The AI-Native Data Platform

When such AI capabilities are combined, they form an entirely new kind of data platform where intelligence is embedded at every layer.

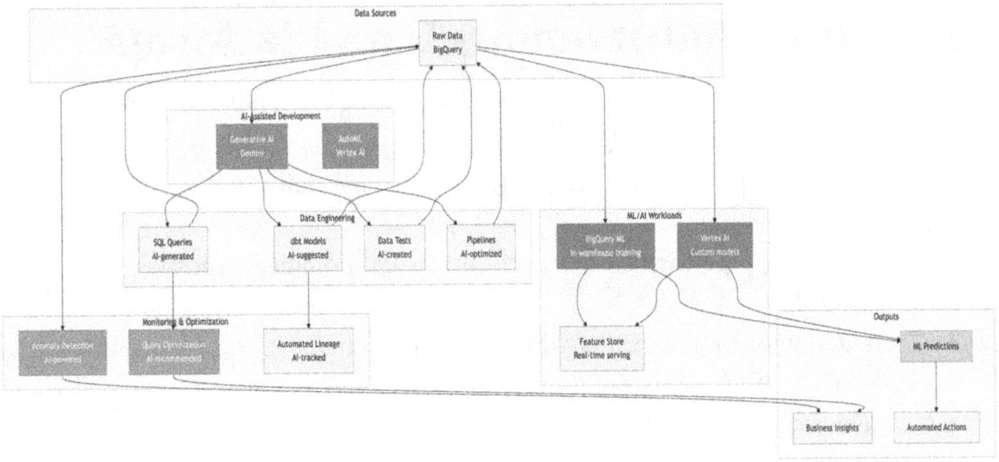

Figure 15.3: *AI-Native Data Platform Architecture*

Note: *GenAI assists with development,* AutoML *trains models automatically, and* AI-*Powered monitoring detects anomalies as well as optimizes queries.*

In this architecture, AI is not just analyzing data, but it is also building the platform itself.

Practical Applications Today

You can start using AI-driven data engineering now with the following steps:

1. **Use Gemini for SQL Assistance:**

```
-- Type a comment describing what you want:
-- "Show me the top 10 customers by revenue in the last 30 days"
-- Gemini will suggest the complete query
```

2. **Automate Feature Engineering with BigQuery ML:**

```
CREATE OR REPLACE MODEL `project.dataset.auto_features`
OPTIONS(
  model_type='AUTOML_REGRESSOR',
  input_label_cols=['target'],
  budget_hours=1.0
) AS
SELECT * FROM training_data;
```

3. **Use Vertex AI Pipelines for MLOps:** Automate the entire ML lifecycle–from data prep to model deployment–with Kubeflow pipelines that integrate BigQuery and Vertex AI.

The Future: Autonomous Data Platforms

The trajectory is clear: data platforms are becoming increasingly autonomous. In the coming years, we will see the following:

- **Self-optimizing warehouses** that automatically adjust partitioning, clustering, and materialization strategies.
- **Self-healing pipelines** that detect and fix data quality issues without human intervention.
- **Self-documenting systems** where lineage, schemas, and business logic are automatically generated and maintained.
- **Conversational interfaces** where you describe what you need in natural language and the system builds it.

This does not mean data engineers become obsolete; rather, it means that the role shifts from writing boilerplate code to designing systems, defining business logic, ensuring that AI-generated solutions align with organizational needs.

Automation-First Workflows

The third major trend reshaping data engineering is the elimination of infrastructure management through serverless frameworks and automated pipelines.

Serverless ELT Frameworks

The evolution of data transformation tools reflects a broader trend in cloud computing: the shift from infrastructure management to pure business logic. In *Chapter 7, ELT with dbt and BigQuery*, we introduced dbt as a framework for managing SQL transformations. Yet, even dbt required managing Python environments, installing dependencies, and configuring deployment infrastructure.

That is now changing. Serverless ELT frameworks are eliminating infrastructure concerns, allowing you to focus solely on writing transformations and defining data quality rules.

dbt Cloud: Managed dbt

dbt Cloud takes the open-source dbt framework and wraps it in a fully managed service, as demonstrated in this section:

What dbt Cloud Provides:

- **No Infrastructure to Manage:** No Python environments, no servers, and no deployment scripts.
- **Built-in Integrated Development Environment (IDE):** Write, test, and run dbt models in a browser.
- **Integrated Scheduler:** Schedule dbt runs without Airflow or Cloud Composer.
- **Automatic Documentation:** dbt docs are generated and hosted automatically.
- **Semantic Layer:** Define metrics once, query them anywhere (such as Looker, Tableau, Python, and more).
- **CI/CD Integration:** Automatic testing on Pull Requests (PRs).
- **Observability:** Built-in monitoring, alerting, and lineage tracking.

The dbt Cloud Workflow is as Follows:

1. Write dbt models in the browser IDE.
2. Test locally with a dev dataset.
3. Commit to Git (such as GitHub, GitLab, or Azure DevOps).
4. dbt Cloud automatically runs tests on PRs.
5. Merge to main triggers automatic deployment to production.
6. Scheduled jobs keep data fresh.

This eliminates the need for:

- Python virtual environments,
- CI/CD pipeline configuration (GitHub Actions and more),
- Deployment scripts, and
- Infrastructure monitoring.

BigQuery Studio: No-Code Transformations

BigQuery Studio is Google's unified collaborative workspace for data practitioners, offering an integrated interface for no-code/low-code data transformation, as described in this section:

The Key Features Include:

- **Visual Query Builder:** Build SQL queries by dragging and dropping tables.
- **Notebook Interface:** Combine SQL, Python, and Markdown in Jupyter-style notebooks.
- **Gemini Integration:** Generate SQL from natural language.
- **Scheduled Queries:** Run transformations on a schedule without external orchestration.
- **Materialized Views:** Automatically refresh derived tables.
- **Data Canvas:** Visual data pipeline builder (similar to Azure Data Factory).

Who It is for:

- Analysts who need to build pipelines without learning dbt or Dataflow.
- Teams that want to prototype transformations quickly.
- Organizations standardizing on Google Cloud's native tools.

The Serverless Spectrum

The data transformation landscape now offers a spectrum of options, as demonstrated in *Table* 15.1:

Tool	Code Required	Infrastructure	Best For
Raw SQL	High	Self-managed	Full control, low engineering capacity
dbt Core	Medium	Self-managed	Open-source, customization
dbt Cloud	Medium	Fully managed	Production dbt, scaling teams
BigQuery Studio	Low	Fully managed	Analysts, rapid prototyping
Dataform	Medium	Fully managed	Google-native, SQL-first teams

Table 15.1: *Data Transformation Options*

Dataform: Google's Native ELT

Google acquired Dataform in 2020 and integrated it into BigQuery. It is similar to dbt but with tighter BigQuery integration.

Dataform Advantages Include:

- Native BigQuery integration (no external tools)
- Built-in scheduling and orchestration
- Automatic dependency resolution
- Incremental table management
- Data quality assertions

Example Dataform Workflow:

```
-- config block defines materialization
config {
  type: "table",
  schema: "analytics",
  tags: ["daily"]
}

-- SQL transformation
SELECT
  customer_id,
  SUM(amount) AS total_revenue
FROM ${ref("stg_orders")}
WHERE status = 'completed'
GROUP BY customer_id
```

Choosing Your Framework

Choose dbt Cloud if:

- You want the largest community and ecosystem.
- You need flexibility to run on multiple warehouses.
- You value open-source foundations.

Choose BigQuery Studio if:

- Your team prefers visual/no-code tools.
- You are standardizing on Google Cloud.
- You want the simplest possible setup.

Choose Dataform if:

- You are deeply invested in Google Cloud.
- You want native BigQuery integration.
- You prefer Google's support and SLAs.

The trend is clear: infrastructure management is disappearing. In 5 years, most data teams will not manage servers, containers, or orchestration platforms—they will write transformations and let the cloud handle everything else.

Automated Pipelines and Quality

The next generation of data pipelines is built on automation: CI/CD for data, automated lineage tracking, and continuous quality monitoring.

CI/CD for Data

As software engineering adopted CI/CD, data engineering is following suit. Modern data pipelines deploy through automated workflows in the following ways:

Automated Testing:

- Every dbt model has tests (for example, **`unique`**, **`not_null`**, **`relationships`**, and so on).
- Tests run automatically on PRs.
- Failed tests block deployment.

Automated Deployment:

- Merge to main triggers automatic deployment.
- Blue/green deployments for zero-downtime updates.
- Automatic rollback on failures.

Automated Documentation:

- Lineage graphs generated automatically.
- Column descriptions synced to BigQuery metadata.
- Data dictionaries published to internal wikis.

Example GitHub Actions Workflow for dbt:

```
name: dbt CI/CD
on:
  pull_request:
  push:
    branches: [main]

jobs:
  test:
    runs-on: ubuntu-latest
    steps:
      - uses: actions/checkout@v3
```

```
      - name: Install dbt
        run: pip install dbt-bigquery
      - name: Run tests
        run: dbt test
      - name: Deploy to prod
        if: github.ref == 'refs/heads/main'
        run: dbt run --target prod
```

Automated Lineage Tracking

Data lineage–understanding where data comes from and where it goes–is critical for:

- **Impact Analysis:** "If I change this table, what breaks?"
- **Root Cause Analysis:** "Why is this dashboard showing wrong numbers?"
- **Compliance:** "Where does this customer's PII appear?"

Modern tools track lineage automatically through the following:

Data Catalog:

- Automatically discovers tables, views, and pipelines.
- Tracks column-level lineage.
- Integrates with dbt, Dataflow, and BigQuery.

dbt Lineage:

- Generates lineage graphs from `ref()` and `source()` functions.
- Shows upstream and downstream dependencies.
- Integrates with Data Catalog.

OpenLineage:

- Open standard for lineage metadata.
- Supported by Airflow, dbt, Spark, and BigQuery.
- Enables cross-tool lineage tracking.

Continuous Quality Monitoring

Data quality is not a one-time check–it is continuous monitoring, ensured by the following:

Automated Anomaly Detection:

- ML models learn normal data patterns.
- Alert when metrics deviate (for example, row count drops 50%).

- Suggest root causes based on lineage.

Data Observability Platforms:

Tools such as Monte Carlo, Datafold, and Soda automatically monitor:

- **Freshness:** Is data arriving on time?
- **Volume:** Are row counts within expected ranges?
- **Schema:** Have columns been added/removed?
- **Distribution:** Are value distributions normal?

Example: Automated Freshness Check in dbt:

```
sources:
  - name: raw_data
    tables:
      - name: orders
        freshness:
          warn_after: {count: 12, period: hour}
          error_after: {count: 24, period: hour}
```

The Automation Stack

A modern automation-first pipeline includes:

1. **Version control:** Git for all code and configuration
2. **CI/CD:** GitHub Actions, GitLab CI, or dbt Cloud
3. **Testing:** dbt tests, Great Expectations, or Soda
4. **Lineage:** Data Catalog, dbt docs, or OpenLineage
5. **Monitoring:** Data observability platforms
6. **Alerting:** Slack, PagerDuty, or email notifications

The goal: pipelines that heal themselves. When data quality issues arise, the system detects them, alerts the right people, and in some cases, automatically fixes them (for example, re-running failed jobs, rolling back bad deployments, and so on).

The Future Data Engineer

With real-time platforms, AI-native tools, and automation handling more technical work, the data engineering role itself is transforming.

The Evolving Role

As automation, AI, and serverless frameworks handle more of the technical work, the data engineering role is evolving. The skills that mattered five years ago are not the same skills that will matter five years from now.

From Infrastructure to Strategy

The day-to-day responsibilities of a data engineer are shifting dramatically as cloud-native tools absorb the operational burden.

What is Becoming Less Important:

- Managing servers and containers.
- Writing boilerplate ETL code.
- Manually optimizing queries.
- Building custom orchestration frameworks.

What is Becoming More Important:

- Designing data architectures (such as Data Mesh, data products, and more).
- Defining data quality standards and SLAs.
- Collaborating with business stakeholders.
- Understanding ML/AI workflows.
- Ensuring data governance and compliance.

The role is shifting from builder to architect–from writing code to designing systems.

The T-Shaped Data Engineer

The most valuable data engineers will be T-shaped:

Depth (the Vertical Bar):

- Deep expertise in one area (for example, streaming, ML, governance, and so on).

Breadth (the Horizontal Bar):

- Working knowledge of:
    - Cloud platforms (such as GCP, AWS, Azure, and more)
    - Data warehousing (such as BigQuery, Snowflake, Redshift, and more)
    - Transformation tools (such as dbt, Dataform, Spark, and more)

- Orchestration (such as Airflow, Dagster, Prefect, and more)
- ML/AI (such as Vertex AI, TensorFlow, PyTorch, and more)
- Data governance (such as IAM, DLP, lineage, and more)

New Roles Emerging

The data engineering field is fragmenting into specialized roles, including:

Analytics Engineer:

- Focuses on dbt and SQL transformations.
- Bridges data engineering and analytics.
- Owns data quality and documentation.

ML Engineer:

- Builds ML pipelines and feature stores.
- Deploys models for production.
- Monitors model performance.

Data Platform Engineer:

- Builds self-serve data platforms.
- Enables domain teams (Data Mesh).
- Manages infrastructure and governance.

Data Reliability Engineer:

- Ensures data quality and freshness.
- Builds observability and monitoring.
- Responds to data incidents.

Skills That Will Always Matter

Regardless of how the field evolves, some skills remain timeless, including:

1. **SQL:** The lingua franca of data.
2. **Data Modeling:** Understanding how to structure data.
3. **Problem-Solving:** Debugging complex issues.
4. **Communication:** Explaining technical concepts to non-technical stakeholders.
5. **Business Acumen:** Understanding how data drives business decisions.

Preparing for the Next Generation

So, how do you prepare for a future that is uncertain? Focus on principles over tools, adaptability over specialization, and continuous learning over static knowledge.

Invest in Fundamentals

Tools change, but fundamentals endure, including:

Data Structures and Algorithms:

- Understanding how databases work internally
- Knowing when to use hash joins versus merge joins
- Recognizing O(n) versus $O(n^2)$ complexity

Distributed Systems:

- CAP theorem and consistency models
- Partitioning and sharding strategies
- Handling failures and retries

Data Modeling:

- Normalization versus denormalization
- Star schema versus snowflake schema
- Slowly changing dimensions

Statistics and Probability:

- Understanding sampling and bias
- Recognizing correlation versus causation
- Interpreting confidence intervals

The preceding concepts apply regardless of whether you are using BigQuery, Snowflake, or whatever comes next.

Build a Learning System

The field evolves too quickly for one-time learning. Build a system for continuous learning in the following manner:

1. **Follow the Right Sources, Including:**
    - Google Cloud Blog (cloud.google.com/blog),
    - BigQuery release notes,

- dbt Community (discourse.getdbt.com),
- Data Engineering Weekly newsletter, and
- Conferences (such as Google Cloud Next and dbt Coalesce).

2. **Experiment Regularly:**
   - Try new features in sandbox projects.
   - Rebuild old projects with new tools.
   - Contribute to open-source projects.
3. **Teach Others to:**
   - Write blog posts about what you learn,
   - Answer questions on Stack Overflow, and
   - Mentor junior engineers.
4. **Build a Portfolio to:**
   - Maintain a GitHub with sample projects,
   - Document your architectural decisions, and
   - Share lessons learned publicly.

Develop Adjacent Skills

The most valuable engineers have skills beyond pure technical work, which are as follows:

Product Thinking:

- Understand user needs (who are your data consumers?).
- Prioritize features based on impact.
- Measure success with metrics.

Communication:

- Write clear documentation.
- Present technical concepts to executives.
- Facilitate cross-team collaboration.

Project Management:

- Break large projects into milestones.
- Manage stakeholder expectations.
- Navigate organizational politics.

Business Acumen:

- Understand your company's business model.
- Know which metrics drive decisions.
- Speak the language of business stakeholders.

Stay Adaptable

The only constant is change. The tools you master today may be obsolete in a few years. What matters is your ability to learn new tools quickly.

Cultivate a Growth Mindset:

- View challenges as learning opportunities.
- Embrace discomfort when learning new technologies.
- Recognize that expertise is built, not innate.

Practice Deliberate Learning:

- Set specific learning goals (for example, "Build a streaming pipeline with Dataflow").
- Seek feedback on your work.
- Reflect on what worked and what did not.

Build Transferable Skills:

- Focus on concepts that apply across tools.
- Learn multiple tools in the same category (for example, dbt and Dataform).
- Understand the "why" behind architectural decisions.

Conclusion

This book began with the fundamentals of BigQuery and data warehousing. We explored how BigQuery stores and processes data, mastered ingestion and transformation patterns, built orchestrated pipelines, implemented real-time streaming, and deployed production-grade ELT systems. Each chapter equipped you with practical skills for building modern data platforms.

However, the field does not stand still. This final chapter looked at where BigQuery and data engineering are heading now. We examined the shift toward real-time analytics as the default, explored how the Storage Write API is enabling sub-second latency, and discussed how Data Mesh architectures are decentralizing data ownership. We saw how AI is becoming embedded in data platforms–not just analyzing data, but also building the systems through tools such as Gemini and Vertex AI integration.

We also explored the rise of serverless ELT frameworks, such as dbt Cloud and BigQuery Studio, that eliminate infrastructure management. We discussed automation-first pipelines in which CI/CD, lineage tracking, and quality monitoring happen automatically. We also covered how the data engineering role is evolving from infrastructure management to strategic architecture.

The trends are clear: real-time by default, AI-native architectures, and automation-first workflows. BigQuery is evolving to meet these demands, and the skills that matter most are shifting from technical implementation to strategic design, from writing code to architecting systems, and from managing infrastructure to enabling teams.

The foundation you have built throughout this book—understanding BigQuery's architecture, mastering transformation patterns, implementing quality checks, and deploying with CI/CD—will serve you well as these trends reshape the field. The specific tools will change, but the principles endure: design for scale, automate everything, test relentlessly, and always keep the business need in focus.

The future of data engineering is not about predicting which specific tools will dominate, but rather about building the adaptability to learn whatever comes next. Stay curious, keep experimenting, and remember that the best data engineers are not those who know every tool, but rather those who can learn any tool quickly and apply it effectively.

Points to Remember

- Continuous Queries transform BigQuery from a passive warehouse into an active engine that processes live streaming data and pushes results to downstream systems in real-time.
- **Data Mesh** is a decentralized architecture where individual business teams own their data as products, while a central platform team provides the infrastructure and automated governance.
- BigLake enables a Lakehouse architecture by letting you query open file formats (like **Parquet, Iceberg, and Delta**) in object storage with BigQuery's performance and security.
- **Vertex AI and Gemini integrations** bring machine learning and generative AI directly into SQL workflows, allowing you to train models, generate code, and analyze text where the data lives.
- Modern data workflows are serverless and automated, using managed tools (like Dataform or dbt Cloud) and CI/CD pipelines to build, test, and document models without managing servers.
- As the data engineering role shifts from managing infrastructure to designing architecture, strong fundamentals in SQL, data modeling, and system design remain the most critical skills.

Multiple Choice Questions

1. What is the primary advantage of BigQuery's Storage Write API over legacy streaming inserts?

    a. It supports larger batch sizes.

    b. It works with older BigQuery versions.

    c. It requires less network bandwidth.

    d. It provides sub-second latency and exactly-once semantics.

2. In a Data Mesh architecture, who owns the data products?

    a. The central data engineering team

    b. The platform team that provides infrastructure

    c. Domain teams (for example, Marketing, Finance, Supply Chain)

    d. External vendors and consultants

3. Which tool provides AI-assisted SQL generation directly in BigQuery?

    a. Gemini in BigQuery

    b. Dataform

    c. dbt Cloud

    d. Vertex AI AutoML

4. What is the primary purpose of serverless ELT frameworks such as dbt Cloud?

    a. To replace SQL with Python

    b. To eliminate infrastructure management and focus on transformations

    c. To provide cheaper compute than BigQuery

    d. To enable multi-cloud deployments

5. In the context of automated data pipelines, what does "data observability" monitor?

    a. Only query performance metrics

    b. Freshness, volume, schema changes, and data distribution

    c. User access patterns and security logs

    d. Cloud infrastructure costs

6. What is a key principle of Data Mesh architecture?
   a. Domain teams own their data as products with SLAs
   b. Only the data team can create data products
   c. All data must be centralized in one warehouse
   d. Data governance is optional for domain teams
7. How is the data engineering role evolving according to current trends?
   a. From strategy to infrastructure management
   b. From architecture to manual coding
   c. From infrastructure to strategic design and architecture
   d. From collaboration to isolated technical work
8. Which skill is becoming MORE important for data engineers as automation increases?
   a. Managing Kubernetes clusters
   b. Writing custom ETL frameworks
   c. Designing data architectures and defining quality standards
   d. Manually optimizing every query
9. What is the primary benefit of BigQuery Continuous Queries?
   a. They reduce storage costs by archiving old data.
   b. They transform BigQuery from passive warehouse to active event-driven engine.
   c. They replace the need for batch processing entirely.
   d. They automatically optimize all existing queries.
10. What is BigLake's main advantage in the Lakehouse Architecture?
    a. It stores data more cheaply than Cloud Storage.
    b. It allows BigQuery to query open table formats such as Iceberg without data duplication.
    c. It replaces the need for BigQuery native tables.
    d. It only works with Google Cloud Storage.

Answers

1. d
2. c
3. a
4. b
5. b
6. a
7. c
8. c
9. b
10. b

Questions

1. Explain how the shift from batch to real-time analytics changes the way data platforms are designed. What architectural patterns become more important?
2. Describe the four principles of Data Mesh architecture. Why might an organization choose Data Mesh over a traditional centralized data warehouse?
3. How is AI being integrated into data engineering workflows beyond just analyzing data? Provide three specific examples of AI-assisted data engineering tasks.
4. Compare and contrast dbt Cloud, BigQuery Studio, and Dataform. What are the key differences, and when would you choose each?
5. Discuss how the data engineering role is evolving. What skills are becoming less important, and what skills are becoming more critical for future success?

Key Terms

- **Storage Write API:** BigQuery's high-performance streaming API that provides sub-second latency and exactly-once semantics for real-time data ingestion.

- **Data Mesh:** An architectural pattern that decentralizes data ownership, treating data as products owned by domain teams rather than a central data engineering team.
- **Data Product:** A dataset owned by a domain team, treated as a product with SLAs, documentation, quality guarantees, and defined consumers.
- **Gemini in BigQuery:** Google's AI-powered assistant integrated into BigQuery Studio that generates SQL from natural language, explains queries, and suggests optimizations.
- **Serverless ELT:** Transformation frameworks (such as dbt Cloud) that eliminate infrastructure management, allowing data engineers to focus solely on writing transformations.
- **Data Observability:** Continuous monitoring of data pipelines for freshness, volume, schema changes, and distribution anomalies to detect quality issues automatically.
- **Analytics Engineer:** An emerging role that focuses on dbt transformations, data quality, and documentation, bridging data engineering and analytics.
- **Federated Governance:** In Data Mesh, governance policies (such as security, privacy, quality, and so on) are enforced automatically by the platform rather than manually by a central team.
- **Committed Streams:** An enhancement to the Storage Write API that allows writing data in a pending state and atomically committing or aborting entire batches.
- **T-Shaped Engineer:** A data engineer with deep expertise in one area (the vertical bar) and broad working knowledge across multiple domains (the horizontal bar).
- **BigLake:** Google's unified query engine that allows BigQuery to execute high-performance queries directly against data in Cloud Storage, AWS S3, or Azure Blob Storage, with native support for open table formats such as Apache Iceberg, Delta Lake, and Apache Hudi.
- **Continuous Queries:** A BigQuery feature that runs queries continuously in the background, processing new data as it arrives and pushing results in real-time to downstream systems such as Pub/Sub or Bigtable, transforming BigQuery into an active event-driven engine.
- **Lakehouse Architecture:** A data architecture pattern that converges data lakes and data warehouses by decoupling compute from storage, allowing multiple query engines to access the same data stored in open formats without duplication.
- **Data Clean Rooms:** Privacy-preserving environments that allow organizations to securely share and analyze data across company boundaries without

exposing underlying PII, important for post-cookie era marketing and cross-organization collaboration.

Closing: The Architecture of You

If I had to summarize your journey throughout this book, it would probably appear in BigQuery in the following manner:

```
SELECT
  reader.skills,
  reader.confidence,
  future.opportunities
FROM `your_career.current_state` AS reader
INNER JOIN `ultimate_bigquery.lessons_learned` AS lessons
  ON reader.determination = lessons.requirements
WHERE mindset = 'streaming_first'
  AND legacy_habits IS NULL;
```

When you started this book, you were looking at the fundamental concepts–the equivalent of raw CSV files sitting in a Cloud Storage bucket. Chapter by chapter, you have transformed those concepts into a structured, optimized, and highly valuable skill set.

However, just as an ELT pipeline is never truly "finished," neither is your growth as a Data Engineer. You now have the foundational knowledge to architect modern pipelines, optimize complex BigQuery models, and adapt to the AI-native architectures of the future. You are evolving from a writer of queries into an architect of systems.

What Happens Next is Up to You

Do not let the momentum stop here. Engage with the broader data community (for instance, the dbt Slack and Google Cloud Innovators forums are fantastic resources), start experimenting in your own development sandboxes, and most importantly, start building.

Thank you for trusting this book as your guide through the Google Cloud data ecosystem.

May your pipelines be robust, your partitions perfectly pruned, and your queries always run fast as well as under budget. Happy building!

Index

C

D

Q

R

S

T

U

V

W

www.ingramcontent.com/pod-product-compliance
Lightning Source LLC
LaVergne TN
LVHW060434061126
851857LV00016B/1621
* 9 7 8 8 1 6 9 6 4 6 2 9 1 *